Appraising Residential Properties

Appraising Residential Properties

  American Institute of Real Estate Appraisers
430 North Michigan Avenue
Chicago, Illinois 60611-4088

Director of Publications: Sally King
Development Writer: Michael R. Milgrim, Ph.D.
Editor: Stephanie Shea-Joyce

For Educational Purposes Only

Library of Congress Cataloging in Publication Data

Appraising residential properties.
   Bibliography: p.
   Includes index.
   1. Real property—Valuation—United States.
I. American Institute of Real Estate Appraisers.
HD1387.A685 1988   333.33'8   88-8122
ISBN 0-911780-95-5

Table of Contents

Foreword

In the past several years it has become evident that the appraisal field has needed a textbook that covers the fundamental concepts and procedures of residential real estate appraisal. The American Institute of Real Estate Appraisal is proud to present this book to fill that need. Since the project was launched by the Publications Committee of the Appraisal Institute in 1985, three goals have directed the effort. The text is designed to instruct students and practitioners in a direct, practical manner. It is broad in scope and provides a step-by-step guide through the valuation process. To enhance its usefulness, the book also contains up-to-date residential applications of the three approaches to value as well as essential information on appraisal reports, the requirements of professional practice, and a host of topical and specialized subjects.

The text represents the collective efforts of a team of expert appraisal consultants whose numerous insights are reflected throughout the work. The contributions of the following individuals are acknowledged with special thanks. Richard Marchitelli, MAI, Chairman of Publications, guided the decision-making process from the inception of the project through the various stages of its development. Saadya Sternberg, an out-of-house writer, prepared the original draft of the manuscript, which was subsequently revised and expanded by Michael Milgrim, the Appraisal Institute's technical writer/development editor. Monty D. McCormick, RM, and Gary P. Taylor, MAI, served as cochairmen of the Residential Project Subcommittee.

Many others acted as reviewers and consultants on the project, reading the manuscript and making helpful suggestions for its revision: Haskell J. Berry, Jr., MAI; J.T. Brewer, RM; Douglas C. Brown, MAI; James H. Bulthuis, MAI; Virginia Craig, RM; Stephen F. Fanning, MAI; Roy L. Gordon, MAI; Patrick C. Kerr, MAI; Patricia J. Marshall, MAI; David Michael Mason, MAI; David Matthews, MAI; Dorothy Mills; Thomas J. Power, RM; Joe R. Price, MAI; Anthony Reynolds, MAI; and Andrew H. Rothstein, MAI.

Sheila Crowell; Frank Harrison, MAI, RM; Richard Marchitelli, MAI; Mary Jo Thomas, RM; and Janice Young, MAI reviewed the final manuscript. The Appraisal Institute is grateful for their dedication and for the time and effort they expended to make this project a success.

Terrell R. Oetzel, MAI
1988 President
American Institute of Real Estate Appraisers

PART I

FOUNDATIONS OF APPRAISAL

1 Introduction to Residential Appraisal

Material comfort, pride, and security can all accrue from the ownership of a home. The durability of a home and the parcel of land on which it is built gives many owners a sense of permanence and attachment.

Purchasers expect many benefits from the ownership of residential property; these benefits may be as diverse as the people making the purchases. Some individuals buy homes so that they can establish and raise a family. Other buyers may seek homes near to where they work, rest, and entertain. Finally, practically all purchasers have an interest in the financial benefits that owning a residence can provide. Sometimes these benefits take the form of rental income, but more commonly the benefits include income tax shelter, the availability of home equity loans, and the anticipation of realizing a higher resale value when the property is sold.

Individuals are not the only ones to benefit from the purchase and ownership of residential property. The community as a whole and the national economy are also enriched. Many home owners invest labor and capital to maintain and improve their properties. Property ownership often gives people a greater sense of community responsibility and civic attachment. In many areas citizens form groups to influence zoning boards and other political bodies for the protection and maintenance of their neighborhoods. Moreover, the purchase of a new home supports the construction industry and adds to the tax base of the local government. Because home ownership has these far-reaching consequences, government organizations often try to improve conditions in the housing market to stimulate the general economy.

THE ROLE OF THE RESIDENTIAL APPRAISER

The rights to own and use real estate must be safeguarded if society is to function. The successful management of this limited resource is an essential activity. Appraisers of real property evaluate the utility and desirability of property and estimate its value for various purposes such as purchase and sale, financing, taxation, investment, and insurance. Residential appraisers consider the

3

utility and value of residential properties. Appraisers help ensure that decisions made by buyers, sellers, government officials, insurers, investors, and others are based on well-informed, carefully reasoned judgments. Therefore, appraisers help promote the stable and orderly development of a fundamental societal resource.

WHAT IS AN APPRAISAL?

Appraisal is the act or process of estimating value. An appraisal provides an answer to a client's specific question about the value of a real property interest. The appraiser's answer is an estimate; it does not establish value of real estate. An appraisal is one person's opinion based on research in the appropriate market, the assemblage of pertinent data, and the application of appropriate analytical techniques. When these activities are combined with the knowledge, experience, and professional judgment of a qualified appraiser, they result in a solution to the client's problem. Because the opinion offered by a professional real estate appraiser is substantiated by relevant data and sound reasoning, it carries considerable weight.

The purpose of all appraisals is to estimate the defined value of a real property interest in real estate. *Value* may be loosely defined as the monetary worth of property, goods, or services. Many people are involved in real estate activities—buyers, sellers, tax assessors, investors, and insurers—and each may have his or her own concerns about a parcel of real estate. Therefore, several different ways to consider the monetary worth of real estate have evolved.

Typically an appraiser is asked to estimate the price at which a property would most likely sell in the market under certain, specified conditions. The appraiser's estimate of market value is a reflection of the probable price that would be agreed upon between knowledgeable parties acting without duress. Appraisers do not establish value; rather, they estimate the most likely value that a competitive market would set. (A more precise definition of the concept of market value is provided in the next chapter.) Most residential appraisal work is devoted to estimating the most likely selling price of residential real estate. This book, therefore, will focus on the background, data, and techniques needed to research and form sound judgments of the market value of residential properties.

APPRAISAL AND ANALYSIS

There are two broad types of assignments that appraiser-analysts may be asked to perform. An *appraisal* is the act or process of estimating value. This may be market value, insurable value, investment value, or some other properly defined value of an identified interest or interests in a specific parcel or parcels of real estate as of a given date. If the problem to be solved is not a question about a defined value, the assignment is considered an analysis rather than an appraisal. *Analysis* is the act or process of providing information, recommendations, and/or conclusions on diversified problems in real estate other than an estimate of value.

Analyses include land utilization studies, supply and demand studies, economic feasibility studies, highest and best use analyses, and marketability or investment studies for a proposed or existing development.

An analyst retained to act as a disinterested third party in rendering an unbiased analysis cannot be compensated in a manner that is contingent on the results of the analysis. However, an analyst may be retained to perform a legitimate business activity such as providing brokerage, mortgage banking, or tax counseling advice for a fee that is contingent on the results achieved, but only when the role being performed by the analyst is clearly disclosed. In accepting an analysis assignment, an analyst must carefully consider and determine whether the service to be performed is, or would be perceived by third parties or the public to be, a service that carries with it an implied impartiality on the part of the analyst. If so, the assignment can only be accepted for a fee that is not contingent on the result of the analysis.

THE APPRAISAL REPORT

Whether the purpose of an assignment is to estimate a defined value of real property or to provide an analysis, the conclusions and methodology employed in the assignment are conveyed to the client in an *appraisal report*. This report may be long or short and it can be presented in a form, letter, or narrative format in accordance with the wishes of the client, the type of property being appraised, and the nature of the appraisal assignment. An appraisal report should contain sufficient information on the data and reasoning used so that it can be objectively reviewed by a third party. The appraisal report should be self-contained and stand on its own merits. Supporting data for oral and letter reports must be kept on file by the appraiser-analyst.

USES OF RESIDENTIAL APPRAISALS

Few people buy and sell residential real estate on a regular basis. Unlike knowledgeable stock investors or seasoned comparison shoppers, buyers and sellers of homes usually have little experience in the real estate market. Consequently, most do not have the talent or judgment needed to consider the utility of the real estate and estimate its value in a reliable manner. The refined, intuitive skills that consumers and dealers bring to the market for most goods and services are the product of years of experience comparing the prices and quality of various commodities. These skills are often lacking when it comes to real estate decisions. The purchase or sale of residential real estate may be one of the largest financial transactions a person will ever make, so the services rendered by the professional appraiser are especially significant.

Each year buyers, sellers, lenders, builders, insurers, brokers, and government officials make real estate decisions that involve billions of dollars; these decisions depend on real estate appraisals. Informed investment or loan decisions based on competent real estate appraisals help prevent business failures. In many ways, appraisals encourage the appropriate use of our nation's land—a limited and valuable resource.

It is extremely important that appraisers exercise objectivity. In many real estate decisions, one or both parties have a strong, vested interest in a particular conclusion, such as a high or a low value estimate. As an objective investigator, an appraiser must provide an unbiased opinion that can be used in court testimony if necessary. Judicious decisions based, in part, on reliable and objective appraisals also help the economy function.

Real estate appraisals are required in a variety of circumstances. Decisions concerning market transactions, tax questions, legal claims, investment planning and counseling, and other real estate-related matters may require the services of a professional appraiser.

Reason #①

Market Transactions

To prepare for a market transaction in which property ownership is transferred, several parties may request separate appraisals to answer specific questions. Both the seller and the potential buyer are typically interested in the real estate's market value. The buyer needs to know the property's market value to decide on an acceptable offering price; the seller, or sales agent, may use the market value estimate to select a price at which to sell or list the property. The buyer and the seller, separately or together, may also want to investigate suitable forms of financing to ensure that the sale goes through. The financial institution from which the buyer requests a loan also needs certain information. Because the amount of the loan is usually based on a set loan-to-value ratio, the institution requires a market value estimate. Financial institutions may also be interested in long-term forecasts of neighborhood stability and conditions in the real estate market because the property will be pledged to them as security for a fairly long period of time. Potential insurers and underwriters of mortgage loans are interested in similar information.

Besides purchases and sales, other transactions may require appraisals. A landlord may want to know typical market rents to establish a profitable rental schedule and a potential tenant may need this information to decide if the rent and lease provisions are fair. Parties who are exchanging real estate, rather than buying and selling, may want market value estimates of both parcels to serve as the basis of their negotiations. Appraisals may also be requested when reorganization or consolidation of the ownership of several properties is contemplated.

Reason #②

Tax Questions

Tax assessors need estimates of real estate values to calculate ad valorem taxes, which are based on property value. Property owners who wish to challenge their tax estimates may hire appraisers. To calculate gift and inheritance taxes on real estate, value estimates of the bequeathed property are required. Various income tax provisions require appraisals as supporting evidence. For example, estimates of historical values may be needed to establish capital gains taxes. The allocation of assets between nondepreciable items

Reason #3

such as land and depreciable items such as buildings may be required to calculate depreciation deductions.

Legal Claims

When the government exercises the right of eminent domain and takes possession of private property for a public use, an appraisal is frequently required to estimate the amount of just compensation to be paid to the owner. Just compensation is sometimes set at the market value of the property taken, but additional compensation may also be required by the law. When only a portion of the real estate is taken, market value estimates may be needed for the property as a whole and for the property that remains after the taking. Many state courts require a valuation of the part taken and an estimate of the severance damage or special benefits to the remainder. Appraisals may also be required for arbitration between adversaries, such as lawsuits over damage to real estate or court division of property after a divorce.

Reason #4

Investment Planning and Counseling

An appraiser's expert opinion on real estate matters is often sought by investors, builders, and government officials. Investors in residential apartment buildings may seek advice on investment goals, alternatives, resources, constraints, and timing from appraisers. Individuals who invest in capital markets may need appraisal advice to decide whether to purchase real estate mortgages, bonds, or other types of securities.

Home owners who are considering renovation work may be interested in an analysis of the costs and benefits involved. Home builders may consult appraisers on the feasibility of a project, its market value, or the marketability of specific design features in the local area. Zoning boards, courts, and planners often need to consult appraisers about the probable effects of their proposed actions.

Other Situations

There are many other situations in which residential appraisals may be required. Financial institutions that are considering whether or not to foreclose on a property may be interested in the price the real estate might bring in a forced sale or auction. Appraisals can facilitate corporate or company purchases of the homes of transferred employees. Questions about insurance often necessitate an appraisal. A home owner may want to know how much insurance to carry and which parts of the property are covered under the provisions of an insurance policy. The insurer may be interested in the value of the insured parts to decide how much to charge for the policy. Value estimates may be needed by the policyholder to support casualty loss claims or an insurance adjuster may hire an appraiser to examine and evaluate the property damage and provide a basis for a negotiated settlement.

These cases do not represent all of the circumstances in which an appraisal may be requested, but they do suggest the broad scope of a professional appraiser's activities.

PURPOSE AND USE OF AN APPRAISAL

The *purpose* of an appraisal is the stated reason for an appraisal assignment—i.e., to estimate a defined value of a real property interest. The purpose of the appraisal reflects an agreement between the client and the appraiser about the appraisal problem to be solved. The information the client seeks guides the appraiser in fulfilling the purpose of the assignment, but any specific conclusion the client hopes to obtain must not.

The client's *use* of the appraisal and its *purpose* are distinct. The use of an appraisal is determined by the client's needs. A client may want to know the market value of a residence to avoid paying too much for its purchase or accepting too little for its sale. A lender may need to know whether the market value estimate justifies a loan of the amount requested. Another client may prefer a low value estimate because the estimate is to serve as the basis for the collection of inheritance taxes. An appraiser's function, however, is to provide an objective value estimate regardless of the use made of the appraisal. The appraiser is an independent third party with a responsibility to provide competent and unbiased service; on this the appraiser's professional integrity and the public trust depend.

SKILLS AND CHARACTERISTICS OF A RESIDENTIAL APPRAISER

Given the broad scope of appraisal activities and the public's trust in the appraiser's opinions, an appraiser obviously needs to possess personal integrity, diligence, and professionalism. However, other skills, education, experience, and qualifications are also essential to a residential appraiser.

Licensing and Certification

Most states do not require that individuals be qualified before they are allowed to perform appraisals. However, there is increased recognition of the need to have professional estimates prepared by persons of integrity, so future licensing or certification of appraisers is likely. In some states, legislation that would require appraisers to meet minimum standards of experience and education is being considered.

The American Institute of Real Estate Appraisers has long encouraged industry self-regulation by awarding the RM (Residential Member) and MAI (Member, Appraisal Institute) designations to appraisers who meet its requirements of experience, competence, and ethical practice. The Appraisal Institute has worked to advance the status of professional real estate appraisers throughout the United States by making the public aware of the quality work performed by designated appraisers, by enforcing the Uniform Standards of Professional Appraisal Practice, and by sponsoring educational programs. Individuals who hold these recognized professional designations find their employment and business prospects considerably enhanced. Professionalism helps regulate the industry and strongly encourages quality appraisal work. In fact, many financial institutions only accept the work of appraisers with recognized professional designations.

Education

A college education can contribute to the success of a residential appraiser, particularly if this education has improved the individual's ability to reason clearly. Few colleges have programs devoted specifically to real estate appraisal, but courses in related fields such as economics, finance, taxation, city and county planning, architecture, urban geography, mathematics, and statistics can provide prospective appraisers with important background knowledge. The Appraisal Institute also offers courses and seminars on a variety of topics which can improve a residential appraiser's grasp of appraisal theory and practical techniques. A college degree is required for the RM (Residential Member) designation of the Appraisal Institute.

Skills

An appraiser must possess strong communication, investigative, and analytical skills. It is essential that an appraiser be able to communicate his or her findings in an orderly, logical, and grammatically correct manner. Clear communication is a sign of clear thinking and sound, considered judgment. Written reports to clients should be clear and persuasive. Jargon, ambiguity, and inconsistency are unacceptable. Furthermore, appraisers must regularly seek essential information from diverse individuals and sometimes from reluctant sources. Therefore, good communication skills are very important.

Good appraisers are like good detectives. They are naturally inquisitive and enjoy knowing where and how to obtain information. An appraiser must be aware of the countless ways in which data can be misleading and be sensitive to new trends and developments in the community. Appraisers must also be open-minded. Market value, which the appraiser seeks to estimate, is shaped by the needs, desires, and motivations of the marketplace, which may not conform to the appraiser's personal preferences.

Analytical skills are also important. Appraisers must know how to analyze the data they collect and draw logical conclusions. They should understand the reasoning behind the three approaches to value—the cost, sales comparison, and income capitalization approaches—and recognize that one approach may be more or less reliable than the others in a particular case. With good analytical skills, an appraiser can divide an assignment into a series of distinct tasks and provide much more efficient appraisal service.

Two attributes are essential in appraisal practice—reasonableness and common sense. These attributes are acquired through experience and help the appraiser gather and analyze data and draw sound, supportable conclusions.

Experience

Education, a knowledge of techniques, and skills are important, but the ultimate test of an appraiser's ability comes on the job. Experience is essential in appraisal and it is generally reflected in the salaries and fees an appraiser can earn. Learning the art of real estate appraisal takes time, but time alone is not enough. The appraiser will benefit from experience only if he or she constantly works at self-improvement through formal education such as the courses and seminars offered by the American Institute of Real Estate Appraisers and other professional organizations.

EMPLOYMENT AS A RESIDENTIAL APPRAISER

To dedicated, qualified professionals, the field of residential appraisal can present stimulating challenges and rewarding opportunities. Each property presents unique problems and each assignment challenges the appraiser to find efficient, creative solutions. The many appraisers who work in public and private institutions receive good salaries commensurate with their experience, ability, and education. Those with effective business skills have the option of entering private practice where they can enjoy the flexibility and greater remuneration that independence can often supply.

In addition to challenging work and monetary rewards, professional appraisers are also important to the community because of the service they provide. The public relies on real estate appraisers' opinions to make decisions concerning investment, land use and development, and critical legal matters. As a result, the integrity, responsibility, and sound judgment of professional appraisers can earn them the respect of the community in which they practice.

USING THIS BOOK

This book can be used as an introduction to residential appraisal by those entering the field, and as a review and reference text for more advanced students and practicing residential appraisers. It provides a practical guide to the essential aspects of residential appraising. Other individuals involved in the field of real estate may also find this book useful. Brokers and sales associates; representatives of lending institutions; housing contractors, developers, and builders; court and government officials; and individuals considering the purchase, sale, rental, leasing, or renovation of residential property could all benefit greatly from the appraisal knowledge contained in this text.

All the essential steps in the valuation process, the procedure that appraisers follow to reach appraisal conclusions, are presented and explained in detail. Many practical examples and illustrations are provided to enhance the reader's understanding.

Chapters 1 through 4 introduce fundamental terms and concepts and provide an overview of the valuation process. Chapter 5 explains how to begin an appraisal assignment and Chapters 6 through 10 describe most of the kinds of data appraisers need to collect and where and how they can be obtained. Chapter 11 discusses highest and best use, a fundamental concept in all appraisals. Chapters 12 through 19 cover the analytical techniques appraisers apply to the data collected to reach a value conclusion. Chapter 20 addresses the final reconciliation of value indications and Chapter 21 describes how appraisal results are communicated to the client. Chapter 22, the final chapter of the book, discusses the problems residential appraisers face when confronted with special types of residences.

Each chapter ends with a short summary and a list of review questions. By answering these questions, appraisers can obtain a better understanding of the material, identify any concepts they have not mastered, and prepare themselves for the topics covered in the chapters that follow. The review questions will also help readers remember the techniques they have learned so that they can apply them more successfully in actual appraisal situations.

SUMMARY

Residential real estate appraisal is a challenging and rewarding field for those who have the skills and sense of responsibility it requires. Practicing appraisers, beginning students, and professionals who work in real estate-related fields can all benefit from learning the appraisal techniques described in this book.

Appraisal is the act or process of estimating value. *Analysis* provides information, recommendations, and/or conclusions on diversified problems in real estate other than an estimate of value. Professional real estate appraisers base their value estimates on market data obtained through careful research. These data are analyzed by applying judgment and the results are communicated to clients in appraisal reports. The appraiser's conclusions and reasoning must be clearly expressed so that the report can be reviewed and understood by an objective third party. An appraisal report should stand on its own merits.

A careful distinction must also be made between the purpose of an appraisal and a client's use of the appraisal.

Appraisals are needed in our society because many market participants do not have the information and experience needed to make wise real estate decisions. The unbiased, professional estimates provided by appraisers allow buyers, sellers, and lenders to make sound economic and legal decisions. Clients need a professional appraiser's informed opinion to answer a variety of questions concerning proposed market transactions, taxes, legal claims, investment plans, and other real estate-related matters.

Appraisers who hold a recognized professional designation indicate that they have the ethical and educational qualifications as well as the experience required to perform assignments competently; designation usually enhances their employment prospects. A college education and training in relevant areas are often essential in residential appraising.

A basic knowledge of residential appraisal techniques can be learned from this text. Communication skills, curiosity, open-mindedness, analytical abilities, reasonableness, and common sense are essential attributes of professional appraisers. Observant appraisers develop additional skills and increase their competence through practical experience on the job.

REVIEW QUESTIONS

1. How do real estate appraisers contribute to the operation of economic and judicial systems?

2. Define the following terms: *appraisal, value,* and *analysis.*

3. Cite specific examples of market transactions, tax questions, legal claims, and investment planning situations in which appraisals may be required. What other matters might require an appraiser's opinion?

4. What type of education and experience can prepare an indivdual for the appraisal profession?

① By setting standards in valuing real estate interest whereas said interest in R.E. can be sold, transferred, finance, etc.

② Appraisal is an estimate of value determined by a
(A) trained, knowledgeable, expert

(B) Value is what is received on interest held in R.E. which is also determined by the purpose of the appraise

(C) Analysis is reporting on the uses, conditions, market of R.E. without determining value.

③ Appraisals needed for Buy sell, Devorice Settlements, Investments, Tax value,

④ Possible college, training in the field, O.J.T.

2 Real Property Ownership and Value

What is valued in an appraisal? Although appraisers investigate and analyze land and structures, these physical entities do not, strictly speaking, possess value or utility. Rather, it is the *right* to use property that has value. The various rights to use real estate are conveyed by a title, deed, or contract. When the ownership of a parcel of real estate is transferred, these rights change hands. To highlight this distinction, property is divided into two legal categories: real estate and real property.

REAL ESTATE

Real estate is the physical land and appurtenances attached to the land—e.g., structures. Real estate is the physical entity, which includes everything that is fixed and immobile. It encompasses all that is given by nature as part of the land as well as all that has been affixed to the land in a relatively permanent way by man.

The concept of real estate incorporates three important elements: land, improvements, and fixtures.

Land is the earth's surface, both land and water, and anything that is attached to it. It includes all natural resources in their original state—e.g., mineral deposits, wildlife, timber, fish, water, coal deposits, and soil.

Improvements are buildings or other relatively permanent structures or developments that are located on, or attached to, land. This category includes both improvements *to* the land such as access and utilities, which prepare the land for a subsequent use, and improvements *on* the land such as buildings and landscaping.

A *fixture* is an item that was once personal property—i.e., a movable possession that is not part of the real estate—but has since been installed or attached to the land or the building in a rather permanent manner.

It is not always apparent whether an item is truly a fixture, and thus part of the realty, or whether it should be considered personalty, and therefore not included in the real estate value estimate. An appraiser may need guidance to appreciate these legal distinctions, which are usually set forth in state law and may vary according to statute. Most courts use the following criteria to judge the status of an item:

1. The manner in which the item is affixed. Generally an item is considered personal property if it can be removed without causing serious injury to the real estate or to itself. There are exceptions to this rule.

2. The character of the item and its adaptation to the real estate. Items that are specifically constructed for use in a particular building or installed to fulfill the purpose for which the building was erected are generally considered permanent parts of the building.

3. The intention of the party who attached the item. Frequently the terms of a lease reveal whether the item was meant to be permanent or whether it was to be removed at some time.[1] For example, an apartment or house lease may specify that items such as bookshelves and venetian blinds may be installed by the tenant and removed as personal property at the termination of the lease.

To ascertain the full extent of the physical entity being appraised, the various components of the property must be distinguished in an appraisal. The appraiser must determine the exact boundaries of the site, the nature of any improvements to and on the site, and the status of any improvements including fixtures. Obviously, the inclusion or exclusion of an item from the appraiser's analysis can increase or decrease the total value estimate. If an appraiser is asked to include the value of certain items of personalty in the final value estimate, the effect of these inclusions must be precisely stated in the appraisal report.

REAL PROPERTY

Real property refers to all interests, benefits, and rights inherent in the ownership of physical real estate. The concept of real property is useful because the ownership of real estate consists of various interests, benefits, and rights, which can be separated without dividing the physical real estate. Real property has been compared to a bundle of sticks in which each stick represents a separate, transferable right. The individual rights to real estate include the rights to occupy the real estate, to sell it, to lease it, to enter it, to give it away, to borrow against it, or to exercise more than one or none of these rights. This aspect of real property divisibility is reflected in the bundle of rights theory.

Because real property rights are divisible, larger or smaller bundles of rights can be created by selling or leasing all or part of the property. These partial bundles of rights are contained in estates. An *estate* is the degree, nature, or extent of interest that a person has in property. Various possible estates are discussed below; each represents a different degree of real property ownership.

---

1. Robert Kratovil and Raymond J. Werner, *Real Estate Law*, 8th ed. (Englewood Cliffs, N.J.: Prentice-Hall, Inc., 1983), pp. 18-23.

Fee simple estates

Most of the properties studied in residential appraisals are held in fee simple. A *fee simple estate* is an absolute ownership unencumbered by any other interest or estate. The owner of a fee simple title possesses all the rights and benefits of the real estate subject only to the powers of government, which include taxation, eminent domain, escheat, and police power. The owner of a fee simple title possesses a complete bundle of rights.

Leased fee estates

When an owner enters into a lease agreement with a tenant, two less-than-complete estates are created: a leased fee estate and a leasehold estate. The leased fee estate is the landlord's estate. A *leased fee estate* is an ownership interest held by a landlord with the right of use and occupancy conveyed by lease to others; the rights of the lessor (the leased fee owner) and the leased fee are specified by contract terms contained within the lease. Specific lease terms vary, but a leased fee generally provides for rent to be paid by the lessee (the tenant) to the lessor (the landlord) under stipulated terms. The lessor has the right of repossession at the termination of the lease, default provisions, and the rights to sell, mortgage, or bequeath the property during the lease period. When a lease is legally delivered, the lessor must surrender possession of the property to the lessee for the lease period and abide by the lease provisions.

Leasehold estates

The leasehold estate is the lessee's, or tenant's, estate. A *leasehold estate* is the right to use and occupy real estate for a stated term under certain conditions as conveyed by the lease. Under a lease, the tenant usually acquires the rights to possess the property for the lease period, to sublease the property, and to improve the property under restrictions specified in the lease. In return the tenant must pay rent, surrender possession of the property at the termination of the lease, and abide by the lease provisions along with the lessor.

Estates encumbered by mortgages

An owner can limit or restrict his or her real property interest in exchange for a mortgage loan. The owner is obligated to repay the loan according to a certain schedule and to pledge the real estate as security. The value of the owner's interest minus the debt, or mortgage, is called *equity*. The lender's interest consists of the right to repayment plus the right to foreclose on the loan if the owner defaults; the lender can legally force a sale of the property to recover all or part of the money owed. Usually a residential appraiser is asked to estimate the value of property as if it were held in fee simple—i.e., without considering any mortgage encumbrances or leases that may exist.

Estates subject to easement

Granting or selling an easement can also create a less-than-complete estate. An *easement* is an interest that conveys use, but not ownership, of a portion of real property. A right-of-way is a common type of easement; it allows the owner of the dominant estate, or tenement, access rights across the servient estate, or tenement. The owner of the servient estate is not permitted to restrict access. Often easements are attached to the land and continue to burden the servient estate even when the property is sold; these easements are called *appurtenant easements*. A utility easement that permits power lines to run along one side of a site is an appurtenant easement. Information on the burdens and benefits of easements can be found in title reports.

Fee simple estates, leased fee and leasehold estates, easements, and mortgages represent only a few of the many ways in which

Figure 2.1   Components of Real Property Rights

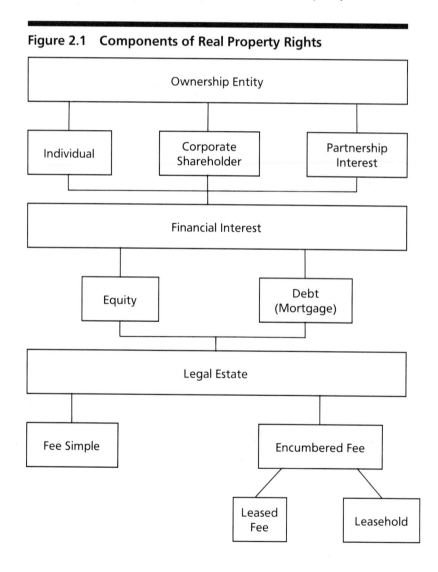

property rights may be divided. Just as various components of the physical real estate must be separated for appraisal purposes, an appraiser must precisely identify which *property rights* are being included in a valuation. The value conclusions reached in appraising the same parcel of real estate may differ depending on whether the fee simple estate or some other estate is being valued.

LIMITATIONS ON PROPERTY USE

Individuals who own estates in real property are limited in their use of the property only by the legal property rights they possess, by the physical characteristics of the real estate, and by economic feasibility. Subject to legal, physical, and economic limitations, owners of interests in real property in the United States have the right to put the property to any use they find desirable. This fact has considerable significance in real estate appraisal because value is created by the expectation of benefits that can accrue from ownership rights. Because various factors limit the potential uses and benefits that an estate can provide, the estate's value is limited as well. Thus an appraiser must carefully study the *legal limitations*, *physical limitations*, and *economic limitations* to which a parcel of real estate is subject. If any of these limitations change, the value of the parcel may change as a result.

Legal Limitations

Legal limitations effectively limit the ways in which property can be used. In the United States, public laws governing the use and development of land accord the owner the fullest possible freedom consistent with the rights accorded to others. However, the government reserves certain powers over property use, which take precedence over the rights of individuals to acquire title to property. Subject to constitutional and statutory requirements, the government can, at any time, exercise four powers for the public benefit. All property ownership is limited by the four powers of government: *taxation, eminent domain, escheat,* and *police power.* Taxation is the right of government to raise revenue through assessments on valuable goods, products, and rights. Under eminent domain, the government can take private property for public use upon the payment of just compensation to the owner. Escheat gives the state titular ownership of a property when its owner dies without a will or any ascertainable heirs. Police power is the right of government under which property is regulated to protect public safety, health, morals, and general welfare.

Under the power of taxation, state and local governments[2] can impose on owners of real property any level of taxes they need so long as these taxes are imposed fairly. Property taxes in different jurisdictions vary, and they can limit or discourage many kinds of development and land use.

---

2. Under the U.S. Constitution, the federal government is prohibited from directly taxing real property.

The power of eminent domain can be exercised by agencies acting under government authority such as housing departments and public utilities. Under this power, the government can take private property and use it for public purposes upon payment of just compensation to the owner. The private use of property can also be restricted by eminent domain. For example, the government can acquire an easement in the property for an underground electrical line or a sewer and water line.

The government's police power is the most direct, comprehensive, and frequently invoked legal limitation on property use. Through its police power, the government has the right to enforce zoning ordinances; building, housing, plumbing, and electrical codes; sanitary regulations; rent controls; historical preservation acts; utility requirements; and many other codes and regulations. These controls can affect almost every detail of property use, from permitted land uses to the size of windows and doors; even the type of finish can be regulated. Often the codes also specify what action is to be taken if the building does not conform to the ordinance requirements. Therefore, it is essential that an appraiser be familiar with all zoning ordinances and other regulations in effect in the area.

In addition to government restrictions on property, private voluntary and involuntary legal limitations exist. Private voluntary limitations include deed restrictions, lease agreements, mortgage notes with provisions that limit property use, and party wall agreements, which grant owners of adjoining properties the common right to use a wall erected on the boundary line. Private involuntary limitations include easements, rights-of-way, and encroachments.

Private legal limitations can restrict the use or manner of development and even the way in which ownership can be conveyed. The purchaser of an encumbered property may be obligated to use the property subject to restrictions. Thus there are many legal restrictions created by private agreement or imposed by government that affect the uses to which real estate may be put.

Physical Limitations

There are also physical limitations on what type of structure can be built in a particular location and in what mannner. The land's physical characteristics and the laws of nature dictate that many conceivable uses of real estate are difficult or impossible to achieve. Obviously a 120-ft.-by-150-ft. mansion cannot be built on a 100-ft.-by-120-ft. tract of land. Furthermore, it is not practical to build houses, raise crops, or construct office buildings in many places on the surface of the earth.

Land with irregular topography, earthquake fault areas, floodplains, areas with the potential for landslides, and excessively cold or hot areas have limited utility for residential users, although some people may be willing to put up with a certain amount of discomfort or risk. Physical factors affect the engineering and design of structures as well. Due to climatic conditions, building design in an area may be limited to a narrow range of building types.

The physical characteristics of real estate and the environment are not influenced by natural conditions only. Man-made conditions also restrict and influence land use. Proximity to roads and highways and access to shopping centers, workplaces, and recreational facilities can affect how a given parcel of real estate is used.

The laws of nature do not change, but the effects of natural conditions on specific locations can be mitigated. The limits of physical possibility are constantly being pushed back through technological advancement. For this reason, appraisers must keep abreast of changing physical conditions in the area as well as developments in science and technology, particularly construction techniques and building design. These factors can all affect the range of possible uses to which real estate may be put.

Economic Limitations

Although a use may be legally permissible and physically possible, it may not be economically practical for an owner to consider. The market strongly discourages uses that are not economically feasible. Conversely, uses that are profitable or beneficial are encouraged by the market so long as they are legally permissible. Chapters 4, 6, and 7 examine economic conditions that affect property use decisions.

Changing economic forces and constraints can alter the balance of legal and physical limitations on property use. If economic pressures are strong enough, existing physical and legal limitations can be overcome or modified. For example, zoning ordinances can be changed if a large constituency will benefit from their revision. Similarly, many difficult physical limitations can be overcome if enough money is available to correct them. Often these funds *will* be spent if there is a likelihood that greater benefits or income can be secured from the projected use of the real estate.

Limitations Combined

Together legal, physical, and economic limitations shape the ways in which real estate can be used. Legal restrictions limit the rights of individuals to use property in specific ways. Physical limitations can make certain uses impossible or difficult. The economic limitations created by market forces also affect property use. These three limitations dictate the number of uses to which a parcel of real estate can be put. In both appraisals and analyses, it is essential to study how real estate can be used profitably. Real estate appraiser-analysts examine these limitations and analyze their effect on the benefits the real property is expected to produce.

THE CONCEPT OF VALUE

As mentioned previously, value can be broadly defined as the monetary worth of goods or services to people. However, this definition is not sufficiently precise for appraisal purposes because "monetary worth" may have different meanings to various people involved in real estate activities. The concept of value may have one meaning to a buyer or seller and another to a lender, owner, investor, insurance adjustor, or tax collector. These different interpretations can be attributed to the fact that different people may focus on distinct aspects of real estate—i.e., different benefits, interests, or possible uses. Consider the following examples.

Buyers and sellers consider the monetary worth (market value) of a residential property in terms of the prices of other, nearby properties that are similar in quality and utility.

Lenders may consider the price a property would bring in a forced sale (liquidation value), rather than the prices obtained for comparable properties under typical market conditions.

Investors with unusual investment criteria may find that a particular property is ideally suited to their needs. For those investors, the monetary worth (investment value) of the real estate may be higher or lower than the value of a similar property to other buyers and sellers.

A property may provide its owner with certain valuable benefits and income that could not be realized by another owner. The monetary worth of the real estate to that owner might then be different than its worth to typical buyers and sellers of similar property. If the property were sold on the open market, the price obtained could be different from its investment value or use value.

Estimates of value may vary depending on the investor's perspective. In defining a residential appraisal problem, therefore, the appraiser *must* specify the precise type of value to be estimated—e.g., market value, use value, investment value, insurable value, assessed value, or some other type of specified value. The value concept selected must be precisely defined at the beginning of the valuation process.

MARKET VALUE

The concept of *market value* is of paramount importance to the business and real estate communities. Vast sums of debt and equity capital are committed each year to real estate investments and mortgage loans based on market value estimations. Individuals involved in real estate taxation, litigation, and legislation also have an ongoing, active concern with market value issues. In virtually every aspect of the real estate industry and its regulation at local, state, and federal levels, market value considerations are of vital importance to economic stability.

For these reasons, the definition of market value used by appraisers and their clients must be clearly understood and communicated. However, definitions of market value can and do represent different beliefs and assumptions about the marketplace and the nature of value. Although market value is basically a simple concept—i.e., an objective value created by the collective patterns of the market—the definition of market value is controversial and debate on the subject continues, sometimes producing rather fine distinctions.

The differences in market value definitions fall into several categories:

1. All cash and terms equivalent to cash versus noncash-equivalent financing terms

2. Specified property rights versus the real estate
3. Price versus the highest price
4. Most probable price versus the highest price
5. Equilibrium value versus market value

Current definitions of market value reflect different opinions about the items listed above. Some appraisers believe that market value is best measured in terms of all cash. This opinion has its origin in the first half of the twentieth century when economic conditions were extremely stable. During that period, mortgage rates remained nearly level, real estate prices rose slowly, and fee simple interests were the subject of most appraisals. Due to stable market conditions, little consideration was given to financing terms and market value in appraisals most frequently implied all-cash transactions.

Another school of thought emerged in the latter part of the twentieth century when real estate financing changed and real property interests became more complex. Today long-term, fixed-rate loans are increasingly supplemented or replaced with more complicated financing instruments. Many clients now request estimates of the market value of property subject to leases, easements, or mortgages. Therefore, real estate analysts must focus more attention on the important interrelationships between debt and equity interests and fee simple, leased fee, and leasehold interests.

Financing terms, which may or may not be equivalent to cash, affect value. The value affected by financing or leases may be market value when it is value created by the activity of the market.

A market value appraisal is always the valuation of specified rights in the subject property, not valuation of the physical real estate. The property rights specified may be the fee simple estate, the leased or mortgaged estate, or some other interest in the real estate.

There is considerable logic in the simple concept of market value as the "most probable selling price." If duress is present in a sale, however, it will be reflected in the transaction price, which may not be market value. Thus, "most probable selling price" has not been widely accepted as market value in some segments of the financial community.

The concept of market value as the "highest price" under a set of specific conditions, as opposed to the average or most likely price under the same conditions, is also controversial. For a market to exist, there must be enough buyers, sellers, and products to provide competition; from this competition a price that represents a central tendency and a highest tendency will develop. The notion of "highest price" was founded in the idea that market value should be the highest possible price represented by the central tendency, not the highest possible price within the range of market data. However, a definition that includes the word *highest* is, perhaps, subject to misinterpretation.

Equilibrium value is the price that would be set by the market if supply and demand were in balance. When the forces of supply and demand are not at equilibrium, market value can and does differ significantly from market value in a more balanced situation. During the Depression, for example, values fell dramatically and many people believed, or wanted to believe, that properties had intrinsic value, although this value was not obtainable in the market. When the market is extremely active, prices rise higher than some people believe is normal or intrinsic. In all cases, however, market value is the price that is available in the market. Intrinsic value and equilibrium value are regarded by some practitioners and theorists as meaningless in relation to market value.

Despite differing schools of thought, it is generally agreed that market value results from collective value judgments, not from isolated opinions. A market value estimate must be based on objective observation of the collective actions of the marketplace. The standard of measurement must be cash, so increases or decreases in market value caused by financing and other terms are measured against an all-cash value.

A good market value definition should incorporate the concepts that are most widely agreed upon—e.g., willing, able, and knowledgeable buyers and sellers who act prudently—and give the appraiser a choice among 1) all cash, or 2) terms equivalent to cash, or 3) other precisely revealed terms. Increments or diminutions from the all-cash market value must still be quantified in terms of cash. Thus market value may be defined as

> The most probable price, as of a specified date, in cash, or in terms equivalent to cash, or in other precisely revealed terms, for which the specified property rights should sell after reasonable exposure in a competitive market under all conditions requisite to fair sale, with the buyer and seller each acting prudently, knowledgeably, and for self-interest, and assuming that neither is under undue duress.

Fundamental assumptions and conditions presumed in this definition are that

1. Buyer and seller are motivated by self-interest.
2. Buyer and seller are well-informed and acting prudently.
3. The property is exposed for a reasonable time on the open market.
4. Payment is made in cash, its equivalent, or in specified financing terms.
5. Specified financing, if any, may be the financing actually in place or on terms generally available for the property type in its locale on the effective appraisal date.
6. The effect, if any, on the amount of market value of atypical financing, services, or fees shall be clearly and precisely revealed in the appraisal report.

If the value being estimated is market value, the Uniform Standards of Professional Appraisal Practice require that the appraiser clearly indicate whether the estimate is the most probable price

    i. in terms of cash; or

    ii. in terms of financial arrangements equivalent to cash; or

iii. in such other terms as may be precisely defined; if an estimate is based on submarket financing or financing with unusual conditions or incentives, the terms of such financing must be clearly set forth, their contributions to or negative influence on value must be described and estimated, and the market data supporting the valuation estimate must be described and explained

Although these requirements include noncash-equivalent financing terms within the scope of the market value of the appraised property rights, these rights are valued in relation to cash. Increases or decreases in market value that are attributable to financing terms are measured against an all-cash standard, and the dollar amount of variance between the financed value and the cash standard must be reported.

In litigation matters, appraisers must use the precise definition of market value that is applied in the jurisdiction in which the services are being performed. Because government and regulatory agencies define or interpret market value from time to time, individuals performing appraisal services for these agencies or for institutions subject to their control should use the applicable market value definition.

The Federal National Mortgage Association (FNMA) and the Federal Home Loan Mortgage Corporation (FHLMC) also use a special definition of market value with which appraisers should familiarize themselves.

OTHER VALUES

Use Value

Along with an increased emphasis on market value, the realities of today's real estate market frequently require that other kinds of value be considered. These other values include use value, investment value, insurable value, and assessed value.

Use value is the value of a specific property for a specific use. This value concept is based on the productivity of an economic good. Use value refers to the value that the real estate contributes to the enterprise of which it is a part, without regard to highest and best use or the monetary amount that might be realized upon its sale. Use value may vary with the management of the property and external conditions such as changes in the business environment. Many real properties have a different use value and market value.

When the property being appraised is of a type that is not commonly sold or rented, it may be difficult to determine whether an estimate of market value or use value is appropriate. *Limited-market properties* can present special problems for appraisers.

Many limited-market properties are improved with structures that have unique physical designs, special construction materials, or layouts that severely restrict the property's utility; generally they are only suitable for the use for which they were built. Consequently, such properties are often called *special-purpose* or *special-design properties*. In some locales, churches and schools may be limited-market properties.

In certain circumstances, limited-market properties may be appraised at their use value based on their current use. In other circumstances, they are appraised at market value based on the most likely alternative use. Because there is a relatively small market for these properties and lengthy market exposure is often required to find a buyer, evidence to support a market value estimate may be sparse. Nonetheless, if a market exists, the appraiser must search diligently for all available evidence of market value.

If a property's current use is so specialized that there is no demonstrable market for the property, but the use is viable and likely to continue, the appraiser may render an estimate of use value. A use value estimate should not be confused with a market value estimate. If no market can be found, or if data are not available, the appraiser cannot conclude a market value and should say so in the report. However, for legal purposes it is sometimes necessary to estimate market value when no market can be found. In these cases, the appraiser must comply with the legal requirement, but will have to reach an estimate of market value by other means.

Investment Value

While use value focuses on the specific use of a particular property, investment value is concerned with the value of a specific investment to a particular investor. In real estate appraisal assignments, *investment value* is the value of an investment to a particular investor based on individual investment requirements. In contrast to market value, investment value is value to an individual, not value in the marketplace.

Investment value reflects the subjective relationship between a particular investor and a given investment. It is distinct from market value, although investment value and market value indications may be numerically the same. When measured in dollars, investment value is the highest price an investor would pay for an investment given its perceived capacity to satisfy a desire, need, or investment goal. In all appraisals to estimate investment value, the specific investment criteria considered in the analysis must be reported.

Investment value appraisals are commonly requested by potential purchasers of existing investments or income-producing properties and by developers of new properties.

Insurable Value

Insurable value is based on the replacement cost of physical items that are subject to loss from hazards. *Insurable value* is that portion of the value of an asset or asset group that is acknowledged or recognized under the provisions of an applicable loss insurance policy.

Assessed Value

Assessed value is applied in ad valorem taxation and is established by the municipal authority legally charged with this responsibility. Assessment schedules may not conform to market value, but they usually relate to a market value base.

SUMMARY

Real estate and real property are distinct concepts, although under some statutes they are considered synonymous. *Real estate* refers to physical land and the improvements to and on the land. *Real property* refers to the benefits, interests, and rights inherent in the ownership of real estate. These rights can be divided and conveyed separately. A *fee simple* title implies full ownership of the complete bundle of rights. Leased fee estates, leasehold estates, estates encumbered by mortgages, and estates subject to easements all represent less-than-complete forms of property ownership.

The uses to which land can be put are limited by the form of property ownership, the physical characteristics of the real estate, and economic feasibility. Legal limitations on the rights and benefits of use are imposed by the four powers of government—taxation, eminent domain, escheat, and police power—and by private voluntary and involuntary restrictions. Zoning laws, building codes, and other regulations are based on the government's police power. Physical limitations on the use of property result from the natural condition of land and the environment in any given location. However, these conditions may change or be overcome through technological advances. Economic limitations seriously influence land-use decisions. Uses that are too expensive or do not produce sufficient benefits are generally avoided. Together legal, physical, and economic limitations restrict the range of beneficial uses to which real estate can be put and substantially affect real estate values.

Because the term *value* has many meanings, a specific value definition must be selected and stated at the beginning of an appraisal assignment. *Market value* is the most widely recognized value concept and it is the type of value most commonly estimated in appraisals. Definitions of market value vary, but the one selected for use in the appraisal must be precisely understood and communicated. One definition that incorporates widely accepted concepts is

> The most probable price, as of a specified date, in cash, or in terms equivalent to cash, or in other revealed terms, for which the specified property rights should sell after reasonable exposure in a competitive market under all conditions requisite to fair sale, with the buyer and seller each acting prudently, knowledgeably, and for self-interest, and assuming that neither is under undue duress.

Under the Uniform Standards of Professional Appraisal Practice, the specification of market value in an appraisal report must include a statement as to whether the estimate is in terms of cash, in terms of financial arrangements equivalent to cash, or in such other terms as may be precisely defined.

Appraisers are frequently asked to estimate other types of value, including use value, investment value, and insurable value. Use value is the value of a specific property for a specific use without regard to its highest and best use. Investment value is the value of an investment to a particular investor based on individual investment requirements. Insurable value is that portion of value covered by casualty insurance. Assessed value refers to the value of property for ad valorem tax purposes and is calculated by applying a ratio to market value.

REVIEW QUESTIONS

1. Explain the distinction between real estate and real property.
2. Identify and describe several different real property interests.
3. How do legal, physical, and economic limitations restrict the uses to which real estate may be put?
4. What different concepts of value are used by buyers and sellers, owners, investors, lenders, insurers, and tax assessors?
5. Discuss the various elements that must be considered in the definition of market value.

3 The Valuation Process

The *valuation process* is a systematic procedure developed to produce well-researched, well-supported estimates of real property value. The process consists of a progressive series of steps, beginning with the definition of the valuation problem. The process proceeds through the collection of data pertinent to the problem's solution, the selection and application of appropriate analytical approaches, the reconciliation of value indications, and the final estimate of value. It concludes when the value conclusion is reported to the client. The steps in the process and the methods of analysis are adaptable to many appraisal situations. Although the valuation process is designed primarily for market value appraisals, it provides a general framework within which most valuation assignments are conducted.

The valuation process consists of seven basic steps, which are graphically illustrated in Figure 3.1. Each phase of the process will be briefly discussed in this chapter; more detailed discussion of specific steps will be presented in subsequent chapters.

DEFINITION OF THE PROBLEM

The first step in the valuation process is to define the problem accurately. An exact definition eliminates ambiguity about what the client requires and alerts the appraiser to the amount and nature of the data that will be needed to solve the problem. The definition of the appraisal problem has seven, specific components:

1. Identification of the real estate
2. Identification of the property rights to be valued
3. Date of the value estimate
4. Use of the appraisal
5. Definition of value
6. Description of the scope of the appraisal
7. Limiting conditions and assumptions

Identification of the Real Estate

The property to be valued must be precisely identified. A street address is often acceptable, but a complete legal description is

Figure 3.1   The Valuation Process

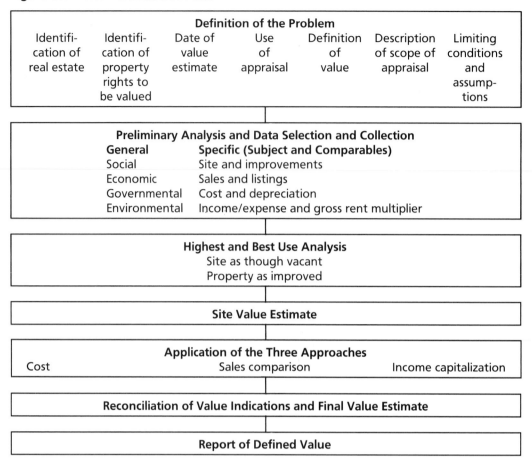

Definition of the Problem						
Identifi-cation of real estate	Identifi-cation of property rights to be valued	Date of value estimate	Use of appraisal	Definition of value	Description of scope of appraisal	Limiting conditions and assump-tions

Preliminary Analysis and Data Selection and Collection	
General	**Specific (Subject and Comparables)**
Social	Site and improvements
Economic	Sales and listings
Governmental	Cost and depreciation
Environmental	Income/expense and gross rent multiplier

Highest and Best Use Analysis
Site as though vacant
Property as improved

Site Value Estimate

Application of the Three Approaches		
Cost	Sales comparison	Income capitalization

Reconciliation of Value Indications and Final Value Estimate

Report of Defined Value

preferred. Legal descriptions are derived from land surveys and maintained in public records under state and local law. They may be found in deeds, abstracts of title, mortgages, plat books, and other public documents.

Land may be described using various systems of identification: the metes and bounds system, the rectangular or government survey system, and the lot and block system. Appraisers should be familiar with the types of legal description that are most prevalent in their area. The three systems mentioned above are described in Chapter 5.

A detailed description and an analysis of the improvements are made later in the appraisal, but some appraisers mention the property type within the definition of the problem. This is a matter of choice and custom. The identification of the real estate should leave no doubt as to the location and identity of the property being appraised.

Identification of the Property Rights to Be Valued

After the real estate is identified, the ownership rights must be precisely defined. Most residential appraisal assignments are per-

formed to estimate the value of the rights of absolute ownership—
the fee simple.

Occasionally appraisals to estimate other rights are requested.
Easements, encroachments, and subsurface mineral rights are examples of fractional rights that may have to be valued separately.
Appraisers may also be asked to estimate the value of partial interests created by the severance or division of ownership rights. Liens
and other limitations of ownership should be identified in the
definition of the appraisal problem. Because real property value
is the value of the rights of ownership, it is important to specify
which particular rights are to be valued in an appraisal.

Date of Value Estimate

A specific date of value is essential because value influences change
constantly. Abrupt changes in the business and real estate markets affect property values. Even without dramatic market shifts,
values are subject to gradual change. Therefore, a value estimate
is only valid for a particular date. Using a specified date enables
an appraiser to isolate and quantify all the factors that influence
value at this time.

Most appraisals require current value estimates and usually
the client and the appraiser agree on the exact date in advance.
The date of inspection is often used as the date of the value estimate if no other date is specified. However, retrospective and prospective appraisals are not uncommon. An appraisal for inheritance
tax purposes usually requires an estimate of value as of the date
of the testator's death. To make insurance adjustments, insurers
may require a value estimate as of the date of casualty. Appraisals
used in lawsuits frequently require a value estimate as of a date
set by the court. In eminent domain proceedings, for example,
value is estimated as of the date when the petition to condemn
was filed, or as of some other date stipulated by statute or the
court. Similarly, appraisals for divorce litigation require value
estimates as of a specified date (e.g., date of filing or dissolution).
Some appraisals prepared for mortgage financing require value
estimates as of a prospective or future date.

Use of the Appraisal

Appraisals may be used in many different ways by various clients.
Lenders may want to know how much money to lend to a home
buyer. Buyers and sellers may want a value estimate to analyze
offers to buy or sell. Courts may use value estimates as a basis for
just compensation in eminent domain proceedings.

An appraiser can often avoid misdirected effort and other difficulties by reaching an advance agreement with the client on the
use and ownership of the appraisal and the form of the appraisal
report.

Definition of Value

Many types of value may be estimated in appraisals—e.g., market
value, use value, investment value, assessed value, and insurable
value. Each of these values has its own definition and special

techniques may be required to estimate the value sought. Therefore, it is essential to specify the value being reported. If this value is market value, the clients or the courts may request that the appraiser use the specific legal or economic definition that is appropriate to the assignment. The Uniform Standards of Professional Appraisal Practice require an appraiser to define the value being considered.

Once the value to be estimated has been identified, the appraiser can select the most appropriate valuation techniques and determine the necessary data to collect. Including the definition of value in the report also communicates the objective of the appraisal to the reader.

Description of the Scope of the Appraisal

The *scope of the appraisal* refers to the extent of the process in which data are collected, confirmed, and reported. The scope is described to protect third parties whose reliance on an appraisal report may be affected by this information. An appraiser determines the extent of the work and of the report relative to the significance of the appraisal problem. The appraiser is responsible for describing the scope of the appraisal in the report.

Limiting Conditions and Assumptions

To complete the definition of the problem, all limitations and assumptions inherent in the appraisal report must be identified. For example, the report might state that the valuation of subsurface rights is not part of the appraisal. Other limiting conditions might specify that no court testimony or attendance in court will be required unless separate arrangements are made, that no engineering survey has been made by the appraiser, that data on the size and area of the property have been obtained from sources believed to be reliable, or that no environmental assessment has been undertaken. All of these conditions limit the scope of the appraiser's obligations in regard to the assignment and must be clearly and prominently set forth in the report.

PRELIMINARY ANALYSIS AND DATA SELECTION AND COLLECTION

The second phase of the valuation process consists of a preliminary analysis of the problem and selection and collection of pertinent data. A plan of the steps needed to complete the assignment is useful in the preliminary analysis; it allows the appraiser to create a schedule for data collection. Each task is allocated a certain amount of time and a place in the sequence. Then a person is selected to complete each task, either someone on the appraiser's staff or an outside specialist. Detailed work plans are especially necessary in long, complex assignments. They can help prevent errors and omissions and may make research trips more productive. A work plan can also be useful when the client and appraiser negotiate the appraiser's fee.

To perform a preliminary analysis, an appraiser investigates the subject neighborhood, itemizes the data that will be needed, and creates a work schedule.

Preliminary investigation

A drive around the subject neighborhood and property will help familiarize the appraiser with the task ahead. Special conditions that may require additional research can be noted. A preliminary investigation may not be necessary if the appraiser has had considerable experience with the neighborhood and the property type.

Data needed

A useful work plan includes a list of all the general and specific data needed. Information on value influences in the region and the neighborhood should be listed along with data on the subject and comparable properties. If information from soil experts, engineers, legal specialists, or other experts will be required, this should be noted.

Work schedule

A work schedule in the form of a flowchart is organized around the steps in the valuation process. The main procedures to be performed and the types of data needed should be listed in the order in which they will be used; the responsibility for completing each task should be properly delegated.

After the preliminary analysis, the appraiser is ready to begin collecting pertinent data. The amount and type of data required will vary with the type of property being appraised, the value being estimated, the presentation of the report, and the intended use of the value conclusion. Depending on the appraisal assignment, a particular approach to value and data collection effort may be appropriate. The valuation approaches are discussed in detail in subsequent chapters.

Most appraisal assignments require information on market transactions of similar vacant and improved real estate; cost and depreciation estimates; and income, expense, and gross rent multiplier data. Data fall into two categories: general data about conditions in the nation, region, city, and neighborhood that affect value and specific data about the site, the improvements, and comparable properties. The accuracy of all data obtained should be verified by cross-checking different sources and inspecting the subject property.

General Data

The collection of *general data* usually involves all or many of the following steps:

1. Compile information on how social, economic, governmental, and environmental forces interact and affect real estate values on national, regional, and local levels. Appraisers need this information to develop an understanding of how these four forces influence the value and use of the subject property.

2. Inspect and observe the neighborhood, identifying its boundaries and major characteristics. Neighborhood inspection is usually performed during the preliminary survey. Because many of the forces that influence value affect most properties in a neighborhood in the same way, identifying neigh-

borhood boundaries is an important step toward selecting relevant market data.

3. Identify the stage in the life cycle of the neighborhood. Neighborhoods typically go through a cycle of changes—i.e., growth, stability, decline, and revitalization—which affect property values. Understanding the reasons behind these value changes can help an appraiser identify the highest and best use of a property.

4. Conduct additional research into the local market. Although some changes that affect values in a neighborhood are immediately discernible, others may require time-consuming study. In particular, appraisers should focus on factors that pertain to the long-term prospects of the area. Neighborhood zoning ordinances, municipal development projects, locally available financing terms, and plans for transportation networks can provide useful indications of how neighborhood values have been evolving. This information may enable an appraiser to forecast future trends.

5. Rate the quality of the neighborhood. Appraisers must try to identify and understand the amenities and shortcomings that make a neighborhood more or less attractive to market participants. This critical step in data collection will allow the appraiser to determine the locational advantages or disadvantages of the subject and comparable properties.

Specific Data

Specific data are collected for the subject property and each proposed comparable. First the appraiser inspects the subject property's site and improvements. Site data include information on the size, shape, and location of the lot; the orientation of the building(s); the topography; available utilities and site improvements; and the property's compatibility with surrounding land uses. The improvements are described in terms of their style, design, and layout as well as their structural and mechanical components. The appraiser rates each component for its quality, condition, functional utility, energy efficiency, and market appeal. Comparable properties are usually analyzed in less detail than the subject, but all factors that affect their values must be analyzed fully and accurately.

The amount of detail needed to describe the subject property depends on which approaches are applied. If sales comparison is the primary approach, the data collected must be sufficient to allow the appraiser to recognize and adjust for differences between the subject and similar properties. When the cost approach is emphasized, the subject property description must be detailed enough to support a valid estimate of the costs of reproducing or replacing the improvements with a comparable structure and an accurate measurement of accrued depreciation. If the real estate produces an income, the appraiser may investigate comparable properties to estimate rents and expenses and to derive income multipliers and overall capitalization rates. The appraiser must determine the degree of comparability between the subject and comparable properties to ensure that their sources of income are the same and that their operating expense ratios are similar.

HIGHEST AND BEST USE ANALYSIS

Highest and best use analysis is essential in the valuation process. The highest and best use of both the site as though vacant and the property as improved must meet four criteria. The highest and best use must be 1) legally permissible, 2) physically possible, 3) financially feasible, and 4) maximally productive. These criteria are usually considered sequentially; a use may be financially feasible, but this is irrelevant if it is legally prohibited or physically impossible.

Highest and best use analysis is performed in two steps. First the site is analyzed as though vacant and available for development. Analyzing the highest and best use of the site as though vacant serves two important functions. It helps the appraiser identify comparable properties. The highest and best use of comparable property sites as though vacant should be similar to that of the subject property. A second reason to analyze the highest and best use of the site as though vacant is to help the appraiser develop an estimate of site value.

In this first analysis, the potential uses of the vacant land are analyzed with respect to the four criteria. Each use is tested to see whether it is legally permissible, physically possible, and financially feasible. Uses that do not pass these tests are eliminated from further consideration. The uses that remain are analyzed and the one that is maximally productive is selected as the highest and best use of the site as though vacant.

The highest and best use of a site may be to remain vacant, or it may be to develop the site. If so, the appraiser seeks to find out what type of building or other improvement should be constructed and when. The conclusion of highest and best use for a site should be as specific as the marketplace indicates.

In the second analysis, the highest and best use of the property as improved is examined. Analyzing the highest and best use of property as improved also serves two functions. The appraiser can ensure that each comparable improved property has a highest and best use similar to that of the subject property. The analysis also helps an appraiser determine whether the improvements should be demolished, renovated, or retained in their present condition. Identification of the existing property's most profitable use is crucial to this determination.

In this second analysis, the existing improvements are considered with respect to the same four criteria. Of the legal uses that are physically possible and financially feasible, the one that is maximally productive is the highest and best use of the property as improved. In analyzing the highest and best use of owner-occupied properties, appraisers must consider any rehabilitation or modernization that is consistent with market preferences. For example, the highest and best use of a residence should reflect all rehabilitation required to provide the amenities that are standard in the given market.

SITE VALUE ESTIMATE

In many market value appraisal assignments, separate estimates of the value of the site are required. Some appraisals are performed to value a site only. Ad valorem tax assessments in some areas require separate estimates of site value and a site value estimate is also essential to highest and best use analysis.

The most reliable method for estimating site value is the sales comparison approach. Sales of similar vacant parcels are researched, analyzed, compared, and adjusted to provide a value indication for the land being appraised. When sufficient data are not available for sales comparison, however, several other procedures can be used to value land: allocation, extraction, subdivision development analysis, land residual techniques, and ground rent capitalization. All six land valuation procedures and the relative merits of each are discussed in detail in Chapter 12.

APPLICATION OF THE THREE APPROACHES

Once pertinent data have been collected, the appraiser is ready to apply one or more of the three approaches to value; each approach will result in at least one separate indication of value. The appropriateness of each approach depends on the nature of the valuation problem and the amount of reliable data available. For example, the sales comparison approach is most applicable when sufficient data can be collected on recent sales of comparable properties. If a property has many special features or no comparable properties have been sold recently, the sales comparison approach may not be very reliable. In these cases, the appraiser might place greater emphasis on the cost approach. If the property being appraised appeals to an active rental market, the income capitalization approach is given serious consideration. All applicable approaches should be used whenever possible.

All three approaches rely on market data and the principle of substitution, which holds that the price or rent that a property is likely to command will closely reflect the prices or rents for which similar properties are selling or renting in the same market. The cost of constructing similar structures, minus accrued depreciation, can be added to site value to produce one value indication. Sales of comparable properties can be analyzed to produce another. Studying the value of properties that have similar gross incomes provides a third method for obtaining a value indication. Because all three approaches are based on an understanding of how buyers and sellers interact, they should yield similar value conclusions.

Cost Approach

The *cost approach* is based on the premise that value is indicated by the current cost to construct a new improvement minus accrued depreciation plus the value of the site.

The cost approach is applied in five steps:

1. Estimate the value of the site as if vacant and available for development to its highest and best use.
2. Estimate the current cost of replacing or reproducing all building and site improvements.

3. Estimate accrued depreciation from all causes.

4. Subtract the estimate of accrued depreciation from the replacement or reproduction cost estimate to obtain an estimate of the depreciated value of the improvements.

5. Add the estimate of the depreciated replacement or reproduction cost of the improvements to the estimated value of the site.

The cost approach is most reliable when the property's improvements are new or nearly new and represent the highest and best use of the site. If the utility and condition of the property are close to ideal, accrued depreciation will be minimal. Because accrued depreciation can be difficult to estimate, the cost approach is less reliable and less convincing when it is used to appraise older properties. When an improvement has special construction features or comparable sales are unavailable, the cost approach is especially useful.

Sales Comparison Approach

The *sales comparison approach* is used to value most residential properties because it is direct and easy to understand. When properly applied, this approach is usually the most reliable and the most persuasive. To apply the sales comparison approach, the appraiser considers the prices of similar properties that have recently been sold. These prices can indicate the value of the subject property once they are adjusted to reflect any differences between the subject and the comparables. The steps are

1. Research and identify comparable properties that have been sold recently, and ascertain the price, property rights conveyed, financing terms, conditions of sale (buyer and seller motivations), and market conditions (time) involved in each transaction. Verify the accuracy of this information.

2. Examine each comparable sale to determine how it differs from the subject property and how these differences affect its value. The elements of comparison include real property rights conveyed, financing terms, conditions of sale, market conditions, and other features such as location, physical characteristics, and income-producing characteristics, if appropriate.

3. Adjust the sale or unit price of each comparable for observed differences between the subject and the comparables. If the subject is superior to the comparable, adjust the price of the comparable upward; if the subject is inferior to the comparable, a downward adjustment is made to the price of the comparable.

4. Reconcile the results of these comparisons into a single value indication or range of values.

Income Capitalization Approach

In the *income capitalization approach*, property value is measured in relation to the anticipated future benefits that can be derived from property ownership. When the property being appraised competes in an active rental market, an appraiser can derive an indication of value by converting the anticipated future benefits into a present value through capitalization. The capitalization technique applied depends on the income characteristics of the subject property and the data available for analysis.

The income capitalization approach is not commonly used to estimate the value of single-family residential properties. However, some residential properties are bought on the basis of their gross incomes. To value these properties, a gross rent multiplier (*GRM*) can be applied to an estimate of market rent. The steps are

1. Research and identify competitive rental properties that have been sold recently and divide the sale price of each by its gross monthly rent at the time of sale to obtain its *GRM*.

2. Estimate the monthly market rent that the subject property should command in light of present and anticipated rent levels and the property's market appeal.

3. Multiply the subject property's monthly market rent by a *GRM* selected from the *GRM*s of competing properties to obtain an indication of the value of the subject property.

To derive reliable *GRM*s, the appraiser must use truly comparable properties that have very similar ratios of operating expenses to gross rent.

Some buildings are bought on the basis of their net operating incomes (*NOI*s). These properties are typically valued with direct capitalization—i.e., a stabilized net operating income estimate is capitalized using an overall rate (R_O). Other, more involved analyses and capitalization procedures may be needed to estimate the value of some income-producing properties.

RECONCILIATION OF VALUE ESTIMATES AND FINAL VALUE CONCLUSION

The last analytical phase in the valuation process is the *reconciliation* of the various value estimates into a *final value conclusion*. Obviously the application of more than one approach will result in more than one estimate of value. Even if only one approach is applied, the range of values derived may need to be refined into a single figure. To perform reconciliation, an appraiser reviews each stage of the valuation process and tests the reasonableness of each conclusion reached. The appraiser asks, which data seem to be the most reliable? Which approach should be given the greatest weight in light of the purpose of the assignment and the information available? Finally, and perhaps most importantly, do the results make sense? These questions must be asked and answered throughout the valuation process, but final reconciliation is the appraiser's last opportunity to perform such a review.

Each valuation approach serves as a check on the other approaches used. A wide variation among the value estimates derived often suggests that one approach is not as applicable as the others or that valuation procedures have not been properly applied. Unrealistic conclusions must be closely scrutinized. Once the appraiser is satisfied that the general range of value estimates is justified, each estimate is weighted according to its appropriateness and reliability. Finally, the appraiser selects a single value estimate or a range of value estimates based on the market data and his or her informed judgment.

REPORT OF DEFINED VALUE

An appraisal is not complete until the conclusion and the reasoning behind it have been communicated to the client, usually in a written report. In addition to the final estimate of value, written reports should include all the pertinent data considered and all the methods of analysis used in the appraisal.

The appraisal report is a tangible expression of the appraiser's service, so its organization, presentation, and overall appearance are important. By signing a report, the appraiser accepts responsibility for the report. Appraisal reports prepared by members or candidates of the American Institute of Real Estate Appraisers must meet certain requirements.[1]

Appraisals may be communicated orally or in writing. Examples of written reports include form reports, letter reports, and narrative reports.

Form reports are preprinted documents which appraisers complete as they proceed through the valuation process. These standardized forms allow users of appraisal reports to compare and consider many appraisals quickly, to discern immediately whether all the required information has been supplied, and to analyze the reported data with computers. Form reports are commonly used by lending institutions, government agencies, and employee transfer companies which must process large numbers of appraisals.

If a client is already familiar with the subject property or, for some other reason, a detailed narrative report is not necessary, a *letter report* may be requested. Letter reports include all the items in the definition of the problem in abbreviated form, a brief outline of how the appraisal was conducted, and the value conclusion. A letter report should be of sufficient length to meet all minimum reporting requirements.

A *narrative report* is the most comprehensive method for communicating the results of an appraisal to the client. This type of report is used when complete, detailed documentation is needed. A narrative appraisal report presents the pertinent evidence and the logic employed to reach the final value estimate in a manner that is simple and convincing. Narrative reports are usually organized to follow the main steps in the valuation process.

---

1. See the Standards Rules Relating to Standard 2 of the Uniform Standards of Professional Appraisal Practice for the specific requirements that apply to reports of value estimates (appraisals) signed by Appraisal Institute members and candidates.

SUMMARY

The valuation process is a systematic procedure that results in a final value estimate. The process begins with a concise statement of the problem. To define the appraisal problem, the appraiser must identify the real estate and the property rights to be appraised. The date of the value estimate, the use of the appraisal, the definition of the value to be estimated, the scope of the appraisal, and all limiting conditions and assumptions must be specified.

Once the problem is defined, the appraiser makes a preliminary investigation of the subject property and the area, itemizes the kinds of data that will be needed, and prepares a work schedule. The amount and type of data required depend on the type of property being appraised, the definition of value, and the use of the appraisal. These factors may influence the valuation approaches applied and the data to be collected. The data collected include general data, which pertain to national and regional influences as well as local community characteristics, and specific data about the subject property and comparable sale properties.

An analysis of highest and best use is crucial to the valuation process. The four criteria of legal permissibility, physical possibility, financial feasibility, and maximum productivity are used as tests. Highest and best use is analyzed for the site as though vacant and for the property as improved. The value of the site as though vacant is estimated through sales comparison or other appropriate procedures. Separate value indications for the property as improved are derived by applying the cost, sales comparison, and income capitalization approaches to value.

To apply the sales comparison approach, an appraiser collects sales data on comparable properties, analyzes differences among the subject and comparable properties, makes appropriate adjustments to the prices of the comparables, and reconciles the resulting value indications. In the cost approach, estimates are made of the value of the land as though vacant, the replacement or reproduction cost of the improvements, and accrued depreciation from all causes. Accrued depreciation is then subtracted from the replacement or reproduction cost to obtain the depreciated value of the improvements, which is added to land value to produce a property value indication. To apply the income capitalization approach, the appraiser derives gross rent multipliers (*GRM*s) from competitive rental properties by dividing the sale price of each by its gross monthly rent. Then the monthly market rent of the subject property is estimated and this figure is multiplied by a gross rent multiplier selected from the range of multipliers indicated by the competitive properties.

One or more of the approaches to value may have greater significance or reliability in a given assignment. The separate value indications derived from the approaches applied are reconciled into a final estimate of value. The data and analysis on which the value estimate is based are communicated to the client in an appraisal report, which may be an oral report or a form, letter, or narrative report. All appraisal reports must meet the requirements of the Uniform Standards of Professional Appraisal Practice.

REVIEW QUESTIONS

1. Identify the basic steps in the valuation process.
2. Discuss the considerations that must be addressed to define the valuation problem.
3. Explain what is involved in a preliminary analysis.
4. Describe the types of information that are considered general data and specific data.
5. What is the purpose of highest and best use analysis?
6. Describe the methodology involved in each of the three approaches to value.
7. What are the purpose and significance of reconciling value estimates?

4 Principles of Real Estate Economics

Every appraiser should be familiar with the fundamental principles of real estate economics. These concepts originate in basic economic theory and have been refined and made practical by real estate appraisers throughout this century. Economic principles provide a theoretical base, although real estate appraisal is not concerned with theoretical matters only. Every objective, professional appraisal must be supported by a solid understanding of economic principles, which govern how value is created and how it changes in the real estate market. To conduct professional appraisals, practitioners must recognize how economic principles operate in particular valuation situations. These fundamental ideas reappear throughout the remaining chapters of this book.

The principles and concepts of real estate economics may be organized into three broad categories:

1. General economic principles, which can be observd in a wide variety of markets;
2. Special characteristics of real estate markets; and
3. Principles relating to the agents of production, which create real estate and the benefits that accrue from the use of real estate.

GENERAL ECONOMIC THEORY

The general principles of economic theory are the laws and concepts that characterize the actions of buyers and sellers who exchange many types of goods and services. These fundamental ideas apply to real estate markets as well as related markets which directly or indirectly influence property values. The fundamental concerns to be addressed are the principle of supply and demand, the concept of competition, the principle of substitution, and the definition of a market.

Supply and Demand

The most fundamental of all economic principles is the law of supply and demand. As applied to real property, the law of *supply and demand* states that the price of real property varies directly, but not necessarily proportionately, with demand and inversely, but not necessarily proportionately, with supply. This principle applies to the prices of all goods and services that are bought and sold in competitive markets. It affirms that, all else being equal, less money will usually be received for an item when it is available for sale in greater numbers, and more money will generally be obtained for the item when less of it is available. Similarly, when the number of items that purchasers demand increases, the prices paid for these items can be expected to rise provided the supply remains constant; if demand decreases, prices can be expected to fall.

In residential markets, supply increases may result from new construction, conversion from other uses, or the actions of many owners who decide to sell at a given time. Decreases in supply usually result from demolition, conversion to other uses, abandonment, slow or limited construction of new residences, and the actions of owners who decide to abstain from selling their property. Changes in demand typically occur more rapidly than changes in supply, so demand is the more critical price determinant.

Figures 4.1 and 4.2 illustrate the operation of the principle of supply and demand in the real estate market. Supply is the schedule of various amounts of a type of real estate available for sale or lease at various prices. As the upward-sloping supply curve in Figure 4.1 suggests, suppliers are usually more willing to supply when prices are higher. Similarly, demand is the schedule of the amounts of a type of real estate demanded at various prices for purchase or rent. The demand curve in the figure slopes downward because more is demanded at lower prices. The point where these curves intersect is the price at which a given property will most probably sell.

Figure 4.2 shows how the real estate market reacts when demand shifts. In this example demand has decreased, so the whole curve moves to the left. If supply remains constant, the curves intersect at a different point and the price at which the property will most probably sell drops.

Four economic factors must be present to create value: desire, utility, scarcity, and effective purchasing power. The interaction of these factors is reflected in the principle of supply and demand. *Desire* is a purchaser's wish for an item to satisfy an actual need or an individual want beyond essential life-support needs. Desire is limited by effective purchasing power.

Utility is the ability of an item to satisfy a human want, need, or desire; it varies with the wants and needs of different individuals. Sometimes improving the usefulness and quality of an item can increase the demand for it. However, changes in utility can only go so far toward augmenting demand.

Scarcity is the present or anticipated supply of an item relative to the demand for it. The availability of an item must be somewhat limited for needs or wants to be perceived. If an item is abundant, its existence will be taken for granted. Air is the classic example of a necessary item that is typically so abundant that it has no definable economic value.

The final factor of value is *effective purchasing power*, the ability and willingness of people to pay for the goods or services that

Figure 4.1 Operation of Supply and Demand

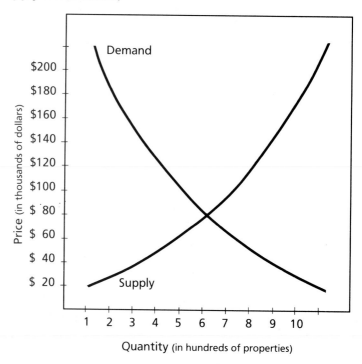

Figure 4.2 Operation of Supply and Demand (Demand Shifts)

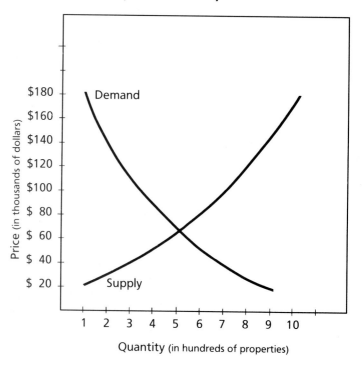

Appraising Residential Properties

they desire. Individuals must have purchasing power to translate their desires into demand. Desire coupled with purchasing power is sometimes called *effective demand*. Often the effective demand for an expensive item diminishes when income levels fall. Changes in purchasing power have a pronounced effect on real estate markets because real estate transactions involve large amounts of money.

Competition

Supply and demand exert their pressure on prices through *competition*. An auction is a familiar example of competition among buyers. Most markets are not like auctions, however, because sellers must also compete. When demand is weak compared with supply, competition between sellers can become especially intense. The quality and utility of the item may be improved and special incentives may be offered to attract the limited number of buyers. In many cases, prices must also be reduced.

Competing sellers hope to make a profit by obtaining prices that are somewhat greater than their expenses for acquiring or producing the item. When a strong demand for an item emerges, the first sellers frequently do make sizable profits. Soon, however, other sellers join the competition, which drives prices down. Sometimes so many suppliers join the market that competition is very intense and prices fall below the cost of production, which undermines profits for everyone. In this situation, some sellers go bankrupt and others refrain from any further production or acquisition until all the oversupplied items have been absorbed, and demand can resume at higher prices.

In the long run, balance is restored in the market, at least in theory. When demand is not strong enough to raise prices, nor weak enough to lower prices, prices stabilize and the forces of supply and demand are in equilibrium. At the point of equilibrium, prices are generally fairly close to the costs required to produce the item and compensate developers with an acceptable margin of profit, called *entrepreneurial profit*.

Substitution

Substitution is another principle that has broad significance in all economic activities. The principle of *substitution* affirms that when several similar or commensurate commodities, goods, or services are available, the one with the lowest price will attract the greatest demand and the widest distribution. Because competition underlies this principle, the prices at which similar items are sold in a market tend to grow increasingly uniform. Sellers who face a shrinking demand for their products are soon forced to lower their prices to prevailing levels if they are to sell at all. Sellers who experience the most intense demand for their products due to their lower prices may raise prices to established levels to reap greater profits.

When the items that different sellers are offering are physically similar, like oranges at a fruit market, it is easy to see how the principle of substitution operates. But substitution works equally well when the characteristics of items of similar utility are more abstract. For example, investors may perceive bond issues, mortgage loans, and other long-term capital instruments to be more or less interchangeable for their purposes; these investments all involve similar levels of risk, tie up money for approximately the same amount of time, and produce similar yields. As a result, these investments directly compete with one another for investors' funds.

Because investments compete for investment capital, conditions in the mortgage market closely follow conditions in financial markets, and the mortgage market is sensitive to developments that affect investment in other financial markets. Appraisers must perceive these market relationships to understand changes in price levels in the residential market. The amount and terms of mortgage money available at any given moment strongly affect the demand for housing.

The principle of substitution is also basic to the three valuation approaches. In the cost approach, a value indication is produced by adding the cost to produce a substitute residence to the value of the land. The reasoning behind this approach is that no one will spend more money for a property than it would cost to buy similar land and erect a similar structure on it without undue delay. In the sales comparison approach, the market value of a residence is estimated by examining the prices at which comparable residences have recently been sold. In the income capitalization approach, market value is based on the economic benefits that a property offers, which are indicated by market-derived rates of return.

Markets

Supply and demand, competition, and substitution are all demonstrated in the operation of markets. A *market* is a set of arrangements in which buyers and sellers are brought together through the price mechanism. A stock exchange, for example, is a market established in a convenient location where buyers come to obtain the goods or services offered by sellers. However, the product does not always have to be brought to market, as the real estate market demonstrates. Real estate markets are not stationary, but they are nevertheless markets because buyers and sellers interact, compete, and effect identifiable changes in real estate prices.

Each market has its own unique characteristics, which depend on the arrangements that buyers and sellers have developed and the patterns of activity that have evolved. Perhaps the most important feature that identifies a specific market is the degree of direct competition among the different items sold in it. When the competition is direct, the activities are considered to be taking place in the same market. The distance between individual properties is not as significant as their substitutability.

Real estate markets have many characteristics which set them off from other markets. Five different real estate markets can be identified in terms of typical users and property types.

1. Residential markets
2. Commercial markets

3. Industrial markets
4. Agricultural markets
5. Special-purpose markets

Each of these markets can be further divided into various submarkets, in which buyers seek and sellers offer properties with specific features, locations, and prices. When the characteristics of the properties are very similar, the result is direct competition among the buyers who represent demand and the sellers who represent supply. Increased similarity makes price relationships closer and the market more focused. Identifying and analyzing smaller markets within a larger market is called *market segmentation.*

CHARACTERISTICS OF REAL ESTATE MARKETS

Real estate markets have the same general characteristics as markets of all kinds, but they have many other features that make them unique. These features can best be illustrated by comparing real estate markets with a perfect, hypothetical market in which supply and demand operate smoothly, freely, and efficiently.

The goods or services in an efficient market are essentially homogeneous items that can be readily substituted for one another. As a result, prices tend to be relatively uniform and predictable. However, each parcel of real estate is unique. No two parcels have identical characteristics; even those that are physically similar differ as to location. The market for these properties often will recognize such differences and react to them with a variance in price. Consequently, the value of one property cannot be automatically inferred from the prices at which other properties have been sold.

In an efficient market, prices are the primary consideration in the buyer's decision to purchase. Quality tends to be fairly uniform, and prices are relatively low and stable. In the real estate market prices are not low. Most buyers cannot afford to purchase housing without obtaining a mortgage loan. Therefore, types of financing, the amount of mortgage money available, interest rates, down payment requirements, and typical loan duration all affect purchase decisions. When mortgage terms are unfavorable, effective demand drops substantially and market activity declines. Some sales will take place with special, favorable financing, but higher prices may result.

Purchasing power in the real estate market is very sensitive to changes in population, wage levels, the stability of income, and employment figures. Construction costs, housing costs, and rent levels are also affected by the ability of market participants to pay.

In an efficient market there is a large number of buyers and sellers who create a competitive, free market and none of these participants has a large enough share of the market to have a direct and measurable influence on price. In real estate there are usually only a few buyers and sellers interested in a particular type of property at one time, in one price range, and in one location. A seller's sentimental attachment or a buyer's personal preferences *can* have a measurable effect on the balance of supply and demand for one type of property in a given area. As a result, prices for similar parcels of real estate can vary greatly.

Real estate markets are not entirely free and open. The government and the Federal Reserve System often manipulate the market by increasing or decreasing the supply of credit and the terms obtainable for home loans and mortgage loans. Their actions alter the free movement of supply and demand for many types of property and affect property prices.

An efficient market is self-regulating. There are very few government restrictions on open and free competition. Real estate markets are not self-regulating. Federal, state, county, and local regulations govern the ownership and transfer of real estate; contractual and deed restrictions may also regulate the sale and purchase of property. The demand for specific uses of real estate is often legally limited through the imposition of zoning laws. Because of these restrictions and regulations, supply and demand do not move freely in real estate markets.

Supply and demand are never far out of balance in an efficient market. Goods are quickly consumed and can be readily supplied in response to increases in demand. As a result, the market can move rapidly toward balance through the effects of competition. Although the supply of and demand for real estate also tend toward equilibrium, this theoretical point is seldom achieved. The supply of real estate for a specific use does not adjust to market demand as quickly as the supply of less durable commodities. It can take months or even years to develop an area, construct buildings, or convert properties from one use to another. Furthermore, shifts in demand may occur while new real estate units are being supplied. These units will probably not be consumed quickly, but will remain on the market for a considerable time, creating an oversupply rather than market equilibrium.

Buyers and sellers in an efficient market are knowledgeable and fully informed about market conditions, the behavior of others, past market activity, product quality, and product substitutability. Any information needed on bids, offers, and sales is readily available. Buyers and sellers in real estate markets are not always well-informed. Most people do not buy and sell real estate frequently, so they may not be very familiar with the procedure or know how to judge a property. Information on bids, offers, and sales of a particular property or similar properties is not readily available to most buyers and sellers. Because detailed information is sometimes lacking, individual sale prices may be well above or below actual market values.

Buyers and sellers in an efficient market are brought together by an organized market mechanism, such as the New York Stock Exchange, and it is relatively easy for sellers to enter into the market in response to market demand. In real estate markets buyers and sellers are not formally brought together. Buyers rarely meet other buyers until they have become neighbors; sellers do not pool their resources and arrange their products for sale at one location and time for the convenience of buyers who wish to comparison shop.

Finally, in an efficient market goods are easily transported from place to place. One of the chief characteristics of real estate is its fixed location. By definition, real estate is immovable. Demand in one place cannot be met by supply in another. One important consequence of this fixity is that a substantial portion of a property's purchase price may be paid for the amenity of living in a particular neighborhood or environment, not for the physical appeal of the actual property. Convenient access to workplaces, shopping, and other services; the prestige that a neighborhood and address provide; and the security of a property investment are among the many benefits that may be purchased along with the real estate.

Although benefits such as these strongly influence the desirability of property, most individual owners have little or no control over these features and little legal recourse when damage to them affects property value adversely. Real estate, more than any other good or service, is affected by externalities—i.e., economies or diseconomies created by people other than those who own or use the property. Property owners have no control over federal highways or the maintenance standards of the neighbors, which are among the many external factors that affect the value of real estate.

As the foregoing discussion clearly shows, real estate markets are not efficient. In fact, many economists believe that real estate markets are among the least efficient markets in existence. Products are not homogeneous. The market is not perfectly competitive. Prices are not low. The government does act to restrict and influence trade. Supply and demand are rarely in balance. Buyers and sellers are not always well-organized and well-informed and external conditions have a very significant effect on value.

The principles of economic theory do apply, but there are many complications. Prices do not rise and fall in real estate markets as smoothly or rapidly as they do in markets for other commodities. Individual sales can occur at prices well above or well below market values. Therefore, in the valuation of real estate, a judicious sifting of the available data is necessary. Because no perfect substitute properties exist, comparable sales cannot be used to obtain value indications until they are carefully adjusted to reflect the market.

The inefficiencies of real estate markets do not make them deficient in contrast to other markets, but they do make value estimation more complex. Because real estate markets are inefficient and real estate transactions are significant, society needs objective, professional appraisers who can study market trends and assess the impact of the many forces that influence real property value.

FOUR FORCES

Appraisers must understand the forces that influence value. The many conditions that limit the use of real property include legal, physical, and economic restrictions. Some of these conditions also influence the utility and value of real estate, but not merely by acting as restrictions. They can also increase, sustain, or diminish property values by affecting the supply of or demand for properties of a specific type in a particular area at any given time. Appraisers consider four broad, dynamic forces that influence value: social trends and standards, economic conditions, governmental rules and regulations, and environmental conditions. The interaction of these forces affects the value of every parcel of real estate available in the market.

Social Forces

Social trends and standards have a major effect on real estate values. A change in demographics, such as an influx into or a migration from an area, directly alters the number of properties demanded in that area. Changes in birth and death rates, marriage and divorce rates, population age, and household formation can also influence the characteristics of real estate in demand. Different types of consumers have different neighborhood and building preferences, and their favor or disfavor is reflected in the prices they will pay for property.

Economic Forces

Many kinds of economic forces influence real property values. A population's purchasing power limits the quantity and quality of affordable real estate and directly influences demand. Purchasing power is determined by economic conditions such as employment and wage levels, industrial contraction or expansion, the community's economic base, price levels, and the cost and availability of credit. On the supply side, influential economic conditions include the stock of available vacant and improved properties, new properties under construction or in the planning stage, occupancy rates, rent and price patterns of existing properties, and construction costs.

Governmental Forces

Governmental, political, and legal actions at various levels can strongly influence property values. The legal climate at a particular time in a specific place may impede the normal operation of supply and demand. The government also provides necessary facilities and services that help shape land-use patterns and, hence, affect the values of properties in certain locations. Such government activity may include

- Public services such as fire and police protection, utilities, refuse collection, and transportation networks
- Local zoning, building, and health codes, which may support or obstruct specific land uses
- National, state, and local fiscal policies
- Special legislation that influences general property values — e.g., rent control laws; statutory redemption laws; restrictions on forms of ownership such as condominiums and timeshare arrangements; homestead exemption laws; environmental legislation regulating new development; and laws that affect types of loans, loan terms, and the investment powers of mortgage lending institutions.

Environmental Forces

Natural and man-made environmental forces also influence real property values. Natural barriers to future development include rivers, mountains, lakes, and oceans; man-made features such as federal and state highways, railroads, airports, and navigable waterways all influence the potential use and value of real estate. Climatic conditions such as snowfall, rainfall, and temperature; humidity; topography; and soil are also important environmental influences. The natural character and desirability of a property's surrounding area or neighborhood are environmental factors that can exert a substantial influence on property values.

Location is a very important environmental influence; access to public transportation, schools, stores, service establishments, parks, recreational areas, cultural facilities, places of worship, sources of employment, and product markets all have a very strong effect on a property's marketability in the eyes of potential buyers. The use of land can be changed if it is economical to do so, but the location of land is fixed. The location of property, therefore, is a critical consideration.

The four forces that affect property value are not distinct, mutually exclusive categories; often they are interrelated. For example, political forces such as the actions of the federal government stimulate the housing market, so they must also be considered economic forces. Classification of these forces is useful in considering the variety of value influences and how they interact to affect supply and demand in real estate markets.

FOUR FORCES IN THE LOCAL RESIDENTIAL MARKET

An appraiser is typically most interested in the market area for the subject property. Within this geographic area or political jurisdiction, alternative, similar properties effectively compete with the subject property in the minds of probable, potential purchasers and users. Outside this area, zoning regulations may differ, locations may not appeal to the same buyers, builders may not incur the same costs, and other value influences will have different effects. Thus the market area is the area where value-influencing forces have similar effects and the principle of substitution has the greatest applicability.

Because the location of real estate is fixed, the area in which buyers and sellers compete directly is often small and can be delineated geographically. People with a certain level of income and demographic characteristics—e.g., age, number of young children—often shop for residences in particular neighborhoods. These buyers compete most directly with other buyers who have the same income level and preferences. Similarly, home sellers usually face the most direct competition from neighbors who have similar property for sale; less direct competition may come from sellers of comparable property in competitive neighborhoods some distance away.

In another context, many of the costs of residential development in an area are determined by competition in local construction and financial markets and by municipal development policy and regulation. Early in the valuation process, the appraiser must find the area in which the four forces affect value in a similar manner and specify the submarket to which the subject property most likely appeals. Recent comparable sales and other indications of value drawn from within the market area generally have the greatest reliability for valuation purposes.

CHANGES IN LOCAL AND REGIONAL MARKETS

An appraiser examines not only the area in which the four forces are exerting similar effects at the present moment, but also the region in which the forces will shift and shape values over a longer period. As people move to seek employment or opportunity in another part of the country, the demand for residential property moves with them. The families that remain grow older and begin to require new services. Tastes change and zoning ordinances are revised in response to new economic pressures. Credit may be available on easy terms, but at a later time it may become tight; new types of mortgage instruments may be introduced. Entire neighborhoods change their composition, size, and character. These and many other changes reflect the complex and dynamic interaction of the four forces that influence value. Changes that affect real estate values are constantly occurring.

Appraisers must study how values change for many reasons. One reason involves the comparability of sale prices as indications of value. The comparable properties used in market value appraisals have been sold at different times. Older sale prices may have to be used and these prices may reflect superior or inferior market conditions, not any real difference in the attributes of the comparable property relative to the subject property. Prices must therefore be adjusted for time, and this process requires knowledge of how the market changes over time.

Another reason appraisers study how values change is to understand trends that affect a broad area over a long duration, which may help explain specific developments in the local market. For example, a study of general trends might lead an appraiser to conclude that new, smaller homes represent the beginning of a local trend toward energy and maintenance efficiency, and that smaller houses will not suffer as much as expected for their modest dimensions.

CREATION AND PRODUCTIVITY OF REAL ESTATE

Real estate is composed of many parts and can be used to produce various kinds of benefits. The value of a property in the market is ultimately the result of buyer and seller interaction. Property value depends on the benefits that market participants seek to acquire through property ownership and on the many costs involved in producing these benefits.

Economic principles and concepts of value are studied by examining how the costs involved in producing, maintaining, and operating real estate relate to the benefits produced. The productivity of real estate is analyzed with regard to several concepts and principles: 1) agents of production, 2) anticipation, 3) contribution, 4) increasing and decreasing returns, 5) balance, 6) conformity, 7) highest and best use, and 8) consistent use. Each concept and principle addresses a particular question about the typical costs and benefits of components of real estate and how these components may be combined to produce the greatest utility and value.

Agents of Production

Economic theory holds that for any good or service to be produced, expenditures must be made for the *agents of production*: land, labor, capital, and coordination.

Land refers to the earth and all its resources, which include water, fish, game, woods, and minerals in their natural state. Land provides the basic space and the raw materials needed for all production.

Labor is the work required to obtain and process natural resources, to shape them into salable products, and to transport these products to a location where buyers will purchase them. Management and highly skilled labor such as that provided by an engineer or architect are not included in this category.

Capital refers to the money committed to the creation and operation of an enterprise apart from the money needed for the other three agents of production. Materials, tools, machinery, warehouses, and buildings, which are the physical parts of the enterprise and not part of the natural land, represent forms of invested capital.

Coordination refers to the knowledge, skill, business acumen, managerial talent, and entrepreneurial ability that are typically required to produce beneficial items efficiently. Successful production of some items requires more or less coordination, but all items require this agent of production in some degree.

Because a limited amount of each of these agents is available in any one area at any one time, production costs are largely shaped by competition in the local market. There is competition for land in real estate markets; for labor in employment markets; for capital in financial markets; and for coordination in markets for trained professionals, skilled entrepreneurs, and effective business managers. Naturally, local markets are often influenced by the broader markets for these agents and by external economic conditions. Therefore, residential appraisers must follow trends that affect local construction costs to analyze supply and understand the data used in the cost approach. These supply-side costs will be discussed further in Chapters 6 and 13.

Anticipation

The agents of production are combined to produce benefits which are used directly by producers or sold in the market. The expectation of future benefits gives an item its value. The concept of *anticipation* affirms that value is created by the expectation of benefits to be derived in the future. According to this concept, the value of a property in the market at a given time is the present value of all the future benefits that people perceive the property will yield.

This understanding of the source of value applies to all types of property, even residential properties in which the expected benefits take the form of home ownership and occupancy. The appraiser applies the concept of anticipation most directly, however, to property that generates a rental income. The application of gross rent multipliers and overall capitalization rates is based on the concept of anticipation. The future benefits of owning these properties take the form of an income stream and a reversion. To apply the income capitalization approach, both the income stream and reversion are capitalized to yield an indication of value. Thus anticipation is the basis of the income capitalization approach.

In light of anticipation, an appraiser recognizes that the present value of future benefits reflects the time value of money. More money or benefits in the future is equal to less money or benefits today. Through the capitalization process, future benefits are discounted to obtain their present value.

Contribution

The concept of *contribution* focuses on the value of separate agents of production. Contribution states that the value of a particular component is measured in terms of its contribution to the value of the whole property, or as the amount that its absence would detract from the value of the whole. According to this concept, value and cost are distinct. A built-in swimming pool may cost the owner $10,000, but it does not necessarily increase total property value by $10,000. It might contribute more value, or it might contribute less. In the eyes of potential buyers, the benefits offered by a particular aspect of a residence may or may not justify a sizable increase in the price they will pay; the production costs incurred by the owner or developer are seldom considered.

Increasing and Decreasing Returns

Typical relationships between the costs of productive agents and their contribution to value can be understood through the concepts of increasing and decreasing returns. The concept of *increasing returns* holds that successive increments of one or more agents of production added to fixed amounts of other agents will enhance income in dollars, benefits, or amenities at an increasing rate until a maximum return is reached. In other words, the amounts of an appropriate agent of production that are added initially tend to produce benefits that are far greater than the cost of the agent. At some point—i.e., the point of diminishing or decreasing returns—these increases cease and the concept of decreasing returns comes into play. The concept of *decreasing returns* holds that once the maximum return has been reached, the increment to value will become increasingly less than the value of the added agent or agents.

Figure 4.3 Increasing and Decreasing Returns

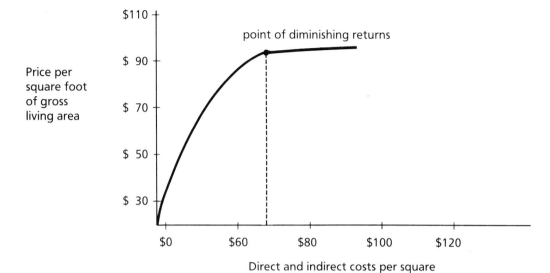

Price per square foot of gross living area

point of diminishing returns

Direct and indirect costs per square foot of gross living area

Figure 4.3 illustrates the law of increasing and decreasing returns. Increases in the direct and indirect costs of creating residential properties—e.g., construction, financing, marketing—are plotted on the graph against the prices the properties are expected to command. Once the point of diminishing returns is reached, continuing cost increments are met with declining demand and cease to produce a corresponding return.

Consider the addition of a bathroom to a single-family residence. In many markets, the value added by a second bathroom will equal, and in some cases exceed, the production costs. However, adding a third or fourth bathroom often will not produce enough extra benefits to warrant the additional expenditure. There is a limit to how desirable extra bathrooms are and how much they may increase the property price. Although a developer may be able to sell an overimproved property at a higher-than-average price, in all probability some of the extra production costs will have to be absorbed.

Balance

The principle of *balance* states that real property value is created and sustained when contrasting, opposing, or interacting elements are in a state of equilibrium. This principle applies not only to the combination of the agents of production in a particular property and the harmonious relationship between a property and its surroundings, but also to many properties and land uses over a long period.

Neighborhoods and regions are thought to go through a cycle of changes—from initial growth and stability to decline and eventual revitalization. The principle of balance suggests that property values on the whole will reach their highest and most lasting levels when the neighborhood is stable. This may or may not be apparent for each and every parcel of real estate.

When an area is first developed, land values are low compared with property values and rapid development is profitable. At this time property values are also relatively low because the attractiveness of the area has not been fully realized. However, if too many units are built in the hope of securing a share of the profit, some of them will suffer from a lack of demand. Until these units are absorbed, economic equilibrium will not be attained. Residential and commercial property in poor condition will have a detrimental effect on the values of other properties nearby.

The neighborhood will probably reach the peak of its attractiveness and value when market participants perceive that there are the right number of stores, residences, schools, places of worship, parks, and other services. Property values will be maintained so long as businesses remain moderately successful, economic growth is sustained, and buildings throughout the area are kept up. In the stable stage, the balance of elements in the neighborhood will conform fully to the preferences and standards of the market.

Conformity

Conformity affirms that property values are generally maximized and sustained when property features conform to the standards of the market. If a property's architectural style, building cost and quality, lot size, and other physical and legal features are reasonably consistent with the characteristics of other neighborhood properties, market conformity is often indicated. Conformity provides the economic basis for the analysis of a property's highest and best use.

To assess conformity an appraiser considers how common a property feature is in the area and how consistent it is with other neighborhood properties. Features that are unique, such as the use of brick in an area where wood construction is typical, often cost more to produce and their uniqueness suggests that there is not a broad demand for such features in light of their production costs. Lack of conformity might, therefore, indicate that the agents of production have not been properly selected and combined in an optimal manner. However, a small, but active, market could exist for these unique features, so conclusions as to conformity must be based on careful analysis. In general, high-quality homes in an area of lower-priced housing will not sell at the same prices they would attract if they were located in more compatible surroundings. Most people who shop in a lower-priced neighborhood usually cannot or do not want to pay a substantial premium for the difference in quality.

In high-priced neighborhoods and resort areas, idiosyncratic architectural design may be the rule rather than the exception. In these areas it may be harder to apply the concept of conformity to property features; uniqueness may itself be prized. Nonetheless, an appraiser who has sufficient experience with these properties can often tell which characteristics do or do not reflect the local market's standards and preferences.

When neighborhoods are undergoing substantial change, it is often difficult to discern the market standards to which the property is expected to conform. Several markets may compete for the property for different uses. In such circumstances, a residential appraiser can only use his or her best analytical skills and judgment.

Highest and Best Use

A land or property use that takes maximum advantage of the site's economic potential is called its *highest and best use*. In the opinion of the market, this use supports the highest value of the vacant land or the improved property. The highest and best use of a property must be legally permissible, physically possible, and financially feasible, and it must result in the highest value.

Many legal, physical, and economic conditions can limit the uses to which property can be put. Legal restrictions on use; the size, shape, and location of the site; existing improvements; available utilities and transportation services; and other factors affect the best possible use of a given property at any point in time.

The highest and best use of a parcel of real estate constitutes the market's standard of expectation for that type of land or property in that location. If a property is not being used to its maximum potential, it will not have maximum value. An expenditure may be required for its adaptation. Depreciation and obsolescence represent penalties on property value according to the market's standard. Highest and best use also reflects the market's perception that value is created by the potential for future benefits, not by past or present uses.

The value of a site depends on its ability to produce the most benefits possible. This potential best use is the *highest and best use of the site as though vacant*. The improvements built on a parcel of land must also be considered in analyzing highest and best use. The optimal use that would take advantage of the existing improvements is called the *highest and best use of the property as improved*. The appraiser considers whether the existing improvement should be renovated, expanded, partially demolished, or left as is.

There are often differences between the potential of a vacant site and the potential of an improved property. These differences are frequently highlighted when a property is located in a transitional area. Many fine residences are built on land which, as a result of changes in the neighborhood, could be used more profitably today for commercial purposes. When such a residence remains on the site until it ceases to contribute to land value, demolition, removal, or conversion to a commercial use are considered. Sometimes, as a result of competition, land values in an area increase so rapidly that eventually land value exceeds property value. Stepped-up demand encourages either the demolition of the improvement or its conversion to a more profitable use.

Consistent Use

As mentioned previously, a property can have different highest and best uses depending on whether it is considered as though vacant or as improved. When the value of the improvements is added to the value of the land, it is important to make sure that the same kind of use is employed consistently. According to the concept of *consistent use*, land cannot be valued on the basis of one use while improvements to the land are valued on the basis of another. If, in the above example, the improvements were valued on the basis of their contribution to the value of the property as a residence through an analysis of other residential properties in the neighborhood, it would be incorrect to add that value to the land's market value based on a commercial use. This methodology would result in an incorrect value estimate. Appraisers must bear in mind the concept of consistent use when adding together the contributions of land and improvements.

SUMMARY

The fundamental concepts and principles of real estate economics provide the theoretical basis for residential property appraisals. Appraisers must understand general economic principles as well as the special characteristics of real estate markets and the concepts and principles that relate to the creation and productivity of real estate.

General economic principles apply to many kinds of markets, including real estate and associated markets. The principle of supply and demand states that price varies directly with demand and inversely with supply, although the variance is not necessarily proportionate in either case. Competition within the market puts pressure on both supply and demand. Substitution makes the prices of similar items in a market more uniform and is the basis for all three approaches to value in real estate appraisal. The substitutability of items is one of the characteristics that defines specific markets.

The special characteristics of real estate markets can be illustrated by comparing them with a perfectly efficient market. Differences stem from a variety of features. Unlike efficient markets, supply and demand are rarely in balance in real estate markets. Individual sales can occur above or below expected levels. Many external forces influence real estate markets. The four forces that are most significant are social, economic, governmental, and environmental. Within a specific market area, the effects of these forces are most similar and comparable data are most reliable. Local and regional changes must also be analyzed in residential appraisals.

The principles and concepts involved in the creation and productivity of real estate relate to the costs and benefits of property. The four agents of production—land, labor, capital, and coordination—are combined to produce beneficial items. Anticipation affirms that value is created by the expectation of benefits to be derived in the future. Appraisers apply this concept in the income capitalization approach by discounting future benefits to present value. Contribution holds that the value of an individual component is measured in terms of its contribution to the whole. The law of increasing and decreasing returns describes how increments of the agents of production successively contribute to value. Although initial amounts may produce many benefits for the expense, after a certain point the increase in benefits falls below the cost and continues to diminish thereafter.

The principle of balance holds that values are positively affected when the combination of the agents of production and the relationship between the property and its surroundings achieve economic equilibrium. A property's conformity to market standards, which is reflected in the similar features of the subject and surrounding properties, usually optimizes value. Highest and best use is the use that maximizes the property's economic potential in the eyes of the market. The highest and best use of a site as though vacant may be different from the highest and best use of the property as improved. If this is so, the concept of consistent use dictates that when land and improvements are valued separately, they must be considered in terms of a consistent use.

REVIEW QUESTIONS

1. Explain the principle of supply and demand. How do competition and substitution contribute to the operation of this principle?

2. Why are real estate markets inefficient? Which specific characteristics of efficient markets do not apply to real estate markets?

3. Describe the four factors that influence real property values. Cite examples in each category. How is a market area delineated by the interaction of these four forces?

4. Discuss how anticipation, contribution, increasing and decreasing returns, balance, and highest and best use relate to the four agents of production.

5. Explain the distinction between the highest and best use of the site as though vacant and of the property as improved. What must an appraiser guard against when valuing land and improvements separately?

PART II

DATA COLLECTION AND PRELIMINARY ANALYSIS

5 Beginning the Appraisal

An assignment to estimate value usually begins when a client contacts an appraiser and they reach an agreement on the character and scope of the appraisal. The client may be a representative of a financial institution, an employee of a relocation company, a property owner, a prospective buyer, or some other party. The appraiser must first find out why the client wants the appraisal. The client may be thinking of making a loan to a home buyer, purchasing a home, or facilitating the transfer of a company employee. Sometimes a client does not know exactly what is needed, and the discussion takes the form of a consultation. Once the nature of the appraisal assignment is established, the valuation process begins.

Appraisal practices vary considerably, so the order in which data are collected and the nature of the information sought can differ widely. The elements discussed below are typical to most appraisals.

The appraiser notes the property owner's name and phone number, the property address, and the legal identification of the property if the client can provide it. Together the client and the appraiser determine the appropriate form for communicating the appraisal conclusion; the appraiser's conclusions can be presented orally or in writing.

The purpose of the appraisal is discussed next. If the assignment is a valuation, the appraiser and the client decide which kind of value is appropriate to the problem. For most assignments, market value estimates are required.

The appraiser asks what property rights are to be considered in the appraisal. The client may be seeking the value of the fee simple estate or the value of a fractional interest created by the legal or financial division of property rights in a lease or mortgage. The appraiser also elicits any pertinent information the client may have about the property—its type, condition, recent sale price, and existing financing. Any items of personal property that will be included in the valuation should be specified. The appraiser also asks the client whether there are any special limiting conditions or assumptions that must be considered in performing the appraisal. In some cases, for example, a value estimate may be contingent upon painting the exterior of the property or completing some other repair. If a value estimate is contingent on an extraordinary condition, the condition will have to be clearly and accurately disclosed in the report.

Based on the client's description, the appraiser carefully considers whether he or she has the knowledge and experience needed to complete the appraisal competently. Most residential assignments are not beyond the abilities of a professionally trained, experienced appraiser. In some cases, however, special expertise may be required. In these instances the Uniform Standards of Professional Appraisal Practice require that the appraiser immediately disclose the lack of knowledge or experience to the client and take all steps necessary or appropriate to complete the appraisal competently.

Next the appraiser ascertains when the client will need the appraisal report. Mortgage lenders and relocation companies, which commission many residential appraisal reports, frequently need reports in three to ten days. Once the appraiser checks his or her schedule and estimates how long the valuation process and the report writing should take, the client and the appraiser can choose a date for the preliminary inspection. Then the appraiser quotes a fee and a financial agreement is reached. The assignment is entered in the appraiser's logbook or computer. The oral contract may be followed up with a written contract or letter of engagement. If the assignment is being performed for a large client such as a bank or government agency, the appraiser may complete the appropriate section of a master contract.

This hypothetical scenario describes how many residential appraisals begin. Although the appraiser and the client have entered into a contract, the definition of the problem is not complete. Seven separate elements are essential to define the appraisal problem.

1. Identification of the real estate
2. Identification of the property rights to be valued
3. Date of the value estimate
4. Use of the appraisal (Why the client needs the appraisal)
5. Definition of value
6. Description of the scope of the appraisal
7. All limiting conditions and assumptions

Of these seven items, only three or four are likely to be well established when the appraiser agrees to begin the assignment: the use of the appraisal, the definition of value, the date of the value estimate, and perhaps the identification of the property rights to be valued. Limiting conditions and assumptions are often not revealed until after the property inspection. Two other elements—the identification of the real estate and the property rights conveyed—should be directly investigated. At this stage the appraiser may have only a street address to identify the property, not a legal description. Similarly, the property rights may have been named by the client— e.g., fee simple, leased fee estate, fee subject to a mortgage—but the specific character of these rights and any limitations imposed by private restrictions and the four powers of government have not yet been established. The scope of the appraisal depends on the requirements of the appraisal problem with respect to the collection, confirmation, and reporting of data.

All seven elements define the appraisal problem and usually must be known before the appraiser can proceed. This detailed information, which is normally collected at the start of the valuation process, is the focus of this chapter.

PRELIMINARY STRATEGY

Specific information about the subject property obtained from the owner or broker can usually provide the appraiser with a preliminary description of the subject. This information may be detailed enough to enable the appraiser to select potentially comparable properties from research data collected before the field inspection. These comparable properties may be improved properties, vacant land, or competitive rental properties, depending on the type of property being appraised. They can be used to obtain the data applied in the sales comparison, cost, and income capitalization approaches. Data that characterize the subject property and potential comparable properties are often compiled initially from the appraiser's data files or from public records. The list of potentially comparable properties is narrowed down to actual comparables after the subject property has been inspected. If the comparable data are not adequate, other sales may need to be considered.

By applying this strategy an appraiser can study the neighborhood, the subject property, and potentially comparable properties all in a single field inspection. Many appraisers use this method for routine residential appraisals, but some precautions are necessary. To use this strategy the appraiser must have a good sense of the kinds of data that will be needed and why they are relevant. Specific data describing the subject and potentially comparable properties can only be collected once the appraiser has identified the value influences operating in the neighborhood and the region at the time of the appraisal. Perhaps more importantly, the appraiser must also fully understand the concept of *comparability*, which is central to real estate valuation. Appraisers must be able to recognize when the sale price of one parcel of real estate can provide a useful indication of the value of another parcel and when it cannot. They must know when to make adjustments to the price of a comparable and how to make these adjustments. Some basic requirements for property comparability are discussed here; sales comparison and adjustment techniques are more fully developed in Chapters 17 and 18.

The appraisal strategy described in this chapter is just that—an appraisal *strategy*. It is not a specific procedure to be applied in every circumstance, but a description of the steps followed to collect data in many residential appraisals. Appraisers are contractually bound to fulfill the services agreed upon with their clients; they also have a duty to the public, to third parties using the appraisal report, to the appraisal profession, and to themselves to perform appraisal services in accordance with high ethical and professional standards. Within these parameters, however, appraisers have considerable leeway. Appraisal clients have different needs. Different real estate arrangements, political entities, and legal practices are found in different areas of the country. In various markets different types of information will be more or less reliable. Finally, each appraiser has developed his or her own methods for researching and compiling data. With these differences in mind, the data collection steps usually followed at the beginning of the valuation process are discussed below.

OBTAINING DATA FROM THE OWNER OR SALES AGENT

The appraiser needs to collect reliable data on the subject property from informed sources within a brief period of time. The most knowledgeable source is usually the property owner, who may also be the occupant, or in the case of rental property, the property manager. Sales agents and brokers often have detailed information on property characteristics; a representative of a financial institution that holds the property mortgage may also be a good source. Often an appraiser with good communication skills can secure the cooperation of these important personal sources.

Several kinds of information can be obtained from the owner or agent by asking questions about the sales history of the subject. When was the property last sold? If the sale occurred within the past year or two years, what was the reason for the sale? What was the sale price and what type of financing was involved? Is there a current listing, option, or agreement of sale? If so, what is the price and what are the terms?

Knowing the subject property's sales history can be vital in an appraisal. The statements and actions of actual buyers and sellers of the property may be more indicative of the property's value than the patterns revealed by the sales of other properties, even the most comparable ones. Indeed, the Uniform Standards of Professional Appraisal Practice require that this type of information be considered if it is available. Information on current listings, offers, or agreements of sale can suggest a probable range of value within which the appraiser's final conclusion of value may fall. Usually a sale is concluded at a price that is lower than the seller's offering price, but higher than the buyer's initial bid.

The appraiser asks a second set of questions to obtain a preliminary description of the subject. What type of house is it? How many stories does it have and how many bedrooms and bathrooms? How old is it and are there any additions to the original structure? What is the size of the lot? Does the owner or agent have a legal description or a recent survey of the property? Are there any additional improvements to the site such as a pool, guest house, or barn?

The answers provided by the owner or agent help the appraiser form a general picture of the property to be appraised. This preliminary description will enable the appraiser to select comparable properties for analysis.

The appraiser will also want to determine if non-realty items of property should be considered. Are items of personal property to be included in the sale? If the appraiser has agreed to consider these items as part of the estimate of value, they must be identified. The question of personal property is relevant if the appraisal has been requested for a sales transaction. The appraiser may also ask the owner about non-realty items during the property inspection. The inclusion of personal property will affect the value conclusion and therefore must be specified in the appraisal report. In appraisals needed for lending purposes, appraisers are often specifically requested to omit personal property.

After the sales history and preliminary description have been established, the appraiser makes an appointment to inspect the property. Appraisers should be very courteous to home owners and maintain good relations with brokers and agents because these individuals can be important sources of vital data now and in the future. The information obtained from these interested parties must be verified by checking with other sources and inspecting the property. An examination of public records and an onsite inspection of the subject property provide data that are essential to property analysis.

SCHEDULING AND DELEGATING APPRAISAL TASKS

Now that the appraiser has a general definition of the appraisal problem and a preliminary description of the property to be appraised, a schedule for data collection can be developed. Experienced appraisers who are familiar with the type of property being appraised can review the necessary steps mentally, but appraisers with less experience and those performing complex assignments should list the kinds of data needed and draw up a schedule for the collection effort. Written schedules are particularly helpful if the services of additional staff or outside professionals will be needed.

Appraisers who delegate tasks should recognize that they are personally responsible for any work conducted in their name. To ensure that clients, the public, and third parties are not misled, the Uniform Standards of Professional Appraisal Practice require that an appraiser certify in the report, when applicable, that no one provided significant professional assistance to the person signing the report; if there are exceptions, the name of each individual who provided significant professional assistance must be stated.

IDENTIFYING COMPARABLES

Comparable properties are identified to provide data that can be applied in each of the three approaches to value. To gather data for the sales comparison approach, the appraiser identifies improved properties that have been recently sold and are competitive with the subject property. To apply the cost approach the appraiser needs data on unimproved property, or vacant sites, that have been recently sold and are comparable to the subject site. Site sales may indicate site value, to which depreciated improvement costs are added to provide an indication of the value of the total property. The income capitalization approach usually requires data on comparable or competitive rental properties. These properties must be identified to determine market rents and sales prices and to derive gross rent multipliers. *Market rent*, the rent that the subject rental property should command in the open market, is multiplied by an appropriate gross rent multiplier to yield a value indication. Thus, the appraiser must identify comparable improved, vacant, and rental properties.

Selecting properties that are *truly* comparable to the subject property is an essential step in all three valuation approaches. Chapter 16 provides a detailed description of the requirements a comparable must satisfy. For a property to be comparable, it should be similar in features to the subject property and competitive with it. In other words, the comparable property should appeal to many of the same people who would consider purchasing the subject property. It should be located within the subject property's market area and must have been sold recently. If a property does not meet all of these requirements, it is not comparable to the subject property for appraisal purposes.

Data Sources for Comparables

An experienced appraiser needs true skill and talent to locate possible comparables. Sources of information on a particular type of property in a given area may be many or few. The appraiser wants to collect as much information as required and make sure that the information ultimately used is reliable. Data can be verified by consulting and cross-checking several sources. Some of the many data sources that can be used to identify comparables are listed below.

Multiple Listing Service (MLS)

Multiple listing services are extremely useful to real estate appraisers. These services are usually sponsored by local boards of REALTORS® or individual brokers. Listings received by participating brokers and completed sales transactions are collected in the MLS and made available by subscription, often to members only. Current listings and sales information are available by computer. MLS computers can be accessed using a modem. Subscribers to the MLS can enter the description of a property and receive a printout of matching properties within specified parameters. Listings and sales data are also published in a book and an index of recently sold properties is included at the end. Books published quarterly or annually summarize all sales activity and indicate which listings have expired or been withdrawn from the market during that period. Property descriptions may specify house size and type, the number and type of rooms, the year built, and the lot size; information on zoning, taxes, the school district, and utilities may also be cited. The sale price of each property is indicated and sometimes the financing is specified; the broker's name is listed and often a photograph of the house is included. Much of this information is collected from property owners. Information is only as reliable as its source. Often property owners do not know the precise square foot area of the plot or the exact date of construction. In general, however, an MLS can be extremely useful as an initial source of information.

Figure 5.1 Sample Data Sheet from MLS

Listing 1

ML# 5-035599-3			$ 99,900	REFRIG *	OV/RA *	DW *	DISP
ADDR 35W486 FOX RIVER DR				WASHER *	DRYER *	SOFTN *	SUMP
CITY ST CHARLES				WIND TREAT	ANT *	CABLE *	EDO *
SUBD FOX RIVER ESTATES				DRY WALL *	PLASTER *	PANEL	
SCHOOL ST-CHRL303		ZN FARM		CARPET *	TILE/VY *	HW	CER
P# 09-10-402-001		TX $1,854 R		ST & SC *	AL	WOOD	THERMO *
LSZ 105X250		ACR	MOL	DR	COMB	EL	SEP
RMS 5	BR 3	BA # 1 ½ 1		M BATH	UP	DN	BSMT
SQ FT	EST AGE 31-50 YR (YR)			FP LR	FF	BDRM	BSMT
EXTERIOR STUCCO	STYLE 1 STORY			CA	HUMID	220V	POOL
GAR 2 CAR	BSMT FULL			PORCH	PATIO	DECK *	FEN YD
OWNER HAINES					***INFORMATION DEEMED RELIABLE, BUT NOT GUARANTEED***		
LR 25x14 M	M BR 13x12 M	OT 36x12 B		WST SEPTIC			
DR	BR2 13x12 M	OT 2		WATER WELL			
KT 22x14 M	BR3 10x 9 M	FP# 1		HEAT FORCE AIR			
FR 36x13 M	BR4			FUEL GAS			HORSES N
UT	BR5	SP FIN CONVEN					

A DELIGHTFUL RANCH IN THE TREES–NEW CUSTOM KITCHEN. TERRIFIC 2
LEVEL DECK. FINISHED BASEMENT. NEW ANDERSEN WINDOWS & PATO DOORS
WALK TO THE RIVER–TASTEFULLY DECORATED WITH'LOTS OF CHARM–POOL
TABLE STAYS & JENAIRE STOVE–FURNACE 3 YEARS OLD.

LOFF BOBBIE KING REALTY, INC.	LA KING, BOBBIE	PH 377-9077

99,900   17 01/11/88 03/11/88 AML   187

Listing 2

ML# 5-030871-3			$ 129,900	REFRIG *	OV/RA *	DW *	DISP *
ADDR 42 LAKEWOOD CIR.				WASHER *	DRYER *	SOFTN *	SUMP
CITY ST. CHARLES				WIND TREAT *	ANT *	CABLE	EDO
SUBD WILDROSE SPRINGS				DRY WALL *	PLASTER *	PANEL	
SCHOOL WILDROSE		ZN RESIDEN		CARPET *	TILE/VY *	HW	CER *
P# 09-21-452-038		TX $2,246		ST & SC *	AL	WOOD	THERMO
LSZ 0		ACR	MOL	DR	COMB	EL	SEP
RMS 5	BR 2	BA # 2 ½		M BATH	UP	DN	BSMT
SQ FT	EST AGE 1-5 YR. (YR)			FP LR	FR	BDRM	BSMT
EXTERIOR CEDAR	STYLE TOWNHOUS			CA	HUMID	220V	POOL
GAR 2 CAR	BSMT SLAB			PORCH	PATIO	DECK *	FEN YD
OWNER ON FILE					***INFORMATION DEEMED RELIABLE. BUT NOT GUARANTEED***		
LR 18x20	M BR 13x17	OT 10x12		WST SEWER			
DR 12x10	BR2 12x10	OT 2		WATER CITY			
KT 12x 9	BR3	FP#		HEAT FORCE AI			
FR	BR4			FUEL GAS			HORSES N
UT	BR5	SP FIN CONVEN					

LUXURY TOWNHOME. BACKS UP TO BEAUTIFUL WOODED AREA DINING AREA
OFF KITCHEN IS 12X10. VAULTED CEILING IN LIVING ROOM PROVIDES
DRAMATIC EFFECT. BEAUTIFUL MASTER BEDROOM WITH DRESSING AREA AND
SKYLIGHT. DEN/LOFT AREA IS 10X12

LOFF GROSSKLAG B. H. & G -ST. CHAR	LA TINMAN, PAULINE R	PH 377-9200

124,900   0 06/07/86 08/07/86 CNV   111

Listing 3

ML# 5-035166-3			$ 198,500	REFRIG	OV/RA *	DW *	DISP
ADDR 5N400 FENCE RAIL				WASHER	DRYER *	SOFTN *	SUMP *
CITY ST CHARLES				WIND TREAT	ANT *	CABLE *	EDO *
SUBD MIDDLECREEK				DRY WALL *	PLASTER *	PANEL *	
SCHOOL ST-CHRL303		ZN RESIDEN		CARPET *	TILE/VY *	HW	CER
P# 09-16-354-005		TX $3,159 R		ST & SC *	AL	WOOD	THERMO *
LSZ 174X386X146X322		ACR	MOL	DR	COMB	EL	SEP *
RMS 9	BR 5	BA # 2 ½ 1		M BATH *	UP	DN	BSMT
SQ FT 2850	EST AGE 6-10 YRS (YR)			FP LR	FR	BDRM	BSMT
EXTERIOR CEDAR	STYLE 2 STORY			CA *	HUMID	220V	POOL
GAR 2 CAR	BSMT FULL			PORCH *	PATIO *	DECK	FEN YD
OWNER ANDREW					***INFORMATION DEEMED RELIABLE BUT NOT GUARANTEED***		
LR 12x19 M	M BR 12x18 U	OT		WST SEPTIC			
DR 11x13 M	BR2 12x10 U	OT 2		WATER WELL			
KT 11x20 M	BR3 10x13 U	FP# 1		HEAT FORCE AIR			
FR 12x20 M	BR4 15x17 U			FUEL GAS			HORSES N
UT M	BR5 10x12 U	SP FIN CONVEN					

LARGE FAMILY ROOM WITH FULL WALL BRICK FIREPLACE. SCREENED PORCH.
NOTE SIZE OF BEDROOMS. WOOD SHAKE ROOF. STONE FRONT AND CEDAR SIDE
WILDROSE GRADE SCHOOL. FIRST FLOOR LAUNDRY ROOM. QUIET CULDESAC
LOCATION. LANDSCAPPED WITH TREES. YARD UTILITY BUILDING.

LOFF FIRST UNITED REALTORS	LA KELKER, JACK	PH 584-2600

193,000   63 12/14/87 01/28/88 AML   32655

Listing 4

ML# 5-035294-V			$ 224,850	REFRIG	OV/RA	DW *	DISP
ADDR 3010 KILDEER LN				WASHER	DRYER	SOFTN	SUMP *
CITY ST CHARLES				WIND TREAT	ANT	CABLE	EDO
SUBD THORNLEY ON THE FOX				DRY WALL *	PLASTER	PANEL *	
SCHOOL ST-CHRL303		ZN RESIDEN		CARPET *	TILE/VY *	HW *	CER
P# 09-22-101-006		TX $2,742 R		ST & SC *	AL	WOOD	THERMO *
LSZ 190X225X190X189		ACR	MOL	DR *	COMB	EL	SEP *
RMS 9	BR 4	BA # 2 ½ 1		M BATH *	UP	DN	BSMT
SQ FT	EST AGE 6-10 YRS (YR)			FP LR	FR	BDRM	BSMT
EXTERIOR ALUMINUM	STYLE 2 STORY			CA *	HUMID	220V	POOL
GAR 2 CAR	BSMT FULL			PORCH	PATIO	DECK *	FEN YD
OWNER MERRILL LYNCH					***INFORMATION DEEMED RELIABLE BUT NOT GUARANTEED***		
LR 19x13 M	M BR 19x15 U	OT 17x16 M		WST SEPTIC			
DR 13x12 M	BR2 15x12 U	OT 2		WATER CITY			
KT 22x12 M	BR3 15x12 U	FP# 2		HEAT FORCE AIR			
FR 18x15 M	BR4 13x12 U			FUEL GAS			HORSES N
UT 14x 7 M	BR5	SP FIN CONVEN					

QUALITY-BUILT ATTRACTIVE COLONIAL ON LARGE WELL-LANDSCAPED LOT 3
MINUTES FROM DOWNTOWN ST CHARLES. BEAUTIFUL YEAR-ROUND SOLARIUM
W/ CERAMIC TILE & BEAMED CEILING/WET BAR. NEUTRAL DECOR FEATURES
COVE MOLDINGS, 6 PANEL DOORS. HARDWOOD FLRS & BOOKSHELVES IN FAM

LOFF LAND OF LINCOLN PARTNERS REAL	LA BELL, JIM	PH 584-1818

215,000   78 01/15/88 02/16/88 CNV   32655

Source: Fox Valley Board
of REALTORS®, Aurora,
Illinois.

Figure 5.2 Sample Assessment Roll

LIST OF TAXABLE REAL PROPERTY IN THE TOWNSHIP OF ___
IN THE COUNTY OF KANE AND STATE OF ILLINOIS FOR THE ASSESSMENT
YEAR 19 ___

FARM VALUE AS MADE BY ASSESSOR OR
REVISED, CORRECTED, MADE OR EQUALIZED BY SU-
PERVISOR OF ASSESSMENTS, OR CORRECTED, MADE
OR REVISED AND EQUALIZED BY BOARD OF REVIEW.

ASSESSED VALUE AS MADE BY ASSESSOR OR
REVISED, CORRECTED, MADE OR EQUALIZED BY SUPER-
VISOR OF ASSESSMENTS, OR CORRECTED, MADE OR
REVISED AND EQUALIZED BY BOARD OF REVIEW.

OWNER NAME	TAX CODE	PARCEL NUMBER / HIE AMOUNT	ACRES	USE CODE	FNF ACRES	FARM LANDS/LOTS	FARM IMPROVEMENT	ASSESSING AGENCY	NON-FARM LANDS/LOTS	NON-FARM IMPROVEMENT	TOTAL	HIE YR REVISED VALUE
1												1
2												2
3												3
4												4
5												5
6												6
7												7
8												8
9												9
10												10

PAGE TOTALS

Source: Kane County
Assessment Office,
Geneva, Illinois.

Title insurance companies

Title insurance protects property owners from the possibility that their title will be contested. To do this, title insurance companies obtain copies of many public records relating to the real estate, including assessment records and a detailed history of past sales of the property. Title companies issue *title reports*, which summarize their findings. Many title companies will research sales in an area for an appraiser; generally a fee is charged, but if the research is limited, their services may be free. Title companies can be an extremely valuable source of information for identifying comparables.

Transfer records

Most jurisdictions have a public office or depository for deeds where transactions are documented and made public. This process, known as *constructive notice*, ensures that interested individuals can research and, when necessary, contest deed transfers. Most county recorder's offices keep index books to deeds and mortgages so that the book and page on which the deed is recorded can be located.

Deeds contain important information on potentially comparable properties, including a legal description of the real estate and the date the deed was recorded. Deeds also list the names and addresses of people who can be contacted to verify the transaction. The names of the buyer, the seller, and the title company; mailing addresses for the buyer, the buyer's attorney, and the broker; a lender loan number; and the buyer's new tax billing address may all be found in a deed.

Some deeds indicate the cash *consideration*, the actual price for which the property was transferred; others have a stamp that indicates the transfer tax paid, from which the cash consideration can be calculated. However, these figures may not always reflect the actual sale price. Some purchasers deduct the estimated value of personal property from the true consideration to reduce the amount of transfer taxes paid. If these personal property values are inflated, the recorded consideration for the real property may be less than the true consideration. In other circumstances, the recorded consideration may be overstated to obtain a higher loan or understated to justify a low property tax assessment. Some states require that the true and actual consideration be reported on the deed, but other states allow a minimal recording such as "$1.00 and other valuable consideration." The appraiser should verify that the recorded consideration corresponds to the actual price for which the property was transferred. If it does not, the circumstances that the recorded consideration reflects should be determined.

Tax records

Another important public record is the tax assessment roll, which is usually kept with other tax records at the municipal or county assessor's office. All privately owned property in the county or district is listed on the assessment roll, which indicates the taxpayer's mailing address, the assessed value of the property, and often the date of the most recent transfer of ownership. Other records kept by the local tax assessor may include property cards with land and building sketches, area measurements, and sale prices. Because most tax information is computerized, however, sketches of the properties are being eliminated. Furthermore, some of the information on property cards may be dated and unreliable. Tax assessment data can be quite useful, however, for preliminary identification of comparables.

Published news

Most city newspapers feature real estate news. Although some of this news may be incomplete or inaccurate, an appraiser may be able to confirm the details of transactions by contacting the negotiating brokers and the parties involved, who are usually listed.

REALTORS®, appraisers, managers, and bankers

Real estate and financial professionals often have information about real estate transactions and can provide valuable leads. These sources may be definitive, but if the information obtained is third-party data, the appraiser should try to verify it independently.

The appraiser's files

Whenever possible appraisers should accumulate information on listings of properties offered for sale. They can request that their names be added to the mailing lists of banks, brokers, and other individuals who offer properties for sale. Classified ads can provide information on asking prices and may indicate the strength or weakness of the local market for a particular type of property and the trend of activity in a particular area. Offers to purchase are also useful and may be obtained from brokers or managers. Generally, listings are higher than eventual transaction prices and offers are somewhat lower.

ESSENTIAL PROPERTY INFORMATION

Certain critical information must be collected for the subject property and for each proposed comparable.

1. A legal description of the real estate
2. The property rights conveyed, and any public or private use restrictions
3. The tax status of the property, including tax rates, tax burdens, and assessed values

Legal Descriptions of Real Estate

A legal description of real estate describes the parcel of land, which may be called a *lot*, *plot*, or *tract*, in such a way that it cannot be confused with any other parcel. Legal descriptions of real estate are based on precise surveys and are maintained as public records in accordance with local and state laws. They may be found in the deed filed in the public recorder's office or in the copy held by the owner. Because legal descriptions of real estate are the most accurate, they are the form of identification required in most appraisals.

There are three principal systems of legal description: the metes and bounds system, the rectangular or government survey system, and the lot and block system. Each system is used in a different part of the country and combinations of these systems are used in some areas.

Metes and bounds system

The *metes and bounds system* is the oldest form of real estate identification currently in use. The system dates back to a time centuries ago when a buyer and seller would pace around the property, note boundary markers, and make property measurements. Most states still use this system today, often as a supplement to other systems of legal description.

In the metes and bounds system, a point of beginning (POB) serves as the initial reference point. The location of this point is established and related by survey to a survey benchmark. The boundaries of the land tract are described by proceeding from the POB along a certain course measured in degrees, minutes, and seconds. The distance between the POB and a subsequent point is measured in feet or another appropriate surveying measure. The surveyor continues to measure along the boundary line until the entire property is enclosed. If the survey is accurately conducted, the last line should return to the exact POB, a process called *closing*.

Points are often monuments that can be exactly located. They may be metal or concrete monuments set in the ground or geographic landmarks. Monuments make it easier for the surveyor and others to identify the boundary lines quickly. If no monuments are established, however, the entire property can be surveyed using only the POB and the metes and bounds description.

Metes and bounds descriptions based on competent surveys can be quite accurate, but they can also be extremely long. They may be cumbersome to use and difficult to understand in routine transactions. There is also an increased possibility of typographical errors. Nonetheless, they provide the most precise descriptions of irregularly shaped parcels. A metes and bounds description can also be used to calculate the area of a parcel by entering the measurements into a special engineering calculator or a suitable computer program.

Figure 5.3 is an example of a metes and bounds description of a parcel of land.

Figure 5.3 Metes and Bounds System

Description of Tract: Commencing at the Northwest corner of Section 12 thence South along the section line 21 feet; thence East 10 feet for a place of beginning; thence continuing East 34 feet; thence South 62 degrees, 30 minutes East 32 feet; thence Southeasterly along a line forming an angle of 8 degrees, 04 minutes to the right with a prolongation of the last described course 29 feet; thence South 13 degrees, 0 minutes to the left with a prolongation of the last described line a distance of 49 feet; thence East to a line parallel with the West line of said Section and 180 feet distant therefrom; thence South on the last described line a distance of 65 feet; thence due West a distance of 82 feet; thence North 1 degree West 39 feet; thence North 58 degrees West a distance of 49 feet; thence Northwesterly along a line forming an angle of 163 degrees as measured from right to left with the last described line a distance of 49 feet; thence North the place of beginning.

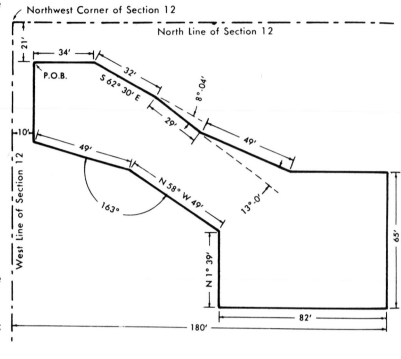

Rectangular or government survey system

On May 25, 1785, the government passed a land ordinance establishing the rectangular survey system, which is also known as the *government survey system*. This system became the principal method of legal description used for most land west of the Ohio and Mississippi Rivers; it was also adopted in Alabama, Florida, and Mississippi. The rectangular survey system was established to facilitate the rapid sale of land that the government had acquired through purchases and treaties.

When the rectangular survey system is applied, a tract of land is identified by specifying the portion of a map grid to which it corresponds. Each map centers on *initial reference points* established by the Commissioner of the U.S. General Land Office. Through these points on the map, intersecting east-west lines, called *baselines*, and north-south lines, called *meridians* or principal meridians, are drawn. Each meridian is identified by name.

Range lines are drawn parallel to each meridian at intervals of six miles. Similarly, *township lines* are drawn at six-mile intervals parallel to the baselines. The intersection of range lines and township lines forms a grid of six-mile squares; each square identifies one township. Thus, the term *township* has two meanings. It identifies the location of a line north or south of a baseline, and it also refers to a square of land measuring six miles by six miles. Township squares are identified by counting the number of lines from an initial reference point.

Townships are further divided into 36 *sections* by the north-south and east-west lines spaced one mile apart. Thus, each standard section is one-mile square and contains 640 acres. Sections are numbered in a back-and-forth, or serpentine, manner as shown in Figure 5.4. They may be divided into *quarter sections,* and quarter sections are divided further into smaller fractions. The description of a particular parcel of real estate begins with the most specific units and proceeds to identify the baseline and meridian. Figures 5.4 and 5.5 illustrate applications of the rectangular survey system.

The rectangular survey system is complicated by several factors, the most important of which is the curvature of the earth. Because the earth is round, lines drawn parallel to meridian lines tend to converge as they approach the North and South Poles. Consequently, the upper part of each township is narrower than the lower part, by as much as 50 feet in many areas of the country. This difference and other problems caused by inaccurate survey measurement are allowed for by adjusting the most westerly half-mile of the township. In addition, the curvature of the earth is compensated for by resetting the grid every 24 miles—i.e., every four township and range lines—along *guide meridians* and *standard parallels.* These lines run parallel to the principal meridian and baseline, respectively. Resetting the grids ensures that groups of townships remain more or less square and do not become increasingly narrower as one proceeds northward.

The rectangular survey system is used in the U.S. Government's Geodetic Survey and Geological Survey programs, which compile information on elevation and other land characteristics to create topographic maps. These maps, called *quadrangles*, contain much information that may be useful to appraisers. Quadrangles can be used to locate legally described parcels because they show township and range lines; they also illustrate important natural and man-made features.

The natural features commonly depicted in these maps include land elevations represented by topographic contour lines at specified intervals as well as rivers, lakes, intermittent streams, other bodies of water, poorly drained areas, and forests. Man-made features include improved and unimproved roads, highways, bridges, power transmission lines, levees, railroads, airports, houses of worship, schools, and important buildings. Appraisers may find such information quite useful when they are considering environmental influences on the subject property and proposed comparable properties.

Figure 5.4 Government Survey System

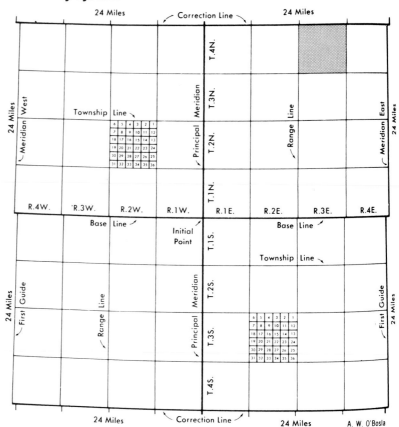

Description of the shaded township: Township 4 North, Range 3 East (T.4N., R.3E.). The township is four township rows north of the baseline and three range lines east of the principal meridian. (The township is located in northern California, so the baseline and principal meridian may be further identified as Mt. Diablo Base and Meridian.) Source: John S. Hoag, *Fundamentals of Land Measurement* (Chicago: Chicago Title Insurance Company, 1976), p. 8. Reprinted through courtesy of Chicago Title Insurance Company.

Lot and block system

The lot and block system is a simple method of legal description used to identify small parcels in many areas. The system is based on subdivision maps. When developers subdivide land—i.e., create streets and prepare individual lots for sale—they are required by law to submit a map of the development and all lot divisions. The subdivision map is based on an authorized survey, which begins from an established benchmark and measures the lots and the blocks of lots that have been staked out. Lot and block lines are recorded on the map and each lot and block is labelled with a letter or number. Thus when the map becomes public record, each lot in the development can be precisely identified by its lot and block number.

Because lot and block descriptions are generally short and easy to understand, they are used for many routine transactions. Lot and block maps identified by the subdivision name or number may be found by searching map records in the public recorder's office, which are indexed by volume and page. A complete legal description is expressed by stating the lot number, the block number, the name or number of the subdivision, and then either the location of the subdivision in a survey system or the volume and page number of the map record. Figure 5.6 is an example of a lot and block land description.

Figure 5.5 Division of a Section of Land

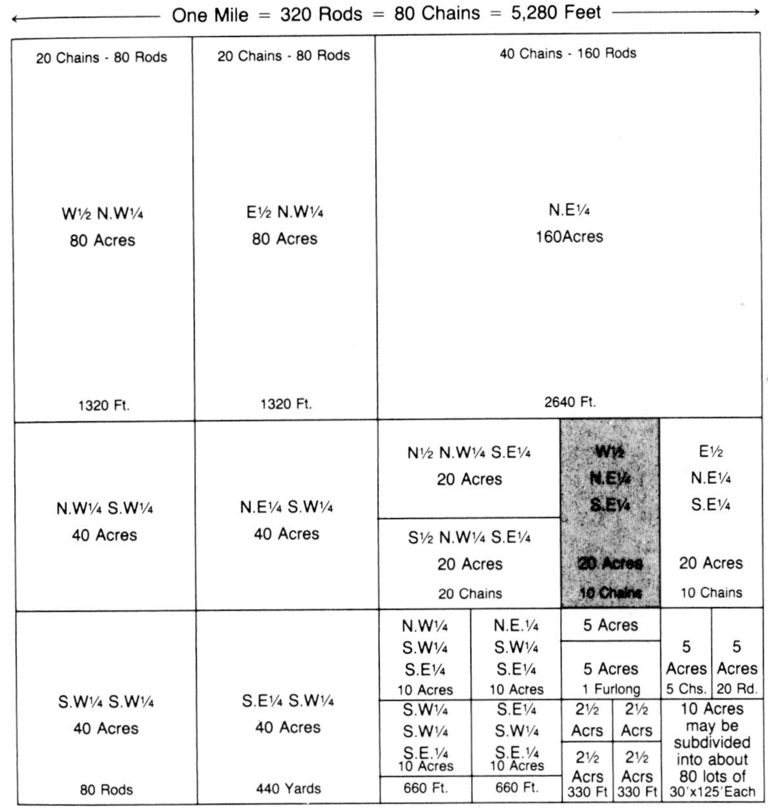
One Mile = 320 Rods = 80 Chains = 5,280 Feet
20 Chains - 80 Rods
20 Chains - 80 Rods
40 Chains - 160 Rods
W½ N.W¼
80 Acres
E½ N.W¼
80 Acres
N.E¼
160Acres
1320 Ft.
1320 Ft.
2640 Ft.
N½ N.W¼ S.E¼
20 Acres
S½ N.W¼ S.E¼
20 Acres
20 Chains
W½
N.E¼
S.E¼
20 Acres
10 Chains
E½
N.E¼
S.E¼
20 Acres
10 Chains
N.W¼ S.W¼
40 Acres
N.E¼ S.W¼
40 Acres
S.W¼ S.W¼
40 Acres
80 Rods
S.E¼ S.W¼
40 Acres
440 Yards
N.W¼
S.W¼
S.E¼
10 Acres
N.E.¼
S.W¼
S.E¼
10 Acres
S.W¼
S.W¼
S.E.¼
10 Acres
660 Ft.
S.E¼
S.W¼
S.E.¼
10 Acres
660 Ft.
5 Acres
5 Acres
1 Furlong
2½ Acrs
2½ Acrs
2½ Acrs 330 Ft
2½ Acrs 330 Ft
5 Acres 5 Chs.
5 Acres 20 Rd.
10 Acres may be subdivided into about 80 lots of 30'x125' Each

Description of the shaded 20-acre parcel located in the southwestern part of the section: The west half of the northeast quarter of the southeast quarter of Section 10, Township 4 North, Range 3 East (Mt. Diablo Base and Meridian).

Figure 5.6 Lot and Block System

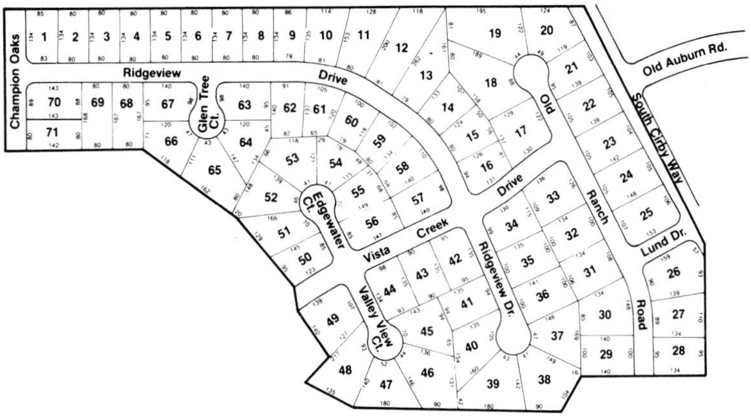
Champion Oaks
Ridgeview
Drive
Glen Tree Ct.
Edgewater Ct.
Vista
Creek
Valley View Ct.
Ridgeview Dr.
Drive
Old Ranch Road
Old Auburn Rd.
South Cirby Way
Lund Dr.

Description of a lot in the rectangular survey area: Lot 10 of Woodridge Creek Unit (Block) 1, a Subdivision of the Southeast quarter of Section 18, Township 10 North, Range 7 East (Mt. Diablo Base and Meridian).

(Owner: Sunrise Properties, Sacramento, Calif.; engineer: Morton and Pitalo, Sacramento, Calif.)

Some government authorities use a variation of the lot and block system to identify property for taxation purposes. Individual lots are called *parcels* and are grouped together in blocks. Survey descriptions of the parcels are found in coded map books maintained by the assessing authority. These descriptions are referenced with the number of the map book, the page, the block, and the parcel number. Although a tax parcel cannot be used as a legal description for property conveyance in most jurisdictions, it may provide useful data for appraisers. Moreover, some form reports also provide a space for recording the tax parcel number of the subject property.

In summary, three types of legal description—i.e., metes and bounds, rectangular or government survey, and lot and block—can be used to identify subject and comparable properties. Appraisers must understand the type of legal description used in their areas to identify properties and their boundaries correctly in their appraisal reports.

Property Rights Conveyed

Identification of the property rights to be appraised begins with specification of the legal estate to be valued—i.e., the fee simple interest or a partial interest created by the legal or financial division of interests in a lease or mortgage. The Uniform Standards of Professional Appraisal Practice require that the real property rights appraised be clearly identified.

Public Limitations

Zoning ordinances and a variety of building, plumbing, fire, and electrical codes are among the many public limitations which restrict property rights. These restrictions are imposed under police power, which gives the government the right to regulate land use and development for the public's benefit. Zoning laws may originate at the city or county level, but they are often subject to regional, state, and federal control.

Generally land is zoned to allow a specific type of use—e.g., residential, agricultural, commercial, industrial, or special-purpose. Along with the type of use, a maximum intensity of use may also be indicated. Special zoning ordinances are imposed in zones subject to floods, earthquakes, and other natural disasters; zoning laws also restrict new construction in coastal areas and historic preservation districts.

Zoning ordinances and building, plumbing, and electrical codes may specify building height; front, side, and rear yard requirements; density of use; building setback; construction materials; and the architectural detailing of improvements. These regulations may also influence room sizes; floor plans; heating, plumbing, sanitary, and electrical systems; and many other details. In short, zoning ordinances and other legal codes derived from police power can regulate almost any aspect of property use.

Zoning regulations frequently specify the action to be taken if a property does not conform to a particular ordinance. This information is significant in appraisals because a property that does not conform to legal requirements usually may not be replaced if the property suffers major damage. Many zoning codes allow a nonconforming use to continue only if the property suffers less than a certain percentage of damage. Thus in some cases a nonconforming property may be subject to a value penalty in comparison with conforming properties. Chapter 11 will cover the subject of nonconforming use in more detail.

Data sources

Property rights are identified in property deeds and abstracts of title. A copy of a deed can be found in the public records office or obtained from the property owner. Information on the police power limitations applicable in an area can be requested from local zoning offices and county or municipal planning offices. Maps are used to show areas where specific requirements apply, and books are used to describe the corresponding laws in detail. Many appraisers acquire copies of the maps and regulations in effect in the areas where they work for office use.

Zoning laws are not static. They can and do change in response to strong community and economic pressures. Consequently, an appraiser should be aware not only of the ordinances that are currently in effect, but also of the possibility that these regulations will change. The market for the subject property will take the probability of zoning changes into account, and may hold different ideas about the highest and best use and value of the property than the existing zoning would suggest. However, an appraiser who relies on the likelihood of such a change in a valuation must usually collect documentary evidence to support this argument. Information on the probability of zoning changes can normally be obtained from local zoning or planning boards.

Private Agreements and Restrictions

Private agreements can also limit the rights to use property. In certain areas of the country—e.g., Houston, Texas and much of Alaska—private deed restrictions are preferred to zoning laws as a means to regulate property use. In addition to private agreements, restrictions arising from eminent domain proceedings limit property use. Some examples of private agreements and restrictions follow.

Easements and rights-of-way

Easements and rights-of-way are rights extended to nonowners of property usually for specific purposes. For example, easements or rights-of-way may be granted to neighbors. They may also be acquired by the government, upon payment of just compensation, through eminent domain proceedings to construct electrical transmission lines, underground sewers, and tunnels or to allow for flowage, aviation routes, roads, walkways, and open space. These restrictions generally run with the land and continue to encumber the property even if it is sold. An easement or right-of-way across a neighboring property that benefits the subject property constitutes an enhancement, not a limitation, on the property rights of the subject.

Other deed restrictions

Other restrictions on use may be described in property deeds. Developers frequently impose such restrictions as part of the initial sales agreement to protect the value of other properties in the development. For example, a sales agreement may include clauses that prohibit the sale of gasoline or alcohol on the premises.

Party wall agreements

A party wall agreement may be needed when improvements are erected so that a common wall is used by owners of abutting properties. Because many party wall agreements are not recorded in writing, party walls must be examined during field inspections.

Riparian and littoral rights

Riparian and littoral rights are concerned with the use of water or a shore by an owner whose land borders a stream, river, lake, ocean, or other body of water. Riparian rights may include the right to construct piers, boathouses, and other improvements over the water or to use the water for fishing and recreational purposes. Littoral rights pertain to the use and enjoyment of the shoreline and safeguard the owner against artificial interference that might change the position of the shoreline. Riparian and littoral rights can have a substantial effect on the value of the land, so they must be considered carefully.

Data sources

Title reports and abstracts of title may contain some information about restrictions on property rights, but they do not always go into detail. A copy of the property deed or other conveyance should be obtained from the county recorder so that all limitations imposed on the property can be thoroughly identified.

Tax Status

Like public and private restrictions, taxes constitute a legal limitation on property rights. The burden of taxation can also influence the highest and best use of property and its market value. In certain school districts, for example, taxes may be disproportionately high. These taxes may discourage buyers who have no school-age children from purchasing a home there. Because taxes can affect property values, comparing the tax burdens of the subject property and each proposed comparable property can reveal important clues about their differences. If taxes are found to influence the values of comparable properties differently, the appraiser can adjust for the difference as part of the adjustment process.

The *tax burden* of a property is calculated from two variables—the *assessed value* of the property and the *tax rate* applied in the particular jurisdiction. The property's assessed value may be of interest to mortgage lenders.

A property's assessed value, or assessment, is the value of the property according to the tax rolls. Taxes are assessed in relation to this value, hence the term *ad valorem* (according to value) *taxation*. Tax rolls often show the assessed value of the property as a whole as well as an allocation of value between the land and the improvements. In some areas different tax rates are applied to the assessed values of these two property components.

Assessed value usually bears some relation to market value, but the assessed value of a property often differs from its market value for several reasons. First, assessed value may be based on a percentage of market value—e.g., 80% rather than 100% of market value. This percentage is called an *assessment ratio*. Second, and more important, properties are assessed in many communities at infrequent intervals by understaffed tax officials. Consequently, unless a property has been revalued recently, its assessed value may not bear a realistic relation to market value. Appraisers do sometimes use assessment data such as land-to-improvement value ratios to derive market value conclusions, but only when there is little other evidence available and then only with extreme caution.

The *tax rate* is the ratio between the taxes levied and the assessed value. Tax rates may be expressed in dollars owed per $1,000 of value, called a *mill rate* (one mill = $0.001) or in dollars owed per $100 of value (1% = $0.01). Thus the tax burden of a property can be calculated by multiplying the tax rate by the property's assessed value. Consider the following example.

Assessed value	$ 50,000
Mill rate	25 ($0.025 × $50,000)
Taxes	$ 1,250
Assessed value	$100,000
Mill rate	40 ($0.04 × $100,000)
Taxes	$ 4,000

This system is sometimes confusing and makes it difficult to compare the taxes in one community with the taxes in another. Very different assessment ratios and mill rates can produce the same tax burden, depending on their combined influence. Appraisers must recognize this to compare the tax status of different properties correctly.

Special assessments

Special assessments may be levied by a district taxing authority for a finite period of time to pay for public improvements such as sewers, street paving, and sidewalks. Usually the tax assessment is based on the benefits that the property will derive from the improvement, not the cost of providing the improvement to a specific property. Thus, if two lots are assumed to derive a similar value enhancement from the installation of a sewer line, they will probably be subject to the same special assessment even if the installation costs for one property are higher than the costs for the other.

Special service areas are contiguous areas within counties or municipalities that are provided with special public improvements. These improvements are paid for by levying a tax on all properties within the area for a designated period. Generally, this special tax levy is added to regular property taxes for a specified period of time and can be deducted from the property owners' income tax. Appraisers must identify special service areas and analyze how special tax levies affect property values. If the tax bill on a particular property seems abnormally high compared with the taxes on competitive properties, the appraiser should investigate the cause.

Data sources

Just as an appraiser may be interested in future zoning laws, future trends in property taxes must be investigated along with current assessments. A short history of tax assessments and tax rates can help an appraiser form a conclusion about the probable trend in property taxation. Discussions with tax officials can give the appraiser a sense of the probability of revaluation and the likely direction of future assessments.

INFORMATION ON THE SUBJECT PROPERTY AND COMPARABLES

The subject site and improvements must be inspected to determine the highest and best use of the property, collect data on the property's physical characteristics, and establish criteria for the selection of comparables. The procedures followed in the onsite inspection of the subject property and the descriptive data that an appraiser obtains in this inspection are discussed in depth in Chapters 8, 9, and 10.

After the potential comparables have been narrowed down, the appraiser will want to verify the sales data on the remaining comparable properties. Later adjustments will be made to the sale price of each comparable to reflect its differences from the subject property. The information needed to verify comparable sales data and make adjustments is normally collected at the outset of the appraisal.

Data Verification

Sales prices and financing terms are often indicated by multiple listing services. The transfer tax stamped on a deed may also indicate the sale price, but this information must be used with caution. Title companies also supply this type of data. In all cases, however, it is best to verify information with the parties involved in the transaction—the buyer, the seller, the sales agent or broker, attorneys for both parties, or the mortgage lender. Not only are these sources often more reliable, but these individuals can answer important questions about the conditions of the sale. What were the specific financing terms? Was the sale affected by duress? Was any personalty included in the transaction? How long was the property on the market—and did it receive enough exposure? Were the buyer and seller related or unusually motivated? Was the sale atypical for any other reasons? The conditions of the sale can affect the property price and, therefore, its reliability as an indication of market value. Often only an individual involved in the sale can supply this type of information. The names and addresses of the parties involved in a transaction can be found in the MLS, title records and abstracts, and public records—particularly the property deed.

Descriptive Data

Finally, an appraiser collects descriptive information on the characteristics of each comparable property. What are the size and shape of the lot? Does the property have a favorable or unfavorable location in the neighborhood? What is the composition of the soil? What is the topography in the area? How old are the structures, and of what type are they? Does the property have any special feature such as a remodeled basement, a desirable view, or a built-in kitchen? Are there any problems with the property?

Appraisers rarely have the opportunity to inspect the interiors of comparable properties. Much of their information must be obtained from parties to the transactions. It is wise to collect as much data as possible and then contact knowledgeable parties for further information or clarification. Additional data can be found in plat books, topographical maps, soil maps, floodplain maps, street and highway maps, and utility maps. These maps are discussed further in Chapter 8.

SUMMARY

A residential appraisal usually begins with a meeting between the appraiser and a client, who arrive at a mutual understanding as to the purpose, use, and effective date of the appraisal. During this discussion, some additional information may be supplied. To define the appraisal problem, the real estate must be precisely identified, usually by specifying a legal description, the property rights to be appraised, the scope of the appraisal, and all limiting conditions and assumptions. Then the client and the appraiser agree on a fee and the appraiser follows up the oral contract with a written contract. If the assignment is being performed for a large client such as a bank or a government agency, the appraiser often completes the appropriate section of a master contract.

The real estate and the property rights to be appraised are always identified at the start of the appraisal. Public records are consulted to verify the relevant data. The appraiser can often obtain information on the physical characteristics of the subject property and its recent sales history from the owner or the owner's representative. Data on comparable properties are collected from MLS books or computer services, title insurance companies, in-house files, and interviews with brokers. All data should be verified by cross-checking sources.

The appraiser inspects the subject property and comparable properties to collect descriptive data and determine their comparability. By studying the descriptive data, the appraiser can narrow the list of potential comparables. These properties should be competitive with the subject property, recent in time of sale, similar in terms of physical characteristics, and located within the same market area.

The appraiser usually collects pertinent data about the subject property and similar data about each comparable. Necessary information includes a legal description of the real estate, prepared with the metes and bounds, rectangular or government survey, or lot and block system; all zoning and private deed restrictions that limit property rights such as easements, rights-of-way, party wall agreements, and riparian and littoral rights; and the property's tax status, including assessments, special assessments, and service tax levies.

A variety of other information is collected for each comparable property: the sale price, date of sale, financing terms, physical characteristics, and the names of the parties involved in or associated with the transaction. With this information the appraiser can verify sales data and later begin adjusting comparable sales prices to yield a value indication for the subject property.

REVIEW QUESTIONS

1. How does an appraisal assignment usually begin? What questions are asked at this time and what agreement is reached?

2. List the elements that constitute the definition of the appraisal problem.

3. Discuss the various kinds of information that an appraiser might obtain from a property owner or occupant, a property manager, a sales agent or broker, or a representative of the financial institution to which a property is mortgaged.

4. What requirements must a property meet to be considered a comparable?

5. Identify the most common sources for data on comparable properties.

6. What are police power limitations and how can an appraiser investigate these property restrictions?

7. Cite five examples of private agreements and other restrictions that limit property rights.

8. Why do assessed values often differ from the market values of properties? How are assessment ratios and tax rates applied?

9. What information does an appraiser need to select comparables?

6 Market Conditions in the City and Region

An appraisal report must discuss market conditions in the city and region where the subject property is located. A description of prevalent conditions helps the reader of the report understand the motivations of participants in the market for the subject property. An economically depressed region exhibits a certain pattern of real estate transactions, and a region with a growing population and an expanding economic base exhibits another. Broad market conditions provide the background for local and neighborhood market influences that have direct bearing on the value of the subject property.

General data about the city and region are usually collected in the appraiser's files, where they are available for use in specific assignments. These files must be updated frequently and all data should be examined in the context of the specific assignment. In most circumstances an appraiser will be familiar with the general condition of the local real estate market. Comprehensive analyses may require extensive research.

To conduct a *market study*, for example, the general market conditions that affect a specific area or a particular property type must be studied. A careful investigation of historical and potential levels of supply and demand may be needed. Similarly, to perform a *marketability study*, an appraiser investigates how a particular property or class of properties will be absorbed, sold, or leased under current or anticipated market conditions. Marketability studies are often requested by developers and entrepreneurs who need to know the risks involved in subdivision, condominium, or retail projects.

Even the simplest valuation assignments must be based on a solid understanding of prevalent market conditions. Market analysis serves two important functions. First, it provides a background against which local developments are considered. For example, property values in an area may rise because the area is becoming more economically attractive than the areas that surround it. To develop an understanding of the conditions in the subject area and surrounding areas, an appraiser interviews market participants and relates their perceptions to statistical data.

Second, a knowledge of the broad changes that affect supply

and demand gives an appraiser an indication of how values change over time. Changes in residential real estate values do not relate only to the local market. The supply of and demand for housing are affected by broader trends and cycles as well. Recognizing that these broader changes cause values to shift over time, appraisers carefully scrutinize price trends that have affected the region over a long period of time.

Market Influences

Changes that affect real estate values can originate at international, national, regional, municipal, community, and neighborhood levels. When a specific area is being considered, the influences on value are most relevant. This chapter examines city and regional factors that influence the supply and demand of housing, the trends and cycles that affect real estate markets, and the patterns of growth and change that characterized the development of American communities.

In a market study, present conditions of supply and demand are investigated and the social, economic, governmental, and environmental forces that cause these conditions to change are analyzed. Trends and cycles at national and regional levels affect many types of real estate and often provide the standard against which local market fluctuations are measured. Therefore, an appraiser's analysis usually relates these broader trends to conditions in specific geographic areas. The markets studied are defined in terms of location, type, size, age, condition, and the price range of the properties considered. The following list identifies value influences and indicators at different levels.

International
- Comparatively low or high land prices
- Comparative stability or instability of governments
- Oil embargos and high energy costs
- Balance of foreign trade
- Rates of foreign exchange
- Foreign interest rates
- Commodity price levels, industrial production levels, and volume of retail sales

National
- GNP and national income
- Balance of payments to other countries
- Federal Reserve credit regulation and fiscal policy
- Domestic interest rates

Regional
- Regional price level indexes
- Interest rates
- Aggregate employment and unemployment statistics
- Housing starts, building permits issued, and dollar volume of construction

- State laws governing development, environmental protection, and low- and moderate-income housing

Community

- Local population
- Long-term and seasonal employment
- Income and wage rates
- Diversity of employment
- Interest rates
- Net household formation
- Household income
- Availability of mortgage money
- Competitiveness with other communities
- Adequacy of utilities and transportation system
- Zoning, subdivision regulations, and building codes

Neighborhood

- Age
- Stage in life cycle
- Rates of construction and vacancy
- Market activity levels, absorption rate, turnover rate, volume of sales
- Motivations of buyers and sellers
- Property use before and after sale
- Features desired in the neighborhood
- Presence of desired amenities
- Maintenance standards
- Economic profile and age of occupants

The amount of research required usually increases as the market becomes more defined. Ultimately, a specific market area is delineated. The most useful comparable data analyzed in an appraisal are drawn from the specific market area because it is within this area that alternative, similar properties effectively compete with the subject property.

HOUSING DEMAND

To study the demand for housing, an appraiser examines present levels of demand as well as recent and anticipated factors that may influence demand. The number of new households being formed in an area is a key statistic because it indicates the perceived need for new housing units. The rate of new household formation and other factors that influence demand are shaped by changes in population and purchasing power.

Population

Area population changes as a result of natural growth or decline and movement into or out of an area. Migratory patterns can be studied internationally, nationally, and within specific communities. Although many factors influence an individual's decision to move, the most compelling impetus may be economic necessity.

People move to areas where they can live and work in security and comfort and where their children will have the best economic future. In the 1970s the population trend in the United States was toward the Sunbelt states and away from the industrial states of the Northeast. Economic conditions in particular areas of the country have altered this picture. The shift toward a service- and research-based economy has revitalized regions such as the Boston area, but the decline in oil production and agriculture has left others such as Texas in an economic recession. Different regions of the country, and even certain areas within individual states, have very different economic characteristics. This variation is more extreme today than it has been for most of this century.

Birth and death rates, the age at which people start families, and the number of children in a typical family all affect population size in the long term. Marriage and divorce rates also influence the rate of new household formation. Furthermore, appraisers are interested not only in the numbers of units desired, but also in the kinds of units desired. Specific population characteristics can explain differences in demand. Young families with children, single professionals, and older adults often have different preferences as to housing features and neighborhood amenities. These segments of the population also tend to have different levels of income, which allow them to make their preferences felt. Thus, the ages, number of children, gender, occupation, and income of residents are all likely to be relevant in a study of the market population.

Purchasing Power

Purchasing power is the second essential component of effective demand. The demand for housing can increase or decrease substantially with a change in purchasing power, even if the size of the population remains the same. Overall shifts in the level of demand may occur when people have more money to spend on housing needs. The type of housing desired may also change.

Purchasing power depends on the *disposable income*—i.e., personal income that remains after taxes and other payments to government—that a household wants to allocate to housing expenditures. It also varies with the size of these expenditures. Employment, income, and savings levels as well as the average number of wage earners in a household should be considered. Tax levels indicate how much money is available to purchase goods and services of all kinds; the prices of other basic goods suggest how much money can be spent on housing. Housing expenditures include the price of residences, mortgage financing, property taxes, and maintenance costs.

The terms of available mortgage financing may represent the single most essential housing expense considered in the study of demand. Most of the money used to buy residential properties is borrowed from savings and loan institutions and commercial banks. When these primary sources have little credit available or the terms of the credit are too restrictive, the demand for housing contracts. High interest rates translate into high monthly payments. If these payments exceed the portion of monthly household income that can be spent for housing, increasing numbers of home owners will default and others may be discouraged from entering the real estate market. Sellers may offer creative financing arrangements, which call for monthly payments that are lower than those required with typical financing.

The availability and terms of mortgage financing are affected by economic decisions and changes on many levels; appraisers should carefully track each influence and consider its effects. The Federal Reserve can increase or decrease the supply of credit to its member banks, which will result in monetary expansion or contraction. The amount of credit that banks and savings and loan institutions can offer home buyers also depends on how much money other individuals have deposited with them. The savings level, in turn, reflects national, regional, and local business conditions. The size of the national debt is another influence affecting credit availability. The U.S. Department of the Treasury strongly competes with private sources to obtain a share of the country's available credit. When the government borrows heavily to pay its bills, the credit supply may shrink and interest rates may rise.

To provide greater liquidity for mortgages when capital is in short supply, government and private agencies have created the *secondary mortgage market*. The Federal National Mortgage Association (FNMA), the Federal Home Loan Mortgage Corporation (FHLMC), and the Government National Mortgage Association (GNMA) are the main participants in the secondary mortgage market. When these organizations decide to purchase packages of mortgages from primary sources, more money is available for home buyers.

Organizations such as FNMA, FHLMC, and GNMA generate the greatest amount of secondary mortgage market activity, but banks and insurance companies in the private sector are also substantial sources of mortgage money. These institutions sell loan portfolios and shares to private investors. Real estate investment trusts (REITs) purchase mortgages, providing lending institutions with greater liquidity.

Certain federal agencies either guarantee or insure home mortgages. The Veterans Administration (VA) provides a wide range of benefits, which include guaranteed mortgage loans. The Federal Housing Administration (FHA), which is part of the Department of Housing and Urban Development (HUD), acts primarily as an insurer of mortgages made by private lenders. To qualify for FHA insurance, a property has to comply with FHA criteria and the mortgage must meet FHA standards regarding interest rates, lending practices, and review procedures. Because FHA mortgages call for lower down payments and interest rates, they stimulate home ownership among first-time buyers.

An appraiser may find printed data on current interest rates and the availability of financing in the survey updates of multiple listing services and title companies. Most local newspapers provide comprehensive listings of interest rates on everything from Treasury bills to mortgages. Local lending institutions can quote the rates on conventional, VA, and FHA loans, and indicate how many points are charged. Local REALTORS® can supply information on the financing arrangements involved in their most recent transactions. Appraisers need broad knowledge of national and local developments to understand the full implications of specific market conditions in the immediate area.

HOUSING SUPPLY

Appraisers are equally concerned with supply—the amount of real estate likely to be placed on the market in any given period of time. Familiarity with the property type, construction cost, age, condition, and price or rent levels of properties now on the market will help an appraiser better understand the amounts and kinds of property that are likely to be put on the market in the future. Changes in the inventory of existing and planned properties must be observed and analyzed to study supply. The stock of housing is increased by new construction and conversion from other uses; it is decreased by demolition, abandonment, and conversion to other uses.

Supply increases that result from recent construction activity can be studied by analyzing new housing starts. The number, location, type of unit, and price or rent of the new units constructed should be considered. An appraiser can use data on housing starts supplemented with information on proposed construction activity and projected demand to form a picture of the relationship between supply and demand in the market and decide whether an oversupply or undersupply is likely to be created by current construction. An analysis of trends for the past several years may be helpful. These data may show a balanced supply-demand relationship at present, but project an oversupply in the future.

Housing stock is usually a local matter, but local situations may reflect national trends. Data on the numbers of properties available for sale and lease can be obtained from multiple listing services and realty advertisements in newspapers. Local and regional planning agencies and departments of development can provide data on projected expansion and authorized construction permits. On a national level, housing starts are analyzed in the *Economic Report of the President* published by the Council of Economic Advisors. The U.S. Department of Commerce, Bureau of the Census, publishes the *Census of Housing* and the *Annual Housing Survey,* which contain information on housing completions, housing authorized by permits, and other housing statistics. The U.S. Department of Housing and Urban Development also issues reports on FHA starts and housing programs administered by the department.

Vacancy rates are a good indication of how supply relates to existing demand. Some vacancy is normal in all markets, but vacancy rates vary considerably from area to area. A vacancy rate that is low compared to historical levels indicates that demand is strong compared to supply. A high vacancy rate often indicates an oversupply. Rates of property turnover and conversion can also be used to analyze changes in market supply.

By observing cost trends in each of the agents of production—labor, land, capital, and coordination—an appraiser can obtain indirect information on the likely pattern of housing supply. If a developer expects these costs to rise faster than the sales prices for the completed units, profits will be diminished and supply will probably decline. Such information can be used to prepare both short-term and long-term supply forecasts.

Labor costs tend to rise when economic conditions improve and unemployment levels decrease. Land costs usually rise as the supply of desirable vacant land shrinks; this usually occurs toward the end of a phase of heavy building in an area. Government restrictions on land use for purposes such as coastal or scenic preservation can also limit supply and increase the cost of salable land. Coordination expenditures such as architects' fees and managers' costs, which vary from area to area and change over time, also affect the costs of producing residential real estate.

Capital costs are reflected in the loans developers and builders take out to subdivide land and construct houses. Because loans provide most of the capital invested in home construction, the pace of building tends to slacken when interest rates rise. Fluctuating interest rates affect both the supply of and the demand for residential real estate, so they have an extremely important impact on market activity.

Costs of all kinds are influenced by inflationary pressures. International developments such as the balance of trade can affect inflation; tariffs on imported building materials such as lumber can increase domestic costs for building materials. Generally all material and labor costs are largely determined by regional and local availability.

Appraisers can obtain data on local vacancy and occupancy levels from chambers of commerce, builders' boards, and real estate management companies. For information on costs, appraisers should consult local builders and developers and refer to cost-estimating services, which also provide multipliers for adjusting national cost data to local conditions.

CHANGES, TRENDS, AND CYCLES

Most of the changes that affect supply and demand in real estate markets are not random. An appraiser must understand why the market is changing because this knowledge may affect the outcome of the appraisal assignment. Changes that are pervasive or relate to many other changes that are occurring are called *trends*. A trend is a series of related changes brought about by a chain of causes and effects. A trend reflects the momentum of the market and develops in recognizable patterns. An appraiser can analyze these patterns to make forecasts.

For example, the increase in energy costs in the 1970s produced a major trend which affected the general economy and had a pronounced impact on real estate. Some of the consequences of this trend were recessions in energy-dependent regions of the country, high inflation and interest rates throughout the nation, and increased demand for smaller, energy-efficient housing.

Many important trends that affect real estate prices occur in cycles. Frequently real estate values follow the familiar business cycle; fluctuations in value are related to the rise and fall of the real gross national product. This cycle is repeated every three to five years on average. Another influential cycle is the neighborhood life cycle of growth, stability, decline, and revitalization. This cycle is usually much longer than the business cycle.

Seasonal cycles also affect real estate values. In many areas of the country, for example, construction slows down during the winter, thus decreasing supply. In some areas, people prefer to sell their homes when the landscape is most attractive, usually in late spring or summer. Market activity generally increases during these periods. Many leases turn over on an annual basis, in early autumn in some areas. Neighborhoods near large universities may have rent cycles tied to segments of the school year. The length of vacancies may depend on the actual lease periods. The presence of tenants at the time of purchase often influences the price a buyer will pay for income-producing property.

Real Estate and Business Cycles

The real estate cycle, which exerts a dominant influence on real estate values, operates in tandem with the business cycle. This composite cycle includes four phases: expansion, peak, contraction, and trough. The intensity, duration, and character of the cycle change over the years. Furthermore, this cycle never repeats itself in exactly the same way. The phases described below provide a general model of the sequence of the cycle. Although the impact of the cycle is national in scope, its effects may vary considerably from region to region.

Expansion

In the early stages of economic expansion, demand and savings that have been building up since the previous economic downswing are unleashed. Production resumes and sets the cycle in motion. Increased activity in industrial and service sectors leads to greater employment, which enhances purchasing power and fuels spending. Interest rates and inflation, which is characterized by price escalation and an increase in the volume of money, are comparatively low. Together with the increase in demand, these factors stimulate new construction of residential dwellings and an increase in the subdivision of land. Expansionary activity is often instigated by the Federal Reserve and encouraged by secondary mortgage market financing.

As the volume of retail sales picks up, more plants and stores may be needed. In a short while rents begin to rise and, with them, the profitability of constructing rental units. The development of business blocks, shopping centers, and office buildings may also become more attractive.

Because wages rise in periods of expansion, labor and production costs begin to rise. This phenomenon is known as *cost-push inflation.* At the same time, the increased demand for goods and services also causes prices to rise. This type of inflation is called *demand-pull inflation.* Both varieties of inflation tend to occur as the economy expands. As individuals and companies seek to finance new projects, the demand for money and credit increases and the cost of borrowing money, the interest rate, rises. Lenders may also feel that they have to compensate for their losses to inflation, which exerts more upward pressure on interest rates.

Peak

Expansion begins to slow down as money becomes less available or credit becomes obtainable only at high rates. To control high inflation, the Federal Reserve uses its credit-regulating power to reduce the amount of money member banks have to lend. Spending and then production decline as the expansion reaches its peak.

The peak is usually short-lived. People who have not anticipated the peak, or do not recognize that it has come, keep on producing. Houses continue to be built, but because there is no new demand for them, an oversupply results. In the oversupplied market, many sellers may at first resist lowering prices, waiting to see if the market will pick up again. Ultimately, however, prices do fall.

Contraction

A phase of economic decline begins. Businesses start to fail or contract due to a drop in demand. Workers are laid off, and people have less money to spend or invest. More businesses contract and workers who have kept their jobs grow anxious about the future and the high rate of inflation. If they respond by cutting back on spending, the economic difficulty is compounded. Interest rates are high, which lessens the demand for housing. Unemployment is rising and wage hikes have ceased, so many potential buyers cannot afford the payments that banks charge for mortgages. Foreclosures also increase, especially on rental properties that were financed at high interest rates. If the recession continues or has an especially strong impact on a particular region, mortgages on single-family residences are also foreclosed. High interest rates and diminishing demand discourage new construction and market activity declines.

Trough

The lowest point of the business cycle is called the *nadir,* or *trough.* At this point, many foreclosures occur. After these foreclosures, the financial wreckage is cleared away. Homes are refinanced and interest rates come down. High unemployment begins to abate, savings that accumulated during the recession are spent, and a new period of economic recovery begins.

The business cycle has always had a substantial influence on real estate. Appraisers should be aware of the elements that characterize each phase in the cycle and their immediate local impact to recognize the market trends that these indications signal.

Since the mid-1960s greater financial volatility has made market behavior and business cycles more difficult to predict. The increasingly higher, long-term inflation rates since 1966 and the very intense inflation that characterized 1979-1981 have further complicated matters by successively driving up both price and value levels. Over the past two decades, three economic recessions—i.e., 1969-1970, 1974-1976, and 1980-1982—have been accompanied by significant erosion in the demand for real estate.[1] In the mid-1970s and early 1980s, a profusion of variable- and adjustable-rate mortgage terms and creative financing arrangements were made available to stimulate depressed demand and protect lenders from high inflation. Beginning in the early 1980s, an affordability crisis was created in specific market segments by the discrepancy between soaring housing prices and the depressed income levels of many younger households.

ORIGINS AND GROWTH OF AMERICAN COMMUNITIES

The forces that affect property values can often be best understood by studying how a specific community has evolved in shape and character. How do the various neighborhoods in a city affect one another? Does the subject neighborhood lie in the path of an expanding, wealthier community or are residents moving to locations that offer access to workplaces on less congested routes? An appraiser notes the community's *siting factor*—i.e., the reason the site was originally chosen for settlement—as well as the reasons for subsequent growth, patterns of change, and factors likely to encourage, direct, or restrict future development. This information can help the appraiser complete the analysis of market conditions in the city and region and begin to focus on market conditions in the specific neighborhood.

Siting Factors and Economic Base Analysis

Historically, people settle in locations because of their particular advantages: defensible terrain, access to water, location on trade routes or at intersections where goods could be profitably traded, availability of economic resources such as arable or mineral-rich land, and proximity to political centers. Many of these considerations influenced the sites selected for early American communities and affect where new communities are developed today.

In addition to the original siting factor, an appraiser is interested in what makes an area a desirable or undesirable place to live now. The economic health and stability of the region or community is particularly important. The economic soundness of an area is formally studied in an *economic base analysis.* An economic base analysis examines which local business activities draw purchasing power into the area and which activities serve the local population. Such an analysis also assesses the diversity of

---

1. For a more complete discussion of trends in real estate and their impact on the appraisal profession, see "Trends in American Real Estate," *Real Estate Valuing, Counseling, Forecasting: Selected Writings of John Robert White* (Chicago: American Institute of Real Estate Apppraisers, 1984) and John Robert White, "The Real Estate Appraiser—The Elusive Goal of Professionalism" and "Profile of the Modern Real Estate Appraiser," *The Appraisal Journal,* July 1987 and October 1987.

the economy in the area and its ability to weather cyclical fluctuations. If an area's economic base is concentrated on a single industry, the area may be susceptible to resource depletion, imitation products produced elsewhere, or technological developments that supplant the need for its products. Similarly, areas that cannot weather cyclical economic fluctuations will present greater risks to lenders, who will be forced to raise rates; this will discourage growth and demand in the area. By contrast, areas that have a diversity of basic industries and occupations tend to fare better over the long term.

Sometimes an appraiser must consult specialists with expert information on the region's economic base, particularly if a long-term study of supply and demand or a marketability study is needed. For most residential appraisals, however, a detailed, formal analysis of the area's economic base is not required. Nonetheless, appraisers should be sensitive to changes in the economic climate of a region, especially changes that may not have been anticipated by market participants. The sudden arrival or departure of a major employer, for example, can have a substantial effect on the demand for housing in an area.

Important technological, economic, and political developments also influence the shape and character of American communities. With an understanding of these factors an appraiser can develop a useful perspective on ongoing trends that affect many cities and regions in the United States.

The Shape of Communities

Access to markets and resources has long been an essential siting factor, but the development of new forms of transportation continues to change the nature of accessibility. Sites along inland waterways and near coastal harbors were favored in America's early history. The development of steamships and the construction of canal systems that linked these waterways reinforced the locational advantages of these sites. The national railroad system, which was constructed from the 1840s through the 1890s, radically changed siting patterns.

Transportation changes also altered the configuration of cities. In the seventeenth, eighteenth, and early nineteenth centuries, land transportation was on foot, on horseback, or by animal-drawn vehicles capable of carrying only a few passengers or tons of freight. Cities were rarely more than three to five miles in diameter.

Development of the short-run steam railroad and the horse-drawn streetcar capable of carrying 20 passengers marked the beginnings of commuting in America. Dormitory suburbs sprang up at the end of transportation lines. Cities rapidly grew, expanding along commuter lines in a star-shaped pattern. The development of cable-powered cars, electric trolleys, and later the automobile, bus, and truck reinforced the growth of cities along radial lines.[2]

---

2. There are various conceptual models of urban growth: the concentric zone theory, the sector (wedge) theory, the multiple nuclei theory, and the radial (axial) corridor theory. For a historical overview of the development of these theories, see W. B. Martin, "How to Predict Urban Growth Patterns," *The Appraisal Journal*, April 1984.

Downtown areas, called *central business districts* (CBDs), developed to serve the expanded cities, and congestion increased. Manufacturers who needed to transport bulky goods left the center city and relocated in outlying industrial districts along railroad lines. Zoning laws, which were unconstitutional until the 1920s, also came into existence and were used to protect public health and to maintain the identity of business districts. In the city core, this promoted the process of segmentation. One area was an extensive retail district and another housed banks, insurance companies, and office buildings. New building technology using steel framing and curtain-wall construction introduced the era of the skyscraper and allowed higher population densities in the CBDs.

The pressure of crowded urban environments led to the development of garden cities and planned suburbs for the wealthy. Poorer inhabitants were concentrated in the industrial districts. Middle-class residents lived in neighborhoods beyond the poorer, industrial areas and the upper classes lived on the fringe of the town, far from the crowded conditions of the urban center.

Development of contemporary communities

The Depression provoked widespread concern about the economic health of American communities. At this time the federal government started to become involved in urban development through the various programs of New Deal legislation. Government's increased involvement with urban development had substantial effects on real estate transactions.

The Home Owners Loan Corporation (HOLC) was established in 1933 and remained in existence until 1951. This organization helped families prevent the loss of their homes through mortgage foreclosure. The FHA was created in 1934 to insure mortgage loans made by private lenders, thereby helping to reduce their risks. Interest rates fell dramatically. Before the creation of the FHA, mortgage rates generally were set at 6% to 7% for a five-year term and down payments of 50% of property value were common. Thereafter rates were reduced to about 4%, 25-year terms became typical, and down payments declined to 25% of property value or less. The use of amortizing mortgages also became prevalent.

Labor legislation reduced the work week to 40 hours. Many blue-collar workers joined the ranks of white-collar commuters and had more leisure time to spend on home improvements. In 1937 slum clearance and public housing programs were initiated by the newly created U.S. Housing Authority, a forerunner of the Department of Housing and Urban Development. Under federally sponsored work programs, funds were allocated to massive highway projects across the nation. All these activities fostered the growth of cities and changed the pattern of real estate uses.

In the postwar period after 1945, the trend toward suburban growth and urban decline intensified. The VA provided mortgage guarantees for returning GIs and the demand for housing was enormous. The development of mass-produced tract houses in the 1950s expanded suburbia and shopping centers proliferated.

The growth of the suburbs has continued to the present day. Now 40% of all Americans live in suburban communities.[3]

During the 1950s and 1960s, inner-city areas continued to decline despite federal urban renewal programs.[4] Due to overcrowded schools, unsuccessful housing projects, and rising crime levels, many cities became less desirable places to live. With high-wage industries and middle-income residents migrating to the suburbs and lower-income families moving into the cities, the tax base on which cities could draw was reduced, compounding urban difficulties.

Changes in technology, which were stimulated by World War II, accelerated in the 1970s and transformed the kinds of industry that formed the economic base of the nation. Traditional heavy manufacturing declined because foreign competition eroded its position in domestic and international markets. High technology industries that require fewer raw materials and a more highly trained work force grew rapidly. Electronics, computers, chemicals, aircraft and aerospace, defense, and various research and development industries have all experienced good growth. The service sector of the economy has also expanded, providing a variety of services demanded by business, financial, and professional communities.

Many high technology and service industries are concentrated in suburban areas and industrial park developments. During the 1970s the southern and western regions of the United States experienced an economic boom. These locations were favored for their pleasant climates and recreational advantages. Since 1983, however, economic expansion in the Sunbelt has slowed down.

In the past two decades, federal involvement in community development has continued. The Department of Housing and Urban Development (HUD), which was created in 1965, issued a ban on housing discrimination. The regulatory powers of government agencies established in the 1970s such as the Environmental Protection Agency (EPA), the Occupational Safety and Health Administration (OSHA), and the Department of Energy have affected housing and community development.

American society is changing and so is the character of American communities. Lifestyles have become more varied. The baby-boom generation, people born between 1946 and 1966, have grown in age and political force. Gentrification, the purchase and renovation of properties in older neighborhoods by higher-income people, has gained momentum and produced both positive and negative effects. Conversion of rental properties to condominiums and cooperatives has enabled more urban residents to own the units in which they live. The proportion of single people in the population has increased and their preference for smaller residential units has been felt in real estate markets. Suburbs built up in

---

3. For a comprehensive history of the decentralization of the nation's urban population, see Kenneth T. Jackson, *Crabgrass Frontier: The Suburbanization of the United States* (New York: Oxford University Press, 1985).

4. In *The Death and Life of Great American Cities* (New York: Random House, 1961), Jane Jacobs presents a strong indictment of the urban renewal program from the perspective of a contemporaneous critic.

the postwar years are aging and becoming empty-nester communities; retirement communities have proliferated, especially in the Sunbelt.

Although civil rights legislation has slowly begun to improve employment prospects for minorities, segregation of lower-income groups in housing remains a problem. Many neighborhood and citizens' groups were formed in the 1970s, spawned by a grass roots activism that the civil rights movement and the War on Poverty had generated. New urban politics have begun to play a role in revitalizing the inner city.

Perhaps the most dramatic of all contemporary social and economic changes has been the influx of women into the work force. This trend has transformed the character of domestic life. Many households require two incomes to meet expenses. Households are also becoming smaller and working couples want housing that requires minimal maintenance. Affluent double-income households may have the disposable income to satisfy their demand for more residential amenities.

The demographic and social trends discussed in this chapter, and others that will emerge in the future, are reflected in the planning and development of the communities in which we live and work.

SUMMARY

Although data on market conditions in a city and region are often collected and kept in the appraiser's file, these data must be updated and considered within the context of the specific appraisal assignment. Analyses that call for market or marketability studies may require more extensive research. To perform appraisals an appraiser must have a solid understanding of market conditions. In analyzing the market for a property, pervasive influences that affect the broader housing market are considered. International and national trends, regional and community influences, and local and neighborhood factors are analyzed. At each level the conditions of supply and demand and the forces that affect these conditions are examined.

Demand is studied primarily by analyzing the current and anticipated conditions that affect population and purchasing power. Population analysis focuses on the number and rate of new household formation, the characteristics of residents, and their housing preferences. Purchasing power is studied chiefly in terms of income and employment levels, tax levels, price levels, and housing expenditures. Mortgage payments are a key housing expense. The terms and availability of mortgage financing are shaped by government policies, secondary mortgage market activities, and the decisions of local lenders. An appraiser should examine trends that affect how homes are financed at all levels.

Supply is studied by analyzing the inventory of various types of existing housing as well as new and proposed construction. Vacancy and turnover rates and the costs of construction—i.e., the prices of labor, land, capital, and coordination—are significant in the study of supply.

Interrelated changes in supply and demand produce trends, which often occur in cycles. Business and real estate cycles experience periods of expansion, peak, contraction, and trough. Sales and rentals of residential real estate are influenced by the economic changes wrought by these cycles.

In addition to cyclical influences, an appraiser must consider the evolution of the region and the community and the directions in which they are likely to grow. Economic base analysis can be used to forecast future trends. An understanding of the history of the area and characteristic patterns of community growth can also help an appraiser assess the market conditions that affect real estate.

REVIEW QUESTIONS

1. Describe value influences at international and national, regional and community, and local and neighborhood levels. Cite several examples of each.

2. Identify the two approaches used to study housing demand. What kinds of data will an appraiser use to analyze housing trends?

3. How do the following organizations and institutions influence the availability of financing: the Federal Reserve System, the U.S. Department of the Treasury, the secondary mortgage market, and federal agencies such as the VA and the FHA?

4. Describe the various phases in business and real estate cycles. Identify the characteristics of each phase.

5. Define economic base analysis. What three questions must be considered in such an analysis?

7 The Neighborhood and Local Market

Appraisers regularly update their files to include new data on the area in which they usually work. As mentioned in Chapter 6, much of the background research on the local and neighborhood market is conducted in advance; then additional data are collected as part of the specific assignment. If the appraiser is not thoroughly familiar with the neighborhood or the type of property being appraised, much more research will be required. Typically, an appraiser draws upon information available in office files, makes additional inquiries to supplement and update these data, and completes the research for the assignment by examining the characteristics of the neighborhood during the field inspection.

The in-house research, supplemental inquiries, and field investigation are undertaken to answer interrelated questions concerning

- The basic characteristics of the residential real estate market, including price levels, price changes, supply and demand relationships, and market activity patterns
- The features, locations, and possible alternative uses of residential properties, which contribute to or detract from value in this market
- The boundaries and major characteristics of the neighborhood where the subject property is located
- The competitive advantages and disadvantages of the neighborhood in light of the amenities, facilities, and appeal of comparable neighborhoods
- The present mix of land uses and the likely pattern and direction of future changes in land use

The conclusions drawn in neighborhood and area analysis are likely to affect all aspects of the appraiser's subsequent analyses. An understanding of the market area, market characteristics, neighborhood land uses, and anticipated changes is essential to every other facet of the appraisal. This preliminary analysis affects the selection of appropriate market data, the determination of highest and best use, the adjustment of comparable property prices, the estimation of accrued depreciation, and the derivation of income and expense information. Consequently, the appraiser must be both sensitive and careful to perform the analysis properly.

At one time lenders were accused of contributing to discrimination against minorities by unfairly penalizing neighborhoods because of the low income and racial background of their residents; this practice is known as *redlining*. The integration of neighborhoods was mistakenly thought to signal the beginning of a decline in their life cycles. Some banks refused to make mortgage loans in certain inner-city areas due to their high default rates, rather than basing their discussions on individual investment risks. This practice was held to be unlawful by the courts and by federal agencies that have regulatory authority over lending institutions.

Proper neighborhood and area analysis can ensure that the appraiser does not use inappropriate data or double-count—i.e., consider a value influence in more than one category and make two adjustments to a price for one value influence.

NEIGHBORHOODS, DISTRICTS, AND MARKET AREAS

A neighborhood is defined by certain characteristics which differentiate it from other neighborhoods and adjacent areas. Often neighborhood residents have common social characteristics such as age, income, and lifestyle. Many neighborhoods are identified by landmarks and defined boundaries; properties may have similar architectural styles or a particular blend of styles. A neighborhood can also be characterized by the mix of amenities and services that appeal to the people who choose to live there.

These features are not constant or uniform in all neighborhoods and they usually change over time and in different ways in each particular case. The character of a neighborhood is continually evolving in response to changing social, economic, governmental, and environmental conditions. The life of a neighborhood frequently follows a cyclical pattern and is affected by many factors, including its age, its position within the larger community, and the appeal of competitive neighborhoods.

The idea of a neighborhood is familiar to most people, but appraisers use the term in a specific sense. For appraisal purposes, a *neighborhood* is an area of complementary land uses. One essential aspect of this definition is the concept of a variety of land uses that function as a unit. Most residential neighborhoods contain a variety of land uses; different areas are improved with detached single-family dwellings; apartment buildings; and amenities and services such as parks, churches, cinemas, schools, and businesses. All of these elements tend to function together in a neighborhood, and the state of each part can often strongly affect the state of the whole. As the principle of balance suggests, failing businesses, poorly maintained residential blocks, an inappropriate mix of land uses, and other detrimental conditions that affect segments of a neighborhood can directly reduce the appeal of the other neighborhood properties. These conditions often signal a pattern of change in a neighborhood, which may affect the value of all properties within its boundaries.

A *district* is a type of neighborhood that is characterized by homogeneous land use. Districts are commonly composed of apartments, or of commercial, industrial, or agricultural properties. In large cities, an apartment district usually covers an extensive area; in smaller cities, an apartment district may be limited in size. The apartment buildings in a district may be multistory or single-story, high-rise or row, garden or townhouse. Individual units may be rented or privately owned as cooperatives or condominiums.

The concepts of neighborhood and district overlap, but a necessary distinction exists. The term *neighborhood* suggests a variety or balance of complementary land uses, while the term *district* refers to an area where one type of use predominates. Sometimes a neighborhood is composed of various districts. Often, a commercial district marks the edge of a residential neighborhood.

The *market area* is the area in which properties effectively compete with the subject property in the minds of probable, potential purchasers and users. The residential market area usually includes much of the subject neighborhood; occasionally, however, only a segment of the neighborhood may be in the market area. The market area can also extend beyond the neighborhood when other neighborhoods compete with the subject neighborhood in the minds of potential purchasers. Often these other neighborhoods are near the subject neighborhood or located a similar distance away from a major employment center. Rural estates belong to a market area that is far more extensive than the market areas for urban or suburban properties. A market area is defined by the type of property, the type of transaction—e.g., rental or sale—and the geographic area in which competition is effective.

NEIGHBORHOOD BOUNDARIES

The unity or consistency that characterizes a neighborhood can be expressed in many ways. Similar building types and styles, population features, occupant economic profiles, and zoning regulations that affect land use may be found within neighborhoods. Similarity in the dominant form of land use, rent and occupancy levels, the credit ratings of occupants, and the ages of buildings all tend to differentiate certain areas from others. Home buyers may consider these factors when selecting where to purchase property.

Frequently the limits of a neighborhood are visibly represented by a change in physical characteristics. Features such as transportation arteries (highways, major streets, railroads), bodies of water (rivers, lakes, streams), and changes in elevation (hills, mountains, cliffs, valleys) may mark neighborhood boundaries. Changes in prevailing land uses, types of structures, street patterns, vegetation, and lot sizes can all suggest that one neighborhood has ended and another has begun. Often the neighborhood of a house located in a single-family subdivision ends when the dominant land use changes to commercial, apartment, or industrial use.

Appraisers are also interested in another kind of boundary—the limit of value influences that affect the subject property. Often the limit of these value influences coincides with the geographic boundary of the neighborhood, but this is not always the case. If the subject property is located at the edge of a neighborhood, it may be affected by outside conditions that do not affect most other neighborhood properties. Fumes and noise from a highway, traffic from a commercial district, or an unfavorable view can negatively affect value. If the subject property is near the border of another residential neighborhood, it may be subject to certain value influences from that neighborhood.

An appraiser should extend the geographic search of the market area far enough to encompass all influences that the market perceives as affecting the value of the subject property. The physical points at which value influences affecting the subject and surrounding properties stop set the boundaries for market analysis.

Whether or not the limits of the neighborhood are clearly set off by physical features, an appraiser must explicitly explain how the boundaries of the neighborhood were identified in the appraisal report.

Different areas within a neighborhood, sometimes called *subneighborhoods*, may be regarded differently by the market population due to perceived advantages and disadvantages. The immediate neighborhood of the subject and comparable properties is critical in an appraisal and should be carefully examined along with the neighborhood as a whole. It is important for an appraiser to note the individual locations of comparable properties within a neighborhood because different subneighborhoods may be regarded in different ways by the market population. (See Figure 7.1.)

NEIGHBORHOOD LIFE CYCLES

Most neighborhoods go through a cycle of changes, which affect their character, their desirability, and the value of real estate located there. Neighborhoods go through periods of growth, stability, decline, and revitalization.

Growth

A neighborhood begins its life when buildings are constructed on vacant, newly cleared land or when properties are converted from a different use. This development may create a new community or it may expand an existing community to accommodate new demand for real estate. Neighborhoods often begin their growth during periods of local economic expansion. When employment prospects are good and interest rates are relatively low, developers are motivated to construct new units.

A neighborhood's growth period may be short-lived or it may last several years. Growth may continue as long as the neighborhood is perceived as a good value. Growth may stop when the demand for new housing diminishes as a result of shifts in buyer preferences or when the supply of housing is restrained by high construction or financing costs. If the neighborhood is successfully developed, new construction will attract new inhabitants. As the neighborhood gains public recognition and favor, demand is sustained. As long as vacant land is plentiful, land prices will usually remain low in comparison to improved property prices. In a successful development, prices for both vacant land and improved properties usually increase as growth continues.

Figure 7.1 Neighborhood Map Showing Comparable Sales

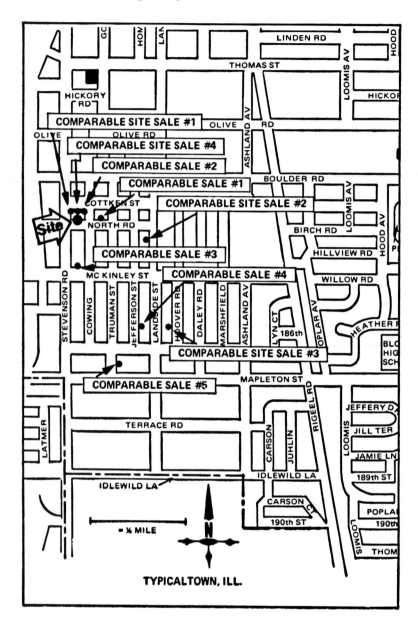

Because neighborhood growth frequently coincides with expansion in the local and regional economy, funding for public works to support the development often increases. Public works are not usually profitable on a small scale; a sewer trunk line, which may open thousands of acres for development, is generally not extended in small units. Public restrictions on development often accompany public funding. In many cases further development must conform to detailed land-use plans drawn up by local government and municipal agencies.

During the growth period of a neighborhood, activity is generally vigorous in comparison with its periods of stability and decline.

As a result, the buildings constructed during this period tend to be relatively similar in appearance; they reflect the building practices and market preferences of a particular time. The economic history of a city can often be discerned by studying the dominant architectural styles of its neighborhoods.

Stability

Neighborhood growth ends when it is no longer profitable to build or when other neighborhoods become better values. The neighborhood enters a relatively stable period. A period of stability can also occur after a period of revitalization, when it is no longer profitable to convert properties from one use to another or to renovate them. In the stable phase, changes do not usually stop completely, but they proceed at a slower pace. New construction may continue on a limited basis once demand increases or financing terms improve.

Neighborhood stability is characterized by the absence of marked growth or decline. The neighborhood settles into a comfortable pattern of activity. Because the number of businesses, schools, and churches is sufficient to meet the needs of the residents, change is not encouraged. The various parts of the neighborhood, and the neighborhood's relationship to the larger community, are in balance. The demand for both new and existing units is generally balanced with the supply. Many residents remain, so property turnovers are relatively low. Real estate values stabilize and may even appreciate depending on the neighborhood's popularity and the strength of demand. Zoning codes are enforced and there is strong economic and social pressure for dwellings to conform to neighborhood and legal standards. The boundaries of the neighborhood are usually clearly demarcated.

This period of stability may last for some time. Buildings are aging, but residents have enough income to meet these maintenance costs; deterioration is not substantial. Neighborhoods have no established life expectancy, so decline is not imminent in all older neighborhoods.

Decline

A period of decline begins when a neighborhood can no longer compete with comparable neighborhoods. Maintenance costs may become too high due to the age of the dwellings or, more likely, the location, style, and utility of residences have lost their appeal.

During this period, prices may fall to attract buyers. "For sale" signs appear more frequently and turnovers increase. Neither new nor older residents have enough money to maintain the buildings adequately. Because residents cannot support the community businesses and services that were formerly in demand, building maintenance declines, vacancies increase, and businesses change hands. During a period of decline, building codes and zoning regulations may not be enforced. The boundaries of the neighborhood become less distinct and the number of rental units often increases in comparison with owner-occupied units.

Revitalization

Neighborhood decline ends when the dominant land use changes or a period of renewal begins. The decline in values ceases and a new balance is struck. Deteriorated buildings are torn down, other buildings are converted to more intensive uses, and the neighborhood is ready to begin its cycle of change once more.

When revitalization occurs, it is usually the result of changing preferences and community patterns. For example, economic growth in the larger community may increase the demand for housing in the neighborhood. Organized community efforts such as redevelopment programs and historical renovation may contribute significantly to revitalization or revitalization may begin spontaneously, without planning or formal municipal assistance.

A relatively recent phenomenon in neighborhood revitalization is *gentrification,* in which middle- and upper-income people purchase properties in urban neighborhoods to renovate or rehabilitate them. These properties may be of marginal quality and used for residential or other uses. Often apartment buildings are upgraded, converted to condominiums or cooperatives, and removed from the rental stock. This type of activity can change the orientation of the entire neighborhood.

Gentrification appears to stem from the preponderance of single people and small families in metropolitan areas, who want to live in proximity to urban activities. As a consequence of gentrification, poorer residents are displaced due to high rents and rising prices. These lower-income groups may have moved into older city neighborhoods when others found them unappealing and unattractive. Two or more poorer families may have occupied units that were designed for single households. These groups are edged out of the local market by gentrification. Their plight has been compounded by the decrease in federal funds for low-income housing.

A period of revitalization, like a period of decline, is often marked by increased change and greater disparity between values in different parts of the neighborhood. Revitalization usually proceeds block by block. Once the effort gathers momentum, more remodeling is undertaken by residents who foresee a substantial rise in property values. The changes that accompany revitalization are usually noticeably different from the changes brought about by decline. Neighborhood revitalization usually fosters an atmosphere of hope as large numbers of tradesmen and homeowners work to repair or remodel neighborhood properties.

These four stages describe how neighborhoods and districts evolve, but they should not be taken as rigid guides to market trends. Changes do not necessarily follow in sequence. Decline may proceed at a barely perceptible rate. At any time in the cycle, major changes can occur to interrupt the order of the neighborhood life cycle. An external influence such as a new highway that changes traffic patterns can bring about decline or revitalization. A neighborhood that is in a stage of growth may decline suddenly rather than stabilize. An area that is developing as a residential neighborhood may, due to a sudden external change, begin to grow as a commercial district. An appraiser can only reach a conclusion about the stage of a neighborhood and the likely trend in its property values after he or she has conducted careful market observation and research. Discussions with local residents, merchants, brokers, bankers, appraisers, municipal planners, zoning officials, and other knowledgeable persons can contribute greatly to the appraiser's understanding of neighborhood development.

STEPS IN THE NEIGHBORHOOD ANALYSIS

There are two major steps in neighborhood analysis: 1) planning the analysis effort and collecting pertinent market information and 2) inspecting the neighborhood and, when necessary, conducting additional research to resolve questions raised by the field inspection.

Planning the Analysis and Collecting Data

Essential data needs

An appraiser begins neighborhood analysis by determining what data are needed to answer the appraisal problem, where these data can be obtained, and how they can best be collected. The data required depend on the purpose of the assignment and the use to which it will be put. The purpose of most appraisal assignments is to reach a market value conclusion, so this discussion will focus on the data needed for these appraisals. In ordinary market value appraisals such as those used by mortgage lenders, neighborhood analysis is performed to fulfill the following objectives:

1. To form an understanding of market preferences and price patterns on which a market value estimate can be based. This understanding is developed by analyzing data on price and rent levels for properties of different ages with various features and by studying construction costs, supply and demand levels, anticipated changes in supply and demand, and market activity patterns.

2. To reach a general conclusion concerning the highest and best use of the site as though vacant, which is required for site valuation. Many characteristics of the neighborhood—e.g., its zoning, tax assessments, accessibility, schools, and cultural facilities—contribute to the determination of the highest and best use of the site as though vacant.

3. To consider which specific improvements within the general use category would constitute the highest and best use of the site as though vacant. Generally, the ideal improvements for the subject property are suggested by the characteristics of other neighborhood property improvements.

4. To determine the highest and best use of the property as improved, considering the structures already on the site as well as neighborhood and market standards.

5. To identify the primary area from which comparable properties are to be selected. Several parts of the subject neighborhood or other neighborhoods may be acceptable for this

purpose, but locations nearest the subject property and most similar in character are generally the best.

6. To discern if and why different locations in the same neighborhood have different values. This knowledge provides a basis for adjusting comparable sales for locational differences within the neighborhood.

7. To consider the positive and negative value influence of land uses of neighboring properties.

8. To identify various value influences in the neighborhood and rate the neighborhood in comparison with other, competitive neighborhoods. This information will allow the appraiser to use comparables from competitive neighborhoods if necessary and make the necessary adjustments for neighborhood location. It may also help the appraiser understand the neighborhood's most probable future.

9. To learn about recent changes in the neighborhood that may have affected values since the dates when comparables were sold. This information provides a basis for making adjustments for market conditions (time).

10. To examine the long-term prospects of the neighborhood to decide whether the subject property will qualify as security for a long-term loan. This objective is particularly important when the client is a lender or loan underwriter.

If the appraisal is to be used in a land utilization study or for site selection, a different emphasis may be required.

Once the appraiser has reviewed the objectives of the neighborhood analysis, necessary data must be collected and analyzed to identify value influences. Some data will be compiled from census tables, utility line maps, and MLS sales. Other data will be obtained from interviewing people familiar with the neighborhood— buyers, sellers, brokers, property owners, and officials responsible for public services in the neighborhood. The picture the appraiser forms from this descriptive and numerical information will be tested and refined during the field inspection of the neighborhood. The condition of the improvements and the proximity of other uses will also become evident from the field inspection.

Data on standardized or statistically defined areas such as cities, counties, tax districts, census tracts, and special enumeration districts are available from municipal and county sources. The areas covered rarely conform to the neighborhood boundaries that the appraiser has identified. Thus, during inspection of the neighborhood, corroborative research is often necessary to ascertain whether the general data collected are appropriate for the market area being studied. If an appraiser is unfamiliar with a given neighborhood, the field inspection is often the best place to start collecting data.

Collection tools

In addition to a vehicle and a map of the area, the appraiser may use a form or checklist to facilitate the collection of needed data. Such a list may suggest many important items that might otherwise be overlooked. If the appraisal is to be communicated in a form report, the appraiser should take the form when he or she conducts the neighborhood inspection.

Form reports are requested by organizations, business firms, and federal agencies that wish to have the results of appraisals presented in a standard format. The most widely used form, the Uniform Residential Appraisal Report (URAR), is used by the FHLMC and the FNMA for appraisals of properties with mortgages that these agencies may purchase. (See Figure 7.2.) Appraisal report forms include space to record many variables important to neighborhood analysis.

Although the checklists provided on these forms serve an important purpose, they should not limit the appraisers' analysis. There may be important value influences in the specific neighborhood that the form does not list. However, each form has a space for comments, and any considerations not mentioned in the checklist should be addressed there. Many appraisals submitted on form reports require further explanation or clarification, which may not fit on the form. In these cases, the appraiser provides additional narrative material on an attached addendum sheet, which is considered part of the appraisal.

Neighborhood Inspection

The next stage in neighborhood analysis is the visual inspection. The inspection is conducted in several steps.

1. Inspect the area's physical characteristics. An appraiser drives or walks around the subject area to develop a sense of place and observe the degree of similarity among land uses, types of structures, architectural styles, and maintenance levels in the area.

2. Draw preliminary boundaries on a map. On a map of the area, the appraiser notes points where the physical characteristics of the land and properties change perceptibly. A copy of this map may be included in the appraisal report. These points generally mark the limits of the market area. The appraiser also identifies any physical barriers such as major streets, hills, rivers, and railroads that coincide with or are near the market area's boundaries. Neighborhood occupants, business people, brokers, and community representatives may be questioned to obtain their perceptions of how far the neighborhood extends and what features characterize its different parts.

3. Observe land uses and signs of change. An appraiser looks for signs of change in the neighborhood and tries to assess the direction of change, its likely effects on the subject property, and recent changes that may have affected comparable properties. These trends are noted on the map for future reference.

4. Rate the neighborhood for quality. The appraiser should rate various aspects of the neighborhood in comparison with other neighborhoods that appeal to the same market population.

Figure 7.2 The Neighborhood Section of the URAR

NEIGHBORHOOD

LOCATION	Urban	Suburban	Rural
BUILT UP	Over 75%	25-75%	Under 25%
GROWTH RATE	Rapid	Stable	Slow
PROPERTY VALUES	Increasing	Stable	Declining
DEMAND/SUPPLY	Shortage	In Balance	Over Supply
MARKETING TIME	Under 3 Mos.	3-6 Mos.	Over 6 Mos.

PRESENT LAND USE	%	LAND USE CHANGE	PREDOMINANT OCCUPANCY	SINGLE FAMILY HOUSING
Single Family		Not Likely	Owner	PRICE $ (000) / AGE (yrs)
2-4 Family		Likely	Tenant	
Multi-family		In process	Vacant (0-5%)	Low
Commercial		To:	Vacant (over 5%)	High
Industrial				Predominant
Vacant				

NEIGHBORHOOD ANALYSIS	Good	Avg.	Fair	Poor
Employment Stability				
Convenience to Employment				
Convenience to Shopping				
Convenience to Schools				
Adequacy of Public Transportation				
Recreation Facilities				
Adequacy of Utilities				
Property Compatibility				
Protection from Detrimental Cond.				
Police & Fire Protection				
General Appearance of Properties				
Appeal to Market				

Note: Race or the racial composition of the neighborhood are not considered reliable appraisal factors.

COMMENTS:

A neighborhood is never rated in absolute terms; its quality is rated only in comparison with other neighborhoods. The rating suggests the neighborhood's appeal to market participants who are shopping for houses in that neighborhood and competitive neighborhoods.

NEIGHBORHOOD VALUE INFLUENCES

In collecting data and inspecting the neighborhood, the appraiser attempts to identify major value influences, observe how they are changing, and relate these conclusions to the subject property and potentially comparable properties. For purposes of analysis value influences are classified as social, economic, governmental, or environmental. Although these influences often overlap, it is helpful to consider each category separately. Most appraisal reports refer to the four forces that influence value.

Social Influences

Social influences on neighborhood property values include 1) population characteristics and trends, 2) the quality and reputation of the establishments that serve the neighborhood, 3) community and neighborhood organizations, and 4) the absence or extent of crime and litter.

Population characteristics

The population characteristics that strongly affect neighborhoods are the current population, the size and composition of households, and the population makeup. For example, changes in the average size of neighborhood households and the age of family members can indicate a demand for houses of a particular size and style and for specific neighborhood services. Other relevant population characteristics include population density, which is usually important in areas dominated by high-rise residences; occupant employment profile; and educational, skill, and income levels of residents.

Population data can be obtained from the U.S. Census Bureau, utility companies, local chambers of commerce, county offices, school districts, and visitors' bureaus. If census figures are not up to date, the population of a neighborhood can be estimated by multiplying the number of electric or water meters in the area by the ratio of population to number of meters that was calculated at the time of the last census.

Population characteristics are important and appraisers should identify and quantify the trends they suggest. For instance, if a neighborhood is becoming increasingly attractive to households with young children, residences with extra rooms and play areas may be in great demand. If middle- and upper-income professionals prefer city neighborhoods close to restaurants and cultural facilities, low-maintenance properties in particular neighborhoods may become especially desirable. Trends can be identified by observing price changes for different types of residences and neighborhoods over several years. Understanding the social forces behind these price changes can help the appraiser forecast a neighborhood's future. However, such forecasts must be based on factual evidence that is clearly stated in the appraisal report.

Quality of services and establishments

The appraiser should investigate how residents and potential buyers rate the quality of businesses and other establishments that serve the neighborhood, in comparison with the services provided in competitive neighborhoods. Do they think there are enough restaurants in the area? Is parking a problem? Are shopping facilities, medical facilities, and recreational areas adequate? How good are the neighborhood schools and places of worship? How do potential buyers feel about area establishments and the neighborhood's future?

Community and neighborhood associations

The presence of neighborhood and community groups can affect the stability of a neighborhood and the value of its residential property. Some neighborhood groups are legal entities formed by the original developers or by the home owners themselves; they are concerned with maintaining common areas and providing certain services such as garbage disposal, snow removal, water supply, and police and fire protection. Voluntary associations such as block clubs and crime watch groups organize neighborhood crime protection efforts; lobby against undesirable rezoning or development; and sponsor revitalization projects, block parties, and street fairs. Community spirit can make a neighborhood more stable and may even reverse a trend toward declining property values.

Crime and litter

When a neighborhood is reputed to have a high crime rate, some residents may move and potential residents may decide not to purchase homes there. Local police departments usually have information on the number and types of crimes reported in an area. Better street lighting, increased police protection, and effective neighborhood crime watch groups can improve a neighborhood's crime problem to some extent.

The absence of litter in public and private areas suggests that property owners care about their neighborhood. The presence of an unusual amount of litter suggests neighborhood apathy and may indicate a change in the neighborhood's occupancy characteristics. The level of crime in the neighborhood and the presence of litter should be stated in the neighborhood section of the appraisal report.

Economic Influences

Economic influences center around neighborhood occupants' financial ability to rent or own property, to maintain it, and to renovate or rehabilitate it when necessary. The physical condition of individual properties indicates the relative financial strength of area occupants and how this strength is translated into neighborhood upkeep. The economic characteristics of occupants may also reflect present conditions and future trends in real estate supply and demand.

Appraisers may consider these economic influences: 1) the economic profile of residents; 2) the types and terms of financing available locally; 3) property price and rent levels; 4) the amount of development, construction, conversions, and vacant land; 5) the extent of occupant ownership; and 6) vacancy rates.

Economic profile of residents

There is a direct relationship between the income and employment profile of neighborhood residents and price and rent levels. The type, stability, and location of employment all have a strong impact on the value of residential property because employment determines the ability of individuals to purchase or rent in a particular area. Income levels tend to set a range of property values in a neighborhood. Information on income levels can be found in recent census data and newspaper surveys.

Local business conditions must also be considered. State employment services, local chambers of commerce, local employers, and monthly business reviews published by academic and financial institutions can provide useful information. Relevant data on local business activities include retail sales levels, real estate transfers, and new housing starts.

An appraiser may compile a wealth of information on local businesses, but these data are only useful if they can be used to relate recent or likely future changes in the economy to specific changes in the demand for a specific type of real estate. For example, upper-income housing in an area may respond to a factory closing differently than lower-income housing. Similarly, business fluctuations may not affect rent levels in the same way they affect the prices of single-family residences.

Types and terms of financing

To assess how the income of a population affects its purchasing power, an appraiser considers the requirements of mortgage lenders who serve the market population in the area. What types of financing are available? Are VA or FHA loans common? What interest rates and points are being charged? What is the typical loan-to-value ratio and loan term?

Mortgage information can be obtained from local savings and loan institutions, banks, and mortgage companies.

Property price and rent levels

Price and rent levels of neighborhood properties usually demonstrate a high degree of conformity. The value of a subject property is strongly affected by the prices at which similar, nearby properties have been sold. Neighborhood prices and rents constitute the primary source of market data for appraisal analysis. Price and rent levels indicate the interaction of value influences. If price levels are changing, an appraiser should fully investigate what is causing this change.

Development, construction, conversions, and vacant land

Vacant land suitable for construction of additional houses may exist within a neighborhood simply because the owners do not wish to sell or develop the land. However, the presence of vacant land may also indicate a lack of effective demand or suggest the likelihood of future construction activity.

If there are only a few vacant lots in a neighborhood, their development usually will not have a substantial impact on most other neighborhood properties. However, if these lots are specifically zoned for nonresidential use or variances are granted to permit nonresidential construction, the presence of an atypical use may have an adverse effect. If a neighborhood has many vacant lots, the values of existing properties will be more significantly affected by the anticipated development of these lots. Similarly, if many neighborhood properties are likely to be converted to residential use, existing residential properties may be affected.

In performing neighborhood analysis, an appraiser should obtain information about buildings under construction and proposed future development as well as the existing supply of properties. Detailed, block-by-block information can help pinpoint the direction of growth or change.

Extent of occupant ownership

Neighborhoods in which most residences are owner-occupied are often more stable and pose less investment risk to lenders than neighborhoods with many tenant-occupants. Owners generally maintain their properties better than tenants. When the ratio of owner-occupied to tenant-occupied residences in a neighborhood changes, decline or revitalization may be indicated.

Vacancy rates

If the vacancy rate in a neighborhood is high in comparison with historical levels, prices and rents may fall and new construction may decline. When the vacancy rate falls, rents and prices increase and entrepreneurs are encouraged to add more units to the market.

If the vacancy rate in the subject neighborhood is relatively high, the appraiser should try to find out why. Do these rates reflect short-term fluctuations or indicate long-term change? A high vacancy rate indicates an oversupply of properties and suggests that prices have been falling or are about to fall. Thus, the appraiser must discern whether prices have bottomed out or will probably continue to fall. This information may be needed to adjust the prices of comparable sale properties for changes in market conditions that occur over time.

Vacancy information can be obtained from local real estate boards, the post office, local public utility companies, newspapers, and property managers. During the neighborhood inspection, the appraiser should note any boarded-up buildings or other signs of vacancy. Vacancy rates for different property types should be considered separately because one property type may be in short supply while another is plentiful.

Government Influences

Government and legal influences on property values include the laws, regulations, and taxes imposed on neighborhood properties and the administration and enforcement activities associated with these constraints. Important factors to be considered are: 1) taxation and special assessments in relation to the services provided and in comparison with other neighborhoods in the community, 2) public and private restrictions, 3) schools, 4) the quality of fire and police protection and other public services, and 5) government planning and development activity. The appraiser gathers data on government influences in the subject neighborhood to get a picture of how the situation in this neighborhood compares with that of other, competitive neighborhoods.

Police power regulations, private restrictions, and taxes can restrict the rights of property ownership and influence property values. In neighborhood analysis an appraiser tries to ascertain:

1. How the benefits produced by local regulations stand in relation to the burdens they impose. The local situation is then compared with the situation in competitive neighborhoods;

2. How much governmental provisions and their enforcement add to or detract from the stability of the neighborhood; and

3. How these provisions relate to the neighborhood or community master plan. The likelihood and effect of future changes in legislation are also assessed.

Taxation and special assessments

Tax burdens can vary significantly and variations in taxes may significantly influence the decisions of potential buyers. Divergent tax rates often affect market value. Local taxes may favor or discriminate against certain types of property. Community development programs may depend on tax revenues. The appraiser should examine local assessed values and tax rates, compare the burdens created by various taxes, and measure their effect on the values of different real estate.

Special assessments are directly related to the additional services or advantages provided; they may pay for private beaches or extra fire protection. Properties subject to high special assessments may or may not be penalized. A special assessment lien may reduce the value of a house by approximately the amount of the lien, or it may have no effect on value.

Counties and cities may have the authority to impose optional taxes such as sales and earnings taxes on residents. When competing communities are subject to different sales and local earnings taxes, the relative desirability of the communities may be affected. These variations often have a more significant effect on the marketability of commercial and industrial real estate than ad valorem taxes do. Such variations can also indirectly influence residential real estate values.

Public and private restrictions

Zoning regulations and building codes are important to the stability of a neighborhood. They provide legal protection against adverse influences, nuisances, and hazards. Some buyers seek out neighborhoods that have effective zoning laws, building codes, and housing and sanitary codes. The enforcement of these codes, regulations, and restrictions should be effective and equitable in comparison with enforcement in competitive neighborhoods.

When zoning variances are obtained easily and without consideration of their effect on surrounding houses, the value of these properties may be decreased. When existing zoning and building regulations are not enforced, neighborhood property values may be decreased. Zoning violations often include illegal signs, illegal business uses, and conversion of properties to a density of use that is higher than the density permitted by the zoning.

Changes in zoning may have positive or negative effects on the neighborhood as a whole, and they can have different effects on individual properties in the neighborhood. For example, rezoning a corner site from residential to commercial use might have a negative effect on the neighborhood as a whole, although it increases the value of that particular property. Appraisers are concerned with both of these effects. The probability of zoning changes in transitional areas should be explored through discussions with zoning officials. Anticipated zoning changes can affect the highest and best use, and hence the value, of the subject and potential comparable properties. Interim uses, temporary uses to which properties may be put until they are ready for their highest and best uses, may be considered.

Deed restrictions often protect properties from the negative impact of an incompatible use. If these restrictions are not enforced, lower values may result. However, some deed restrictions written long ago may be obsolete or unenforceable. Generally, any deed restriction that is against the public interest cannot be upheld.

Schools

Schools are a strong attraction for prospective homebuyers. Many families choose a neighborhood for the quality of its schools. Schools are of immediate concern to families with children. Because today's economy is oriented toward service and high technology industries, which require well-trained workers, communities with educational facilities and institutions of higher education are increasingly favored by business and industry. The reputation and probable future of a neighborhood's schools should be considered.

Fire and police protection

Government-provided services are vital to the maintenance and preservation of neighborhoods and communities. The type of fire-fighting service, the size of the fire district, and the distance of the residence from the firehouse may all influence the decision of a potential home buyer. The reputation of the local police force and its effectiveness in preventing crime can also help shape purchase decisions.

Planning and development activity

Planning for the future development of communities is an important task of government. Good planning can maintain the integrity and character of existing neighborhoods and provide ideas for the future use of undeveloped areas. Poor planning for recrea-

Figure 7.3 Zoning Map

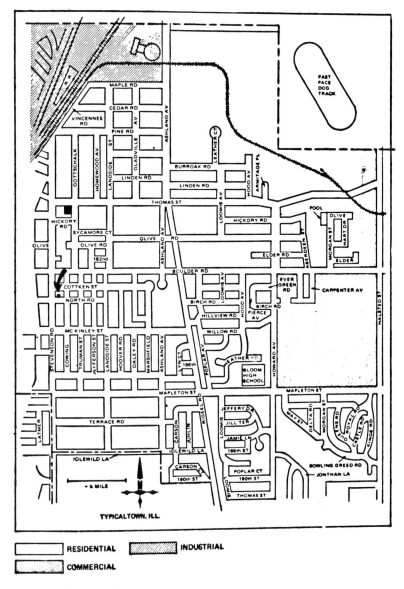

RESIDENTIAL   INDUSTRIAL

COMMERCIAL

tional facilities, schools, and service areas may contribute to neighborhood disintegration. The requirements imposed on developers influence the type and quality of services available to home owners, and have a strong effect on the value of existing structures. By protecting open space areas, the government can deter developers from modifying the environment to maximize the number of units built.

Federal, state, and local government agencies oversee community development activity and can provide important information on trends in land use and housing supply. The Bureau of the Census and the Bureau of Labor Statistics compile useful data on construction volume and labor costs. City and county building and planning commissions, as well as real estate boards and builders' organizations, can provide detailed information on existing and proposed units.

Building permit information, which is usually obtainable from the municipal building inspection department, indicates the types of housing most popular in the area. Municipal planning departments have information on existing and proposed subdivisions to supplement permit information. If the community being investigated is too small to have a planning department, the township clerk or the public works department may have this type of information.

Development activity may be indicated by analyzing current market sales, absorption trends, expected returns, marketing problems, and future development plans. By comparing the number of lots being platted to the number of building permits issued, an appraiser can assess the relative oversupply or undersupply of subdivision lots.

Larger communities have land-use planning facilities. Existing or proposed land-use plans can be consulted to learn of anticipated future development. Many states have statutes requiring that city governments control land use according to approved plans.

The Council of Governments (COG), which is composed of representatives from several municipal and county governments, is another source of information on supply trends. These facilities vary in terms of staffing and funding. Transportation plans and land use records can be obtained from COGs and some COGs also keep detailed housing information.[1]

Environmental Influences

Natural and man-made features that affect the neighborhood and its location are environmental influences. Important environmental considerations include: 1) the location of the neighborhood within the community; 2) the transportation system and important linkages; 3) services, amenities, and recreational facilities; 4) the topography, soil, climate, and view; 5) patterns of land use and signs of change in land-use patterns; 6) the age, size, style, condition, and appearance of residences and neighborhood facilities; 7) the adequacy and quality of utilities; and 8) the presence of hazardous wastes.

Location within the community

Changes occurring in a neighborhood are usually influenced by changes in the larger area of influence. Therefore, a neighborhood may benefit or suffer because of its location. A neighborhood adjacent to a growing business district, for example, may benefit from nearby shopping and municipal services, but it may also suffer from increased crime and congestion. The rapid growth of one neighborhood or district may adversely affect a competitive neighborhood or district. Areas located in the direction of growth may benefit, while other areas may suffer.

---

1. This discussion has been adapted from J. R. Kimball and Barbara S. Bloomberg, "The Demographics of Subdivision Analysis," *The Appraisal Journal,* October 1986.

Transportation systems and linkages

Transportation systems provide important linkages, which have a strong influence on the desirability of specific neighborhoods. An appraiser should consider the destinations to which typical occupants commute as well as the distance, time, and quality of the transportation services available. If adequate facilities are not available, the neighborhood will be at a disadvantage compared with competing neighborhoods with better linkages. In studying location and transportation, an appraiser should consider both existing and proposed transportation facilities, as well as all existing and planned facilities to which residents may be expected to commute.

For the occupants of single-family residential neighborhoods, linkages to workplaces, schools, and shopping areas are usually the most important; recreational facilities, houses of worship, restaurants, and other stores are somewhat less important. A nearby shopping center can enhance a neighborhood's value. Heavy, slow traffic on highways can reduce values in some areas, particularly if these highways are the primary linkages between the neighborhood and major centers of employment. Some linkages have special importance to certain groups of people. Proximity to schools may be a priority for people with children, while public transportation and services are important to the elderly.

Public transportation is crucial to people who do not own automobiles or prefer not to use them for commuting. Even in areas where most families own two or more cars, unstable energy costs, high maintenance and insurance, and the convenience of public transportation make linkages an important consideration.

The transportation characteristics of the neighborhood usually apply to most properties in the neighborhood. However, the walking distance to and from public transportation can be an important variable if residents are expected to use these facilities frequently. Urban apartment dwellers usually prefer to be within walking distance of public transportation. The territory through which commuters must pass is also important; people dislike walking through poorly lighted streets and rundown areas.

The street pattern of the neighborhood has a significant bearing on a property's location in the community and transportation linkages. Contemporary neighborhoods are planned with curving streets, cul-de-sacs, and circular drives. These features take up valuable space and can increase land costs, but they do add privacy and reduce traffic hazards that are often found in older neighborhoods with square-block street patterns. Streets should be designated to make use of natural contours, wooded areas, and ponds. Traffic in residential areas should move slowly and easily. Ideally, expressways and boulevards should be outside residential neighborhoods, but offer convenient access to local streets.

Appraisers should also note the quality of street lighting, pavements, sidewalks, curbs, and gutters. Well-maintained streets and shade trees contribute to the overall desirability of a neighborhood. In congested areas, the availability of street parking can also influence property values.

Amenities, services, and recreational facilities

Amenities and services can have a substantial impact on the desirability of a neighborhood, particularly in more affluent areas. The businesses, schools, cultural facilities, and houses of worship that serve the neighborhood affect its desirability. More prosperous neighborhoods provide recreational facilities such as parks, beaches, pools, tennis courts, country clubs, and libraries. These facilities can help a neighborhood attract new residents. Community home owners' associations can keep a neighborhood in good condition by helping maintain recreational facilities and other amenities that increase the neighborhood's desirability. The presence, location, and accessibility of recreational facilities and services should be noted in the appraisal report.

Topography, soil, climate, and view

Topography and climatic conditions can have a positive or negative effect on neighborhood property values. The presence of a lake, river, bay, or hill often provides a scenic advantage. A hill may mean little in a mountainous region, but an elevated or wooded section in a predominantly flat area can enhance property values. A river, lake, or park may act as a buffer between a residential district and commercial or industrial areas and reinforce the neighborhood's identity.

Topographic and climatic features can also be disadvantageous. A river that floods penalizes the value of homes along its banks. Severe changes in elevation can make access difficult and construction more costly. The soil in an area may have poor bearing quality, absorption, or drainage characteristics. Climate can also have a negative effect. Although a neighborhood usually shares the same climate as competitive neighborhoods, the subject neighborhood may suffer from special conditions such as increased wind, fog, or rain. Conversely, some neighborhoods may offer protection from such adversities.

The desirability of certain types of topography depends on the kind of residential development that is present or contemplated. For expensive homes, large hillside or wooded sites are often desired. Tract developers, however, usually seek a level area or plateau, which is better suited to subdivision construction and can be developed less expensively. Generally, an area slightly higher than surrounding neighborhoods is preferred.

Patterns of land use and signs of change

In a stable neighborhood the mix of land uses is balanced and conforms to market standards. Each use has a clearly defined area and these areas are well buffered from one another. The neighborhood's boundaries are usually explicit and buildings generally conform to one another and to their immediate environment. Excessive homogeneity can detract from value, but a balanced mix is typical and desirable in the market area.

Neighborhood change is often signaled by a poor mix of land uses; considerable variation in construction, maintenance standards, and ownership status; or indistinct neighborhood boundaries. Values may be rising, falling, or about to shift; the neighborhood may be entering a stage of decline, revitalization, or conversion to another type of neighborhood.

To optimize property values, residential areas should be protected from the hazards and nuisances of nearby land uses. Excessive traffic and odors, smoke, dust, and noise from commercial and manufacturing enterprises limit a residential neighborhood's desirability, as does a location near a local airport, a nuclear power plant, or a toxic waste disposal site. Neighborhoods suffering from these conditions may have stable values, particularly if the adverse conditions have been present for some time, but property prices and values in these neighborhoods are likely to be lower than values in similar or competitive neighborhoods that do not suffer adverse influences.

Age, type, size, condition, and appearance of residences

The character of a neighborhood is reflected by its "average" house. The stuctural and architectural quality, age, and condition of typical residences are physical characteristics that have a substantial effect on the desirability of a neighborhood. In stable neighborhoods, this average house suggests the type of improvement that constitutes the highest and best use of the subject site. An appraiser should also note the sizes and shapes of typical sites and typical land-to-building ratios in the neighborhood.

The condition of individual homes and their architectural compatibility influence the general appearance of a neighborhood. Well-kept yards, houses, and community areas reflect good maintenance. Landscaping, trees, open space, and the proper maintenance of vacant lots also make a neighborhood more desirable. Public and commercial establishments should present a neat, compatible appearance. Poorly maintained public areas, vacant stores, and excessive graffiti on buildings detract from a neighborhood's desirability and often indicate a period of change.

Adequacy and quality of utilities

Gas, electricity, water, telephone service, and storm and sanitary sewers are essential in municipal areas to meet contemporary standards of living. The absence of any of these services tends to decrease values in a neighborhood; unusually high costs for these services also influence values. The availability of utilities affects the direction and timing of neighborhood growth and development.

Presence of hazardous wastes

Hazardous wastes are substances that can cause serious illness to people or damage to the environment. The Environmental Protection Agency defines hazardous wastes by the following characteristics: ignitability, corrosiveness, reactivity, and toxicity in extraction. The abatement of hazardous substances is regulated by federal and state statutes and agencies. Two federal statutes, the *Comprehensive Environmental Response, Compensation, and Liability Act* (CERCLA) of 1980 and the *Superfund Amendments and Reauthorization Act* (SARA) of 1986, contain important provisions regarding the liability associated with environmental contamination of property. In recent years, the principle of absolute liability has been upheld in cases where product defects have resulted in human injury. The liability of environmental assessment experts has not yet been addressed by legislation or the courts.[2]

The responsibility of the appraiser in determining the impact of environmental hazards on value has not yet been legally established. The Appraisal Institute takes the position that "the responsibility of the appraiser in such matters must be balanced with the knowledge and training of the appraiser. The duties placed on the appraiser must not be duties that only an environmental engineer or expert can perform. Rather, they should reflect the appraiser's frame of reference, which is that of an ordinary knowledgeable buyer."

Certain signs may indicate that the presence of hazardous wastes should be investigated. An appraiser may want to recommend or retain the services of an environmental assessment expert if the presence of hazardous materials is suspected. If the residence being appraised is situated on or near a site that was once used as an industrial property, solvent or chemical seepage may be present in the ground or the water supply. The site of a commercial property may be polluted with PCBs, asbestos, or seepage from underground storage tanks (USTs); agricultural land and nearby sources of drinking water may be contaminated with pesticides.

During the site inspection, the appraiser should look for warning signs such as an oily sheen on puddles or drainage ditches, discolored vegetation, and cans or drums that may contain paints, coolants, or solvents. Basements, sheds, storage areas, and garages should be checked for hazardous waste. Asbestos-containing materials (ACMs), which were once commonly used to insulate walls and pipes, can become carcinogenic when the asbestos fibers are distributed in the air by crumbling or pulverization (see Chapter 10). Building interiors can be monitored for radon. Radon gas is released from radium, which is produced by the radioactive decay of uranium in ores underground. It can cause lung cancer. Radon percolates up through the soil and infiltrates homes. Weatherizing a residence to save energy seems to increase radon levels, because the gas cannot escape from a tightly sealed house.

Research on former tenants of the residence may also alert the appraiser to the possibility that hazardous wastes are present. If the present owner once leased the property, his or her records should reveal the nature of enterprises conducted on the property in the past. Assessor's records, aerial photographs, and employees of former enterprises may be consulted. Local and regional agencies might also be able to provide information on any permits acquired, complaints filed, and enforcement activities.

---

2. Property owner liability is joint and several—i.e., each and any owner may be charged with cleanup costs. Liability is also retroactive and unending. Environmental polluters may be ordered to reimburse cleanup expenses incurred by the Superfund, pay a penalty for regulatory noncompliance, or compensate for damages arising in a tort suit.

THE LOCAL MARKET

Patterns and Trends

By gathering data on neighborhood value influences, an appraiser forms a picture of the local market, its preferences, and its manner of operation. The appraiser sifts through the data and selects information that relates to the subject property and the particular appraisal problem for further analysis. Usually to make this selection, various kinds of information must be organized and patterns and trends must be isolated. Significant market patterns and trends include 1) price levels for properties with different characteristics, 2) price changes, 3) supply and demand trends, and 4) market activity patterns. These elements provide basic indicators of market characteristics, which are used in many phases of the valuation process.

Price levels

In the market area, house prices and associated costs for construction, maintenance, utilities, and tax assessments are of primary importance. To select comparable properties, an appraiser identifies real estate characteristics in the subject and comparable properties that have the most similar appeal to potential purchasers in the market area. Different property features, condition, and location will be reflected in the different prices purchasers are prepared to pay. To form a picture of the opinions of value held by the local market, the prices of properties with a variety of characteristics must be studied.

For example, an appraiser is likely to compare the prices of older homes with the costs incurred by local contractors and developers to construct similar improvements. This information can indicate how the market discounts the value of properties for the age of the improvements. The appraiser may also want to answer the following questions:

- What value does the market ascribe to the addition of a bathroom or swimming pool?
- How do prices in this market area compare with prices in other market areas?
- Where in the neighborhood are houses selling at a premium? Where are values affected by negative influences?
- How do specific architectural styles appeal to market participants?
- How does the size of the lot affect the property price?
- Does a higher tax burden tend to lower the property price? By how much?
- What percentage premium is being paid in sales that involve atypical or creative financing instruments?

The appraiser answers these questions by comparing sales of properties that are similar in every characteristic but the one being investigated and examining the variance in their prices. Each property is unique, so it is often difficult or impossible to isolate a single variable for analysis. Nevertheless, an appraiser can usually get a sense of the market by observing price trends and making appropriate statistical inferences. Appraisers try to understand the basic preferences of the market and how these preferences relate to prices; this is the basis of the sales comparison approach to value.

Price changes

The pattern of change in price levels over several years is also important. For example, an appraiser might want to determine whether the prices of properties that have a particular feature such as a kitchen with built-in appliances are rising faster than the prices of properties without the feature. Does growing demand for built-in appliances signal a trend? Is the trend in prices related to costs? Are the costs of construction in the area rising faster than property prices? What about the cost of vacant land? If the cost of vacant land is rising faster than property prices, supply is probably about to decline. The appraiser might also want to know how real estate price movements compare with changes in wage levels and the cost of living. These movements can indicate a shift in demand. The rate of change may be equally important. Is change accelerating, stabilizing, or slowing down? With an understanding of the economic and social forces, this information can be used to interpret the present market and forecast future conditions.

Supply and demand

An appraiser needs to study the present supply and demand for properties that are comparable to the subject property. The appraiser forecasts future conditions of supply and demand by considering the combined influence of all the value-influencing forces observed during neighborhood analysis.

One indication of supply and demand in the local market is the relationship between the number of new listings in a specific period and the number of sales during the same period. This information is generally available from newspaper advertisements and sales brokers. Another indication of present supply and demand conditions can be obtained by comparing the market vacancy rate to historical levels.

Appraisers should be alert to conditions that signal probable future changes in the balance of supply and demand. Changes in construction costs, the amount of land available for construction, financing opportunities, and current or planned construction can indicate a change in supply. On the demand side, important variables include population size, employment and income levels, and the terms of available mortgage financing.

Market activity

Market activity patterns are closely related to supply and demand. Market activity, which refers to the efforts of buyers and sellers to conclude sales, is reflected in the volume of listings and sales per period, and in the typical marketing time.

The quantity of buyer and seller activity is reflected in the volume of sales per period compared to past periods. A decline in activity may indicate a very stable market population with demand on the rise and price increases in the near future. It may also signal a weakening market and an imminent drop in prices. Sellers who do not receive acceptable offer levels often hold out for a while in the hope that demand will recover. They may remove their properties from the market, which produces a decline in the volume of sales. Sometimes demand does resume at the old prices. If demand does not pick up, however, sellers eventually give in and listing prices are reduced until a new price level is established. Sales then resume at this new price level. Thus, a decline in the volume of sales may signal trouble in the market. If an appraiser concludes that trouble is ahead, he or she will probably not want to use the prices of sales that occurred in an earlier, more active period without first adjusting them to reflect the change in conditions.

Other significant patterns of activity are *marketing time*, the length of time it takes to sell or rent a particular type of property, and the *listing-to-sale* or *listing-to-rent range*, which is the difference between the initial listing price and the actual sale price or rent of a property. If marketing time or listing-to-price ranges are increasing in comparison to past periods, a weakening market and a drop in prices in the near future may be indicated. Appraisers should also be aware of any change in the number of "for sale" signs visible in the market area. If these signs increase without a corresponding increase in demand, downward pressure on prices may soon be felt. Conversely, an increase in the number of people appearing at open houses or looking at property offered for sale may indicate an increase in demand and an expected rise in prices.

Reporting Conclusions of the Neighborhood Analysis

An appraiser specifically describes all beneficial and detrimental conditions revealed in the neighborhood analysis. A general reference to "pride of ownership" in the neighborhood is too vague and subjective; it does not indicate an actual effect on property values and ascribes motives and attitudes to people. Rather, the appraiser should record precise, impartial observations made during his or her personal inspection of the neighborhood. Descriptive phrases such as "many broken windows, tall weeds on site, no litter present, or well-kept lawns" directly convey meaningful information on value-influencing factors at work in the neighborhood.

SUMMARY

By analyzing the neighborhood and local market, an appraiser identifies the market area of the subject and comparable properties, the value influences affecting the neighborhood, the advantages and disadvantages of the neighborhood in comparison with competitive neighborhoods, current local market conditions, and the direction of future change. A neighborhood is an area of complementary land uses; a district is a type of neighborhood characterized by homogeneous land use; and the market area is the area in which properties effectively compete with the subject property in the minds of probable, potential purchasers and users. At the start of neighborhood analysis, the appraiser should define the neighborhood boundaries and try to identify the stage of the neighborhood's life cycle.

The data needed for neighborhood analysis depend on the use and purpose of the appraisal. The appraiser performs the analysis to understand market preferences and price patterns, to reach general and specific conclusions regarding highest and best use, to define the area from which to select comparables, to examine the effect of different locations within the neighborhood, to determine the influence of nearby land uses, to identify the value influences affecting the neighborhood, to pinpoint the most recent changes affecting values, and to forecast the neighborhood's long-term prospects. In addition to collecting pertinent data, the appraiser makes a visual inspection of the neighborhood to observe physical characteristics, note the neighborhood boundaries, identify land uses and signs of change, and rate the quality of the neighborhood.

The appraiser studies social, economic, governmental, and environmental value influences. Social characteristics include population and demographic trends—e.g., current population, size and composition of households, age distribution; the quality of neighborhood services and establishments; the existence of community or neighborhood associations; and the levels of crime and litter in the area. Economic influences relate to the economic profile of neighborhood residents; the types and terms of financing available locally; property price and rent levels; the amount of development, construction, conversion, and vacant land; the extent of occupant ownership; and vacancy rates. Government influences focus on tax burdens and special assessments, public and private restrictions, schools, fire and police protection, and planning and development activities. Environmental influences include the location of the neighborhood within the community; transportation systems and important linkages; amenities, services, and recreational facilities; topography, soil, climate, and view; patterns of land use and signs of change; the age, type, size, and condition of neighborhood residences; the adequacy and quality of utilities; and the presence of hazardous wastes.

By collecting and analyzing these data, the appraiser should be able to form an accurate picture of the local real estate market. Important market patterns and trends are indicated by the price levels of properties with different characteristics, price changes, supply and demand, and the volume of market activity. In neighborhood analysis, the appraiser should dismiss unfair or arbitrary judgments and carefully construct a detailed, impartial description of the conditions observed in the neighborhood.

REVIEW QUESTIONS

1. What characterizes a neighborhood? Why is the specific location of a property within a neighborhood of special importance?

2. Describe the four stages in the neighborhood life cycle. Explain gentrification.

3. Discuss the specific steps involved in neighborhood inspection.

4. Explain the meaning of the following terms: linkage, land-use mix, rate of household formation, economic profile of neighborhood residents, relationship of special assessments to benefits provided, and Council of Governments (COG).

5. In local market analysis, what sort of indicators does an appraiser use to establish price changes, the relationship between supply and demand, and market activity levels?

8 Site Description

An important distinction exists between the terms *site* and *land*. Land, or raw land, refers to the condition of a plot in its natural state. A site is land that is improved so that it is ready to be used for a specific purpose. Both onsite and offsite improvements can make a plot ready for its intended use or development. Sewers, grading, drainage, utility lines, and access to roads are all examples of improvements that convert land into a site.

Site value often differs from the value of a parcel of raw land. Often site value is higher; the presence of improvements means that less work must be done to develop the property. If the improvements are faulty, inadequate, or otherwise inappropriate to the property's highest and best use, site value may be lower than land value. A lower value may also result if a valuable surface resource has been stripped away in clearing the land.

Because of this possible difference in value, an appraiser should use concepts consistently when researching land or site value. If sales of sites rather than raw land are used to derive a value indication, the appraiser should recognize that site value, not land value, is obtained. In ordinary usage, land and site are often treated synonymously. This is acceptable so long as it does not lead to inappropriate or inconsistent reasoning and the appraiser describes the steps used to convert the indication of land value into an indication of site value.

SITE IMPROVEMENTS

The description and analysis of the site begin with an inspection of the site and all site improvements. Generally, site improvements included in site value are treated in the site description; all others are described with the building improvements. Appraisers should observe the practices commonly used in their market area to avoid misleading the client or other readers of the appraisal report. The final value estimate of the property as a whole should not be affected by how various improvements are classified for analysis. In calculating depreciation for income tax purposes, improvements that are part of the site are usually not considered depreciable.

Site improvements include clearing, grading, draining, public utilities installed, site access routes, sidewalks, curbs, landscaping, septic systems, wells, driveways, parking areas, courts, fences, walls, lights, and poles.

PURPOSES OF THE SITE DESCRIPTION AND ANALYSIS

There are several reasons why an appraiser describes and analyzes the site. A detailed description of the site being appraised is presented in the appraisal report and descriptive data are required on site dimensions, area, zoning, location, topography, utilities, site improvements, present use, and highest and best use. The appraiser considers the conformity of the site size and whether the location of site improvements meet zoning and building setback requirements. The site description also helps the client and third parties form an opinion as to how the highest and best use of the site was determined.

The appraiser also uses the site description to establish criteria for the selection of comparable properties. Comparable properties should be similar in size and other physical characteristics. In most cases the sites of comparable properties will have the same or a similar highest and best use as the site of the subject property. Transitional properties may pose special problems.

The site description and analysis provide much of the data needed to form a separate estimate of land or site value. This separate estimate is needed for the cost approach and provides the basis for any site adjustment needed in the sales comparison approach. A separate land or site value estimate may also be required when the appraisal is being prepared for casualty loss estimates, local tax assessments, or eminent domain proceedings. Site valuation techniques are described in detail in Chapter 12.

Site analysis gives the appraiser an understanding of how the property is currently being used. The general relationship between the building and the site and the pattern of zones into which the improved site is divided both affect the desirability of the property as a whole. Maintenance and landscaping can also affect property value. Site analysis combined with building analysis indicates how the property as a whole can be used most profitably in its improved state and what effect its present condition has on the total property value.

A final purpose for site analysis is to form a basis for determining the highest and best use of the land as though vacant. Having studied the neighborhood and the local market, the appraiser is in a position to understand how the physical and legal characteristics of the site interact with its surroundings to shape its maximum economic potential. This maximum economic potential, or highest and best use, is the key to estimating the market value of the property.

If the lot being appraised is unimproved, vacant land, detailed data on various characteristics may have to be collected as part of site analysis. Often developers want highest and best use or feasibility studies performed before they prepare land for a particular use. These studies examine the quality of the soil and the cost of bringing utilities to the site, among other items. When the property is already improved, the appraiser may assume that the soil is suitable and the site is physically usable, but these assumptions and their effects must be clearly stated in the appraisal report.

STEPS IN THE SITE DESCRIPTION AND ANALYSIS

The site description and analysis involves several steps, which may be grouped into two general tasks.

1. The appraiser prepares for the field inspection by gathering the necessary tools and equipment and reviewing legal, tax, and assessment information on the property. Using this information, the appraiser notes the legal description of the property and all public and private restrictions that limit property use.

2. The appraiser then makes a field inspection of the site. In describing the site, the appraiser observes how site characteristics combine to shape the highest and best use of the site and notes any problems or special advantages that may affect site value. The site description includes a plot plan of the site.

PRE-INSPECTION PREPARATION

Assembling Essential Tools and Equipment

Before making the actual field inspection, the appraiser gathers all the tools and equipment necessary for this phase of the assignment. The appraiser will probably want to collect information on the subject site, the subject improvement, and potential comparables all in one trip, so careful planning is beneficial. Useful tools for data collection and subsequent steps in the analysis include measuring equipment, photographic equipment, maps and plats, calculators, dictation equipment, carrying equipment, and miscellaneous office supplies. Most appraisal offices have many of these items on hand.

Measuring equipment

To measure the building and site improvements, the appraiser may want to bring a 50- to 100-ft. wind-up tape measure and a 12- to 20-ft. tape measure that can be worn on a belt. A carpenter's folding rule may also come in handy. The appraiser should take measurements consistently.

To transfer measurements to scale drawings, the appraiser may use a straight edge, an architect's scale, an engineer's scale, and graph paper. A template and protractor can be used to draw curved lines and measure their angles.

Photographic equipment

An automatic camera can be used to take instant photographs. These reference shots can be used while photos taken with more professional equipment are being processed. An instant camera can also be used to document particular problems or record noteworthy features during the inspection.

Many appraisers use 35 mm cameras which produce clearer pictures. Because various kinds of photographs are required, the camera might be equipped with a regular lens, a wide-angle lens, and a telephoto lens as well as a flash attachment for interior photographs.

Maps and plats

Maps and plats can serve as useful references for the field inspection. Copies of these maps may be included as supplements to the appraisal report. Many appraisers have maps of the areas they regularly appraise in their office files. These maps may include street and highway maps, address maps, municipal maps, plat books, census maps, soil maps, topographical maps, floodplain maps, zoning maps, survey plats, and subdivision maps.

Calculators

An inexpensive pocket calculator is convenient for simple calculations. A portable financial calculator may be needed for more complex calculations.

Dictation equipment

The appraiser can use dictation equipment to record a running description of the property during the inspection, which is later transcribed. A variety of equipment is commercially available. The appraiser should select equipment that is compact, portable, and compatible with the transcription equipment in his or her office.

Carrying equipment

Briefcases are functional and present a professional appearance; portfolios, catalogue cases, and file folders are also used frequently. Clipboards are very convenient for taking notes during the inspection. The appraiser may want to bring a tool box to carry additional equipment such as a screwdriver, a pocket knife, an ice pick, a chisel, a flashlight, and a level to check surfaces.

Miscellaneous equipment

It is wise to have a change of clothing and extra supplies available in the office. With hiking boots, waterproof boots, and work clothes, an appraiser is prepared to inspect rough terrain.

Any forms the appraiser is likely to need should be kept on hand; these include inspection forms as well as appraisal forms.

Reviewing Legal, Tax, and Assessment Information

One reason to review legal information on the property is to identify the precise area to be valued in the appraisal. Often the appraisal assignment will be to value the fee simple interest in a detached, single-family dwelling with access from a public street. The site is the area identified in the legal description of the real estate. The appraiser should verify that the legal description corresponds to the property being appraised. Sometimes other areas must be investigated as well. For example, if a right-of-way across an adjoining property runs with the title, this property should be examined to verify the ease of access.

The appraiser should review the deed or abstract of title to the property, which specifies the property rights conveyed and any limitations on these rights. The records of the county tax assessor or tax collector should be examined for information on the property's assessed value, annual tax burden, and any special assessments.

FIELD INSPECTION

An appraiser inspects the physical characteristics of the site to describe its principal features and any additional advantages or disadvantages the market is likely to consider. The appraiser then determines how the site can best be used, given its legal and physical limitations and its relationship to its surroundings. Assuming the site is put to its highest and best use, the appraiser considers how the physical characteristics of the site and the present condition of the existing site improvements add to or detract from property value. Value influences are examined in light of neighborhood and local market preferences.

Many physical characteristics of a site are considered in the site description, including

- Size and shape
- Topography, soil, and drainage
- Location, access, and environmental influence
- Onsite and offsite utilities
- Site zones and site improvements

Size and Shape

To describe the size and shape of a site, an appraiser notes the site dimensions, including frontage, width, and depth. The appraiser plots the site's shape to calculate its area. Dimensions are usually expressed in feet for easy calculation; area is usually expressed in square feet or sometimes in acres. The appraiser also considers whether plottage, the combination of two or more sites, is desirable and whether excess land is present.

Dimensions

The site's width is the distance between the side lines of the lot. When the shape of a lot is irregular, the *average width* is often used. Many communities prescribe a minimum width for detached, single-family residential lots. Another important measurement is the *width at the building line*. Many zoning regulations specify a minimum width at this line so the site can be used to construct a particular type of improvement.

Frontage refers to the length of a site where it abuts a thoroughfare or accessway. Minimum frontage is often specified by zoning requirements. In the valuation of residential lots, *front footage* is sometimes used as a unit of comparison, but the importance of frontage varies from one location to another. Consequently, care must be exercised in using this unit of comparison for residential lots. Frontage in excess of the standard frontage considered acceptable in the neighborhood may not add proportionate value to the value of the lot.

Most residential neighborhoods have a standard lot depth. Lots that have less depth generally sell for less and lots with excess depth sell for more, but the premium or penalty is rarely proportionate to the dimensions involved. In many communities, a zoning ordinance specifies the minimum depth for detached, single-family residential lots. The minimum depth for attached, single-family residential lots varies, but these lots usually need not be as deep as detached, single-family residential lots.

Tables and formulas are used by assessors to calculate how lot depth affects property value in local markets. Similar tables and formulas are available to calculate the effects of lot size and corner influence. However, using these tables to value single-family residential property is risky. These tables and formulas cannot usually be applied to more than one neighborhood or market and the data used to compile the tables may not be current. Because tables can be misleading and are often misapplied, it is preferable to use more accurate sales data that reflect the appraiser's research and analysis of the specific market.

The size and shape of a site affect the uses to which it can be put and therefore its value. For instance, an odd-shaped parcel may be appropriate for a dwelling, but inappropriate for commercial or industrial use. Zoning, neighborhood standards, and community development goals all have an impact on how sites of various sizes and shapes may be used. Given a particular use, the appraiser can determine how the size and shape of a site affect its value by analyzing sales or lease data on parcels of various sizes and shapes. If the subject property has a characteristic that is unusual for the neighborhood, this should be noted.

An appraiser considers not only the overall dimensions of the site, but also how different parts of the site can be developed. A regularly shaped parcel may have a swamp, stream, or cliff within its borders that limits its utility. All such features should be described and their effects on value carefully considered.

Size

The size or area of a parcel is determined by its linear dimensions and by its shape. An appraiser can consider both of these variables by drawing a scale figure of the site, dividing the drawing into standard geometric figures, and calculating the area of each figure. Specialized computers and software programs are also available for readily computing the areas of both the site and improvements. Appraisers should be familiar with the geometric formulas for calculating areas, which are used to compute site size and to measure improvement characteristics. Some basic formulas are described and illustrated in Figure 8.1.

Figure 8.1   Basic Formulas to Calculate Area

A square is a four-sided figure with sides of equal length that meet at right angles—i.e., angles of 90 degrees. The area of a square is the length of one side squared.

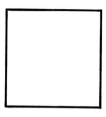

Area of square = length × length

A rectangle is a four-sided figure with sides that meet to form right angles. Parallel sides of a rectangle are of equal length. The area of a rectangle is its length times its width.

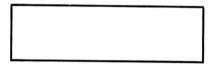

Area of rectangle = length × width

A triangle is a three-sided figure. The height of a triangle is measured by drawing a line from one of its corners to the side facing it, called the base, to intersect the base at a right angle. The area of a triangle is its height times its base divided by two.

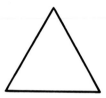

$$\text{Area of triangle} = \frac{\text{height} \times \text{base}}{2}$$

A trapezoid is a four-sided figure with two parallel sides and two sides that are not parallel. The angles that join the sides in a trapezoid are not usually right angles. The area of a trapezoid is the sum of the lengths of its parallel sides, multiplied by the height, and divided by two.

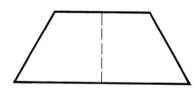

$$\text{Area of trapezoid} = \frac{(\text{side } 1 + \text{side } 2) \times \text{height}}{2}$$

A circle is a curving figure in which all points along the curve are of an equal distance from one central point. This distance is called the circle's *radius*. A *diameter* is a line that passes through the center of the circle and divides it in half; it is always twice as long as the radius. The area of a circle is 3.1416 times the radius squared.

Area of circle = $3.1416 \times \text{radius}^2$

(continued)

Figure 8.1 continued

A slice of a circle is a pie-shaped area bounded by two radius lines and an arc of the circle. As the angle between the radius lines grows larger, a broader arc and larger area of the circle are sliced out. A circle has 360 degrees, so to calculate the area of a slice, divide the angle by 360 and multiply by the area of the circle.

$$\text{Area of slice of circle} = \frac{\text{angle subtended}}{360°} \times \text{area of circle}$$

To measure the area of a fragment of a circle, compute the larger area of the slice that corresponds to its arc and then subtract the excess triangular area. The area of the slice is calculated as described above. The area of the triangle can be calculated by measuring the base and height and applying the standard triangle formula—i.e., base × height/2.

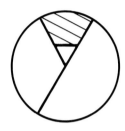

$$\begin{array}{ccc} \text{Area of} & = & \text{area of} & - & \text{area of} \\ \text{circle fragment} & & \text{corresponding slice} & & \text{triangular shape} \end{array}$$

Plottage and excess land

In analyzing how site size affects site value, the appraiser must also consider plottage and excess land. *Plottage* is an increment of value that results when two or more sites can be assembled or combined to produce greater utility and value. A parcel has plottage value when its highest and best use is realized by combining it with one or more other parcels under a single ownership or control. If the parcels have a greater unit value together than they did separately, plottage value results. Analysis of neighboring land uses and values will indicate whether the property being appraised has plottage value.

Excess land is the opposite of plottage. A vacant site or a site considered as though vacant is said to include excess land if some of the land is not needed to accommodate the site's highest and best use. In regard to an improved site, excess land is the surplus land not needed to serve or support the existing improvements. Excess land may have its own highest and best use or it may allow for future expansion of the existing or anticipated improvement. In any given market, the land and improvements that form an economic unit reflect a typical ratio. If an improved property has excess land, this land may not add a proportionate amount of value to the value of the property. Depending on its size, configuration, and location, the excess land may be considered separately from the land that supports the improvements. If the excess land is marketable or has value for a future use, its market value as vacant land constitutes an addition to the estimated value of the property.

Topography, Drainage, and Soil

To evaluate the topography of a site, an appraiser examines land contours, grades, natural drainage, drainage systems, soil conditions, and general physical utility.

Land contours

All variations in elevation should be described. Sites tend to have lower values if extreme topographical conditions increase the cost of building improvements. Steep slopes are more susceptible to landslides and may increase construction costs or preclude construction altogether. In some cases, however, the disadvantages of a high elevation may be offset by an excellent view.

An ideal residential lot may have a slope that rises slightly from the street to the improvement and then gently falls off. However, what is desirable in one neighborhood is not necessarily desirable in another. A lot that is higher or lower than the level of the abutting street may create additional costs for owners due to poor drainage, erosion, or diminished accessibility. If the site is unimproved, these features can limit the usefulness of the site for development.

Drainage

Drainage depends on natural topography and the ability of the soil to absorb water. Natural drainage may be a problem if the site is downstream from properties that have a right to direct excess flows onto it. Some system must be provided to drain the site of surface water and groundwater. Storm sewers should be present in the water disposal area. In some cases, a simple swale may efficiently channel the water from the surface of the lot to the street or into natural drainage; a system of tiles can remove surface and subsurface water from some sites. When the site is located in a designated flood hazard area, the appraiser must consider whether any of the topographical features of the site increase or decrease its susceptibility to flooding in comparison with other neighborhood properties.

The appraiser should be particularly concerned with how the site's drainage characteristics may affect the improvements. A house with a basement must have drains to carry the water out from under the basement and prevent leaks from developing. If a house is built on a slope, special precautions must be taken to keep the runoff water away from the sides of the house.

Soil conditions

The character of the *subsoil* can have a substantial effect on the usefulness of a site and the cost of preparing it for building. Subsoil quality can also affect where improvements can be constructed on the site and influence building design. If bedrock must be blasted or the soil is unstable, the cost of improving the site will increase. Similarly, extra expenses may be incurred for building foundation walls or sinking piles if a site must be filled in. Percolation, permeability, and the absorption capacity of the soil must be considered to assess the site's suitability for septic and storm water systems.

In many areas the *surface soil* of a site is important because the lawn and landscaping surrounding the property are important to its marketability. The appraiser notes whether the soil appears to be suitable for cultivation and typical of the surrounding neighborhood. When appraising a new subdivision, an appraiser determines whether or not the natural surface soil, the topsoil, will need to be replaced after construction with better soil. If the topsoil is naturally sandy or rocky topsoil, it may need to be replaced.

Frequently subsoil conditions are known to local builders and developers. An appraiser may ask that an engineer trained in soil mechanics be retained to test the qualities of the soil for construction, but an expensive soil study is not necessarily needed as part of the appraisal. If the soil-bearing capacity is in doubt, however, the appraiser should inform the client of the need for a soil study. If soil tests are not made, the appraiser must describe the assumptions made concerning soil characteristics in the limiting conditions and assumptions section of the report.

Location, Access, and Environmental Influence

The study of location includes analysis of 1) the relationship between the site and transportation routes and neighborhood facilities, 2) the type and orientation of the lot within the existing street pattern, 3) access to the site, 4) street improvements, 5) environmental hazards and nuisances, and 6) view and climate.

Transportation

The highest and best use of the site and therefore its value are strongly affected by the site's location in relation to transportation routes. Lots that are far away from major transportation routes or accessible only from narrow streets are less appealing to commercial and industrial users. Lots with easy access to schools, workplaces, and recreational facilities often have greater appeal to residential users. Both vehicular and pedestrian access should be considered.

The quality of highways and the density of traffic during rush hours are also important considerations in the study of transportation. The availability, proximity, and quality of public transportation systems are also significant, particularly if many neighborhood residents commute. An appraiser is especially interested in any aspects of the site that make it different from other neighborhood sites and from comparable properties.

Lot type and orientation

Some common types of lots are interior, corner, cul-de-sac, and flag lots.

Interior lots have frontage on only one street. The main access to the lot is usually from that street, although rear alleys may also provide access. Interior lots are often the most regular in shape, particularly if the neighborhood is designed in a grid format. When inspecting interior and cul-de-sac lots, the appraiser should note the distance and direction to the nearest intersection(s).

Corner lots have frontage on two or more streets—often a main street and a side street. These lots often appeal to commercial users because of their increased visibility, greater frontage, and more convenient access from the rear.

If the highest and best use of the site is for residential use, a corner location may pose both advantages and disadvantages. A corner site can have an automobile entrance on the side street, thus reducing driveway areas. This can be especially advantageous in areas where interior lots have little frontage. Corner lots may also allow greater flexibility in the building layout and provide more light and air than interior lots. However, corner lots may also have disadvantages such as less privacy, less security, and greater susceptibility to traffic hazards and nuisances. Corner lots may have two building setback lines, one from each street, which reduces the area on which improvements can be built. Corner sites may also be subject to higher special assessments because they have more sidewalk area and street frontage. Corner sites have both advantages and disadvantages in the market, so an appraiser must assess the impact of a corner influence by studying market data.

Cul-de-sac lots are located at the end of dead-end streets where circular turn-around areas are common. These lots are generally tapered, have very little frontage, and are somewhat irregular in shape. Parking may be more difficult on cul-de-sac lots, but there may be compensatory advantages. Cul-de-sac lots may have bigger backyards and less street traffic, so they may be particularly desirable to families with children.

A flag lot is a rear lot with a long narrow access. The lot and access route resemble the shape of a flag on a pole. Flag lots have greater privacy, but a residence built on such a lot may be difficult to find and have poor access.

Figure 8.2   Types of Lots

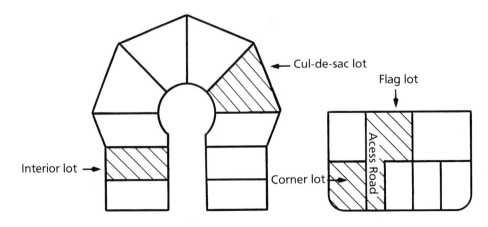

Appraising Residential Properties

Access to the site

Access to the site is closely related to lot type. Access may be provided by a public street or alley, a private road or driveway, or a right-of-way across an abutting property. When access depends on a private road, the appraiser should find out who maintains the road and whether the lending institutions serving the neighborhood write mortgages for houses without a public street address.

The ease of entry to the lot by car is also noted. The grade of the driveway should provide reasonably convenient access. Lots with driveways that slope up to the street are often less desirable than lots with driveways that are level or slope down. It is dangerous to back into traffic or enter traffic when oncoming cars cannot be seen well. The market often penalizes a site for access problems.

Street improvements

The quality and condition of abutting streets and street improvements also affect the value of a site. A description of street improvements includes information on the width of the street or alley, the type of paving, and the condition. The direction of traffic and the number of lanes are also important, as are the quality and condition of gutters and storm sewers, curbs, street lights, sidewalks, trees and plantings, and bicycle lanes. In some areas lenders may require additional information if the property frontage is on a private road.

Nuisances

Convenient service facilities contribute to the value of a site, but they can detract from site value if they are too close. Hospitals, firehouses, gas stations, public schools, stores, restaurants, and medical offices are desirable if they are nearby, but not immediately adjacent to the property. The presence of industrial plants, large commercial or office buildings, noisy highways, utility poles and high-tension wires, motels and hotels, and vacant houses in a residential neighborhood generally has a negative effect on nearby property values. Uses that do not mix well or do not conform to neighborhood standards and properties that are poorly maintained or produce odors, noises, and pests can decrease the value of residential properties and may suggest an alternative highest and best use for the site.

Hazards

Heavy traffic is the most common hazard in residential neighborhoods. The market often recognizes this problem and properties located on heavily traveled streets are penalized for their proximity to noise, fumes, congestion, and accidents. Within the same neighborhood, lots bordering streets with different volumes of traffic can have substantially different values. Families with small children are particularly concerned about traffic hazards. Speed controls, speed bumps, and well-maintained sidewalks to schools and play areas can reduce traffic hazards.

Other hazards are presented by floods, potential landslides, earthquakes, ravines, bodies of water, subsurface mines, gasoline storage tanks, toxic wastes, and railroads. If hazards are observed in the neighborhood, the appraiser investigates what measures have been taken to protect the subject property from danger.

In some areas radon gas, which can cause lung cancer, percolates up through the soil and infiltrates homes. High concentrations of radon may be found in the soil surrounding a residence, but experts do not yet know how to predict whether the interior of the house will have a high level of radon as well.

Flood hazards are especially important in appraisals because in many parts of the country lenders cannot issue a mortgage in a flood hazard area unless the mortgagor purchases flood insurance. If an appraiser learns that the site being appraised is in an identified flood hazard area, he or she should investigate the availability and cost of flood insurance. The potential for flooding in the subject property and comparable sites must be discussed in the appraisal report.

Local government offices often maintain flood maps and officials will know whether or not a site is in a flood zone. It is wise to obtain copies of local flood maps for regular use. These maps indicate different kinds of flood zones such as an area of 100-year flooding or an area of 100- to 500-year shallow flooding. Maps are also available from insurance companies serving the area; the names and addresses of these companies can be obtained from the National Flood Insurers Association.

Climate

Most climatic conditions affect the subject property and comparable properties in the same way, so general climatic conditions are described with community and neighborhood characteristics. However, a particular site may benefit or suffer from a special climatic characteristic, such as high wind. If so, this must be noted in the site description. Climatic conditions may suggest the best orientation for building improvements. If the position of the site relative to the street precludes a building orientation that suits climatic conditions, a value penalty may result.

The significance of climate and its effect on property value may differ depending on the highest and best use of the site. The appraiser must consider how climatic considerations and other environmental influences affect the highest and best use of the site.

View

The view from a property can substantially affect its value. Lots in the same neighborhood that are similar in all respects except their locations and orientation often have different values attributable to the difference in view. Views of water, mountains, or valleys are most popular. A commanding view of the surrounding landscape can sometimes compensate for adverse topographic or climatic characteristics. Conversely, a poor view can produce a value penalty. An appraiser should also consider the likelihood of the property's view being obstructed in the near future.

Figure 8.3 Flood Map

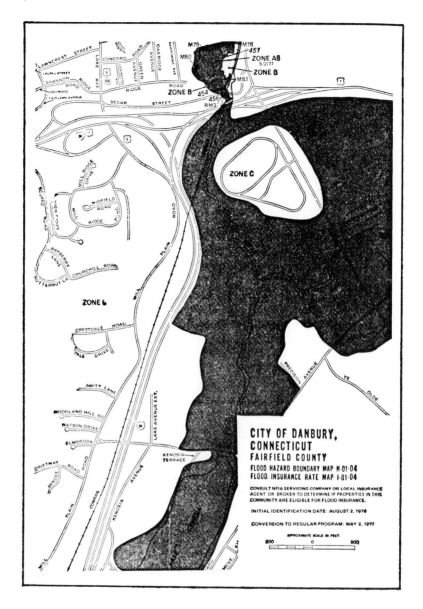

Onsite and Offsite Utilities

An appraiser inspects the utilities present on the site and those that are available nearby. Water, electricity, natural or propane gas, telephone, sewerage, trash collection, and cable television are essential utilities in many residential markets. If the utilities on the site are inadequate, the availability and cost of obtaining utility service must be considered. Both highest and best use and site value may be strongly affected by the availability of utilities.

Water

For residential use a site must have an adequate supply of acceptable water. Water may be obtained from a municipal or private company or from a well. The FHA Minimum Property Standards require that a public water supply should be used if it is available. Some residents obtain water directly from rivers, streams, or lakes or from rainwater collected and stored in tanks on the roof. These houses are not considered satisfactory by FHA standards because they do not have a consistent, adequate supply of safe water.

When water is supplied by a public or publicly regulated company, the appraiser usually checks its availability on the site and determines if the water pressure is sufficient. When water is supplied by an unregulated company, the appraiser must report this fact and investigate the dependability of the water supply. Shallow or artesian wells should be capable of sustaining a flow of five gallons per minute. The water should meet the bacterial and chemical purification requirements set by local health authorities.

When appraising vacant land that is not linked to a public water supply, an appraiser should check the wells dug on surrounding properties to determine the likelihood of finding an adequate water supply for the site.

Sewage disposal

When available, connection to a municipal sewage system is usually desirable, but many areas have no sewer system. Almost 50 million people in 15 million homes in the United States depend on septic systems for their waste disposal; of new houses being constructed, 25% are not connected to municipal sewerage systems. If no public sewers exist, a percolation test may be required to determine whether the soil on the site can absorb the runoff from a septic system. If a percolation test is not made, this fact should be reported in the appraisal report.

Garbage collection

Some sites are not served by garbage collection services because they are located on private roads or in rural areas. If these services must be purchased separately, a value penalty may result depending on the expectations of market participants in the area.

Easements

An easement is an interest in real property that conveys use, but not ownership, of an owner's property. A common type of easement is an easement for utilities. Easements tend to limit the uses to which a site can be put and the types of improvements that can be built on it. During inspection the appraiser examines the site for any evidence of easements. Easements are almost always identified when title or record data are researched, but some easements may not be recorded. The appraiser should also investigate compliance with private restrictions and any potential infringements.

Figure 8.4 Septic System

A typical septic system consists of a large concrete tank buried in the ground. Waste materials from the house drainage line enter the tank and separate into three parts. Solid wastes, which are only about 1% of the total, sink to the bottom. Grease, usually not more than 1% of the total volume of waste, rises to the top. The rest is liquid. Bacteria in the tank decompose the solid waste and grease, and a relatively clear liquid flows from the opposite end of the tank through the drain line to a distribution box, which directs the liquid into a network of buried perforated pipes called a leaching field, or into a seepage pit. From here the liquid runs off into the ground and is absorbed.

Courtesy of
Frank E. Harrison

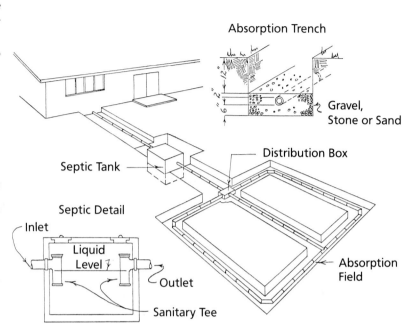

Site Improvements

Landscaping, walls and fences, walks, driveways and parking areas, pools and ponds, waterfront improvements, and recreational facilities are all site improvements.

Landscaping modifies the natural site to achieve a functional or decorative effect. Landscaped lawns can be seeded or sodded; gardens may be either flower gardens or vegetable gardens. Planting areas may include flower beds, planter boxes, and compost heaps. Landscaping often improves the overall appearance of a property and enhances its value. However, the desirability of plants is a matter of individual taste. The more elaborate the garden, the more care it will require. The effect on value produced by landscaping depends on the character and standards of the neighborhood.

Some trees and shrubs are considered part of the raw land, not site improvements. An appraiser considers the maturity, health, and overall appearance of trees and notes any risk of damage that might result from dead trees or branches falling or striking the residence in lightning or wind storms. Trees and shrubs are planted for practical as well as aesthetic reasons. Deciduous trees are best placed on the western side of a property where they will provide shade from the hot afternoon sun in the summer, but allow the sun's warmth to shine through in the winter. Trees also help maintain moisture in the air. Conifers planted on the northern side of a house can act as windbreaks.

Outdoor lighting and sprinkling systems can contribute to the residents' enjoyment of an outside area. Special yard improvements such as statuary, barbecues, planters, fountains, and bird baths tend to give a residence an individual character. However, if these improvements seem in poor taste given the standards of the neighborhood, they may discourage buyers and this must be considered.

Walls and fences built of stone, wood, or metal form barriers around the perimeter of a lot. Walls and fences can vary greatly in terms of cost and condition, and they can provide varying degrees of privacy, decoration, and security. Appraisers should recognize that walls and fences may encroach on neighboring properties and that the walls and fences of abutting properties may encroach on the subject site. If encroachment is evident, it must be reported in the appraisal report and its probable effect on value must be noted.

Walks provide access from streets and from driveway and parking areas to the entrances of the house. Walks can be made of concrete, brick, stone, or patio blocks. They should provide convenient access to the entrances and not become muddy when it rains.

Driveways and parking areas provide access from the street to the garage. They may be made of a variety of materials including gravel, stone, concrete, asphalt, or earth. The slope of a driveway should facilitate access and both driveways and parking areas should be pitched to drain water away from the improvements. Parking areas must allow adequate space for a driver to turn around.

Pools may be heated or unheated and vary in size and quality. Pool construction, depth, equipment, and maintenance requirements will influence the value contributed by a pool. Ponds and lakes may be shallow or deep. Their shoreline features, construction, erosion, accretion, stocking, and manner of use should be considered. An appraiser should also note where water enters and leaves ponds and lakes and examine the potential for flooding.

Waterfront improvements include breakwaters, seawalls, piers, boat hoists, and beaches. An appraiser notes the condition, quality, and effectiveness of these improvements and considers any riparian or littoral rights.

Recreational areas include terraces, tennis courts, bridle paths, golf courses, and whirlpool baths. These amenities should always be considered in light of the probable market for the subject property.

DRAWING A PLOT PLAN

The appraiser draws a plot plan which shows the boundaries of the lot, all topographical features, and the location of all improvements. A good plot plan is drawn to scale, with lot dimensions indicated on the boundary lines. In addition to the house and the garage or carport, the plot plan should show sidewalks, driveways, patios, and pools. Any rights-of-way, easements, or encroachments should also be indicated on the plan.

SUMMARY

A site is land that is improved so that it is ready to be used for a specific purpose. The value of the raw land can be different from the value of the site. Both onsite and offsite improvements prepare a plot for its intended use or development. Site description and analysis are performed to 1) collect data for a detailed description of the site in the appraisal report, 2) establish criteria for the selection of comparables, 3) provide data for a separate estimate of land value, 4) gain an understanding of how the property is being used currently to determine if the site and improvement are combined in a complementary, maximally productive way, and 5) establish a basis for concluding the highest and best use of the land as though vacant.

To describe and analyze a site, an appraiser gathers the necessary equipment; reviews legal, tax, and assessment information; and conducts an inspection of the property, noting the site characteristics and any special problems or advantages. Before setting out on the inspection, the appraiser assembles measuring and photographic equipment, maps and plats, and equipment for making calculations and recording field notes. The appraiser should review the legal description of the real estate, a deed or title abstract specifying the property rights conveyed and any limitations on these rights, and tax assessment information. The site of a detached, single-family residence held in fee simple is generally the area included in the legal description of the real estate.

The physical characteristics of the site to be considered are: 1) site dimensions, area, and the possibility of either plottage or excess land; 2) topography, drainage, subsoil and topsoil; 3) transportation and access, lot type and orientation, and environmental influences such as street improvements, nuisances, hazards, climate, and view; 4) onsite and offsite utilities; and 5) site improvements such as landscaping, walls and fences, walks and driveways, and waterfront and recreational facilities.

The appraiser should prepare a plot plan drawn to scale, showing lot boundaries, topographical features, the location of improvements, and any legal limitations on property rights.

REVIEW QUESTIONS

1. Why can the value of a parcel of raw land and the value of a site differ? If site value is greater than land value, what does this suggest about the existing site improvements? If site value is less than land value, what does this suggest about the existing improvements?

2. Discuss the various purposes of site analysis.

3. What data does the apppraiser review before inspecting the property?

4. Define plottage and excess land.

5. What type of environmental influences does an appraiser consider in describing the physical characteristics of a site?

6. What physical features of a site and legal limitations on property rights does a plot plan illustrate?

9 Building Description

Once the site has been examined, the appraiser is ready to begin the inspection of the improvements. An appraiser describes improvements by noting the size, style, design, and layout of all buildings. The appraiser examines the construction quality and maintenance condition of the building, describing the structural components, materials, and mechanical systems as well as the quality and condition of each component. Any special problems are noted. The appraiser considers how the building elements observed combine with the site's characteristics to shape the highest and best use of the property as improved. Any problems or deficiencies in the present condition of the improvements that might prevent the property from realizing its highest and best use must be described.

The building description is an important step of the valuation process. To complete this step properly, an appraiser must be familiar with building design and construction. The purpose of the building description, the background data and materials needed, and the steps normally taken to complete this stage in the valuation process are discussed in this chapter. Architectural style, building design and layout, and the house zones and rooms found in residential properties are also covered. Chapter 10 rounds out this discussion with information on building construction and the mechanical systems used in residential properties. Specific structural components, equipment, and attachments are covered in depth.

PURPOSES OF THE BUILDING DESCRIPTION

A building description can help an appraiser select suitable comparable properties from a preliminary list of potential comparables. In the sales comparison approach the appraiser uses the complete building description of the subject property to make adjustments for differences between the subject and each of the comparable properties. The building description also provides the data needed to estimate reproduction or replacement costs and accrued depreciation in the cost approach and operating and maintenance expenses in the income capitalization approach. Thus, the quality of the building inspection and description directly affects the reliability of all three approaches to value.

Background Data and Building Inspection Tools

Much of the background data and building inspection materials used in the site inspection is needed again for the building inspection. The following items are especially important.

Zoning and building codes

The appraiser should be thoroughly familiar with all zoning regulations, building codes, and private restrictions that are applicable to the subject property. This information is needed to determine whether existing or potential property uses conform to local codes. The design and construction of buildings are regulated by building, plumbing, electrical, and mechanical codes, and may be limited by deed restrictions as well.

During the building inspection the appraiser should look for current uses that do not conform to legal requirements and consider how these uses might affect the property's value. If, for example, a garage has been remodeled without a building permit, it may now require upgrading to meet building code standards. A building that does not comply with local codes probably has less value than a similar building that does. Making a building conform to the standards set forth in the code may produce additional expenses for its owners and limit the future use of the building.

Blueprints or plans

When building blueprints or plans are available, they can help an appraiser identify the structural and mechanical details of an improvement. Plans and blueprints may also be used to verify the dimensions of a building, but an appraiser cannot rely on plans for size calculations. The appraiser must measure the improvements during the building inspection because the plans may not have been followed accurately or, more likely, alterations and additions may have been made after the plans were prepared.

An appraisal form or checklist

The appraiser may want to bring a checklist to the building inspection to rule out possible oversights.

Other materials

Additional equipment used in an inspection might include a flashlight, a camera with film and batteries, a level, a 100-ft. measuring tape or wheel, an ice pick, a pocket knife, a screwdriver, and a chisel. A clipboard, a pencil, and graph paper should be brought so the appraiser can draw a scale diagram of the building.

DESCRIBING AND RATING THE IMPROVEMENTS

With the data requirements in mind and the necessary materials at hand, the appraiser is ready to begin inspecting the improvements. At each step of the inspection, the appraiser performs two tasks: the appraiser describes and classifies the building element being studied and rates the element. Each physical component must be rated for quality and for condition to determine its effective age as opposed to its actual age. (Both of these terms are defined in Chapter 15.) The rating process is called a *quality and condition survey.* Layouts and designs are also considered for their *functional utility.* The appraiser determines how the functional utility of the building relates to its construction quality and maintenance.

In the context of building description, *quality* refers to the character of construction and the materials used in the original work. The physical deterioration of the improvements is not considered in rating its quality. When well-chosen materials are applied in a suitable manner with sound construction techniques and good workmanship, quality is produced. Published cost-estimating guides provide four quality ratings—low, average, good, and very good to excellent—and indicate separate costs for each category.

On a practical level, economy of construction results in an improvement that produces amenities for a tenant-occupant or rental income for a landlord commensurate with the cost of the improvement over its economic life. A structure may have a functional layout and attractive design, but be constructed with inferior materials and poor workmanship. These deficiencies increase maintenance and utility costs and affect the marketability of a property adversely. Conversely, a building can be too well constructed—i.e., its cost is not justified by its utility. Most purchasers will not want to pay excess costs even though they may be recaptured through reduced maintenance expense.

An excess in the capacity or quality of a structure or structural component, as determined by market standards, is called a *super-adequacy.* Superadequacies should be considered in the quality survey, as should the related concept of overimprovement. An *over-improvement* is an improvement that does not represent the most profitable use of the site on which it is placed because it is too large or costly and cannot develop the highest possible land value.

The *condition* of an improvement refers to the extent to which physical deterioration or structural defects are present. Overall wear and tear and the level of maintenance dictate a building's condition. An appraiser generally distinguishes between items that must be repaired immediately and those that may be repaired or replaced at a later time.

Functional utility is the ability of a property or building to be useful and to perform the function for which it is intended, according to current market preferences and standards. The term also refers to the efficiency of a building's use in terms of architectural style, design and layout, traffic patterns, size and type of rooms, and energy efficiency. A building may have functional utility, but an undistinguished architectural style; another building may have an admired style, but little utility. Form and function should work together to create successful architecture. An appraiser considers the functional utility of a building in relation to its construction quality and condition.

STEPS IN THE BUILDING DESCRIPTION

There is no set order of steps in the building description that works for all appraisals. Different types of properties and different appraisal styles may require that varying procedures be used to inspect improvements. The following steps are presented in a sequence common to many appraisals.

The appraiser begins by observing the general placement of the improvements on the subject site and considering the effects of their location. The exterior is examined in detail, starting with the foundation, framing, exterior covering, and the roof of the residence. (These structural components are discussed in the next chapter.) The building features and the materials used are noted and each feature is rated for quality of construction, condition, and market appeal. The appraiser measures the exterior dimensions of the main improvement and draws a scale diagram of the improvement on a sheet of graph paper. Photographs of the improvements are taken, the architectural style of the main improvement is identified, and the compatibility of the residence with its use and environment is considered.

The interior of the residence is inspected next. The appraiser notes the number and type of rooms and considers the functional utility of the layout. The quality of workmanship and the materials used in the interior finish are examined. Potential problems are carefully studied, and their cause and cost of repair are evaluated. Photographs are often taken of the interior of the improvement.

During the inspection of the interior the appraiser also checks the mechanical systems—heating, cooling, electrical, plumbing, hot water, and waste disposal. (Mechanical systems and equipment will be covered in the next chapter.) Air-conditioning, insulation, and energy efficiency are investigated and any built-in equipment is inspected.

Building additions such as porches, patios, decks, and balconies are examined and wall attachments, stairs, roof attachments, special rooms, basements, and attic areas are inspected. Finally, the appraiser returns outside and examines the garage and any outbuildings. These structures are rated for construction quality, condition, and market appeal.

Orientation and Placement of Improvements on the Site

As mentioned previously, an appraiser observes the location and orientation of the improvements on the site at the outset of the building inspection. In examining the improvements, the appraiser notes how the residence is situated in relation to the sun and how it is adapted to the benefits or constraints of the site location.

During the summer, the sun rises in the northeast, travels in a high arc, and sets in the northwest. During the winter, it rises in the southeast, travels in a low arc, and sets in the southwest. A well-designed house takes advantage of the movement of the sun with a southward orientation and small or few windows to prevent air leakage. A large roof overhang shades the house in the summer months when the sun is high. In the winter when the sun is low, the warmth of the sun can enter the windows of the house.

Outbuildings, trees, and vegetation that are appropriately placed can shelter the main improvement from the sun, wind, or noise.

Size Measurements, Diagrams, and Photographs

Measuring size

Determining the size of a building is sometimes a formidable task. Methods and techniques for calculating building size vary regionally and according to property type; local practices may reflect biases that significantly affect value estimates. Appraisers must be familiar with the measurement techniques used in their areas as well as those used elsewhere in the market. Appraisers must also be consistent in their use, interpretation, and reporting of building measurements within each assignment. Failure to do so can adversely affect the quality of their appraisal reports.

The most common building measurement, gross living area, is always calculated. The dimensions of a building can be ascertained from plans, but these dimensions should be checked against the actual building measurements. The area of attached porches, detached garages, and minor improvements is calculated separately.

Standards for measuring residential properties have been developed by several federal agencies, including the FHA, VA, FNMA, and FHLMC. Because these agencies are closely related to the mortgage market, their standards are used in millions of appraisals. Gross living area is the standard measure applied to single-family residences. *Gross living area* is defined as the total area of finished and above-grade residential space. It is calculated by measuring the area within the outside perimeter of a house and includes finished and habitable, above-grade living area only. Finished basement or attic areas are not included in total gross living area.

The gross living area of a rectangularly shaped house is measured by attaching the end of the tape measure to one exterior corner of the residence, measuring the distance to the next corner, and then repeating this process until all exterior walls have been covered. After noting the measurements on a rough diagram of the house, the appraiser checks to see whether the measurements of parallel sides of the structure are equivalent. This procedure is known as *squaring the house*. The total front building measurements should equal the total rear measurements; the total left-side measurements should equal the total right-side measurements. Minor discrepancies may suggest that the corners of the structure are not perfect right angles; greater discrepancies may be attributable to errors in measuring or rounding inconsistencies.

If there are attachments to the house or the house has an irregular shape, the appraiser sketches the shape of the house and measures each side. Once all the measurements have been verified, the appraiser divides the figure drawn into smaller geometric units, calculates the area of each, and adds the areas together. Areas not normally considered part of the gross living area such as attached garages and entryways must be excluded from the calculations. Computer programs are available for calculating areas, but the appraiser must still "square" the property for the measurements.

An appraiser should never accept a statement as to the size of the subject without verification. Sizes of comparable properties are often obtained from tax records, real estate brokers, and other appraisers.

The method of calculation used must also be determined. If an unverified statement of property size is applied in a value analysis, the resulting estimate could be erroneous. Differences in local and regional market descriptions further complicate the situation. For example, a comparison of condominiums based on square footage may produce inaccurate results if the size of the subject property is expressed in terms of net living area, which is measured along interior walls, and all market data are expressed in terms of gross salable area.

Sketch of the house

A sketch or floor plan of a residence and its garage or carport showing the location of doors, windows, and interior walls is sometimes included as part of an appraisal report. Many appraisers take pride in their ability to draw professional diagrams, but detailed drawings are not required for most residential appraisals. Simple, neat sketches drawn to approximate scale are usually requested by lenders. These sketches should indicate the placement of interior walls and show the same dimensions used to calculate the gross living area.

Photography

Photographs are an important part of an appraisal report. Photographs that are out of focus or badly developed are not acceptable. Instant photographs are acceptable on some occasions, but more professional photographs taken with a 35mm camera are generally required. Color photographs have become a standard part of appraisal reports in many parts of the country.

There is no general rule as to what property features should be photographed. As a minimum, appraisal reports should include photographs of the front and rear of the house, showing the sides as well, and photographs of any major site improvements and a street scene. If the assignment warrants the additional expense, photographs of construction details and the interior of the house should also be included.

ARCHITECTURAL STYLES

In the building description, an appraiser identifies the architectural style of the main improvement and considers its effect on property value. *Architectural* style is the character of a building's form and ornamentation. A wide variety of architectural styles may be identified. An appraiser uses the system of description or identification prevalent in the specific market area so that the client and other users of the appraisal report will understand the style identification. One such system is the Class, Type, Style (CTS) System, which is illustrated by the chart in Figure 9.1.

Architectural Compatibility

One important factor affecting the desirability of a particular architectural style is its conformity or compatibility with the standards of the market. *Compatibility* indicates that a building is in harmony with its use or uses and its environment. This harmony applies to form, materials, and scale of the structure. Styles of different periods frequently clash. A cubistic dwelling would not harmonize with eighteenth-century colonial buildings. A monumental or ostentatious building is out of place in a modest setting. Market value is frequently diminished by incompatibility of design.

Figure 9.1 The CTS System of House Description

The class, type, style (CTS) system was designed to provide a uniform method of describing residential construction. Class denotes the number of occupants per dwelling, type refers to the structural nature of the house, and style refers to the decorative design of the house based on historical or contemporary architecture.

THE CTS SYSTEM (CLASS, TYPE, STYLE)
A UNIFORM METHOD FOR DESCRIBING HOUSES

# CODE	DESCRIPTION	ABBREVIATION
	CLASS	
1	One family, detached	1 FAM D
2	Two family, detached	2 FAM D
3	Three family, detached	3 FAM D
4	Four family, detached	4 FAM D
5	One family, party wall	1 FAM PW
6	Two family, party wall	2 FAM PW
7	Three family, party wall	3 FAM PW
8	Four family, party wall	4 FAM PW
9	Other	OTHER
	TYPE	
1	One story	1 STORY
2	One and a half story	1½ STORY
3	Two story	2 STORY
4	Two and a half story	2½ STORY
5	Three or more stories	3 STORY
6	Bi level	BI LEVEL
6	Raised ranch	R RANCH
6	Split entry	SPLT ENT
7	Split level	SPLT LEV
8	Mansion	MANSION
9	Other	OTHER
	STYLE	
100	COLONIAL AMERICAN	COL AMER
101	Federal	FEDERAL
102	New England Farm House	N E FARM
103	Adams	ADAMS CO
104	Cape Cod	CAPE COD
105	Cape Ann	CAPE ANN
106	Garrison Colonial	GARR CO
107	New England	N E COL
108	Dutch	DUTCH CO
109	Salt Box	SALT BOX
109	Catslide	CATSLIDE
110	Pennsylvania Dutch	PENN DUT
	Pennsylvania German Farm House	GER FARM
111	Classic	CLASSIC
112	Greek Revival	GREEK
113	Southern Colonial	SOUTH CO
114	Front Gable New England	F GAB NE
114	Charleston	CHARLES
114	English Colonial	ENG COL
115	Log Cabin	LOG CAB
200	ENGLISH	ENGLISH
201	Cotswold Cottage	COTSCOT
202	Elizabethan	ELIZ
202	Half Timber	HALFTIM
203	Tudor	TUDOR
204	Williamsburg	WILLIAMS
204	Early Georgian	E GEORG
205	Regency	REGENCY
206	Georgian	GEORGE

# CODE	DESCRIPTION	ABBREVIATION
300	FRENCH	FRENCH
301	French Farm House	FR FARM
302	French Provincial	FR PROV
303	French Normandy	FR NORM
304	Creole	CREOLE
304	Louisiana	LOUISIA
304	New Orleans	NEW OR
400	SWISS	SWISS
401	Swiss Chalet	SWISS CH
500	LATIN	LATIN
501	Spanish Villa	SP VILLA
501	Italian Villa	IT VILLA
600	ORIENTAL	ORIENT
601	Japanese	JAPAN
700	19th CENTURY AMERICAN	19th CTY
701	Early Gothic Revival	E GOTH
702	Egyptian Revival	EGYPT
703	Roman Tuscan Mode	RO TUSC
704	Octagon House	OCTAGON
705	High Victorian Gothic	HI GOTH
706	High Victorian Italianate	VIC ITAL
707	American Mansard	MANSARD
707	Second Empire	2nd EMP
708	Stick Style	STICK
708	Carpenter Gothic	C GOTH
709	Eastlake	EAST L
710	Shingle Style	SHINGLE
711	Romanesque	ROMAN
712	Queen Anne	Q ANNE
713	Brownstone	BROWN S
713	Brick Row House	BR ROW
713	Eastern Townhouse	E TOWN
714	Western Row House	WEST ROW
714	Western Townhouse	W TOWN
715	Monterey	MONTEREY
716	Western Stick	W STICK
717	Mission Style	MISSION
800	EARLY 20th CENTURY AMERICAN	EARLY20C
801	Prairie House	PRAIRIE
802	Bungalow	BUNGALOW
803	Pueblo	PUEBLO
803	Adobe	ADOBE
804	International Style	INTERNAT
805	California Bungalow	CAL BUNG
900	POST WORLD WAR II AMERICAN	POST WW2
901	California Ranch	C RANCH
902	Northwestern	NORTH W
902	Pudget Sound	P SOUND
903	Functional Modern	FUN MOD
903	Contemporary	CONTEMP
904	Solar House	SOLAR
905	"A" Frame	A FRAME
906	Mobile Home	MOBILE
907	Plastic House	PLASTIC

There are several types of incompatibility. The various elements of a structure can be incompatible with one another. A structure can be incompatible with its site or its location in the neighborhood. Compatibility is influenced by a variety of factors, including zoning, construction and maintenance costs, land value, physical features of sites, architectural trends, and technology. Sometimes these influences impose conformity.

The materials used in a structure should be in harmony with one another and with the building's architectural style. A building designed to be built of a particular material will not necessarily be effective if it is constructed of another material. An architectural design should not combine distracting features or building materials that vary excessively.

Architectural design and building materials should be well-integrated and in harmony with the site. A frame building in a wooded, hilly area will probably harmonize with its setting more than a brick building. A frame residence located in a neighborhood of brick homes usually suffers a value penalty.

Perhaps most important, the architectural style of a building should be in harmony with the styles of neighborhood structures and with market standards. Often the predominant uses and building styles in an area can be readily observed; however, the trend of development may be more difficult to forecast. An architectural style that appears atypical may actually indicate the direction of a trend.

The impact of a nonconforming building design should be carefully considered. A somewhat unusual design that is attractive and generally in harmony with other buildings in the area may command a higher price than its more typical neighbors. A house with an incongruous design, however, will probably sell at a price below the general market level. If it does not, it may have special features that compensate for its lack of conformity.

Evaluating the value effect of a nonconforming design may require appraisal judgment. There may be sufficient demand for a detached dwelling in a row-house neighborhood to mitigate any value penalty as a result of incompatibility. Sometimes functional utility may override design as a primary market requirement. If the general proportions and scale of an atypical building are in harmony with its surroundings and the structure has functional utility, the unusual design may not impose a value penalty. In any case, the positive and negative effects of a building's nonconformity should be carefully considered.

Trends in Architectural Styles

Neighborhood properties that conform to the standards of the local market generally have the highest value in relation to construction costs. Although there is room in a free market economy for individual expression and taste, commonly shared tastes characterize the major portion of the real estate market. These commonly shared tastes form the standards of the market, but market standards do change over time.

Market tastes and standards are influenced by both the desire to preserve tradition and the desire for change, variety, and efficiency. Architectural trends respond to the desire to preserve tradition by incorporating elements of past architectural styles; new elements of architectural design are developed in response to the desire for change.

When an architectural style becomes extreme, tastes may shift back to past styles. Extreme ornateness is often replaced with simple forms. A reactive shift provides contrast to the dominant architectural style that precedes it. Changing tastes produce avant-garde or experimental building styles, which are ultimately tested in the market. An experimental style eventually is abandoned or becomes accepted. Design elements discarded in a reactive swing are not lost forever, however. Old forms may disappear for a time and later reappear in a modified form. Figure 9.2 illustrates some common architectural styles identified in the CTS System.

Changes in architectural style often correspond to the economic life cycles of buildings. Major revisions in architectural styles typically occur at the end of a building life cycle, or about every 30 to 50 years.

Newly constructed buildings, which may or may not be designed by professional architects, tend to have broad market appeal. When a building is no longer new, however, it will be compared with other buildings in terms of the quality and functionality of its architectural style. Form and structure are the most basic components of architectural style; they define the possible uses and modifications of a building and their influence on value increases as time goes by.

Various architectural styles are found in different parts of the country. These style differences can largely be attributed to the availability of natural materials such as wood, stone, and clay and differences in climate. Changes in building technology have made styles more uniform in recent years and have changed the way buildings are designed and constructed.

The development of the Franklin stove, for example, modified the layout of rooms in residences because fireplaces were no longer needed to provide heat. The introduction of household appliances in the early twentieth century eliminated the need for root cellars, pantries, and large laundry rooms, reducing the number of rooms of homes and changing other room arrangements.

The prevalent use of central heating and air-conditioning in the mid-twentieth century has resulted in the standardization of architectural styles throughout the country. Regional building styles that were developed to use local building materials and meet the demands of climate have been almost obliterated. The thick, mud masonry walls and small windows of Southwestern architecture were well-suited to the hot, dry weather of the region. Overhanging roofs were used on homes in the rainy Northwest so that windows could be opened for ventilation without admitting the rain. The saltbox houses of New England were windowless and steep-roofed on one side to provide protection against the harsh north wind.

Figure 9.2   Common Architectural Styles

Cape Cod

Garrison Colonial

Dutch Colonial

Southern Colonial

Tudor

Georgian

French Provincial

Spanish Villa

Eastern Brick Row Houses

Western Row Houses

Queen Anne–Victorian

Bungalow

California Ranch

Contemporary

With the development of central heating and air-conditioning, many of these differences in regional styles became unnecessary. In the mid-1970s, however, energy considerations became more important and builders began once again to incorporate structural defenses against climate into new construction. Thus, an energy-conscious market has prompted climate-compatible design to resurface. Energy-saving features must be considered in estimating market value because consumers have become increasingly interested in these elements of building design.

Types of Houses

To describe the architectural style of a residence and evaluate its conformity or compatibility with market tastes and standards, appraisers should be familiar with the advantages and disadvantages of various types of houses. Common house designs include one-story, one-and-one-half-story, two-story, bi-level, and split-level houses; these types of houses and others are discussed below. Figure 9.3 illustrates different house types.

One-story house

A one-story house may be a ranch, a rambler, or a bungalow. The entire living area in this type of house is on ground level. The house may be built over a basement or crawl space or on a slab or pier foundation. One-story houses have proven acceptable in the resale market. They generally have a simple design that can be adapted to any type of topography. Because most of the exterior is accessible, a one-story house is easier to maintain and attachments can be made at ground level. The absence of stairs is appealing to many purchasers.

A one-story house has disadvantages too. All the living area is on one level, so noise spreads throughout the house. In some communities, a single-story design is associated with tract developments which may have limited appeal. A one-story house generally requires a wider lot than other house designs and houses of this type have the highest ratio of foundation and roof area to living area, which results in higher construction costs. Furthermore, without sufficient screening or proper site placement, a one-story house may lack privacy.

One-and-one-half-story house

A one-and-one-half-story house, which is called a Cape Cod in some areas, usually has its main rooms and one bedroom and bathroom on the ground floor. Other bedrooms and bathrooms may be located on the second floor, or the entire second floor may be unfinished and used for storage. The building can be built on a slab or a pier foundation or over a crawl space or basement.

One advantage of a one-and-one-half-story house is its compactness. This type of house is less expensive to heat than a one-story residence with the same square foot area. A one-and-one-half-story house also has visual appeal; houses with dormers can be especially attractive. During the 1950s and 1960s, many of these homes were built and sold with only the first floor finished. The second floor was often completed later to provide extra living

Figure 9.3   Types of Houses

One-Story House

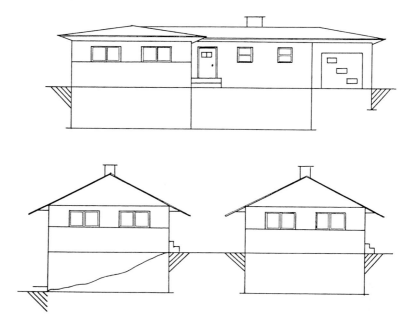

One-and-One-Half Story House

Courtesy of
Frank E. Harrison

(*continued*)

Figure 9.3 continued

Two-Story House

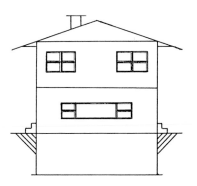

Bi-Level House

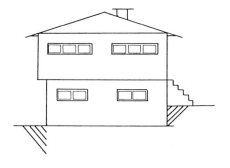

(continued)

Figure 9.3   continued

Split-Level House

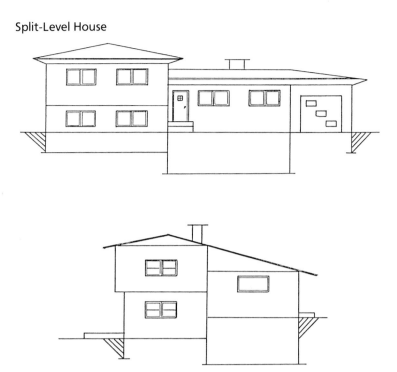

space for an expanding family. These houses provide a practical advantage to growing families with limited means.

In certain markets the one-and-one-half-story house design is regarded as old fashioned. The design has other disadvantages. The stairways to the second floor in these houses are often narrow and steep. They were built to take up as little room as possible on the ground floor, but these stairs make it very difficult to move furniture upstairs. Often these houses have much wasted space because only a portion of the second floor has an adequate ceiling height to be used as living area; the space under the eaves is usually a storage area. The rooms are small in many one-and-one-half-story homes and there are rarely more than two bedrooms on the ground floor. A house without dormers may have lighting and ventilation problems and the upper level may lack temperature control and insulation. It can be quite expensive to finish this type of house, particularly if electricity, plumbing, and other services have to be extended to the upper level after construction.

Two-story house

Two-story houses may be built in several architectural styles. In most two-story homes, the main rooms and sometimes a guest bedroom and bathroom are located on the ground floor; other bedrooms and bathrooms are on the upper floor. A two-story house can be built over a basement or crawl space or on a slab or pier.

A main advantage of a two-story house is that living and working areas are separated from private areas. Many buyers prefer these houses because they suggest the gracious living style of the American past. A two-story house can be built on a smaller lot, but provides the same amount of living area as a one-story house. Foundation and roof costs are lower for the same total floor area.

The stairway that connects the ground level to the private areas of a two-story house can pose problems. Closets and storage areas can make good use of the space under the stairway, but rooms on the second level have no direct access to the exterior. This can be hazardous in the event of a fire or emergency. Furthermore, a two-story design is not easily adapted for expansion upward or outward.

Bi-level house

A bi-level may also be known as a *raised ranch* or *split-foyer* house. The living area in a bi-level house is all on the upper level; the lower level may serve as an extra family room, recreation room, or spare bedroom. A bi-level house usually rests on a concrete slab with foundation walls that rise four feet or less above ground level. The remaining one and one-half stories are built over the foundation walls.

This type of house provides additional living area at the lowest cost. In most markets, the lower level is not regarded as a basement, but as part of the gross living area. Both levels lend themselves to a variety of attachments; part of the lower level can be converted into a garage or finished after the upper level is completed. The lower level may have windows to provide light and ventilation and doors to allow exterior access and more convenient traffic patterns.

The main disadvantage of a bi-level design is that the lower level is sometimes cold and damp and may require special heating and insulation. Heat rises from the lower level through the split entry and warms the upper level. Heating costs can be high if the house is poorly designed.

The ductwork in a bi-level house is hard to install because the foundation level is a functional living area, not a basement or crawl space. All traffic between the two levels must go by way of the interior stairs, which are usually located in the center of the house.

Because of its design limitations, the bi-level house poses challenges for architects. In a poorly designed bi-level house, the division of interior zones may be clumsy or the exterior may be visually unappealing.

Split-level house

Split-level houses include tri-levels and quad-levels which have basements. This type of house allows its residents to live on several levels; two levels are normally finished prior to occupancy. A split-level house consists of a two-story portion, which is constructed like a bi-level, and a one-story portion. The two-story portion is built over a slab and a partial basement; the one-story portion sits on a slab or above a basement or crawl space. The design of the structure can be described as side-to-side, front-to-back, or back-to-front, referring to the relative placement of the one-story and two-story sections.

The upper level of a split-level house, which is separated from the middle level by a half flight of stairs, is reserved for bedrooms and bathrooms. The middle level, which is separated from the upper and lower levels by half flights of stairs, contains a living room, a dining area, a kitchen, and a laundry area. The lower level has additional living areas such as a family room, a recreation room, a den, or extra bedrooms. The lower level usually provides access to the garage.

A split-level home provides additional living area at a very low cost. In most parts of the country, the lower level is considered part of the gross living area, not a basement. The design lends itself to irregular topography, and both the middle and lower levels can accommodate exterior attachments. All the zones within the residence are well set off from one another, yet easily accessible. The traffic pattern is efficient. The lower level provides convenient access to the garage and can be finished after the middle and upper levels are complete. The design can accommodate an overhanging upper level, if desired.

A split-level house may have the same heating and insulation problems that afflict bi-level houses. Because heat rises, the upper levels tend to be warmer than the lower level. The architectural limitations of the bi-level are also found in the split-level design, although split-levels have more versatility. Split-level houses may have less visual appeal if the topography of the site is flat.

Other types of houses

Two-and-one-half-story houses are generally not built today, but the style can be observed in older construction. These houses are similar to two-story dwellings but they have attic areas that are used for storage. This upper area can be added to the design at a relatively low cost, but the extra stairs, wasted space, and limitation on further expansion offset its advantages.

Three-story houses share many of the advantages and disadvantages of two-story houses. They are large enough to house more than one family, and thus have greater potential for rental income. Older homes and mansions of various styles are elaborations on two-story and three-story designs. Modern design housing includes earth-sheltered homes, solar homes, log cabins, and geodesic domes. Attached house designs can be observed in brownstones, rowhouses, townhouses, and semi-detached houses. These less common types of residences are discussed in Chapter 22.

HOUSE ZONES

As part of the building inspection, an appraiser examines the interior layout of a house. A house can be divided into three zones and various circulation areas. The *private-sleeping zone* contains the bedrooms; family, master, and private bathrooms; and dressing rooms. The *living-social zone* consists of the living room, the dining room, the family or recreation room, the den, and any enclosed porches. The *working-service zone* consists of the kitchen, the laundry, the pantry, and other work areas. Corridors, stairways, and entrances are considered circulation areas. Figure 9.4 shows the zone divisions in a well-designed house.

The three zones within a home should be separated from one another so that activities in one zone do not interfere with those in another. The private-sleeping zone should be insulated from the noise of the other two zones. Occupants should be able to move from bedrooms to bathrooms in the private zone without being seen from the other areas of the house.

The working-service zone is the nerve center of the house where most household chores are performed. Someone working in the kitchen should be able to monitor the guest and family entrances as well as activities in the private zone, the porch, the patio, and the backyard.

The guest entrance should lead into the center of the house. This entrance should have a guest closet and provide easy access to the guest lavatory. Ideally the entrance leads directly to the living-social zone and is separated from the private-sleeping area by a noise and visibility barrier. Hard flooring in the guest entrance will withstand mud and dirt tracked in from the outside.

The family entrance should lead into the kitchen from the garage, carport, or breezeway or from a circulation area such as a porch or deck. Traffic from this entrance should not have to pass through the work area in the kitchen. Residents should also be able to move from the family entrance through the service zone to the private-sleeping zone without going through the living-social zone.

A house with a basement may have a separate, outside entrance to the basement. The basement entrance should lead to stairs and hallways that have direct access to the private-sleeping zone, the living-social zone, and both the guest and family entrances. Circulation areas such as the main hallway, a bedroom hallway, stairways, and a rear or service hallway should provide access to the different house zones without passing through individual rooms. Circulation areas should be well-lit, wide, and contain closets and storage space in strategic locations.

Floor plans depend on the size and value of the individual residence and vary from region to region. In a national survey of home owners, the following design problems were noted by many respondents:

- Front door opens directly into living room
- No closet in front hall

Figure 9.4 House Zones

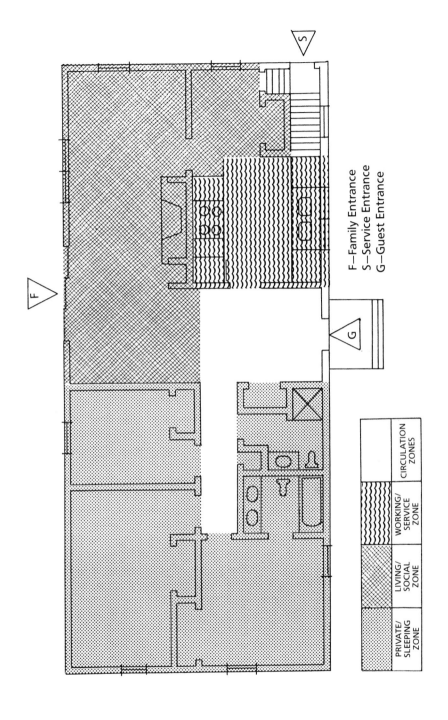

F—Family Entrance
S—Service Entrance
G—Guest Entrance

PRIVATE/ SLEEPING ZONE	LIVING/ SOCIAL ZONE	WORKING/ SERVICE ZONE	CIRCULATION ZONES

- No direct access from the front door to the kitchen, bathroom, or bedroom without passing through other rooms
- Rear door does not lead directly into the kitchen and does not provide convenient access to the street, driveway and garage
- No comfortable eating area in or near the kitchen
- No convenient access from the kitchen to the separate dining area
- Stairways are located off a room, not off a hallway or foyer
- Bedrooms or bathrooms are visible from the living room or foyer
- Recreation or family room is poorly located and not visible from the kitchen
- No access to the basement from outside
- Walls between bedrooms are not soundproof
- Outdoor living areas such as decks and patios are not accessible from the kitchen

ROOMS IN RESIDENTIAL PROPERTIES

In the inspection of the interior, an appraiser studies the specific dimensions and characteristics of the individual rooms in the structure and notes any problems with the building's design.

Living Rooms

Until the middle of this century, the living room was considered the center of a house. More recently, the status of the living room has undergone change. Many home owners socialize, relax, and entertain in their family rooms, patios, and kitchens, rather than in living rooms. These other areas have expanded, and the size and importance of the living room has diminished.

The living room may be located in the front of the house or, if the view or access to outdoor areas is better, at the back or side of the house. Often the dining room is located at one end of the living room, usually adjacent to the kitchen. Ideally the living room should be located away from the traffic patterns to other rooms, but easily accessible from the guest entrance.

In a three-bedroom house, the living room should be at least 11 feet by 16 feet, or approximately 170 square feet in area. A maximum width of 14 feet is desirable, but if traffic crosses the living room area, the width should be at least 15 to 16 feet. If a dining area is located at one end of the living room, the minimum dimensions are 16 feet by 26 feet. Regardless of its size, the living room should be able to accommodate a conversation circle that is 10 feet in diameter.

Living rooms can be square, rectangular, or L-shaped. Square living rooms make furniture arrangement difficult and are the least desirable. Rectangular living rooms should be neither too narrow nor too wide. Living rooms combined with dining areas are usually L-shaped. A living room should have at least one wall with windows for a view and ventilation and another wall long enough for a couch and other furniture. Many home owners complain that too many breaks in the walls of rooms for doorways, windows, and fireplaces make it difficult to arrange furniture comfortably. Sufficient outlets should be available for lamps and appliances. Traffic should not have to pass through the conversation circle in the living room.

Kitchens

The kitchen is the most important room in the house. It serves more functions than any other room and at least 10% of the total cost of the house is normally spent on the kitchen. More than 120 miles are walked each year in the average kitchen during the preparation of just two meals a day; a well-designed kitchen can eliminate 40 miles from this route.

The best location for the kitchen depends on many factors, including the lifestyle of the household and the size of the family. The kitchen should have access to the dining area and to the front or rear entrance. If outdoor areas are used for meals, the kitchen should also have access to them. If the house has a family room, the kitchen should be visible from this room and allow convenient access to it. The kitchen is ordinarily close to, but separated from, the dining area.

The size of the kitchen depends on the space available in the house and the desired equipment or appliances. A kitchen should be at least 8 feet by 10 feet; approximately 10 feet by 10 feet is average. A spacious kitchen is 12 feet by 14 feet or larger. A large kitchen is usually combined with a dining area.

Kitchens should be well-ventilated and well-lit. The window area should be no less than 10% of the floor area and a window over the sink is ideal. All kitchens with more than one counter have a work triangle as an essential design feature. In addition to the work areas, cabinets, storage space, appliances, and built-in equipment are needed. A kitchen may also accommodate a family activity center, a dining area, a laundry area, a trash storage area, or a pantry.

Most kitchen layouts are based on the three points of the work triangle: the sink/food preparation area, the refrigerator, and the cooking area. In a well-designed kitchen, the cumulative length of the legs of the triangle does not exceed 23 feet.

The sink area is the place where food is prepared, dishes are washed, and garbage is disposed of. This accounts for 40% to 45% of kitchen activity. Appliances in the sink area may include a dishwasher, a trash compactor, and a garbage disposal. Single-basin sinks are generally adequate and are common in new construction when dishwashers are installed. Double-basin sinks are better suited to washing dishes by hand. Counters at least 18 inches deep are required on either side of the sink. The space beneath the sink is used to store cleaning products and utensils.

The sink area should be lit by a window above the sink and overhead lighting. Wall cabinets are useful nearby and the dishwasher should be no more than 12 feet away. The sink should be approximately four to six feet from the cooking area and four to seven feet from the refrigerator.

Usually perishable foods are stored in a combination refrigerator and freezer. The refrigerator is ideally located at the end of a counter adjacent to 36 to 42 inches of uninterrupted counter space. The refrigerator should be near the food preparation area and close to a spigot that supplies water if it has an icemaker. It should also be convenient for unloading groceries. For energy efficiency, the refrigerator should be located away from the cooking area.

The cooking area in a kitchen combines a range/cookstove with a conventional oven. Many homes now have microwave ovens as well. Counters at least 15 inches deep are useful on each side of the stove and they should be made of a heatproof material. Gas or electricity power the cooking appliances. The cooking area should never be near a window. Curtains can catch fire, reaching across a range to get to the window is dangerous, and cleaning above the range can be difficult. All cabinets should be at least 30 inches above the range. A ventilator or fan over the range is desirable to remove smoke and cooking fumes. Many fire-related injuries and accidents occur in the cooking area, so a fire extinguisher should be close at hand.

Cooking practices are changing, so kitchen layouts and appliances are changing too. Today many people cook on barbecues and outdoor grills or with microwaves, woks, and other appliances which represent personalty rather than realty. Although this style of cooking may only be a passing phase, the conventional oven has become the least used appliance in the kitchen.

Kitchens may be U-shaped or L-shaped with one counter or two counters. Larger kitchens may have an island in the center. Figure 9.5 illustrates the layout of several common types of kitchens.

In a U-shaped kitchen, cabinets and counters are located along three walls. This design requires the most space, but it is considered to be the most efficient. The work triangle is compact so it is easily separated from traffic patterns through the kitchen. The sink is at the base of the U and the refrigerator and cooking area face each other on the arms of the U. The counter space is continuous and storage space is ample.

Some U-shaped kitchens have certain disadvantages. Too compact a triangle cramps the work area; too open a triangle necessitates too much walking.

The L-shaped kitchen has counters and work areas arranged in two perpendicular, adjacent lines. The sink is usually centered on the long side of the L, with the refrigerator at the end of this counter; the cooking area is along the perpendicular side. This design is best for small kitchens. It also works well for large kitchens because the work triangle is separated from traffic and the rest of the kitchen can be used for other purposes. This design is popular because it is adaptable to various arrangements. Its major disadvantages are the placement of appliances, the potential for wasted space, and the distance between the work centers at the extremities of the L.

Figure 9.5 Typical Kitchen Designs

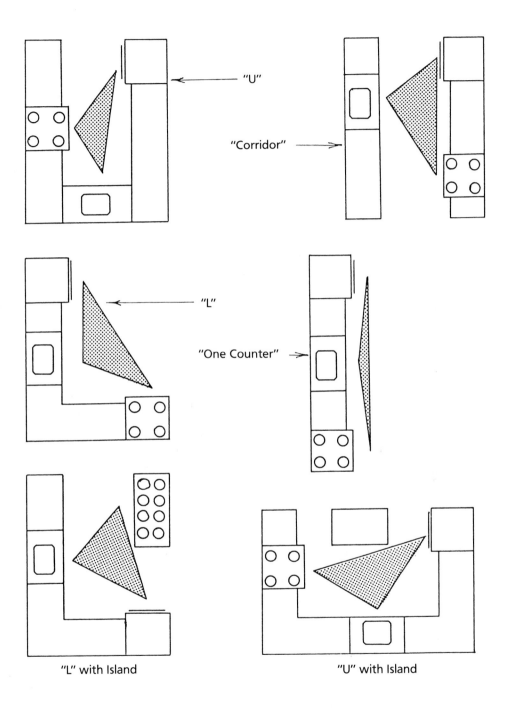

"U"

"Corridor"

"L"

"One Counter"

"L" with Island

"U" with Island

The two-counter kitchen, which is also known as the *corridor,* *galley,* or *pullman kitchen,* has cabinets and work areas on two opposite walls. The work triangle also serves as a passageway for traffic through the kitchen. The sink and cooking area are on one side and the refrigerator is on the opposite side. There should be at least four feet between the counters so that cabinets and appliances can be opened.

The one-counter kitchen, which is also known as the *strip kitchen,* has all the work areas aligned along one wall. This design does not create a work triangle, but it suits scaled-down appliances and works well when kitchen space is limited to less than 12 feet along the wall. The sink should be centrally located, with the refrigerator and the range at opposite ends of the wall.

Island kitchens may be U-shaped or L-shaped. One-counter kitchens may have an island in the center—usually for the sink or the cooking area. Because the island reduces the area of the work triangle, islands are usually used in larger kitchens. In larger kitchens the island may also set off an informal eating area.

Some kitchens have additional areas located outside the work triangle. A separate food preparation area, for example, may require counter space, extra electrical outlets, and storage for cooking utensils. A work desk or personal computer area may be included in a kitchen if space permits. This area may include a desk, a personal computer, a telephone, a calendar, and other home management needs.

Some kitchens have special working surfaces for baking and extra storage for baking goods. Homes in which occupants entertain frequently may have wet bars and areas to store bottles and glasses. A serving or buffet counter in a pass-through area between the kitchen and dining room can facilitate informal meals. A barbecue inside the kitchen may be handy for special cooking, but this equipment must be located near an exhaust fan or hood. Special kitchen features may constitute overimprovements, depending on the standards of the market.

Many kitchens suffer from the following problems:

- Insufficient base cabinet storage
- Insufficient wall cabinet storage
- Insufficient counter space
- No counter beside the refrigerator
- Not enough window area
- Poorly placed doors that waste wall space
- Traffic through the work triangle
- Too little counter space on either side of the sink
- No counter beside the range
- Insufficient space in front of cabinets
- Too great a distance between the sink, range, and refrigerator
- Range under a window

Dining Areas

Most houses built before the middle of this century had separate dining rooms. Many newer houses have dining areas that are part of another room; eat-in kitchens, breakfast nooks, and living room-dining room combinations are examples. Most homebuyers prefer a house with a family room and an eat-in kitchen to one with a formal dining room and no family room.

The dining room is part of the living-social zone of a house. It should be directly accessible to the kitchen, but separate from it. The dining room should be at least 9 feet by 11 feet, and ideally no less than 10 feet by 12 feet. More area may be required if traffic passes through the room. Three-and-one-half feet of space is needed behind each chair and the area should accommodate a table that seats six persons. Extra room is needed to store dishes, silver, and glassware and artificial light is usually provided by a chandelier.

Floor plan problems that can affect dining areas include stairs that open into the dining area; inadequate outlets, switches, lighting, and ventilation; no partition between the kitchen and dining areas; traffic passing through the dining area; and insufficient space for furniture arrangement.

Bedrooms

The number of bedrooms in a house is an important design consideration. The standard may be indicated by neighborhood analysis. Two- and three-bedroom houses have wide acceptance in the market. Houses with four or more bedrooms may represent an overimprovement in many areas; they usually appeal only to large families. Of course, luxury homes may have five bedrooms or more.

Privacy is important, so bedrooms should be located in the most secluded parts of the house. They should be accessible from a central hallway, which connects the other zones of the house. Bedrooms should be insulated from noise produced in other zones of the house and from street noise outside. Placing closets along bedroom walls can minimize the transmission of sounds from adjacent rooms.

The largest bedroom is usually the master bedroom, which often has access to a master bathroom. Other bedrooms may be used for children and guests. Extra bedrooms may be converted into dens, studies, or family rooms.

A bedroom with a single bed must measure at least 8 feet by 10 feet. This size will only be satisfactory if the layout is efficient. The minimum size for a bedroom with a double bed is 10 feet by 11½ feet. In some markets, bedrooms are expected to exceed the minimum size; in others buyers will not pay extra for larger bedrooms. Each bedroom should have at least one closet that is two feet deep, three feet wide, and high enough to accommodate five feet of hanging space. Each closet should also have interior lighting, a pole for hangers, and a shelf not more than 74 inches above the floor with at least eight inches of space above the shelf.

Some bedrooms also have extra space for clothes storage and dressing areas. Because cross ventilation is important, corner bedrooms are preferred. Bedrooms should have adequate natural and artificial lighting. For safety, each bedroom should have a window that provides exterior access and be equipped with or near to smoke and fire detectors. Bedrooms may suffer from the following design problems:

- Insufficient room to arrange furniture
- Not located near a hallway or bathroom
- Serve as passageway to basement, attic, or another room
- Not adequately separated from other house zones
- No soundproofing
- Insufficient closet space
- Lack of lighting in bedroom or closet

Bathrooms

Bathrooms are the smallest rooms in the house and they often seem to be the least adequate. Each residence should have at least one full-size bathroom. However, houses with only one bathroom are obsolete in many markets. Neighborhood analysis will indicate the standard for the area. With the exception of low-priced and resort residences, one and one-half baths are the minimum standard for housing. Two bathrooms are standard for two-story residences in many areas. A bathroom may be identified as the family bathroom, a powder room, or a master bath.

The terminology used to describe bathrooms and lavatories varies in different parts of the country. In most areas a full-size bathroom consists of a room with a toilet or water closet, a washbasin or sink, and a tub. A three-quarter bathroom has a toilet, a wash basin, and a stall shower. A half-bath or two-thirds bath, which is also known as a *lavatory, lavette,* or *powder room,* has a toilet and a washbasin. The number of fixtures present and the sufficiency of the plumbing should be noted.

There should be at least one bathroom on each floor of a multilevel residence. The best location for bathrooms is determined by the plumbing and the room layout. The family bathroom and the master bath are part of the sleeping-private zone; the powder room is usually part of the living-social zone. Entry to the bathroom should be private and walls shared by bathrooms and other rooms should be soundproofed.

A full-size bathroom must be at least five feet by seven feet. The minimum size for a powder room is four feet by five feet. The ideal size for a full-size bathroom is six feet by eight feet or larger. There should be enough space for doors to open.

Bathrooms require the most heat and the best ventilation of any rooms in the house. A window may not be necessary; interior bathrooms without windows are cheaper and generally acceptable in the market. Ventilation can be provided by a vent to the outside or with a fan that starts automatically when the light is turned on.

Family or Recreation Rooms

The concept of a family room evolved in America after World War II. A family room is the area set aside for recreation and relaxation away from the more formal living room. The first family rooms were finished basements or attics; later enclosed porches and extra bedrooms were converted into family rooms. Today, a family room may be used as a den, a study, a guest room, a nursery, a library, a TV room, or a game room.

Ideally a family room is near the kitchen, but it may be located wherever space is available. If possible, it should be toward the rear of the house to provide access to the outside. A family room should have a minimum width of 10½ feet. The typical size is 12 feet by 18 feet, but the room can be much longer. There are no standard layouts of a family room.

A badly designed family room may have poor access to the kitchen and the outside, insufficient heating, too few electrical outlets, or too many walls and doors that do not allow for suitable furniture arrangement. The floor covering may be carpet or vinyl; its condition should be checked.

Laundry Areas

The laundry area and kitchen make up the working-service zone of the house. The location of the laundry room is a matter of convenience; several locations are acceptable in the market. The laundry area can be on the same level as the living area or on another level. Ideally the laundry area should be a separate room that is accessible to the kitchen and the exterior of the house. Laundry facilities may be located in a closet or pantry, an enclosed porch, a mudroom, a breezeway, an attached garage, a detached garage connected to the house by a breezeway, a bedroom/bathroom area, or a basement. The main consideration is the location of the plumbing fixtures needed for the washing machine. There should also be ventilation for the dryer and room to fold clothes.

SUMMARY

In the building description, the appraiser notes the size, style, design, layout, construction quality, and maintenance of the improvement(s). Analyzing the improvements helps the appraiser decide whether the elements of the building contribute to the highest and best use of the property as improved and identifies any problems or deficiencies that may prevent the property from realizing its highest and best use. The building description also lays the groundwork for the selection of comparables, the estimate of reproduction or replacement costs, and the collection of data on operating and maintenance expenses.

To prepare for the building inspection, an appraiser gathers background information and building inspection materials. Background information on zoning and building codes are examined along with blueprints and building plans; an appraisal form or checklist and measuring and calculation equipment are needed for the field inspection.

The appraiser rates building components for their quality, condition, and functional utility. Good materials, sound construction techniques, and a high level of workmanship contribute to quality. A *superadequacy* is a building component that exceeds market standards; an *overimprovement* is an improvement that does not represent the most profitable use of a site because its cost or size precludes the optimization of value.

Condition refers to the amount of physical deterioration in a structure, which determines the effective age of a property. Functional utility is the ability of a structure to be useful and perform the function for which it is intended according to current market standards. The building's efficiency in terms of style, design, layout, traffic patterns, size, and type of rooms also relates to functional utility.

As part of the inspection of the exterior, the appraiser notes the orientation and placement of the improvements on the site and measures the size of the residence. A scale diagram of the building is drawn. Most houses are measured in terms of gross living area, the total area of finished, above-grade residential space. Even when building plans are available, actual measurements must be taken. A sketch of the layout of the house is included in the appraisal report along with photographs of the front and rear of the house showing the sides, any major site improvements, and a street scene.

An appraiser identifies the building's architectural style and considers whether the building is compatible or in harmony with its uses and environment. Modifications in architectural styles occur approximately every 30 to 50 years, corresponding to the economic life cycles of buildings. Modern technology has standardized architectural styles throughout the country, but energy considerations have prompted some builders to reincorporate building features that act as structural defenses against the climate.

Common house types include one-story ranches, ramblers, and bungalows; one-and-one-half-story Cape Cods; two-story houses; bi-level raised ranches and split-foyer houses; and split-level houses with three or four levels. Each type of design has advantages and disadvantages.

As part of the interior inspection, the appraiser notes how the house is divided into zones. The private-sleeping zone includes bedrooms, bathrooms, and dressing rooms. The living-social zone consists of the living room, dining room, family or recreation room, den, and any enclosed porches. The working-service zone contains the kitchen, laundry area, and other work areas. Corridors, stairways, the guest entrance and the family entrance make up the circulation areas. Each zone should be separate, yet accessible to the others. The specific dimensions and characteristics of the rooms that make make up these zones should be studied. The appraiser should also know which design features are acceptable to home owners in the market area and which are not.

REVIEW QUESTIONS

1. What purposes does the building description serve? Why are the improvements analyzed?

2. What background information does an appraiser need before he or she begins the building inspection?

3. Discuss the meaning of *quality, condition,* and *functional utility* in regard to construction and structural components.

4. What characterizes a reactive shift in architectural trends? How does such a shift relate to the economic life cycle of a building?

5. Describe the common types of houses and the advantages and disadvantages of each design.

6. Identify the zones into which a residence is divided. List some common problems with the zone layout of a residence.

7. How does an appraiser measure the area of a house? Define *gross living area.*

10 Analysis of Building Construction

A complete building description includes detailed information about the construction of the building and the condition of its exterior, interior, and mechanical systems. There is no prescribed method for describing all buildings, but it is often useful to describe components in the sequence in which they were constructed. This practice allows an appraiser to note problems that may have arisen at each stage of construction. An appraiser might use the following format to describe the construction and condition of residential improvements.

I. Exterior
   A. Substructure
      1. Clearing and stake out
      2. Test boring
      3. Excavation
      4. Footings
      5. Foundation walls
         a. Slab on ground
         b. Crawl space
         c. Basement
         d. Pier and beam
      6. Grading
   B. Superstructure
      1. Framing
      2. Exterior covering and trim
         a. Exterior walls
         b. Exterior doors
         c. Windows, storm windows, and screens
         d. Roof covering and drain system
         e. Chimneys, stacks, and vents
      3. Insulation
      4. Ventilation

(continued)

II. Interior
   A. Interior covering and trim
      1. Floor covering
      2. Walls and ceilings
      3. Doors
      4. Stairs
      5. Molding and baseboards
      6. Painting, decorating, and finishing
      7. Cabinets
      8. Fireplaces
   B. Protection against decay and insect damage
III. Equipment and mechanical systems
   A. Plumbing system
      1. Piping
      2. Fixtures
   B. Hot water
   C. Heating system
      1. Warm or hot air
      2. Hot water
      3. Steam
      4. Electricity
   D. Heating system fuels
   E. Air conditioning and ventilation system
   F. Electrical system
   G. Miscellaneous systems and equipment
IV. Attachments, garages, and outbuildings

Each of these components is discussed within the context of building construction.

EXTERIOR

Substructure

The *substructure* is the portion of the building that supports the superstructure. Typically, most of the substructure is located below grade, or ground level. To construct the substructure, the site is cleared and staked out. Test borings are then drilled and the site is excavated. Footings and foundation walls are installed and the site is graded.

Clearing and stake out

Before construction can begin, a bulldozer must clear the land. Unwanted vegetation is removed or burned and care is taken to preserve the trees and vegetation that will remain on the site. A contractor or surveyor then stakes out the site and the building lines, marking elevations and building corner lines on stakes and batter boards. If the stake out is inaccurate, the building's corners will not be square. Building lines should conform to setback requirements and the building should be placed to take advantage of the sun and be protected from the wind and rain. The building's placement should also create useful and pleasant site zones.

Test borings

Engineers drill test borings to specific depths in all parts of the site to determine the character of the subsoil and the location of bedrock. If soil problems are found, the added expense of constructing special foundations may result in an overimprovement. Nevertheless, test borings must be drilled and necessary expenditures must be made for correction; uncorrected soil problems can cause the foundation of a house to tilt, sink, or buckle.

Excavation

The land is excavated to accommodate the building foundation. The foundation must rest on undisturbed earth, so the main excavation is dug to the level of the foundation floor. Other trenches are dug lower to accommodate foundation footings along the building's perimeter and footings for piers and chimneys. Excavation may also be necessary to install water, electricity, and sewer lines. If a septic system is planned, septic tank trenches, tank holes, and absorption fields must be dug.

Footings

Footings are support parts used to prevent excessive settlement or movement of the structure. The most common form of footing, a wall footing, is a perimetric base of concrete that rests on undisturbed earth below the frost line. A wall footing distributes the load of the walls over the subgrade. Properly constructed footings extend out from both sides of the foundation walls they support. A drain tile is a specially designed pipe that is laid outside the wall footings to drain ground water to a storm sewer or dry well. Column footings, which are generally square in shape, are used to support vertical columns and posts as well as fireplaces, furnaces, and chimneys. Stepped footings, which consist of connected footings at different heights, are used to support structures on lots that slope. Spread footings are frequently used if the soil has poor load-bearing capacity.

Footings are generally made of concrete which is poured into clean trenches or wood forms. If an extra load is to be supported, column footings may be made of concrete reinforced with steel rods or mesh. The size and depth of footings are dictated by code and the intended load.

Foundation walls

Foundation walls form an enclosure for basements and crawl spaces as well as support walls, floors, and other structural loads. Most foundations are made of poured concrete walls or concrete-and-cinder-block walls that rest on concrete footings. These foundations are the least expensive and the most popular. In older structures foundation walls may be made of cut stone or stone and brick. These walls are more costly and require more skill to install. Treated timber is sometimes used, but these walls do not meet building codes in certain areas. Columns and posts of various materials provide the central support for the building's beams and superstructure. Older buildings may have costly wood posts, masonry posts, or wood beams; many newer structures are built with inexpensive steel lally columns and steel I-beams.

To inspect foundation walls an appraiser looks for evidence of bulges or cracks. Cracks in the foundation almost always go completely through the wall and may cause leakage. Holes, crumbling, or poor interior surfaces may suggest that the concrete was not poured properly. Foundations may be built on a slab on ground, over a crawl space or basement, or on piers and beams.

Slab on ground. Slab-on-ground foundations are either permanent foundations built on footings, or floating foundations, which are used on unstable soil or in areas with poor drainage. Floating slab-on-ground foundations are also called *mat and raft foundations.* They are made of concrete slabs heavily reinforced with steel so that the entire foundation acts as a unit.

A level layer of sand or gravel is applied over undisturbed soil to form the base of a slab-on-ground foundation. Insulation and reinforcing mesh is laid on top of this base to act as a vapor barrier. The concrete is then poured to a depth specified by code and the foundation is finished with a rough trowel. The floor must be pitched to direct drainage to floor drains and the sump pit. Water lines, sewer lines, and radiant floor heating should be installed before the concrete is poured.

Figure 10.1 Footing and Foundation Walls (Basement/Pier-and-Beam Construction)

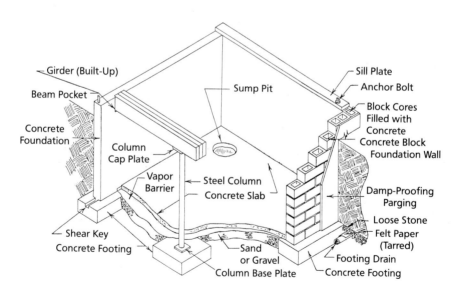

Figures 10.1 through 10.10
Courtesy of Frank E. Harrison

A slab-on-ground foundation has several advantages. It is the most economic type of foundation and eliminates the need for first-floor framing. It is also suitable for mass production in tract or prefabricated housing. Slab-on-ground foundations have several disadvantages as well. Without heating coils, slab-on-ground foundations can be cold. In extremely cold regions of the country, they may be regarded as underimprovements. Furthermore, the mechanical systems in buildings with slab-on-ground foundations must be placed in the walls, the attic, or in separate rooms. Flooding can also be a problem. Flooding is likely to occur if there are no drain tiles around the perimeter of the foundation, if the floor has an inadequate pitch, or if the finish grade of the site does not slope from the slab.

Crawl space. When a foundation is built on a crawl space, foundation walls, columns, and other framing members are supported on footings. The floor of the crawl space may be sand, gravel, concrete, or undisturbed soil. Access to the crawl space is provided by interior hatches or exterior crawl hatches. If a crawl-space foundation is used, the building's systems need not be put on the ground floor. Ductwork can be run below the floor framing, which reduces costs. In a crawl-space foundation, the ground floor is elevated above the exterior ground line and foundation walls are shorter, so costs are lower. However, crawl spaces may be damp or hold standing water. An appraiser should look for such physical problems during the building inspection.

Basement. Basements are similar to crawl spaces, but they are seven to eight feet deeper. A house with a basement may have an interior stairway to the living area as well as exterior access. Adequate light, ventilation, and escape routes are needed. Basement walls are often finished to match the building interior.

Basements provide extra living area at a minimum cost. They can be used for recreation and laundry rooms and can house the building's mechanical systems. However, basements must be effectively waterproofed and ventilated if they are to be used as living area. During the building inspection, an appraiser checks for evidence of mineral sediment on basement walls, which indicates that walls or window wells leak or that the basement has flooded in the past. Mineral powder stains on the floor may indicate cracked floors or clogged basement drains; a musty odor or other evidence of mildew suggests leakage and inadequate ventilation.

Basements are more costly than crawl spaces and are not required in many warmer climates. A basement in the Deep South might well constitute an overimprovement; the cost of this feature will probably not be recaptured when the property is resold.

Pier and beam. In a pier-and-beam foundation, piers resting on footings support beams or girders, which in turn support the superstructure. Because pier-and-beam foundations are very inexpensive in comparison with other types of foundations, they are often used for resort houses and for outbuildings and porches. Columns or piers and beams are also used in other types of foundation for extra support. Pier-and-beam foundations are not often used for conventional homes because many building codes prohibit their use.

Grading

Grading establishes the final level or slope of the site. After the forms for the foundation walls have been removed, the excavated soil is pushed back into place with a bulldozer to fill the depressions along the outer foundation walls. This is the rough grading. The filling in must be done carefully and, if necessary, finished by hand to avoid caving in the foundation walls. During the inspection, an appraiser checks for any interior bulge in the foundation wall, which could indicate excessive pressure from faulty grading.

The finish grading is put down after the residence is constructed during the site cleanup. It is generally done by a landscape contractor using lighter equipment. After the site improvements are completed, topsoil is spread for landscaping and the soil is seeded or sodded. The grading of the site should slope away from the improvements to provide drainage.

Much of the substructure of a building is visible only during construction. An appraiser must obtain information about the substructure from building plans or from architects and contractors. Footings that are improperly designed or constructed can often cause settling and excessive wall cracks. By examining the plans and inspecting the property an appraiser determines whether structural problems exist and what their effect may be on property value. When the problems found can be corrected, the cost to do so is estimated. Some defects are not recognized by the market, so they have little effect on value; others may result in a substantial value penalty. Market research can indicate how various structural problems affect value.

In addition to physical problems, an appraiser looks for functional problems that affect the substructure. In general, the foundation should conform to the type found in the neighborhood; if it does not, an underimprovement or overimprovement may result. If repair is needed, outdated, costly materials such as fieldstone or brick would probably be replaced with less expensive materials. An irregularly shaped foundation adds significantly to the cost of construction; these costs may exceed the value the shape contributes to property value.

Superstructure

Superstructure refers to the portion of the building that is above grade. The superstructure includes the frame of the building and all elements of the exterior structure. A building description typically includes information on each part of the superstructure.

Framing

The structural frame is the load-bearing skeleton of a building. The floors and ceilings, exterior and interior walls, and roof of the building are attached to the frame. The structural frames of most houses in the United States are made of wood, including many homes with brick veneer siding. The three most common types of wooden frame construction are platform, balloon, and post and beam. Of the three, platform framing is the most common.

When *platform construction* is used, one story of the building is constructed at a time and each completed story serves as the platform for the next story. Studs are cut at the ceiling height of the first story, horizontal plates are laid on top of these studs, and more studs are cut for the second story. Usually walls and partitions are preassembled and tilted up into position; special framing is used for doors and windows.

Balloon framing, so named because of its lightness, was popular in older, multistory buildings with brick, stone, or stucco veneer. Long studs run from the top of the foundation wall to the roof. The studs are notched to receive a horizontal framing member at each upper-floor level. Balloon framing is rarely used today because the long studs needed cost a great deal and the framing has poor fire resistance.

Post-and-beam framing is constructed of wood beams that are spaced up to eight feet apart and supported on posts and exterior walls. The framing members used in post-and-beam framing are much larger and heavier than those used in other framing systems. The post-and-beam system was used in colonial houses and

---

Figure 10.2　Platform Construction

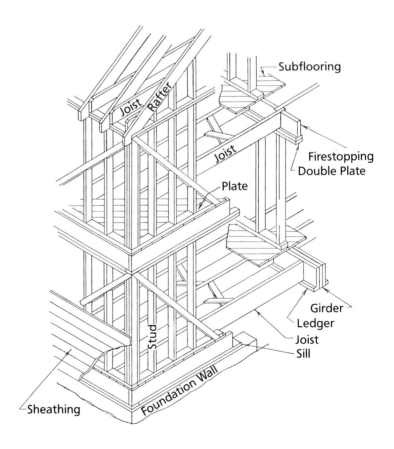

barns; it regained popularity in the mid-1970s when it was used in building designs that include exposed-beam ceilings.

Another, relatively recent method of framing makes use of prefabricated panels of framing members, siding, and subflooring. Construction begins on the ground and, as it proceeds, materials are lifted in units and installed in place. Some buildings are constructed with solid masonry exterior walls, which act as part of the framing system. These walls are often two layers thick or have a face layer backed by masonry of another material; the two layers are joined by metal ties and mortar. Other buildings have hollow masonry walls filled with insulation material. In these buildings interior framing may be made of steel beams or reinforced concrete. Older masonry buildings had interior framing of wood beams and posts.

In the frame of a building, floors are constructed to provide support for the superstructure and for interior partitions. Floors reduce vibrations transmitted through the walls and equalize the expansion and shrinkage of a building. Often the floor finish is built over a subflooring of either plywood or tongue-and-groove planking. The subflooring is nailed to the floor joists, which may be held apart by bridging to prevent sideway deflection. The subflooring is often supported by beams or girders which run mid-

Figure 10.3 Plank-and-Beam Framing

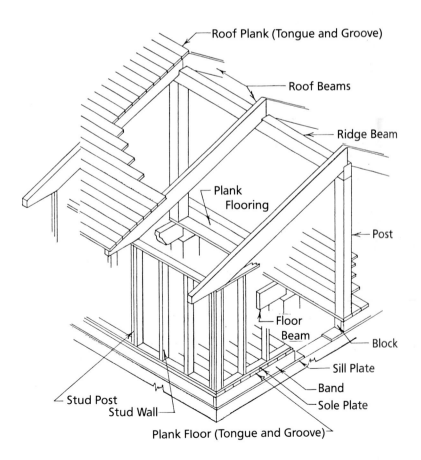

Roof Plank (Tongue and Groove)

Roof Beams

Ridge Beam

Plank Flooring

Post

Floor Beam

Block

Sill Plate

Band

Sole Plate

Stud Post

Stud Wall

Plank Floor (Tongue and Groove)

way between opposite foundation walls. Vertical posts or beams set over footings in the below-grade foundation may provide additional support.

Ceilings are framed with joists and beams. Floor joists for each level often serve as ceiling joists for the level below. The joists are usually thicker on lower floors. Joists extend from the exterior walls over the load-bearing partitions to the center of the house, where they overlap and are braced together.

Interior walls or partitions may be either load-bearing or nonload-bearing. These walls are positioned in accordance with the floor plan and finished on both sides. Partition framing consists of studs running from the sole plate to the top plate. Double studding is used around doors and other openings. Partition frames usually do not contain insulation, but their thickness and center must accommodate the mechanical systems running through the walls and comply with local building codes. By analyzing the building blueprint, an appraiser can determine whether these requirements are being met.

The building frame must also accommodate windows and interior and exterior doors. The sides of doorways and windows are framed with rough jambs attached to vertical studs. The rough jambs, headers, and sills must be plumb and level with the shims.

The frame of a roof is designed and constructed to support its own weight in addition to the weight of finish materials and the pressure from snow, ice, wind, and rain. The method of frame construction used is influenced by the roof type. Common roof types include flat roofs, which are used in industrial and commercial buildings, but less often in houses; lean-to roofs, which are used on sheds and saltbox houses; gambrel roofs, which are popular for barns and Cape Ann and Dutch Colonial houses; and gable, hip, and mansard roofs.

Sloped-joist roof framing is frequently found in flat-roofed homes and prefabricated and low-cost housing. Slightly sloping joists are supported by the building's exterior walls and interior, load-bearing partitions. The sheathing and roof cover are attached to the topside of the joists and the ceiling finish is attached to the underside.

Joists-and-rafter roof frames have joists, which run parallel to the floor and extend from the top plates along the exterior walls to interior, load-bearing partitions. The joists provide the surface to which the ceiling is attached. Rafters that are the same size as the joists are angled to the desired pitch of the roof and support the roof sheathing and cover. The space between the joists and rafters is the building's attic. Rafters from opposite sides join at a ridge beam and are further connected with collar or tie beams running parallel to the joists.

Trusses are sometimes employed for additional support when the joist-and-rafter system of framing is used. Trusses are triangular-shaped components that are attached to the joists and rafters with gusset plates or joints. They are generally preassembled and lifted to the building with a crane. Because they provide extra support, trusses often eliminate the need for interior, load-bearing walls.

Figure 10.4   Roof Types

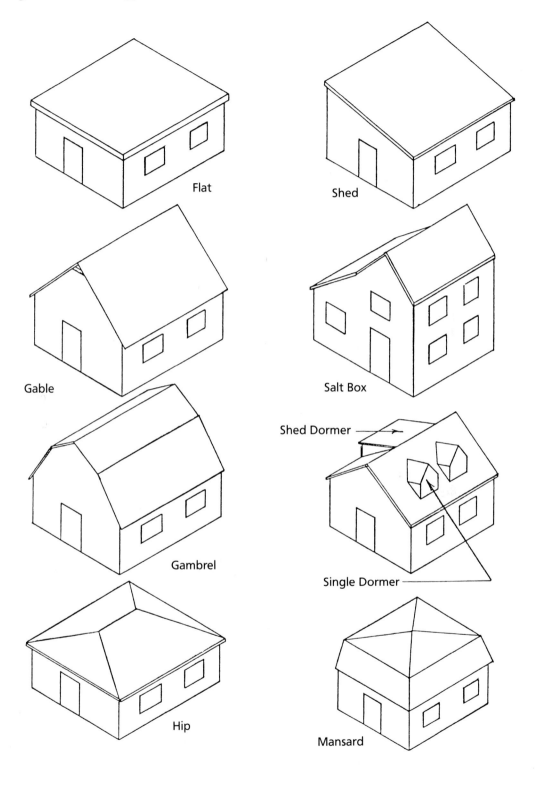

Flat

Shed

Gable

Salt Box

Gambrel

Shed Dormer

Single Dormer

Hip

Mansard

The use of trusses increases flexibility in building design; they lend themselves to gabled architectural styles. However, trusses reduce the space available for attic storage and add to construction costs, which the market may not support.

Plank-and-beam roof framing is employed in buildings designed with exposed ceilings. No joists or rafters are used; instead ridge beams run from the top plate to a central ridge beam. Tongue-and-groove planking and the roof cover are attached to the ridge beams. In place of joists, ceiling beams span the exterior walls. If these beams are functional rather than decorative, they must be supported by interior posts.

When a house is several years old, signs of defective framing may appear. Exterior walls may bulge and girders, roof ridge lines, or rafters may sag. Window sills that are not level and windows that stick may indicate defective framing, poor carpentry, or settling. To conduct a careful house inspection, an appraiser opens and closes each window and checks all doors. Doors should be examined to see if they have been resawed at the bottom. Sagging or sloping floors may be detected visually, or a marble may be placed on the floor to see if it rolls. Defective framing may also be indicated by large cracks on the outside of the house between the chimney and the exterior wall, or cracks running outward at an angle from the upper corners of window and door frames.

Cracks in the walls may be cause for concern, but they do not necessarily indicate framing problems. All houses settle unless they are built on solid rock. Most houses develop some wall and ceiling cracks, but these cracks are serious only if they are accompanied by other signs of defective framing. If major problems are suspected, an appraiser may want to call in professional consultants.

Problems in a new house can often be detected by studying the blueprints. The following functional problems may be observed:

- Floor joists that are too wide and cost more than they contribute to value;
- Floor joists that are too narrow and may later cause the floors to buckle and sink;
- Subflooring made of older materials that are costlier, noisier, and less water-resistant than newer materials;
- Partitions that are improperly sized or improperly placed;
- Use of solid masonry, rather than wood frame or frame and veneer, except where the use of masonry conforms to the market; and
- Walls that are not wide enough to support their intended load or to accommodate sufficient insulation.

Exterior covering and trim

Once the framing is in place, construction begins on the exterior covering and trim, which include the exterior walls, exterior doors and windows, and the roof. Any physical or functional problems with the exterior covering and trim should be noted in the building description.

Exterior walls. Wall sheathing made of wood, plywood, insulated board, or gypsum provides insulation and provides a surface for the wall siding. The sheathing is nailed directly to the studs and may require additional bracing in the corners. Newer materials such as Celotex® are generally cheaper, easier to install, and provide better insulation but they require wooden support in the corners. If the sheathing is not attached properly, it may bulge beneath the siding.

To provide waterproofing, sheathing paper made of felt or aluminum foil is applied over the sheathing. The sheathing paper prevents water from entering the structure, but it allows water vapor to pass through and leave the building. Flashing must be applied where dissimilar materials meet because there is an increased risk of leakage. Flashing is strip metal of galvanized iron or copper which is nailed to the top and bottom of the sheathing where it meets the foundation and roof. During the building inspection, an appraiser notes if flashing is loose or missing along the building walls.

Wall siding is the finish material on the exterior of the walls. Siding may be made of various materials and applied in various patterns. Horizontal siding patterns include bevels or clapboards made of wood, particle board, aluminum, vinyl, masonite, steel, or other materials; tongue-and-groove lap boards; log cabin; and shiplap/Dolly Varden siding. Vertical board and batten siding is applied by nailing vertical boards to horizontal nail strips, which are nailed to the studs; battens cover the board joints. Wood sidings must be stained, sealed, or painted. An appraiser notes whether the paint on the siding is peeling, wrinkling, or buckling and estimates whether a new paint job is needed.

Siding may consist of shingles of wood, asbestos, or asphalt attached directly to horizontal nail strips. Loose shingles should be noted. Stucco siding is also found in residential construction. Furring stips are nailed to the house studs, screening material is attached, and stucco is applied over the screens in three coats. Stucco siding is costly, but it keeps a house cool in warm climates and lends itself to particular architectural styles. Stucco can also be used as an interior finish material. Any cracks in stucco walls should be noted because they are quite expensive to repair.

A house may be sided with a veneer of masonry built of bricks, stones, blocks, or a combination of these materials. Although these materials give an appearance of solidity, they provide no structural support. The veneer is applied from the foundation up in horizontal courses held together with mortar. The masonry is attached to the studs and sheathing with galvanized ties, and spaces between the veneer and the sheathing are vented with weep holes. Stains on masonry veneer may indicate the siding is not suitable to the climate. Panels, glass block, glazed tile, and plastic may also be used for siding. Exterior walls of solid brick, stone, or concrete block may require no additional siding. Concrete block is often considered unsightly. Brick and stone walls must be constructed by special masons and generally are costly to repair.

Exterior doors. Exterior doors may be made of solid wood, metal, or glass. Hollow exterior doors usually signal poor quality construction. Types of doors include panel, flush, combination, batten, Dutch, and sliding glass. Garage doors, stairwell doors, side lights, hatches to the crawl space and coal chutes are also found in residential properties.

The main entrance to a house should be at least 3 feet wide, and 6 feet 8 inches high; service entrances should be at least 2 feet 8 inches wide. An appraiser identifies the type of door and notes any energy-saving materials such as weatherstripping applied around the doors. Air leakage through cracks at the bottom of doors can be stopped with door shoes, weatherproof thresholds, or sweeps.

Windows, storm windows, and screens. Wood was the first material used for windows and it is still the most common material used in houses. Wood provides good insulation, is readily available, takes either a natural or painted finish, and is easily installed and repaired. Aluminum and steel are also popular window materials. When describing a building, an appraiser notes the window type, material, and manufacture. Window types include single- and double-hung, casement, horizontal sliding, clerestory, fixed, awning, hopper, center pivot, and jalousie windows.

Windows have a major impact on the energy efficiency of a structure, so their design and installation have become increasingly important. There is a growing trend among builders to reduce the size of windows and place them higher to conserve energy and increase security. Windows should be tightly sealed with caulking at the joints and between the wall and the window. Insulated glass, multiple glazing, and storm sashes can be used to help keep cold air out and hot air in. An appraiser should identify the energy-saving features of windows in the building description.

Storm doors and windows provide good insulation and can save the owners of a typical house 10% to 20% of their fuel costs. Most modern storm doors and windows are made of aluminum and have permanently installed screens. Wooden storm doors and windows that must be removed and stored during the summer are becoming obsolete. Appraisers find it difficult to judge how much storm windows and doors add to the value of a building in certain markets. However, an analysis of what is typically expected in the area is helpful.

Screens are almost always needed for all windows that open. Most screens have aluminum frames and screening. In residences screens are often combined with storm windows. An appraiser should count all removable window and door screens and note if any are missing.

Roof covering and drain system. The roof frame of a structure must be sheathed, flashed, and covered. Sheathing may be of wood boards, which are costly and difficult to install, plywood, or sheet material attached horizontally or diagonally to the rafters. Roof sheathing must be flush with the ends of overhanging rafters and the wall sheathing of gables. Along ridges, hips, and valleys, sheathing should abut as tightly as possible. A ¾-in. clearance must be

Figure 10.5 Window Types

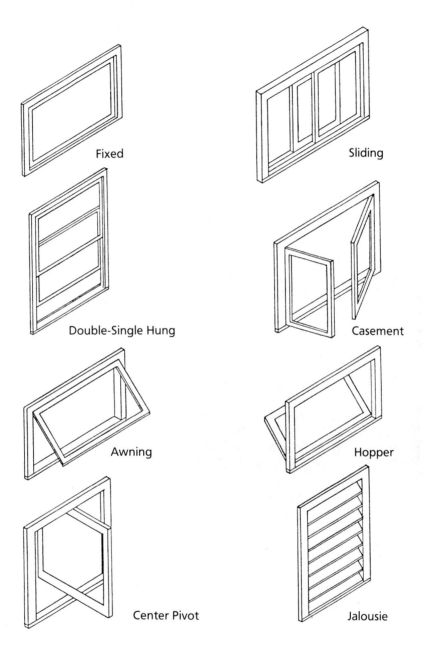

Fixed

Sliding

Double-Single Hung

Casement

Awning

Hopper

Center Pivot

Jalousie

left around chimneys and vent openings. If the sheathing is damaged or applied improperly, the roof may leak. Sheathing paper is nailed over the sheathing in overlapping strips.

Flashing must be applied wherever roof slopes intersect and wherever projections extend through the roof. Flashing is nailed to the sheathing and sealed and waterproofed with an appropriate compound.

Roof covering prevents moisture from entering the building. In most parts of the United States, asphalt shingles are used for residential roofing. These shingles are available in various weights and styles, including lock-tab and seal-tab varieties. Other common roof coverings are shingles or shakes made of wood (usually cedar), slate, metal, and tile. Shingles are nailed in courses with each succeeding course overlapping the nail line; sometimes adhesives activated by the sun are also used. An appraiser notes any loose, torn, broken, or moldy shingles in describing the roof cover.

A built-up roof is completed by applying a final coat of hot asphalt or roofing compound over the sheathing paper; this surface may be topped with gravel or stone. Built-up roofs often blister and generally do not last as long as other roof coverings. They are often used on flat-roofed buildings. Rolled roofing made of asphalt is used when appearance is less important than utility. The roofing material is unrolled over the sheathing paper in overlapping rows and the courses are sealed together with hot asphalt. Other roofs may be constructed of corrugated metal or fiberglass and clay, plastic, or metal tile.

Simple cornices and rake cornices are used when the rafters end at the walls; when the rafters hang over the wall's edge, open or closed cornices are used. Closed cornices have lookouts which join the rafters to the wall siding. A finish is applied to the underside of the roof, called the *soffit*, and to the protruding rafters, called *fascia*. Damage to the soffit and fascia should be noted in the description of the roof.

The water that falls on the roof of a building must be directed to the ground or into the drain system. Gutters and downspouts control water disposal from roofs to prevent damage to exterior walls when roof overhangs are not provided. Gutters or eave troughs catch rainwater at the edge of the roof and direct it to downspouts or leaders; these vertical pipes carry the water to the ground or into sewers, dry wells, drain tiles, or splash pans. Even flat roofs are often slightly pitched to direct water to drains and gutters. Gutters and downspouts may be made of galvanized iron, aluminum, copper, or plastic.

An appraiser considers the overall condition of the roof to determine its remaining useful life. Most roofs need to be replaced several times during a building's life. The condition and age of the roof are considered in the valuation process.

Chimneys, stacks, and vents. The efficiency of a heating system that uses hot air, hot water, or steam depends on the chimney or venting. A good chimney is safe, durable, and tight. Defective chimneys or vents may present serious fire hazards. A chimney can be a simple flue or an intricate masonry structure consisting of heater flues, ash pits, incinerators, ash chutes, fireplaces, and fireplace flues. Regardless of its construction, the chimney is the heaviest portion of the house and must be supported by its own concrete footings. These footings are specially designed so that the chimney will not settle faster than the rest of the building. When chimney walls are exposed to the exterior of the house, they should be eight inches thick and separated from combustible construction. The chimney must extend at least two feet above any part of the roof, roof ridge, or parapet wall within 10 feet of the chimney. At the bottom of the chimney there is usually an ash pit with a clean-out door, into which runs the flue from the fireplaces.

The heart of the chimney is the vertical open shaft, called a *flue*, through which smoke and gas pass to the outside air. A rough surface retards the passage of gas, but a flue lining can overcome this problem. A single flue should not be used for more than one heating device. The flue should extend a few inches above the chimney wall, which is capped with concrete, metal, stone, or some other noncombustible, waterproof material. The cap should slope from the flue to the outside edge. Flues from the furnace and hot water heater may connect to the chimney, but they should not run into the ash pit, because the cold air below the smoke pipe connection will interfere with the draft in the flue.

The furnace and hot water heater are connected to the chimney by a smoke pipe, which should be at least 10 inches below the floor joists. The joists should be further protected with plaster or a shield of metal.

Prefabricated chimneys assembled off the premises may also be installed in residences. These units consist of a flue liner encased in a concrete wall.

Insulation

The presence of insulation in a house provides a number of benefits. Insulation helps home owners economize on fuel and provides comfort in both warm and cold climates. It also reduces noise and impedes the spread of fire. The adequacy of a building's insulation and other energy conservation features are noted by an appraiser in the building description.

Before the 1940s, most buildings were constructed without special insulation materials, although the heavy building materials used at that time provided some insulation. Newer buildings are generally more energy efficient than similar older buildings; many older buildings have been renovated for energy efficiency by adding insulation. Insulation materials are classified according to their form, which may be loose-fill, flexible, rigid, reflective, or foamed-in-place.

Loose-fill insulations are poured or blown by machine into structural cavities. They are manufactured from mineral wool such as rock, slag, or glass wool or from flammable cellulosic fiber such as recycled newsprint, wood chips, or other organic matter.

Flexible insulations are manufactured in batt and blanket form from mineral wool or cellulosic fibers. These insulations may be wrapped with kraft paper on the edges and a vapor barrier on one or both sides, faced with a vapor barrier on one side only, or friction-fit without any covering because the interlaced fibers have enough resilience to remain upright in the cavity. Flexible insulations are generally used in areas where it is not practical to install loose fill or where attached foil or paper facing is desired as a vapor barrier.

Asbestos is a nonflammable, natural mineral substance that separates into fibers. Asbestos-containing materials (ACMs) were widely used in structures built between 1945 and 1970 as thermal and acoustical insulation, or for fireproofing and soundproofing. Other ACMs were used in siding and roofing shingles. Asbestos fibers pose a threat to human health when they are distributed in the air. The potential of any ACM to release fibers depends on its degree of friability—i.e. how easily it is crumbled or pulverized. Dry, spray-on thermal insulation over structural steel is highly friable. Densely packed, nonfibrous ACMs such as vinyl asbestos floor covering and pipe insulation are not considered friable under normal conditions. These materials will become friable if they are broken, sawed, or drilled.

Encapsulation or enclosure of asbestos is only a short-term solution. The Environmental Protection Agency (EPA) has guidelines for the removal of asbestos when a building is being demolished or renovated. However, the EPA has had difficulty enforcing these regulations.

The EPA regulates asbestos under the authority provided by the Clean Air Act and the Toxic Substances Control Act. The National Emission Standards for Hazardous Air Pollutants

Figure 10.6 Insulation

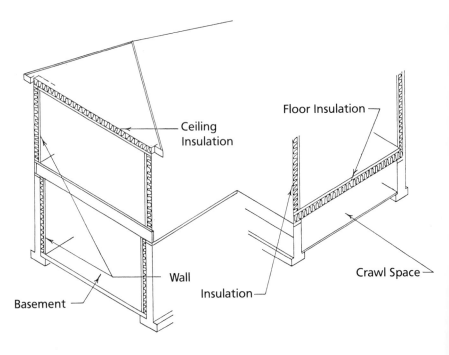

(NESHAP), which were drawn up as part of the Clean Air Act, apply to asbestos emissions in manufacturing, waste disposal, building demolition, and renovation. In 1986 the EPA proposed a ban on asbestos-cement pipe and vinyl asbestos floor tile. The Toxic Substances Control Act was amended by the Asbestos Hazard Emergency Response Act (AHERA) to provide for inspection and abatement of ACMs in the nation's public schools and to promulgate regulations for asbestos removal.

The effect of asbestos on the value of income-producing properties is not yet known. The presence of asbestos has made it more difficult to rent these properties. There is also concern that asbestos legislation will become stricter and that building owners and lenders will be subject to greater liability. Unfortunately, little cost-to-cure data on asbestos abatement are available because relatively few projects have been completed to date. Moreover, each project presents unique problems and building managers and abatement contractors are hesitant to disclose information on projects that often produce cost overruns.

Rigid insulations are popular in new construction. This type of insulation can be used in many parts of a building and comes in four forms: structural wall insulation, fiberboard, structural deck insulation, and rigid board insulation.

Reflective insulation is made of foil so it can reflect heat transferred by radiation. It should be installed to face an air space of at least three-quarters of an inch and should remain free of dust or other substances that could reduce its reflective qualities.

There are two basic types of foamed-in-place insulation: urethane foam insulation and urea-formaldehyde foam insulation (UFFI). Both types are created by a chemical reaction that expands the mixture to approximately 30 times its original size and then solidifies it in about 24 hours.

In April of 1982, the Consumer Product Safety Commission banned the use of urea-formaldehyde foam insulation in residences and schools. The ban resulted from the commission's investigation of the effects of formaldehyde gas, which can be released from the insulation at very high levels, especially immediately after installation. The ban took effect in August of 1982 and was lifted in April of 1983 by a federal court of appeals which held that the health risks had not been proven. The ban was not retroactive, so it did not affect the approximately 500,000 homes that already had urea-formaldehyde foam insulation.

Appraisers must recognize any potential effects that the presence of urea-formaldehyde foam insulation may have on the market value of a structure. They must be extremely careful in valuing properties that are known to have or have had this type of insulation. The obligation to disclose the presence of this potentially harmful substance is imposed on property sellers, real estate brokers, and salespersons representing sellers. Failure to make this disclosure could constitute a breach of a warranty of habitability and entitle the buyer to rescind the sale contract or rental agreement or to recover damages occasioned by the breach.

The ability of all insulation materials to resist the flow of heat is measured in R values. An R value is derived by measuring the British thermal units (Btus) that are transmitted in one hour through one thickness of the insulation. The higher the R value, the better the insulation. There is no universal standard for the amount of insulation required in a building. The amount needed varies from area to area; local building codes establish standards based on the climate and the type of building. For example, overceiling or underroof insulation with an R value of 13 might be satisfactory for a house with gas or oil heat and no air-conditioning located in an area with a mild climate. For buildings with electric heat or air-conditioning located in colder or hotter climates, insulation with an R value of 24 might be necessary. The trend to superinsulate buildings using insulation with much higher R values has recently declined with the fall in fuel prices.

Ventilation

In many buildings ventilation is needed to reduce heat in closed-off areas such as attics and spaces behind walls. Ventilation also prevents the condensation of water that collects in unventilated spaces, which causes building materials to rot and decay. When moisture seeps into insulation, it reduces its R rating. Ventilation can be accomplished with fans and holes that range in size from one inch to several feet in diameter. These holes should be covered with screens to keep out vermin.

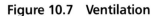

Figure 10.7   Ventilation

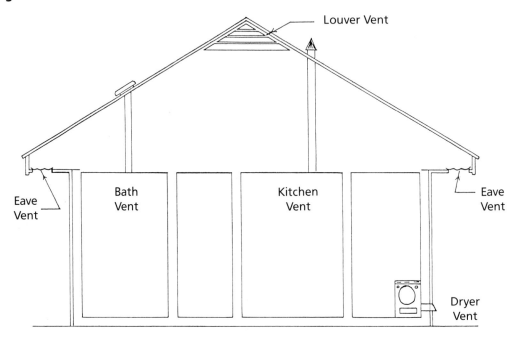

Appraising Residential Properties

INTERIOR

Interior Covering and Trim

The description of the building's interior should provide information about floor, wall, and ceiling coverings and specify the size and location of each room and the number of closets. This information should correspond to the interior floor plan and the rating of its functional utility. Special features should be described and any needed repairs should be reported. Some appraisers describe general construction details and mechanical equipment on a room-by-room basis. However, if these features do not vary significantly from room to room, it is acceptable to describe them for the house as a whole.

Floor covering

Flooring made of strips of hardwood was once the standard in many areas. Today soft woods are used in low-cost houses. More expensive, hardwood floors are attached directly over the subflooring or the joists. Wood block flooring is installed in the same way. Both types of flooring may also be attached to a suitable underlayer with special adhesives.

Wood floors that have been exposed to water may warp and bulge upward. Wide cracks between the floorboards are a sign of poor workmanship or shrinkage that results from drying or storing wood improperly. Wood floors that are rough, discolored, blemished, burned, or gouged can usually be restored with refinishing.

In many homes carpeting is installed over the subflooring. Carpeting over finished hardwood floors may be an overimprovement. Market standards will indicate if this is the case. Padding is important for all carpets. Ceramic tile is popular for bathrooms and lavatories, and may also be found in kitchens. The tiles can be laid in a bed of plaster or attached with a special adhesive to the subflooring. Kitchen flooring may be made of tile or rolled linoleum and no-wax vinyl attached with adhesives.

Concrete slabs may be used for floors with no further treatment, or they may be painted with concrete paint or covered with other materials. Resilient tile glued with special adhesives must be installed over a suitable underlayer, not directly over a board or plank subfloor. Tile floors may be of clay, ceramic, rubber, or vinyl. Terrazzo flooring is made of colored marble chips mixed into cement; it is ground to a smooth surface after it is laid. Slate has an irregular surface, but it is sometimes used for hearths and entry halls, as is brick and stone.

Walls and ceilings

Most interior walls are made of wood studs covered with drywall materials such as gypsum board, wood panels, hardboard, plywood, fiberboard, and ceramic tile. Plaster walls were once popular, but are now used less frequently. The main purpose of wall and ceiling finishes is to provide a decorative, durable cover which is also waterproof in areas subject to moisture.

Gypsum and other wood composition materials can be applied directly onto the studs or masonry. Ceramic tile walls are installed like ceramic tile floors, using cement plaster or special adhesives. Defective grout in the tiles around a bathtub can cause problems; tiles set in plaster or held with waterproof adhesives are less susceptible to water seepage.

A well-constructed plaster wall is quite soundproof. However, plaster walls are costly and susceptible to cracking. As long as cracked plaster adheres tightly to the wall, it may be sufficient to patch and redecorate a crack; bulging ceiling plaster, on the other hand, is dangerous and should be replaced. This defect can often be detected by gently pressing a broom handle against the ceiling to see if there is any give to the plaster.

Doors

Many types of interior doors are considered part of the real estate. Simple, hollow-core interior doors are common and solid doors are found in older homes. The quality of the doors generally corresponds to the overall construction quality of the residence. Hanging doors is a complicated procedure and it is often done improperly. A poorly hung door will usually not close properly or fail to make contact with the edge of its frame when closed. Pre-hung doors are now available.

Stairs

A well-planned stairway provides safe ascent and adequate headroom as well as space to move furniture and equipment. An appraiser notes the amount of headroom; the width of the treads clear of the handrail or the width of the winders in a spiral staircase; the height of the risers, the slope of the stringer, or inclined carriage; and the adequacy of landings, handrails, and railings. Railings should be installed on the open sides of all interior stairwells, including those that lead to the basement and attic. Stairs with risers of irregular height are a safety hazard and violate most municipal building codes. The appraiser should also take note of such functional obsolescence.

Molding and baseboards

Molding is made from a variety of hard and soft woods which are cut, planed, and sanded into desired shapes. Generally the thicker the wood and the more intricate the pattern, the more expensive the molding is. In the past architects designed special moldings for custom houses, but most molding used today is of a standard size and shape.

The interior molding in a modern house may be limited to simple casings around the doors, windows, baseboards, and ceiling. More elaborate residences may have extensive, intricately carved molding. When the lower portion of a wall has a different finish than the upper portion, the lower portion is called the *wainscot* and the finished material is called *wainscoting*. Older homes may have wainscoting that consists of horizontal strips of wood nailed to the wall at chair height to prevent chairs from marring the walls.

Figure 10.8 Interior Doors

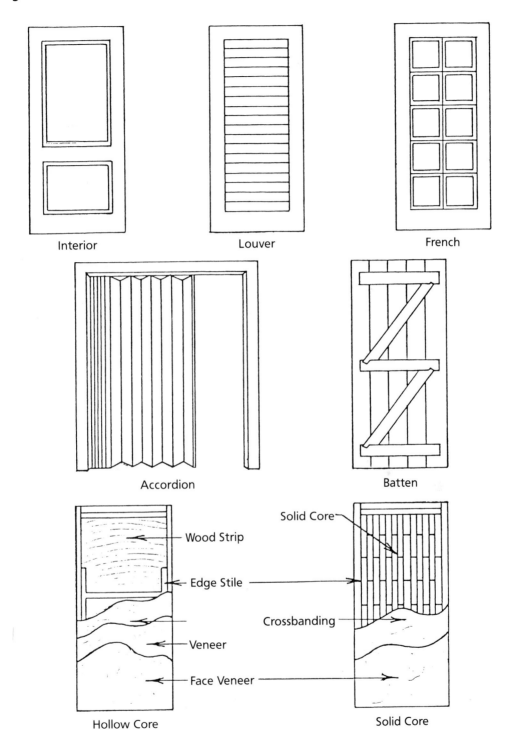

Interior

Louver

French

Accordion

Batten

Wood Strip

Edge Stile

Veneer

Face Veneer

Hollow Core

Solid Core

Edge Stile

Crossbanding

Solid Core

Painting, decorating, and finishing

Interior painting and decorating gives the building an attractive appearance. Latex and oil-based paint, various kinds of wallpaper, paneling, carpeting, and wainscoting can all be used to finish the interior. Most homes are redecorated several times during their useful lives. An appraiser reports the condition of the painting and decorating and estimates when they will have to be redone.

Cabinets

Most cabinets installed before the 1940s were made of wood and custom built at the construction site, but today factory-made wood or metal cabinets are also used. Cabinets must be installed level and plumb to operate properly. They should be screwed, not nailed, to the wall studs, and the screws should go through to the framing members.

Fireplaces

Fireplaces continue to be popular and they are found in many houses. Most fireplaces do not provide a building's primary source of heat; because of their design, many fireplaces have little heating power. Some devices can be installed to make fireplaces better sources of heat. One such device is the Heatilator,® which returns hot air into the room.

A typical fireplace has a single opening with a damper and a hearth. More complex designs feature two, three, four, or more openings. Because fireplaces are difficult to construct, many are poorly built and do not function properly. One common problem is downdraft which may blow smoke into the building when there is wind outside. This can happen if the chimney does not extend at least two feet above any part of the roof within 10 feet of it.

Prefabricated fireplaces or woodstoves and flues are often installed in buildings constructed without fireplaces. These fireplaces must be approved by Underwriters Laboratory and installed according to the manufacturer's instructions or they may be a potential fire hazard. To be safe, a fireplace should be supported by noncombustible material and equipped with a noncombustible hearth that extends at least 16 inches in front of the opening and at least 8 inches on each side. Carpeting or rugs within a few inches of the front of a fireplace may constitute a fire hazard.

Protection Against Decay and Insect Damage

All wood is susceptible to decay and insect damage. Wood decays when it is continually exposed to moisture and water, which enable destructive organisms to propagate on or beneath its surface. The most common of these organisms are aerobic fungi, which thrive when moisture, temperature, and oxygen combine with a cellulose material. Sapwood from all wood species is prone to decay; heartwood may have low to very high susceptibility to decay, depending on its species.

Insects damage wood more rapidly and more visibly than fungi. Several species of insects damage wood, but subterranean, dampwood, and drywood termites are by far the most destructive. Subterranean termites are very adaptable and found throughout the United States. They live in colonies in moist soil and infest both damp and dry wood. Dampwood and drywood termites are only found in certain geographic areas. Drywood termites establish colonies in wood and are extremely difficult to eradicate.

Measures can be taken to protect buildings from decay and insect damage. The ground may be sloped away from the building foundation to provide good drainage; vapor barriers may be installed on the interior sides of exposed walls; the soil in crawl spaces can be covered with polyethylene; flashing may be maintained; gutters, downspouts and splash blocks can be used to carry water away from the foundation walls; poured concrete foundation walls may be laid; masonry foundations can be capped with concrete; wood and soil can be treated with pesticides; buildings can be constructed of dry, naturally durable woods; metal termite shields may be installed; and regular maintenance inspections can be conducted.

EQUIPMENT AND MECHANICAL SYSTEMS

A house cannot provide its residents with adequate shelter and comfort unless its mechanical systems are in good working order. Each item of equipment and mechanical system should be inspected by the appraiser and described in the appraisal report. There is no standard way to categorize mechanical systems and equipment, but most residences have plumbing, hot water, heating, air-conditioning and ventilation, and electrical systems as well as other miscellaneous systems and equipment.

Plumbing System

The plumbing system is an integral part of most buildings. It consists of piping, which is mostly covered or hidden, and fixtures or equipment, which are visible.

Piping

Much of the cost of a plumbing system is spent on piping. Pipes carry water and occasionally other fluids under pressure; waste pipes depend on gravity. The quality of the materials used, the way the pipes are installed, and the ease with which they can be serviced are significant factors in considering the durability of piping and the cost of maintenance. Worn galvanized steel, lead, or brass water pipes may need to be replaced. Copper is an excellent piping material with a long life, and cast iron is a durable material for below-grade waste lines. In many types of buildings, a high-quality piping system can last for the life of the building. However, many buildings have pipes that will not last. An appraiser describes the conditions of the pipes within the structure and notes approximately when they will need to be replaced.

Plastic pipes are commonly used for waste, vent, and water lines. The durability and adequacy of plastic pipes should be checked. Water pipes must be strong enough to withstand the pressure of water flowing through them. Because waste drain lines do not operate under pressure, these pipes must be slanted so

Figure 10.9 Plumbing

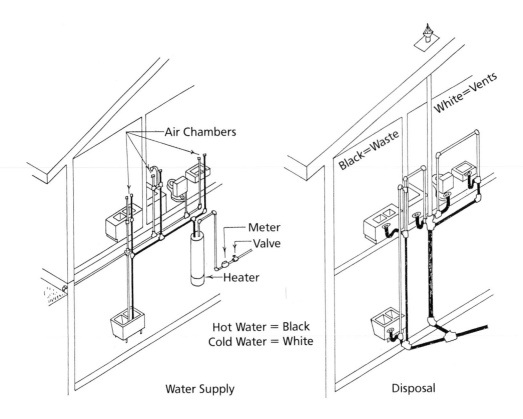

Air Chambers

Meter

Valve

Heater

Hot Water = Black
Cold Water = White

Water Supply

Black=Waste

White=Vents

Disposal

that wastes flow from each fixture through the main line into the sewer or sewage disposal system. Building sewers should be installed to prevent sewers from backing up in heavy rains.

Fixtures

The plumbing fixtures used in bathrooms include lavatories or washbasins, bathtubs, showers, toilets or water closets, bidets, and urinals. Good-quality fixtures are made of cast iron covered with acid-resistant vitreous enamel. Fiberglass and other materials are also used.

The design of bathroom fixtures has undergone substantial change, so old fixtures may become obsolete during the building's economic life. An appraiser reports any modernization that the bathrooms may require. Old fixtures of good quality such as porcelain pedestal basins and legged tubs are often rehabilitated.

Kitchen plumbing fixtures include single or double sinks installed in countertops, garbage disposals, dishwashers, and instant hot water units. Sinks may be made of Monel® metal, stainless steel, enameled steel, or cast iron that is covered with acid-resistant enamel. Some homes have specialized plumbing fixtures such as laundry tubs and wet bars.

Fittings are an important part of plumbing fixtures. Fittings include faucets, spigots, drains, shower heads, and spray hoses. The water in many areas contains minerals such as calcium, magnesium, sulfates, bicarbonates, iron, and sulfur. These minerals react unfavorably with soap to form a curdled substance that is difficult to rinse from clothing, hair, and skin. This hard water often cannot be used unless it is treated. Some residences have automatic, multistage treatment systems to make hard water usable.

Hot Water System

All homes need an adequate supply of hot water. A typical hot water system receives its heat from a furnace or a self-standing water heater, which is powered by electricity, gas, or oil. Houses with inadequate hot water systems suffer functional obsolescence. The size of the hot water tank needed in a residence is determined by the number of inhabitants and their water-using habits as well as the recovery rate of the unit.

Heating Systems

Most common heating systems use warm or hot air, hot water, steam, or electricity. The amount of heat a system can produce is rated in Btus. The Btu requirement for a heating-plant depends on the cubic content, exposure, design, and insulation level of the structure to be heated. An appraiser describes the heating system and analyzes whether is is appropriate for the structure and the local market.

Warm or hot air heating systems

Heating systems based on warm or hot air use either the natural force of gravity or some type of pressure blower to push heated air through heating ducts. The air is heated in a furnace that is fueled with gas, oil, electricity, or coal. The heated air is then distributed through one or more registers directly from the furnace or through ducts connected to registers throughout the building. Air circulation is maintained with a fan and a return duct system. Thermostats, filters, humidifiers, air cleaners, and air purification devices may be included in the heating system.

Some central air-conditioning systems use the same ducts as the heating system. This is not always possible, however, because air-conditioning requires ducts of a different size. Heating registers are generally placed low on the walls, while air-conditioning registers should be placed higher up or in the ceiling.

Older heating systems relied on gravity and had large ducts and simple distribution patterns for circulation. Warm air systems are used in new apartment construction, especially for garden apartments and townhouse developments. When gas is the source of energy, the warm air system may function through unit heaters, radiant gas heaters, wall or floor furnaces, or individual gas furnaces. Gas-fired heating units require adequate ventilation. All open-flame heating sources must have enough air to support complete combustion.

Hot water heating systems

Heating systems based on hot water are also known as *hydronic systems*. Water is heated in a cast-iron or steel boiler. The hot water rises due to gravity in older systems or is pumped by a circulator in modern systems through pipes and radiators where heat is transferred by convection and radiation to the rooms of the house. The colder water then returns to the boiler where it is heated again, and the process is repeated over and over.

Radiant heating is a type of hot water heating. Hot water is circulated by a pump, called a *circulator*, through narrow pipes embedded in floors, walls, and ceilings. The system depends primarily on heat being transferred to an area by radiation rather than by convection, which characterizes conventional systems. In a conventional system, air is warmed as it passes over the heated metal of a radiator and is then circulated in the area of colder air. Radiant heat can also be produced by electric heating elements that are buried in floors, walls, and ceilings.

Figure 10.10   Heating Systems

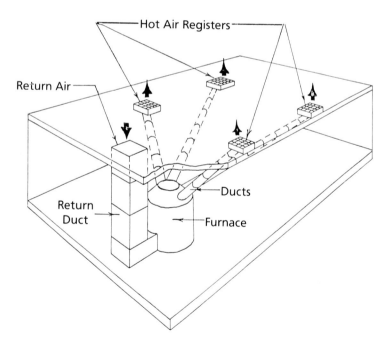

Gravity Hot Air System

(*continued*)

Appraising Residential Properties

Figure 10.10   continued

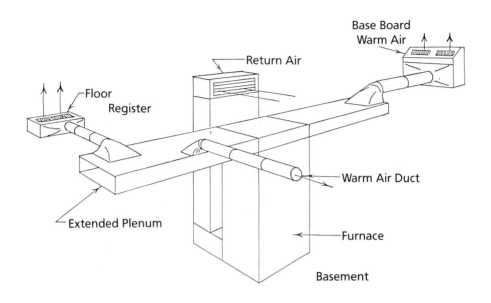

Extended Plenum System

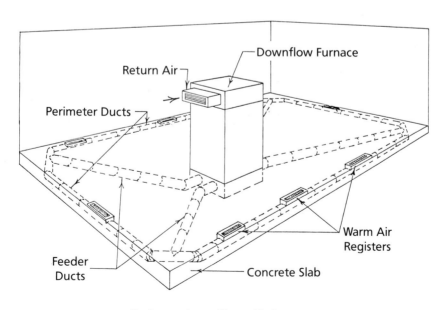

Perimeter Loop Warm Air System

Steam heating systems

Some heating systems use steam heated in a boiler that is fueled by gas, oil, coal, or electricity. Steam is distributed from the boiler with a piping system. In a simple, one-pipe gravity system, which is common in small installations, radiators are served by a single riser from the main pipe. The condensate returns to the boiler through the same riser and is recycled. More expensive, two-pipe systems are found in larger, high-quality installations.

At one time cast iron boilers with vertical sections were used in larger installations; more efficient units were covered with an insulated metal casing or jacket. Low-pressure, fire-tube steel boilers were also used. Steel boilers were heated by combustion gases that passed through tubes inserted into a cylindrical drum containing water. There were several types of two-pass or three-pass steel boilers designed for better efficiency. Small, efficient, package boilers have recently become popular for heating and process-steam generating.

A steam system also uses radiators to transfer heat into rooms by radiation and convection. The common, cast-iron radiator successfully accomplishes this dual process. Steam heating systems are being developed to operate more efficiently. Zone control is now widely used to meet various heating needs in different parts of a building. The amount of heat available for distribution is controlled by separate temperature controls.

Many states require licenses for certain classes of steam boilers. Appraisers must be familiar with boiler license laws in their areas to determine if boiler licenses are current and valid.

Electrical heating systems

The equipment used in electrical heating systems includes heat pumps, wall heaters, baseboard units, duct heating units, and heating units installed in air-conditioning ducts. With this equipment an electrical heating system can heat and cool a building. Electrical heating systems may also make use of radiant floors, walls, and ceilings with panels or cables under the surface; infrared units; and electric furnaces that generate forced warm air or hot water. An electrical resistance system produces heat in the immediate area to be heated. It is the least expensive system to install because it does not require a furnace, furnace room, ducting, flue, or plumbing. However, it does need much more electrical service than would otherwise be needed and a great deal of wiring to each unit in the building.

Heat pumps, which combine heating and cooling functions, are increasing in popularity. A heat pump is actually a reverse refrigeration unit. In the winter the pump takes heat from the outside ground or well water and distributes it in the house. Because the efficiency of the unit decreases when the weather is very cold, it must be supplemented with resistance heating. In the summer the pump cools by ejecting heat from inside of the house like a typical air-conditioning unit.

Finned heating elements called *convectors* are designed to be installed in baseboards or concealed in walls and cabinets. A unit or room heater is a convector combined with a fan. Unit heaters are found in buildings with large spaces to be heated.

The automatic regulation of a heating system contributes to its operating efficiency. A multiple-zone system with separate thermostats is more efficient than a single-zone system with one thermostat. Complex systems provide individual temperature controls for each room. The efficiency of certain systems can be increased by putting a thermostat on the outside of a building. The outside thermostat helps determine how much heat a system needs to produce.

Heating System Fuels

The type of fuel used in a building's heating system is cited in the building description. In certain areas and for certain types of buildings, a particular type of fuel may be more desirable than another. However, the heating systems of many buildings do not use the most economical fuel. For example, during the natural gas shortage in the middle and late 1970s, a moratorium was declared on the use of natural gas. Therefore, buildings constructed then were equipped with heating systems that use other fuels. Now gas is more economical. In a given area for a specific use, different fuels have significant advantages and disadvantages which may occasionally change.

Coal

Throughout much of our country's history, coal was the most popular heating fuel. Today it is still used in stoves and fireplaces. The burning of certain types of coal, however, creates environmental problems.

Fuel oil

In spite of its high cost, fuel oil remains popular because it is easy to transport and store. The common 275-gallon oil tank can be found in millions of houses.

Natural gas

Natural gas is convenient because it is continuously delivered by pipelines, eliminating the need for storage tanks. In many parts of the country gas is the most economical fuel. Liquid petroleum gases such as butane and propane are used in many rural areas. Liquid gas must be stored in onsite tanks and is usually more expensive than natural pipeline gas, but in other respects it is similar to natural gas.

Electricity

Electricity can be used to produce heat in a furnace or to heat water in a boiler. Electric heat is costly, except in a few lower-cost power areas. With good insulation and control, heat loss can be reduced.

An appraiser cannot assume that the existing heating system contributes maximum value to a property. The heating system installed when a building was constructed is often not acceptable to current potential buyers. New technology has continued to reduce the energy consumption of large heating systems.

Many users who formerly depended on gas alone now install alternate, more efficient oil or electric facilities to provide heat during periods when the gas supply is curtailed. Electric heat has become so expensive in certain areas that buildings with electrical heating systems sell for substantially less than similar properties heated with other types of fuel. Buyers are sensitive to energy costs. Buildings with high ceilings, many openings, and poor insulation may be at a disadvantage in the market.

Solar heating systems and solar domestic hot water systems have attracted a great deal of publicity and interest. A variety of solar systems are on the market. Appraisers should keep informed on recent developments in solar energy and its use in particular areas. A building's solar heating system should be fully described and its contribution to property value should be carefully estimated. Residential appraisals reported on FHLMC-FNMA forms must include a separate description and value estimate for solar heating systems and other special energy systems.

Air-Conditioning and Ventilation System

In the past ducts, fans, and windows were used to reduce heat and to provide fresh air in most buildings. Ducts and fans are still used in many buildings. In certain parts of the western United States, humidity remains low during even periods of high heat. In these areas some buildings are cooled with a simple system that blows air across wet excelsior or some other water-absorbing material. Package units that apply this procedure are still manufactured for residential and commercial use. They consume less power and are less expensive than conventional air-conditioning.

In the most common type of air-conditioning system, an electric-powered compressor converts Freon® from a gaseous state into a liquid outside the area being cooled. The heat released in this process is blown away or carried away by water. The compressed Freon® is then directed into thin tubes in a unit in the area being cooled, where it expands and absorbs heat from the air that is directed over the tubes using one or more fans. Some air-conditioners run on gas rather than electricity and use ammonia, not Freon® as the refrigerant.

Air-conditioners range from small, portable units to units that provide tons of cooling capacity. The capacity of an air-conditioning unit is rated in tons of refrigeration. One unit is equal to the amount of heat needed to melt one ton of ice in 24 hours (12,000 Btus per hour).

The appraiser should describe the air-conditioning and ventilation systems in a building and decide if the systems are appropriate for the geographic area and meet current standards. If the appraiser decides that the building has too much or too little air-conditioning, the appraisal report should contain data to support this decision.

Electrical System

A well-designed electrical system should provide sufficient electrical service to power all the electrical equipment in the building. Sometimes a single electrical service supplies power to more than one building.

In an electrical system, power is distributed from the electrical service by wires, or branch circuits, to electrical outlets throughout the building. Each branch circuit starts at a distribution box, where it is separated from the main service by a protective device such as a fuse or circuit breaker. When there is a short circuit or overload in the branch circuit, the fuse or circuit breaker disconnects the branch circuit from the power supply to prevent it from catching fire.

The wiring between the distribution boxes and the outlets in an electrical system can be rigid or flexible conduit. Most houses are wired with BX, or armored, cable. Plastic-coated wire is used in certain areas; knob-and-tube wiring is still found in rural areas and in older buildings, but it is considered obsolete.

Most electrical wire is copper. After the 1940s aluminum wire was used in many homes because the price of copper escalated. However, aluminum's resistance to fire has been seriously questioned and aluminum wiring is now prohibited by law in some sections of the country.

Most houses have a single-phase, three-wire system that provides at least 100 amperes of electricity. Thirty-ampere systems are now obsolete and residences with 60 amperes of service normally sell for less than similar homes with greater electrical service. Service of 150, 200, 300, or 400 amperes is needed to power electrical heating and air-conditioning. Most of these services can provide up to 220 volts by connecting three wires to the outlet.

Wall switches and lighting fixtures are also part of the electrical system. Because lighting fixtures are stylized and styles change, they are often obsolete before they wear out. Incandescent fixtures may be used in smaller rooms or for accent lighting. Some houses have low-voltage switching systems which allow many residents to control many outlets and lights from one place.

Miscellaneous Systems and Equipment

A variety of special mechanical systems and equipment may also be installed in homes. Some residences have intercommunication and sound systems, burglar and fire alarms, automatic doors, elevators, incinerators, laundry chutes, and central vacuum cleaners. Many of these items of equipment may reflect a passing fad or the special interests of the homeowner. The appraiser must determine how much value these specialized items add to the house.

ATTACHMENTS, GARAGES, AND OUTBUILDINGS

Enclosed, screened, or open porches are generally not included in the calculation of gross living area, but they may certainly add to the attractiveness of a home. Porches are usually constructed over some type of foundation. Patios, which are sometimes erroneously described as *open porches,* need not be built onto a foundation. Porches and patios should be located away from street noise, screened for privacy, and, if possible, situated on the south side of the residence. Decks are usually constructed of wood and may be located on the ground level or at upper levels. Decks are adjacent to the house and access is usually provided by sliding glass doors or by a service door. Balconies are railed platforms that project from the face of a building. Breezeways are covered passages between a house and a detached garage. They usually open to the exterior on one or two sides and are constructed and finished to match the residence. Other outdoor attachments include stoops and ramps made of wood, concrete, or masonry.

Wall attachments such as stairwells leading from the exterior to a basement, window wells, oriel windows, and bay windows, and door and window attachments such as awnings and shutters can all add value to a house. Roof attachments include cupolas, skylights, dormers, and antennas. Weather vanes, turrets, and other attachments often lend charm and individual character to a residence. In high-priced residential markets, the value they contribute may be greater than their cost.

Garages are enclosed areas used primarily for car storage, but they may also be used as workshops, laundries, and storage areas. Carports are roofed, open-sided shelters for automobiles. Outbuildings include greenhouses, garden sheds, carriage houses, barns, beach houses, boat houses, recreational facilities, and storage buildings.

The facilities provided for car storage should conform to market standards. A garage in an area where carports are standard is an overimprovement; a carport in an area where garages are considered essential is an underimprovement. An appraiser checks the construction, drainage, ventilation, equipment, and doors of the garage, and notes its size classification. One-car garages must measure at least 10 feet by 20 feet. Two-car garages are at least 18½ feet by 20 feet. Larger garages must provide a minimum of 10 feet by 20 feet for each bay. Oversized garages may be appealing, but they are often overimprovements. Detached garages have become less popular in certain areas of the country. Built-in basement garages are designed to take up a small proportion of the living space and should be constructed of fireproof materials.

OVERALL CONDITION OF THE RESIDENCE

A complete building description includes a quality and condition survey of the main improvements. To describe their condition, an appraiser classifies building components as items requiring immediate repair, items for which maintenance may be deferred, or items that are expected to last for the full economic life of the building.

Items Requiring Immediate Repair

Some homes are exceptionally well maintained, but almost all will contain items in need of repair on the date of the appraisal. Repairing these normal maintenance items should add as much or more value to the property than the cost of repair. When the cost approach to value is applied, these are considered items of curable physical deterioration. The appraiser's repair list should include items that constitute a fire or safety hazard. Many clients request that these items be listed separately in the report. Sometimes the appraiser is asked to estimate the cost of each repair, which is called *cost to cure*. Some of the most common repairs needed are:

- Touching up exterior paint
- Doing minor carpentry on stairs, molding, trim, floors, and porches
- Redecorating interior rooms
- Fixing leaks and noisy plumbing
- Loosening stuck doors and windows
- Repairing holes in screens and replacing broken windows or other glass
- Rehanging loose gutters and leaders
- Replacing missing roof shingles and tiles
- Fixing cracks in pavements
- Doing minor electrical repairs
- Replacing rotted floor boards
- Exterminating vermin
- Fixing cracked or loose bathroom and kitchen tiles
- Repairing septic systems
- Eliminating fire hazards

Short-lived Items

Although a building's paint, roof, and wallpaper may show signs of wear and tear, they may not be ready for replacement on the date of the appraisal. The appraiser must determine whether repairing or replacing the item will add more value to the property than it will cost. If, for example, a house has an exterior paint job that is three years old and exterior paint normally lasts five years, the paint has suffered some depreciation. Repainting the house on the date of the appraisal, however, would probably not add enough value to the property to justify its cost.

The economic life of a building is the period over which the improvements contribute to property value. Items of deferred maintenance will usually have to be repaired at some time prior to the end of the economic life of the building. The remaining economic life of a building component is the estimated period during which the component will contribute to property value. If the remaining economic life of the component is shorter than the remaining economic life of the structure as a whole, the component is known as a *short-lived item.* Some short-lived items are listed below.

- Interior paint and wallpaper
- Exterior paint
- Floor finishes
- Shades, screens, and blinds
- Waterproofing and weatherstripping
- Gutters and leaders
- Storm windows
- Roof covering and flashing
- Hot and cold water pipes
- Plumbing fixtures
- Hot water heater
- Electric service entrance
- Electric wiring
- Electric switches and outlets
- Electric fixtures
- Furnace
- Ducts and radiators
- Air-conditioning equipment
- Carpeting
- Kitchen appliances
- Kitchen cabinets and counters
- Sump pump
- Water softener system
- Washers and dryers
- Ventilating fans
- Fences and other site improvements

An appraiser notes whether the condition of short-lived items is better or worse than the overall condition of the residence.

Long-lived Items

The final step in the quality and condition survey is a description of items that are not expected to require repair or replacement during the economic life of the building. A building component with an expected remaining economic life that is the same as the remaining economic life of the entire structure is a *long-lived item.* Repair may not be required because the components have been built to last and have been well maintained. However, the long-lived items in a building are rarely in exactly the same condition. The appraiser should focus on those items that are not in the same condition as the rest of the building.

Sometimes defective long-lived items are not considered in need of repair because the cost of replacement or repair is greater than the amount these items contribute to the value of the property. A serious crack in a foundation wall, for example, would probably be considered incurable physical deterioration. Incurable depreciation that results from problems in the original design of a residence is considered incurable functional obsolescence.

SUMMARY

A reliable residential appraisal depends on the accuracy and completeness of the building description. To describe a building, an appraiser must possess a good understanding of the various techniques and materials used in constructing residential improvements. The building description notes the materials used, their cost, the quality of workmanship, the maintenance condition of the building, and its conformity to legal and market standards. Physical and functional problems in the design and construction of the building or in its subsequent maintenance are noted in the building description.

Building construction begins when the lot is staked out and building lines are drawn. After test borings are drilled, the site is excavated and the building foundation is laid. An appraiser can inspect some details of the substructure directly, but others must be analyzed by studying house plans and eliciting information from builders.

When the substructure is in place, the builders frame the superstructure. Common types of wood framing are balloon, platform, and post and beam. Masonry and brick walls may also be used to support the superstructure. An exterior covering and trim are applied to the walls and roof, and finish and trim are applied to the interior. The residence is then insulated and equipped with a proper ventilation system. Porches, patios, balconies, and attachments may be constructed by the original builders, or added by subsequent owners. An appraiser notes the quality of construction and the condition of each structural component in the building description.

Mechanical systems and equipment include plumbing pipes and fixtures, a hot water system, a heating system powered by some type of fuel, an air-conditioning and ventilation system, and an electrical system. Garages and outbuildings must also be checked.

To carry out the quality and condition survey of a building, an appraiser describes the condition of items that require immediate repair, short-lived items for which maintenance may be deferred, and long-lived items that are expected to last for the economic life of the building. The character, quality, and appearance of the construction are reflected in each of the three approaches to value. Building features have a major influence on the cost estimate, the estimate of accrued depreciation, the rental income to the property, and the property's comparability with other, competitive properties.

REVIEW QUESTIONS

1. Identify the four major categories used to analyze the construction of a building and describe its structural components.

2. Define the following terms: *substructure, superstructure, exterior covering and trim, interior covering and trim.*

3. What types of insulation are found in residential properties?

4. What measures may be taken to protect a house from decay and insect damage?

5. What items does an appraiser consider in describing the mechanical systems of a residential property?

6. What is the quality and condition survey?

7. Provide examples of items that require immediate repair and short-lived items for which maintenance may be deferred.

PART III

HIGHEST AND BEST USE

11 Highest and Best Use

The data collection effort undertaken by an appraiser provides information that can be used to conduct highest and best use analyses. Analyses of the city and region, the neighborhood and the local market, and the site and improvements all contribute data which can help determine the subject property's highest and best use. The appraiser studies this information and decides which legally permitted, physically possible, and financially feasible use of the property will be most profitable.

The highest and best use of a property reflects the market's perception of its potential. As the concept of anticipation affirms, the potential future use of a property strongly influences its present value. Consequently, highest and best use analysis is an essential step in the valuation process.

This chapter focuses on the purpose of highest and best use analyses, the techniques employed to reach a highest and best use conclusion, and the relationship between highest and best use and the three approaches to value. Special appraisal situations which can complicate highest and best use analyses are also described.

DEFINITION OF HIGHEST AND BEST USE

The current definition of highest and best use in appraisal usage is

> The reasonably probable and legal use of vacant land or an improved property, which is physically possible, appropriately supported, financially feasible, and that results in the highest value.

This definition indicates that two analyses of highest and best use may be undertaken in an appraisal. One analysis focuses on *the highest and best use of the site as though vacant;* the other is concerned with *the highest and best use of the property as improved.* These two analyses of highest and best use are distinct and serve different functions in the valuation process.

Highest and Best Use of the Site as Though Vacant

In analyzing the highest and best use of the land as though vacant, the site is considered as though it were vacant and ready for development. Even if there are improvements on the property, the property is considered as though it were vacant for the purposes of this analysis. The questions to be answered are: If the site is, or were, vacant, what type of building or other improvement, if any, should be constructed on it? When should the improvement be built? How should this improvement be used—for rental income or owner occupancy?

To conduct the analysis, an appraiser considers proposed uses of the land as though vacant, which may include agricultural, residential, commercial, industrial, or special-purpose uses. First each use is tested to see whether it is legally permitted, physically possible, and financially feasible. The test of financial feasibility is applied after the first two criteria are met. Uses that fail any of these tests are eliminated from further consideration. Then, of the uses that remain, the one that is maximally productive is selected as the highest and best use of the site as though vacant.

As the range of possible uses is narrowed, the uses that remain must be scrutinized. If the appraiser concludes that the site as though vacant would be used most profitably for commercial purposes, the client is so informed. At this point the client may want the appraiser to continue the analysis to determine the building characteristics that would create maximum productivity. If a residential use is determined to be the highest and best use of the site as though vacant, the appraiser should identify the specific kind of residential use that would be most profitable. What would be the approximate size, or square foot area, and price of the residence? How many stories would it have? How many bedrooms and bathrooms would it contain? What would the architectual design be?

To form a mental picture of the ideal improvement for the site as though vacant, the appraiser conceives of an improvement that would take maximum advantage of the site's potential and perfectly conform to the current standards of the market. Moreover, all components of this ideal improvement would be suitably priced.

In market valuations analyzing the highest and best use of the site as though vacant and preparing a cost estimate of the ideal improvements serve a variety of purposes. The appraiser's determinations provide information that can be used in all three approaches to value.

In the cost approach, the site must be valued separately from the existing improvements. This requires a separate highest and best use analysis of the site. One technique used to value the site alone is analysis of the sales prices of potentially comparable vacant sites. These vacant parcels can only be truly comparable to the subject site if they have similar highest and best uses.

Existing improvements that do not develop the land to its highest and best use are usually worth less than their cost. A new building that is poorly designed may be worth less than its cost due to functional obsolescence of its design. The improvement that constitutes the highest and best use is the one that adds the greatest value to the site.

In the sales comparison approach, highest and best use analysis serves as a test in the selection of comparables. The sites of comparable properties should have the same or a similar highest and best use as though vacant as the site of the subject property. If they do not, the comparable properties may appeal to somewhat different markets and thus be unreliable indicators of market value.

For income-producing properties, analyzing the highest and best use of the subject site as though vacant helps the appraiser determine which use among competing income-producing uses will produce the greatest income for the site.[1]

A highest and best use study may be performed outside of an appraisal assignment. A client may be interested in a project's feasibility—i.e., the likelihood that the project will satisfy explicit objectives. Most feasibility studies are more detailed than highest and best use analyses conducted for market valuation purposes, but the two are closely related. If the purpose of the appraisal is to study feasibility, a more detailed analysis of alternative uses and market conditions is usually required.

Highest and Best Use of the Property as Improved

To determine the highest and best use of the property as improved, an appraiser compares the existing improvements with ideal improvements. The appraiser attempts to answer these questions: Given the existing improvements on the site, what use should be made of the property and when should this use be implemented? Are any repairs, remodeling, or renovation needed? Would these changes contribute more value to the property than they would cost? How should the existing or renovated structure be used and by whom? Should it be owner-occupied, rented, or used for commercial purposes?

In many appraisal situations, the highest and best use of the property as improved will be the same as, or similar to, the highest and best use of the site as though vacant. The potential benefits that could accrue to the site as though vacant can often be realized by the existing improvements if modest changes are made. This is particularly likely if the improvements are relatively new.

In some cases, however, the presence of improvements alters the property's potential to produce benefits. Consider, for example, a large, older residence in an area which has been rezoned for commercial use. If the site were vacant, it would probably be most profitably used for a commercial establishment. However, because the improvements currently on the site are valuable, the property's highest and best use as improved would probably be continued use as a residential unit, perhaps subject to remodeling. In this case, the improvements contribute value to the property. Improvements can detract from the value of property if they contribute nothing and expense must be incurred to demolish or remove them.

---

1. This method of income capitalization analysis is beyond the scope of the text. Briefly stated, the income allocated to the improvements is deducted from the net operating income for the total property under each proposed use. The income that remains is then capitalized to provide an indication of site value.

To analyze the highest and best use of the property as improved, the four tests are once again applied. Reasonable uses that are legally permitted, physically possible, and financially feasible are contemplated. Of the uses that meet these tests, the use that is maximally productive is selected as the highest and best use of the property as improved.

Alternative uses may involve minor renovation such as replacing radiators or touching up paint, or they may necessitate substantial improvements such as adding a bathroom or finishing a basement. An appraiser may conclude that the existing improvement should be completely demolished and a new structure be built to take its place. In another situation, an appraiser might decide that no structural changes are necessary and determine that the most productive use would be realized by renting out a portion of the building.

The costs of the components in the existing improvement are compared with the costs of the components in the ideal improvement. Analyzing the highest and best use of the property as improved helps the appraiser identify items of accrued depreciation, which must be described in the cost approach. In the sales comparison approach, this highest and best use conclusion helps the appraiser recognize existing and potential characteristics of the subject property which contribute to value in the market area. Potentially comparable properties should have the same or a similar highest and best use as improved or they are not truly comparable.

In the income capitalization approach, analysis of the highest and best use of the property as improved helps the appraiser determine whether the capital expenditure required to remodel or renovate an existing improvement is cost-effective in terms of its contribution to property value. Feasibility studies of improved properties may also be requested by clients who wish to learn whether a specific remodeling or renovation program is cost-effective.

CONCEPT OF CONSISTENT USE

It is critical that the two analyses of highest and best use not be confused in the course of an appraisal. A site value estimate, which is based on a conclusion of the land's highest and best use as though vacant, may not be added to a value estimate of an improvement based on the highest and best use of the property as improved. The concept of consistent use holds that land cannot be valued on the basis of one use while the improvements are valued on the basis of another.

Consider the appraisal of a residential property located on a commercial artery. The site is currently occupied by a dwelling which is in fairly good condition. Recently the site has been zoned for commercial use, which represents the highest and best use of the site as though vacant. Under a commercial use, the land has a market value of $30,000.

The highest and best use of the property as improved is continued residential use subject to minor repairs. Nearby residential properties that are not attractive to commercial users but are otherwise comparable to the subject property have been selling for approximately $70,000. The site value of these properties is estimated to be $10,000, and the value of the comparable improvements is estimated to be $60,000.

An appraiser would violate the concept of consistent use by adding the $60,000 improvement value to the $30,000 land value to obtain a $90,000 total value indication for the subject property. The $60,000 indication of improvement value, which was derived from an analysis of the sales of comparable improved properties, relies on an estimate based on the highest and best use of the property as improved. The $30,000 indication of site value is an estimate based on the highest and best use of the land as though vacant. The two indications are not compatible, so they may not be added together.

An appraiser could properly determine the value of the subject property by analyzing sales of commercially zoned residential properties located on the commercial artery with similar highest and best uses of the site as though vacant.

THE FOUR TESTS

To test for the highest and best use of a site as though vacant or a property as improved, an appraiser must consider all reasonable alternative uses. The highest and best use must meet four criteria, which are sequential and should be considered in the following order: legal permissibility, physical possibility, financial feasibility, and maximum productivity.

Each contemplated use is first tested to determine whether it is legally permissible. Next, uses that are legally permitted are examined to decide whether they are also physically possible. The appraiser then considers whether the use is financially feasible—i.e., produces a return that is at least greater than the investment. Financial feasibility is irrelevant if the use is legally prohibited or physically impossible. Finally, from among the legally permitted and physically possible uses which are financially feasible, the appraiser selects the one use that is maximally productive. This is the highest and best use of the land or the improved property.

Legally Permissible

Site as though vacant

Each potential use must be tested for legal permissibility. Zoning ordinances, building codes, historic district controls, environmental regulations, and other public and private restrictions can all have an impact on the potential uses of land.

To determine whether a use is legally permissible, an appraiser must consider both present and anticipated zoning restrictions. If there is a reasonable probability that a change in zoning regulations will occur soon, an appraiser may consider a use that is not currently allowed under the existing regulations as the highest and best use. However, the appraiser is obligated to disclose all factors pertinent to this determination, including the time and expense involved in securing the zoning change and the risk that the change may not occur.

Changes in zoning regulations can affect the highest and best use of land in another way. When regulations change, existing improvements may cease to conform to the current law. The current use will be permitted, however, and this use may be more profitable than the use allowed under the new zoning. In this case, the highest and best use of the property would be to maintain the legally nonconforming use of the existing improvements.

Building codes can prevent land from being developed to its highest and best use by imposing burdensome restrictions which increase the cost of construction. This is particularly true in metropolitan areas where different municipalities or jurisdictions have different building codes. Residential development trends in metropolitan areas are greatly influenced by offsite requirements specified in building codes. Less restrictive codes typically result in lower development costs and attract developers to an area, while more restrictive codes discourage development.

Increasing concern over the effects of land use has led to environmental regulations, which also must be considered in highest and best use analysis. Appraisers must consider regulations designed to protect clear air, clean water, wetlands, and historic areas and investigate the public's reaction to proposed projects. Opposition from local residents and community groups has stopped many real estate developments.

Property as improved

Many legal considerations that affect the highest and best use of vacant land affect improved property as well. Major remodeling or renovation usually requires a building permit and must comply with the building codes currently in effect. Many communities use their control over permits, codes, and tax incentives to encourage renovation and discourage unwanted conversions. Legal restrictions can have a substantial effect on the highest and best use of property as improved. Commercial or income-producing uses of residences may be restricted by zoning laws or private agreements.

A trend away from demolition and toward preservation of existing structures became evident in the early 1980s. The preservationist trend has led to historic district zoning controls, which make demolition permits difficult or impossible to obtain in some areas. One effect of these controls has been to decrease significantly the number of instances in which the highest and best use of property is to demolish the existing improvements. Moreover, the special tax incentives that are sometimes available for maintaining older buildings may substantially enhance their value and thus influence their highest and best use.

Physically Possible

Site as though vacant

Location has a substantial effect on highest and best use. Commercial and industrial uses frequently require convenient access to transportation networks and proximity to raw materials, labor pools, consumers, and distributors. Commercial enterprises must be located on thoroughfares or in other places accessible to consumers. Residential uses generally require utility service and the amenities and environment provided by a neighborhood.

Analysis of the community and the neighborhood can provide important clues to how the location of a site affects its highest and best use. Current patterns and anticipated trends must both be considered. Location is studied by investigating linkages, access, and the direction of community growth. An appraiser may ask: How is the site situated with respect to roads and utilities? Will the quality of the schools, social amenities, and the reputation or prestige of the area attract residential users of a given income level? How convenient would the site be for other types of uses? How will the pattern of community growth affect the future potential of the site?

Size, shape, and topography can also affect the highest and best use of a site as though vacant. Agricultural and industrial uses may be precluded by the small size of certain parcels, particularly if nearby land is not available for plottage. An irregular shape or uneven terrain can restrict the range of possible uses for a site and may increase the costs of constructing improvements.

The highest and best use of a site may be to combine it with another parcel for a use that requires a larger area. The land would then have *plottage value.* An appraiser must consider the possibility that all or part of the land will be assembled with other parcels. If the highest and best use conclusion is predicated on the likelihood of an assemblage, this must be clearly stated in the appraisal report. Sometimes a site has *excess land,* which is land that either may accommodate a separate highest and best use or represent surplus land. If this is the case, only part of the site will be used for its primary purpose; the rest may have another highest and best use or may be held for future expansion of the anticipated improvement.

When the topography, subsoil, or topsoil conditions of a site make development dangerous or costly, its value is often adversely affected. In a given area the sites available for a particular use compete with one another. If it will cost more to grade or lay foundations on one site than on more typical sites, the site may not appeal to the same users and might have a different highest and best use. Alternatively, the highest and best use might remain the same, but the site could have a lower value.

Property as improved

Physical and environmental conditions also shape the highest and best use of the property as improved. The size, design, and condition of the improvements limit the range of profitable uses to which the property can be put. For example, additions can usually be made to one-story houses more easily than to two-story houses. The property's ability to accommodate the present use is often relevant to the highest and best use conclusion. Obviously the condition of the existing improvements influences the feasibility and cost-effectiveness of various remodeling projects.

Financially Feasible

After eliminating uses that do not meet the criteria of legal permissibility and physical possibility, the remaining uses must be tested for financial feasibility. A use is financially feasible if the income or value benefits that accrue from the use sufficiently exceed the expenses involved. If the benefits exceed the costs by only a marginal amount, a project may not be feasible. To estimate these benefits and costs, an appraiser must carefully examine the supply of and demand for the use in question.

Site as though vacant

The potential highest and best uses of a site are usually long-term land uses or uses that are expected to remain on the site for the normal economic, or useful, life of the improvements. Most buildings are expected to last at least 25 years, and some may last more than 100 years. A building's value or income usually reflects a carefully considered and highly specific long-term use program.

When the primary benefits of a contemplated use take the form of an income stream and reversion—i.e., the lump-sum benefit the investor receives when the investment is terminated—feasibility calculations are based on an analysis of these benefits. If the income[2] can provide the required rate of return on invested capital, the use is considered financially feasible.

Home owners may base their decisions to buy on the anticipation of tax advantages and property appreciation, but the benefits of owning residential property are usually benefits of occupancy and the reversion. The benefits of occupancy are intangible and cannot be calculated, but the anticipated return from the sale of houses in a proposed residential development can be measured. After an allowance is made for the absorption period—i.e., the time it takes to market the developed units successfully—these benefits must be sufficient to justify all construction and other expenses the developer of the vacant site will incur and provide an entrepreneurial profit. In this case, financial feasibility is determined by analyzing the anticipated increase in value rather than an income stream.

To study the financial feasibility of several contemplated uses, an appraiser must make a separate analysis of the market conditions that exist for each use. This market analysis should include an investigation of demand and supply as well as an estimate of the likely absorption period for the improved site. The five steps in market analysis are listed below.

Demand

1. Estimate units of space needed for new growth.
2. Add units of space needed for relocation.

---

2. First the gross income from the contemplated use is estimated. Then vacancy and collection losses and operating expenses are subtracted from the gross income to obtain the probable net operating income (NOI) before debt service.

Supply

   3. Measure vacant competitive units of space.

   4. Add anticipated competitive units of space being planned or constructed.

Absorption

   5. Consider demand-supply relationship.

First an appraiser identifies the competitive market area for the use contemplated and the effective demand within that market area. Because demand is the more volatile of the forces that create real estate value, it is usually studied first. The amount and type of land needed for a specific use can be estimated in relation to projected population size, employment and income levels, and the availability of mortgage funds.

The supply of competing properties in the market area is then examined. Three kinds of properties may compete with the contemplated use of the subject site: existing competitive properties, competitive properties that are being constructed, and competitive properties that are currently being planned. The locations of competing properties should be carefully analyzed. If there is not sufficient demand for the use, given the current and anticipated supply, the use is not reasonably supported and cannot represent a highly probable, profitable use of the site.

If analysis of the supply-demand relationship reveals that the project can be supported in the market, the appraiser estimates the absorption rate for the completed project, the marketing time, and the probable future income. The advantages and disadvantages of the subject property are compared with those of competitive properties. Estimated absorption rates are correlated with projections of population, employment, and income levels in the market. The reasonableness of the appraiser's estimates may be tested against historical absorption rates and the actual marketing time for comparable properties.

Property as improved

The feasibility of renovation or rehabilitation projects is often more difficult to calculate than the feasibility of construction on vacant sites because costs may be harder to estimate. Renovation estimates may be based on unit-in-place costs for new work plus an allowance for the normally higher costs of repair work. Rehabilitation estimates are frequently based on recent costs for the same or equivalent work on similar properties. Home owners and property managers may keep records that include specific bids for renovation work such as exterior painting, roof repair, or exterior decorating.

The cost of repair work on existing improvements may equal the cost of similar work in new construction, but modernizing and remodeling work is usually more expensive for several reasons. Although the quantity of material used may be the same, more labor is involved in repair and the conditions are different. Altering a structure usually involves tearing out old work and performing smaller tasks under conditions that are not conducive to efficiency. If the contractor's estimate is a flat fee, it may be substantially higher than the cost of identical work in new construction because the contractor seeks protection against complications that may arise as the remodeling progresses. Unforeseen complications may necessitate the replacement of existing conduits, pipes, and structural load-bearing members.

The owner must also pay the architect's fee and the cost of supervision, and lose the use of the house while the work is being done. The financial feasibility of renovation or rehabilitation is determined by analyzing whether the costs incurred will be recovered through a higher anticipated sale price or an increased income stream.

Maximally Productive

Of the financially feasible uses, the use that produces the highest price or value consistent with market expectations for that use is the highest and best use. As mentioned previously, the primary benefits of owning many residential properties consist of the intangible benefit of owner-occupancy and the anticipated reversion. Nevertheless, some measure of maximum productivity is indicated. A single-family residence that represents the highest and best use of a vacant parcel of land must command a price which provides the most profitable return on the developer's capital expenditure. To apply the maximally productive criterion to projected rental units, the project's ability to generate the highest anticipated income stream and reversion are analyzed. To test the maximum productivity of improved properties when renovation or rehabilitation represents the highest and best use, the most cost-effective means of modernization is investigated.

SPECIAL SITUATIONS IN HIGHEST AND BEST USE ANALYSIS

The steps described here constitute the basic procedure for testing highest and best use; they are used in many appraisal situations. However, in certain circumstances it may be difficult to determine highest and best use. Interim uses, single uses, legally nonconforming uses, multiple uses, speculative uses, and excess land represent special situations in highest and best use analysis. Many of these highest and best use problems are found in properties located in transitional neighborhoods.

Interim Uses

Often the highest and best use of a site as though vacant or of property as improved may be expected to change in the foreseeable future. A tract of land may not be ready for development now, but urban growth patterns suggest that it will be suitable for development in several years. Similarly, improved urban property may not be renovated until the demand for renovated units is great enough to justify the expense. In neighborhoods that are in transition, the highest and best use of the site as though vacant or the property as improved for the near future may differ from the long-term highest and best use.

The short-term highest and best use is called an *interim use.* Consideration of the interim use of a property is usually relevant in a neighborhood in transition. If the appraiser determines that an interim use is warranted until the long-term highest and best use can be realized, the appraiser must carefully estimate the duration of the interim use, the financial risks and rewards associated with the conversion to the long-term highest and best use, and the benefits or costs that the interim use will contribute to the value of the site or the improved property.

An interim use can affect the value of a site or an improved property positively or negatively. It may produce marginal benefits or income, but will not contribute nearly as much as the long-term highest and best use. Land that is not yet ready for development is often used for agriculture or parking. These interim uses are viable, but other interim uses may constitute a value penalty. For example, an older rental residence which generates less gross revenue than operating expenses does not make a positive contribution to the property's value.

Single-Use Situations

The highest and best use of a site or improved property is generally consistent with other uses found in the neighborhood. For example, a luxurious residence will not generally represent the highest and best use of a site in a neighborhood of low-priced residences. The concept of conformity suggests the type of improvement best suited to the subject site is usually indicated by the type of improvements found in the neighborhood.

Nevertheless, the highest and best use may be unusual or even unique. There may be a strong demand in the neighborhood for one, but only one, convenience store and the neighborhood may support the necessary spot zoning to allow it. An appraiser must proceed cautiously in such situations. If the site is especially well-suited for the single use, this should be noted. Then the probability that the subject site will be selected for that use must be investigated. The demand for the single use must be compared with the demand for a more typical use because the highest and best use of the site is the most profitable among reasonably probable alternative uses.

Legally Nonconforming Uses

A *legally nonconforming use* is a use that was lawfully established and maintained, but no longer conforms to the regulations of the zone in which it is located. A nonconforming use is usually created by the imposition of zoning or a change in zoning ordinances that occurs after the original construction of the improvements. A legally nonconforming use is a use specifically excluded by the zoning revision.

A change in zoning regulations may make an improvement inadequate for the highest and best use of the site. A single-family residence in an area that has been rezoned for commercial use would no longer represent the highest and best use of the land as though vacant. In this case, the legally nonconforming residential use would probably be maintained as an interim use until the existing improvement has depreciated sufficiently to make conversion to a commercial use feasible.

A zoning change can sometimes create a value premium for an improvement. A reduction in the permitted density or a change in development standards may make a nonconforming use more valuable. A country store, for example, might be located in an area which has been entirely rezoned for a low-density residential use. Local zoning ordinances will permit the existing use to continue, but prohibit any expansion or major alteration of the improvements.

Regulations concerning what may or must be done with a nonconforming use differ. Some jurisdictions require that nonconforming uses be phased out over a period of time. If a nonconforming use is discontinued or terminated because the improvements have been damaged by a storm or fire, reestablishing the use may depend on the degree of damage incurred. Because laws vary among jurisdictions, an appraiser must study the regulations that apply to the subject property and each comparable used in the appraisal.

When a zoning change creates a value premium for a nonconforming improvement, continuation of the use often produces more benefits or income than would be possible if the improvement were new. In many nonconforming use situations, the property value estimate reflects the nonconforming use. Land value is estimated on the basis of the legally permissible use, assuming the land is vacant and its value is deducted from the total property value. The remaining value reflects the contribution of the existing improvements as well as any possible premium for the nonconforming use.

Legally nonconforming uses that correspond to the highest and best use of the property as improved are often easy to recognize. In some situations, however, determining whether an existing nonconforming use is the highest and best use of the site requires careful analysis of the incomes produced or values achieved by the nonconforming property and by alternative uses to which the property could be put if it were made to conform with existing regulations.

Because few comparable sales exist for legally nonconforming properties, application of the sales comparison approach is difficult.

Multiple Uses

Often highest and best use includes more than one use for a site or building. One site can serve many functions. Land used for timber or pasture may also provide space for hunting, recreation, and mineral exploration. Land that serves as a right-of-way for power lines can double as open space or a park and public streets may be used for railroad siding or spur track. Buildings can have multiple uses, too. A single-family, owner-occupied home, for example, may have an apartment or office upstairs.

An appraiser often estimates the contributory value of each use on a multiple-use site or in a multiple-use building. In such an appraisal, the appraiser must make sure that the sum of the values of the separate uses does not exceed the value of the total property.

Speculative Uses

Land that is held primarily for future sale may be regarded as a speculative investment. The purchaser or owner may believe that the value of the land will appreciate, but there may be considerable risk that the expected appreciation will not occur during the period the speculator intends to hold the land. Nevertheless, the current value of the land is a function of its future highest and best use.

In such a case, the appraiser should determine the property's probable future highest and best use. Although the appraiser may not be able to predict the exact future highest and best use, the future type of use can often be forecast by analyzing existing zoning and surrounding land-use patterns. There may be several types of potential highest and best uses—i.e., the land may be suitable for single-family or multifamily residential developments. Appraisers usually cannot identify future highest and best uses specifically, but they can discuss logical alternatives and estimate expected levels of income and expenses.

Excess Land

Many large sites have more than one highest and best use. In some situations the highest and best use of a vacant site or a site considered as though vacant may actually consist of two separate economic units. If the portion of the site allocated to one particular use is improved, complies with the zoning requirements, and is suited to the use of the improvement, the highest and best use of this part of the site would be as improved. The highest and best use of the other, unimproved portion of the site would be for development in conformity with zoning regulations.

In other situations excess land may consist of surplus land. Depending on the location of the improvement(s), the site may not be suitable for two economic units, each with a separate highest and best use. Instead the highest and best use of this excess, or surplus, land may be for the future expansion of the existing improvement(s). This excess land may have a different value than the value of the land occupied by the existing improvement.

Some large sites are not considered to have excess land because the acreage that is not needed for the particular use cannot be used separately. An overly large lot in an area that is 100% built up is not considered to have excess land, nor is a site that cannot be divided because of the location of its improvements.

Highest and Best Use in Transitional Neighborhoods

Some of the most difficult residential assignments are appraisals of properties located in areas that are undergoing transition. Transitional neighborhoods present major problems in highest and best use analysis and in the application of the three approaches to value. Many special highest and best use situations are combined in transitional neighborhoods. It is often difficult to select between alternative highest and best uses in these neighborhoods. Interim uses are common and zoning changes and violations are more likely to occur. Multiple uses and unusual uses also increase in frequency. Appraisers using the same valuation techniques and the same market data may arrive at different opinions when valuing properties in transitional neighborhoods.

Neighborhood and area analyses are especially critical when the use of the subject property may be about to change. An appraiser may ask What factors in the neighborhood or the larger community are causing the transition? Where have the most rapid changes been taking place? Where are changes likely to occur in the future?

The appraiser must carefully identify the different markets which may compete for the use of the subject property. If an adjacent neighborhood is expanding, will it grow to encompass the subject property and the subject neighborhood? How strong is the demand for the new use and how will it be met by the anticipated supply? When will the effects of change be felt most acutely? If the subject neighborhood is declining, how and when will the subject be affected? Do potentially comparable properties offer the same prospects to their purchasers? Will the long-term highest and best use of the improvement be conversion to a more intensive use? If so, when might the change occur and how will the interim use contribute to value? These are the kinds of considerations that must be investigated in appraising transitional properties.

In new neighborhoods conformity to surrounding property uses is generally a reliable indication of the highest and best use of the site as though vacant. In older neighborhoods and in transitional neighborhoods in particular, conformity does not reliably indicate the probable highest and best use of the site.

For example, consider the highest and best use of a site as though vacant in a declining residential neighborhood of large, 70-year-old, two- and three-story houses that sell for $30,000 to $40,000. It would not be feasible to replace these houses with similar new improvements because the costs of constructing a large dwelling would probably greatly exceed its expected selling price. The highest and best use of the site might be to build a smaller house that is more compatible with the incomes of current area residents or to put the site to some alternative use.

In the past when the highest and best use of a property in a transitional neighborhood changed, the logical alternative was to raze the improvements and redevelop the site. However, in light of the current interest in preserving older structures, other alternatives should be investigated. Existing improvements can be remodeled, renovated, restored, rehabilitated, or even relocated in some cases. Tax incentives and local regulations may make one of these alternatives more probable, and more profitable, than demolition.

Zoning changes frequently occur in transitional neighborhoods. When a neighborhood is declining, zoning regulations may not be enforced. As the neighborhood begins to stabilize, new ordinances are often put into effect. In growing neighborhoods there may be strong economic pressures to alter existing zoning ordinances. An appraiser investigates the probability and likely content of zoning changes and estimates their effect on the highest and best use of the site or improved property. These factors should be described in the appraisal report.

Appraisals of properties in transitional neighborhoods are often requested by clients who have specific investment criteria. In these cases it is important to recognize that the purpose of the appraisal is to estimate investment value, not market value. To avoid misunderstandings, the definition of value must be clearly stated by the appraiser and fully understood by the client.

HIGHEST AND BEST USE STATEMENTS IN THE APPRAISAL REPORT

All appraisal reports should contain a summary statement which describes the appraiser's highest and best use conclusions. When the appraisal is performed as part of an analysis assignment to determine highest and best use, the analysis and conclusion of highest and best use are described in considerable detail and probable future incomes or returns are calculated. If the purpose of the appraisal is to reach a market value estimate, the highest and best use section is usually briefer. When an appraisal is communicated by means of a form report, the highest and best use of the property is implicit in the type of form report used—e.g., a condominium appraisal would necessitate the use of a condominium report form. In some transitional neighborhoods, the highest and best use of the site as though vacant may be different from the highest and best use of the property as improved. A form report can still be used, but a detailed narrative analysis of highest and best use must be attached as an addendum.

All narrative appraisal reports must explicitly state the reasoning and supporting evidence that led to the highest and best use conclusion. An extensive discussion may be required in appraisal reports concerned with properties in transitional neighborhoods, sites that show the effect of substantial external obsolecence, or properties that indicate interim use, multiple use, use dependent on assemblage, use contingent on a zoning change, or other unusual uses.

The cost approach to value requires a separate site valuation, so a report on an appraisal in which the cost approach is applied must include statements of the highest and best use of the site as though vacant and of property as improved. When a form report is used for an appraisal that employs the cost approach, it is implicit that the highest and best use of the site as though vacant and the highest and best use of the property as improved are the same.

In a narrative report of a cost approach appraisal, the highest and best use of the site should be reported along with a statement that the estimate was made under the theoretical presumption that the land was vacant and available for development. Then the highest and best use of the property as improved should be reported along with a statement that the estimate was made in consideration of the future potential of the existing improvements and site. If the site is already improved to its highest and best use, the appraiser's report should state this explicitly.

Two examples of highest and best use statements in residential appraisal reports follow. The statement used in any individual report must be tailored to the appraisal problem at hand.

Sample Statement
Highest and best use of land as though vacant

This type of highest and best use is employed to estimate the value of a site separately from the value of any existing improvements. It recognizes that any significant elements of accrued depreciation would not be replicated if the site were vacant and a new building were constructed on the site. It is also helpful in identifying comparable properties.

The existing structure is not the highest and best use of the land as though vacant. If the site were vacant, a single-family residence would be the ideal use. The new house would be architecturally compatible with the larger houses built in the neighborhood over the past 10 years and fall within the value range of the neighborhood. It would contain approximately 2,000 square feet of gross living area and would include three bedrooms and two bathrooms.

Sample Statement
Highest and best use of property as improved

This type of highest and best use recognizes that existing improvements should continue to be used until it becomes financially advantageous to demolish the structure and build a new one or to remodel the existing one.

The existing use of the property as a single-family residence is the highest and best use of the property as improved. Because the neighborhood is stable and has been zoned for single-family residential use only, no other use of the property is contemplated. The improvement conforms to the standards of the neighborhood. The existing structure has been properly maintained and is in good repair. It has an effective age of approximately eight years and a remaining economic life of approximately 50 years. The structure was designed as a single-family residence and no other use would be legally or financially feasible.

SUMMARY

Highest and best use is defined as the reasonably probable and legal use of vacant land or an improved property which is physically possible, appropriately supported, financially feasible, and that results in the highest value. This definition reflects two analyses of highest and best use—of the site as though vacant and of the property as improved. To conduct a highest and best use analysis, the appraiser applies four criteria. The use must be

- legally permissible
- physically possible
- financially feasible
- maximally productive

Highest and best use analysis must be completed before the three valuation approaches are applied. In the cost approach this analysis helps the appraiser estimate land value as well as improvement costs and depreciation. In the sales comparison approach, highest and best use analysis facilitates the selection of comparable properties. For income-producing properties, this analysis helps determine which use will produce the greatest income or yield and whether capital expenditures will be required to renovate or rehabilitate the property. Appraisers should be careful not to violate the concept of consistent use by valuing land on the basis of one use and improvements on the basis of another.

A legally permissible use complies with zoning and building codes, environmental regulations, and other public and private restrictions. A legally nonconforming use is a use that was lawfully established, but no longer conforms because of a subsequent change in zoning regulations.

The physical possibility of a use is tested in relation to the location of the site within a community and neighborhood as well as its plot size, shape, and topography. If the highest and best use of a site is to combine it with another site, the site is said to have plottage value. If there is more than enough area to accommodate a separate highest and best use, or to provide surplus land, the site is said to have excess land.

A use is financially feasible if the income or benefits from the use equal or exceed the expenses involved. Financial feasibility may be investigated by analyzing the existing and anticipated demand for and supply of the use within the market area as well as the projected absorption period and marketing time.

Of the financially feasible uses, the maximally productive use that produces the highest price or value consistent with market expectations for that use is the highest and best use. Maximum productivity is measured in terms of profitable return, income, or cost-effectiveness.

Special circumstances can make it difficult to reach a highest and best use conclusion. An interim use is a temporary use to which a site or improved property is put until it is ready to be put to its highest and best use. A single use situation may exist if there is sufficient demand and a reasonable likelihood of realizing an unusual or unique use. A legally nonconforming use can make an improvement inadequate for the highest and best use of the site or it can create a value premium for the improvement. Multiple uses are compatible uses of land or a building, while speculative use describes land held primarily for future sale. Excess land represents another special highest and best use situation. It may be difficult to analyze highest and best use in transitional neighborhoods. Anticipated zoning changes and external obsolescence can be significant factors.

All narrative reports must explicitly state the reasoning and supporting evidence that led to the highest and best use conclusion. When a highest and best use analysis is performed as part of a feasibility study, a detailed explanation of alternative uses must be provided.

REVIEW QUESTIONS

1. Describe the two analyses of highest and best use made by appraisers.
2. Identify the four criteria for determining highest and best use. What does each criterion specifically test?
3. How are these four criteria applied to the land as though vacant and the property as improved?
4. How is highest and best use analysis used in each of the three approaches to value?
5. Define the following terms: *plottage, excess land, legally non-conforming use, interim use, single use, multiple use,* and *speculative use.*
6. What special problems do transitional neighborhoods present to appraisers analyzing highest and best use?
7. What guidelines should be followed in preparing the statement of highest and best use in an appraisal report?

Part IV

THE COST APPROACH

12 Land or Site Valuation

In many appraisal situations, a separate valuation of the land component of a property is required. When an improved residential property is being appraised, a separate land valuation is needed to complete the cost approach. To arrive at a total property value indication using this approach, the value of the land or site must be added to the depreciated cost of the improvements.

A separate land or site valuation can also provide information significant to the sales comparison approach. An understanding of how much value the land contributes to the total value of the subject property can help an appraiser determine the comparability of other properties. Generally a comparable property should have a land-to-property value ratio that is similar to that of the subject property. If a potential comparable and the subject property have dissimilar land-to-property value ratios, their highest and best uses may differ as well.

Land is valued as though vacant and available for development to its highest and best use. Therefore, the land component of a property must be analyzed and valued separately. A developer needs to know the value of vacant or improved land to decide if a project is feasible. Landowners may want to know the value of their land to establish a sale price or to determine *ground rent*, the rent paid for the right to use and occupy the land according to the terms of a ground lease. Land and improvements are sometimes taxed at different rates, so separate valuations may be needed for tax assessment purposes. Separate land value estimates can be used to segregate the value of the improvements so that the appraiser can estimate insurable value or calculate depreciation for income taxes. Typically these values are found by estimating the total value of the property and subtracting the land value component.

SITE AND LAND

Although the terms *site* and *land* are sometimes used synonymously, these concepts must be differentiated in an appraisal. A parcel of land is a portion of the earth in its natural state; a site is land that has been improved—e.g., cleared, graded, provided with utilities, drainage, and access—to prepare it for its intended use. Consequently, a site often has more value than a parcel of raw land.

It is useful to distinguish between site improvements *to* a site and site improvements *on* a site. Site improvements to a site are improvements such as a clearing that transform a parcel of land into a site. They are included in the value of the site as though vacant. Site improvements on a site are improvements such as landscaping that contribute additional value to the site.

Land value and site value should never be confused in an appraisal. If sales of similar properties are used to estimate site value, the appraiser must make sure that these sales are also of sites, not raw land. If an estimate of raw land value is used in the cost approach, the depreciated value of the improvements, which is added to the value of the land, must reflect the value contribution of clearing, grading, drainage, soil compaction, installation of utilities, and other onsite and offsite improvements that were not included in the land value component. Consistency must be maintained throughout the valuation process.

LAND AS A SOURCE OF VALUE

Land is said to *have* value, while improvements *contribute* to value. Land is seen as the value base on which improvements may be built. Improvements can constitute a penalty on land value when they contribute no value as an interim use and their demolition and removal will cost money. Land cannot depreciate in value, although the value of land may change as a result of external conditions and market forces. Only improvements depreciate in value.

Commodities can be manufactured, but land is provided by nature and its supply is relatively fixed. Major changes in the earth's surface have occurred over the centuries, and the supply and quality of land may be slightly modified in one lifespan. Of course, these natural events rarely affect the land with which appraisers are concerned. There are, however, a few notable exceptions.

Land is affected by accretion or erosion along a shoreline, pollution with harmful wastes such as radon and other toxic materials, inundation by volcanic ash and lava flows, exhaustion by improper farming methods, and ecological imbalances that transform agricultural land into desert. Earthquakes and landslides also change the surface of the earth, and faults beneath the surface can create vast sinkholes. These occurrences are fairly rare.

Because land is fixed in supply and location, its value accrues entirely from its potential to serve a profitable or beneficial use for people. A parcel of land may have utility as the site of a building, recreational facility, agricultural tract, or right-of-way for transportation routes. If land has utility for a specific use and there is demand for that use, the land has value to some category of users. Its value in the market depends on its relative attractiveness to prospective purchasers in comparison with other parcels.

MARKET FORCES THAT INFLUENCE LAND VALUES

The forces that affect land values are closely related to those that affect the values of improved properties. A thorough analysis of the market forces at work in the city, region, and neighborhood should yield much information that is relevant to the land value estimate. All major social, economic, governmental, and environmental value influences should be considered in this analysis.

Trends in land values and the values of improved properties do differ. When the real estate market is expanding, land values may increase more slowly than the values of improved properties, and the first developers may reap unusually large profits. As competition increases and profits are cut, however, the rate of change in the values of land and improved property becomes more similar. When improvements are new, land values tend to equal the values of improved properties once all costs of construction and a normal entrepreneurial profit are deducted. When only a few lots remain in a popular location, the value of a parcel of land sometimes increases beyond the level justified by its profitability. In this case prospective owners or owner-occupants may pay higher land and construction costs than the broader real estate market would seem to warrant. Nevertheless, these occurrences are comparatively rare; on the whole, the market tends toward equilibrium.

LAND VALUATION TECHNIQUES

The technique most commonly applied to value land is the sales comparison approach. If sufficient sales of comparable vacant land are not available, less direct valuation techniques can be employed. These alternative procedures include allocation, extraction, subdivision development analysis, land residual, and ground rent capitalization.[1]

Sales Comparison

Of the various techniques available for estimating land value, none is more persuasive than sales comparison. Sales of similar land parcels or sites are analyzed, compared, and adjusted to derive an indication of value for the land parcel or site being appraised. Adjustments are derived from market data using paired data set analysis or other methods and then the adjusted prices are reconciled into an indication of land or site value.

A full discussion of the sales comparison approach to value is provided in Chapter 16. The steps used in land valuation are summarized below.

1. Collect data on sales of similar land parcels or sites and information on ground leases, listings, and offers.

2. Analyze the data to determine the comparability of these land parcels or sites with the subject land parcel or site. Develop appropriate units of comparison and study each element of comparison.

3. Adjust the sale prices of the comparable land parcels or sites to reflect how they differ from the subject.

---

1. Two of these procedures, land residual and ground rent capitalization, involve the application of capitalization rates. Another procedure, subdivision development analysis, uses discounting. Refer to Chapters 18 through 21 of *The Appraisal of Real Estate*, ninth edition, for a more complete discussion of the concepts and techniques involved.

4. Reconcile these adjusted sale prices into a single value indication or range of value indications for the subject land parcel or site.

Collecting the data

Data on land sales and ground leases are available from electronically transmitted and printed data services, newspapers, records of deeds and assessments, and other sources. Interviews with buyers, sellers, lawyers, brokers, and lenders involved in the transactions can provide more direct information. An appraiser identifies the property rights, legal encumbrances, physical characteristics, and site improvements involved in each potentially comparable sale. Sales with special financing or sales affected by unusual motivation must be regarded with caution. For example, parcels that are purchased for assemblage may not provide good indications of market value.

In addition to recorded sales and signed contracts, an appraiser considers offers to sell, offers to purchase, and other incomplete transactions. Offers are less reliable than signed contracts and recorded sales. A final sale price is usually lower than the initial offer to sell, but higher than the initial offer to buy. Negotiation may take place in several stages. Offers may provide an indication of the limits on value for a subject property or neighborhood, but they are not conclusive and are inadmissible in some courts.

To be comparable, a parcel of land or a site should be in the same market area as the subject—i.e., it should effectively compete with the subject property in the minds of potential purchasers. Comparable transactions should be recent and the parcels of land or sites should be substantially similar to the subject in terms of the elements of comparison described below. Each comparable used in the sales comparison analysis should be inspected and described.

Comparable parcels should have the same or a similar highest and best use as the subject parcel. The subject parcel is considered as though vacant in this analysis, even if improvements are located on it. The highest and best use of the subject and the comparables is determined by carefully studying the supply and demand trends in the neighborhood and the market area. All current, anticipated, and potential development activity should be investigated as part of this analysis.

Analyzing the data for comparability

The data collected on each property and transaction must be analyzed to ensure its comparability and consistency with other data. The units of comparison applied to the market data may include price or rent per acre, per square foot, per front foot, per lot. Other units may be used depending on the specific market; land value may also be expressed in dollars per dwelling unit, per room, or per square foot of gross building area.

Usually an appraiser analyzes a sale using as many units of comparison as possible to determine whether any particular unit or units reveal a consistent pattern in the given market. It is often wise to correlate the results obtained using two or more units of comparison to arrive at a land value estimate—e.g., dollars per acre and per lot or dollars per unit and per square foot. If any inconsistency is observed in the data, the cause should be investigated.

The elements of comparison used to analyze sites or vacant parcels include property rights and limitations on use, financing terms, conditions of sale (motivation), market conditions (time), location, physical characteristics, and other characteristics such as zoning. As a general rule, the greater the dissimilarity between the subject and comparable, the less appropriate the comparable will be for deriving a market value indication. When a comparable requires a large adjustment for any element of comparison, the potential for distortion and error in the analysis usually increases.

Market conditions and location are often the most significant elements of comparison. If sale prices have been changing rapidly over the past several months and adequate data are available, the sale dates of the comparables should be as near as possible to the effective date of the appraisal. If an appraiser must choose between sales of properties close to the subject property that occurred several years ago and recent transactions in more distant locations, a balance must be struck. The more recent sales will probably be most indicative.

Size is typically a less important element of comparison than sale date and location. Most types of development have an optimal site size. Excess land may either accommodate a separate highest and best use or represent surplus land not needed to support the existing improvements. Excess land may be sold separately in the market. Because sales of sites of different sizes may have different prices per unit, appraisers ordinarily try to find comparable properties that are approximately the same size as the subject property.

Zoning is often a basic criterion in the selection and analysis of comparables. Sites that are zoned the same as the subject property are more appropriate comparables. If sufficient sales of sites in the same zoning category are not available, data from sites with similar zoning can be used after adjustments are made.

Adjusting sales prices to reflect differences

After comparable data are collected and comparable properties are inspected, sales data must be assembled in an organized, logical manner. Sales data are commonly recorded on a market data grid that has separate rows for important property characteristics. Adjustments for dissimilarities between the subject parcel and each comparable parcel are made to the sale price of the comparable.

Adjustments for elements of comparison can be derived from market data using paired data set analysis or other techniques. To perform paired data set analysis, the prices of comparable parcels that differ from the subject in only one respect are studied to determine how that one variable affects price. Often an adjustment for market conditions can be derived by studying the trend in sales of comparable properties over the past several years; this technique is known as *patterned analysis*. Scatter diagrams and other analytical tools can be used to study the effects of location and physical characteristics. Regardless of the procedure selected, an appraiser must collect and review sufficient data to make the analysis statistically meaningful. One or two paired data sets is not a broad enough market sample to provide reliable results.

Once an adjustment is derived for a difference, it can be applied to the prices of all comparables that differ from the subject in that characteristic. Adjustments may be applied in dollars or percentages. Adjustments are usually made in a particular order; adjustments for property rights, financing, conditions of sale, and market conditions are applied before adjustments are made for location, physical characteristics, and other differences. All adjustments made to comparables should be set forth in the appraisal report in a logical and understandable manner.

Reconciling the results

To reconcile the value indications derived from sales comparison, each step in the analysis is reviewed. The reliability of each data source and analytical method is considered and the reasons for any differences among the sales data compared are investigated. It is especially important to scrutinize the highest and best use conclusion on which the land value estimate is based. How current are the data that support the use conclusion? Do they seem to conform to the pattern of growth in the neighborhood?

Finally, a single value indication or a range of values is selected from the adjusted sale prices of the comparable parcels. The greatest weight is usually given to the comparable sale or sales that are most similar to the subject. The adjustment process is illustrated in the following valuation.

Sales comparison example

An appraiser is asked to estimate the value of a vacant building lot in the Pine Meadows subdivision. Several vacant lots in the subdivision have been sold recently. Analysis of these sales and others in the market area indicates that values have been increasing by 5% per year and demand for vacant lots has been sustained. The appraiser verifies that each comparable sale occurred with market financing and without unusual motivation. The sales are similar in all characteristics except those noted. Data on the subject property and comparable sales are set forth below.

Subject
    Price   ?
    Size   18,000 sq. ft
    Date of sale   Current
    Site location Near river

Sale 1
    Price $12,640
    Size   16,000 sq. ft
    Date of sale   1 year ago
    Site location On hill

(continued)

Sale 2
   Price $14,425
   Size   19,500 sq. ft.
   Date of sale   1 month ago
   Site location   Near river

Sale 3
   Price $15,400
   Size   22,000 sq. ft.
   Date of sale   1 year ago
   Site location   Near river

The appraiser converts each sale price into a price per square foot and then organizes the sales information on a market data grid.

	Subject	Sale 1	Sale 2	Sale 3
Price	?	$12,640	$14,425	$15,400
Size in sq. ft.	18,000	16,000	19,500	22,000
Price per sq. ft.	?	$0.79	$0.74	$0.70
Time	Current	1 year ago	1 month ago	1 year ago
Location	River	Hill	River	River

Next the appraiser isolates the effect of different elements of comparison and makes the appropriate adjustments. Financing for all the sales is typical, so there is no need for a financing adjustment. The first adjustment will be for market conditions (time). Sales 1 and 3 occurred one year ago. An analysis of the change in market conditions indicates they must be adjusted upward by 5%.

Sale 1: $0.79 × 1.05 = $0.83 (rounded)
Sale 3: $0.70 × 1.05 = $0.74 (rounded)

Then the appraiser derives an adjustment for location. Sale 1 differs from both Sales 2 and 3 in location.

	Subject	Sale 1	Sale 2	Sale 3
Price per sq. ft. (adjusted for market conditions)	?	$0.83	$0.74	$0.74
Location	River	Hill	River	River

The hill location is evidently superior. The difference in location is worth $0.09 per square foot ($0.83 − $0.74 = $0.09). Because Sale 1 is superior to the subject, it must be adjusted downward by $0.09.

	Subject	Sale 1	Sale 2	Sale 3
Price per sq. ft. (adjusted for market condtions and location)	?	$0.74	$0.74	$0.74

Now the results can be reconciled. The appraiser gives special weight to Sale 2, which is similar to the subject in all elements of comparison. A value of $13,320 ($0.74 × 18,000) is indicated as the land value estimate by the sales comparison procedure.

Applicability and limitations

Sales comparison analysis is generally the most reliable way to estimate land value. It is easiest to apply and produces the most persuasive results. However, this procedure cannot be directly employed if sufficient data on recent sales of comparable land parcels or sites are not available. Furthermore, current conditions of supply and demand must be considered or the value indication produced may reflect historical, not actual market values.

Allocation

Allocation may be used when data on recent land sales are insufficient and sales comparison cannot be justified. The allocation procedure is based on the belief that a normal or typical ratio of land value to property value is found in competitive or similar properties in comparable neighborhoods—particularly if these neighborhoods are stable. Three steps are involved in allocation.

1. Identify the typical ratio between land value and improved property value in competitive neighborhoods.
2. Find sales of improved properties in the subject neighborhood that are located on parcels of land comparable to the subject parcel.
3. Apply the allocation ratio to the comparable sales prices and develop a value estimate for the subject parcel.

The procedure is demonstrated in the example that follows.

Allocation example

An appraiser is asked to estimate the value of the last vacant site in a developed residential neighborhood. No vacant land sales have taken place in the past several years, but the appraiser does know the recent sales prices of seven improved properties: $84,000, $84,000, $86,000, $90,000, $90,000, $91,000, and $92,000. By studying land-to-property-value ratios in a similar neighborhood, the appraiser estimates that 18% of a property's sale price should be allocated to the land portion of the property.

Applying this ratio to the sales prices of the improved properties indicates a range of $15,120 to $16,560 for site value.

$$0.18 \times \$84,000 = \$15,120$$
$$0.18 \times \$86,000 = \$15,480$$
$$0.18 \times \$90,000 = \$16,200$$
$$0.18 \times \$91,000 = \$16,380$$
$$0.18 \times \$92,000 = \$16,560$$

The value of the subject site should fall within this range.

Applicability and limitations

Allocation is usually applied to residential projects when data on improved property sales are available, but data on sales of vacant lots are not. In densely developed urban areas vacant land sales may be so rare that values cannot be estimated by direct comparison; similarly, sales of vacant sites may seldom take place in remote rural areas. Allocation usually yields less conclusive results than direct sales comparison, but in some situations it may be the only method available.

The appraiser must make sure that both the improved and unimproved parcels from which data are collected are sufficiently competitive with the subject. The allocation ratio can only be used in a fairly stable market and it is generally most reliable when the improvements are relatively new. As improvements age and depreciate, the ratio between land value and total property value tends to increase. However, depreciation may occur at different rates for different properties. As the years pass, the range of land-to-property value ratios for different properties may become increasingly broad and the ratios become less reliable indicators of total property value. When the requirements for allocation cannot be met, the extraction procedure may be more useful.

Allocation ratios are often cited in tax assessment rolls, which show an assessed value for the land, which is nondepreciable, and a separate assessed value for the depreciable improvements. Tax information can be used as a check on other data, but it is rarely used independently because tax valuations are conducted at infrequent intervals and may not reflect all the considerations that affect market value. Mass appraisal data and information from developers of new residential subdivisions can be used in allocation. Quantitative techniques can be applied to find patterns in these data.

Extraction

Extraction is a variant of the allocation procedure. To value land by allocation an appraiser applies a land-to-property value ratio to the prices of comparable improved properties; to value land with the extraction procedure, the appraiser deducts the contributory value of the improvements from the total sale price of each comparable. The extraction procedure is accomplished in three steps.

1. Find recent sales of comparable improved properties. If necessary, adjust the sales prices for financing, market conditions, and conditions of sale.

2. For each comparable property estimate the cost to replace or reproduce the improvements, including an entrepreneurial profit, and deduct an estimate of accrued depreciation from this estimate of cost new. The remainder is the depreciated value of the improvements.

3. Subtract the depreciated value of the improvements from each adjusted sale price. Then the resulting values are reconciled into a land value indication.

The procedure is demonstrated in the example that follows.

Extraction example

An appraiser is retained to estimate the site value of a vacant lot in a fully developed, older neighborhood. There have been no recent sales of vacant lots, and the allocation procedure yields inconclusive results. However, three improved properties on lots near the subject have been sold recently and these lots are identical to the subject in size.

Property 1 was sold for $97,750. The estimated cost new of the improvement was $100,700, and the appraiser estimates that it is 25% depreciated. Property 2 was sold for $74,000 and the appraiser estimates that the depreciated improvements contribute $54,000 to property value. Property 3 was sold for $109,250. The total cost of the recently built residence, including entrepreneurial profit, was $87,000 and the appraiser believes it has no accrued depreciation.

The appraiser extracts the contribution of the improvements from the price of each sale as shown below.

Property 1

Price of improved comparable		$97,750
Less contribution of improvements		
Cost of improvements	$100,700	
Less depreciation		
25% × $100,700	25,175	
		−75,525
Site value		$22,225

Property 2

Price of improved comparable	$74,000
Less contribution of depreciated improvements	54,000
Site value	$20,000

Property 3

Price of improved comparable	$109,250
Less contribution of new improvements	87,000
Site value	$22,250

The range of site values is $20,000 to $22,250. It is reasonable to conclude that the value of the subject site would fall within this range.

Applicability and limitations

Like allocation, extraction is usually less reliable than direct sales comparison. The results are most conclusive when improvements are new and suffer little depreciation. The extraction procedure can also be used to value land in some older neighborhoods where improvements are fairly heterogeneous. Extraction is frequently used to value land in rural areas because the contributory value of improvements is often small and relatively easy to identify. The extraction procedure can be used to check the results of sales comparison analysis.

When extraction is used to estimate land value, the appraiser must remember to include an entrepreneurial profit in the cost new of the improvements. This profit is fair payment for the developer's expertise and assumption of risk; the developer provides coordination, an agent of production distinct from capital, labor, and land. If an appraiser does not allow for an appropriate amount of entrepreneurial profit in the extraction procedure, the land value estimate will be unreasonably high.

To apply the extraction procedure, an appraiser must fully understand the techniques for estimating costs and depreciation; these techniques are discussed in Chapters 14 and 15.

Land Residual

When income-producing properties are being appraised, the income attributable to the land can sometimes be isolated and capitalized into a land value indication. The land residual procedure represents an application of direct capitalization. It can be used to value land when 1) building value is known or can be accurately estimated, 2) the stabilized, annual net operating income to the property is known or can be estimated, and 3) both building and land capitalization rates can be extracted from the market. The procedure is applied in five steps.

1. Determine what improvements represent the highest and best use of the site.

2. Calculate the stabilized, annual net operating income (NOI) to the property by estimating its market rent and deducting operating expenses.

3. Derive a building capitalization rate and a land capitalization rate from market data.

4. Estimate the income attributable to the building using the following formula:

$$\text{Income}_B = \text{Value}_B \times \text{Rate}_B$$

5. Subtract the income attributable to the building from the property's net operating income. The remainder is the income attributable to the land. Capitalize this amount into a value indication using this formula:

$$\text{Value}_L = \text{Income}_L / \text{Rate}_L$$

The land residual procedure is illustrated in the following example.

Land residual example

A developer is considering the purchase of a site for construction of an apartment building. The appraiser retained to estimate the value of the site determines that a four-unit apartment building is the highest and best use of the site. Investigation of the local market indicates that the property can be expected to produce a net operating income (NOI) of $57,000 per year. The building capitalization extracted from the market is 12% and the land capitalization rate is 10%. The value of a new, four-unit apartment building with no depreciation is estimated to be $350,000.

NOI	$57,000
Less income to the building	
($I_B = V_B \times R_B$) $350,000 \times 0.12$	42,000
Income attributable to the land	$15,000
Land value	
($V_L = I_L / R_L$) $15,000/0.10$	$150,000

In this example, the property is assumed to be free and clear of debt. If the purchase of the land or the construction of the building involved the use of borrowed funds, financing would also be considered.

Applicability and limitations

The land residual procedure can only be applied to a property that produces income. Consequently, this procedure is not often applied to residential properties, which usually are not income-producing. When this procedure is applied to land being developed into an income-producing property, a great deal of data must be collected. To apply the land residual technique, an appraiser must first derive a building capitalization rate and a land capitalization rate from the market, perform a highest and best use analysis complete with anticipated income and expenses, and develop a building cost estimate. Because of its extensive data requirements, the land residual procedure is not practical in many land valuation assignments.

Nevertheless, the land residual technique can serve as a check on sales comparison analysis and it is useful when comparable sales are unavailable. The type of investigation used in land residual analysis is perhaps most applicable when the feasibility of alternative uses of a site are being tested.

Subdivision Development Analysis

When the highest and best use of a tract of land is subdivision and development, subdivision development analysis may be used to estimate land value. Land is subdivided in the normal course of residential real estate development. A land developer divides a large plot into smaller parcels and installs utilities, roads, drainage, and other improvements that are required by law. Sometimes the finished lots are sold to other developers at this point; more often the same developer continues the process by constructing residences on the sites and selling off the finished properties.

The developer calculates the development costs, sales expenses, carrying charges, and a reasonable anticipated profit to derive the net proceeds from the sale of the finished units. By simulating the developer's reasoning, the appraiser can discover what price will most probably be paid for the land.

Subdivision development analysis consists of five steps.

1. Estimate the size and number of the subdivided lots.

2. Estimate the value of the finished lots by sales comparison.

3. Estimate the development costs, the development schedule, the anticipated selling period, and a reasonable entrepreneurial profit.

4. Subtract all development costs and the entrepreneurial profit from the anticipated gross sales price to derive the net proceeds of sale after development is complete and the individual lots have been sold.

5. Select a discount rate that reflects the risk incurred during the anticipated development and selling period. Discount the net sales proceeds over this period to obtain the present value of the raw land.

Estimate the size and number of lots. All relevant physical, legal, and economic factors must be considered in these calculations. Legal limitations are imposed by subdivision and zoning regulations. Projected lots must conform to requirements concerning size, frontage, topography, soil quality, and site improvements such as water facilities, drainage, sewage, and streets and curbs. The physical advantages and disadvantages of the subdivision site cannot be ascertained without a survey and engineering studies, which usually are beyond the scope of the appraisal assignment. However, it is not unusual for such valuations to include an engineering study to support the number of units projected and the feasibility of development. A reasonable estimate of the size and number of lots can sometimes be deduced from zoning and subdivision ordinances, or from the number of lots created in subdivisions with similar zoning. In any case, the size and arrangement of the lots should conform to market standards.

Estimate the value of the finished lots by sales comparison. Once it has been determined that the individual sites in the subdivision will conform to zoning requirements, that no physical constraints will impede the development of the sites, and that the projected sites reflect market standards, the proposed development must be considered in terms of the value of the finished lots. By analyzing appropriate comparables from existing, competitive subdivisions that have recently been developed, an appriaser can obtain an indication of the value of the finished lots.

Estimate the costs, development schedule, selling period, and entrepreneurial profit. All costs associated with the development and sale of the improved lots must be calculated. These include the engineering expenses to clear, grade, and finish the land; to build streets, roads, and sidewalks; and to install utilities. There are also carrying charges for taxes, insurance premiums, and inspection fees and expenses for sales commissions and advertising.

The development and selling period must then be projected. Properties are rarely sold off all at once; some remain on the market for a considerable time. The longer a property stays on the market, the greater the costs and risks to the developer. Market analysis is used to forecast development and selling periods and to establish a proper term for discounting the net sales proceeds.

Next, an appraiser calculates the entrepreneurial profit that will be realized by the developer if the project is successful. This is included among the costs to develop the land. An entrepreneurial profit cannot be guaranteed for every development project. However, when subdivision represents the highest and best use of the land, the appraiser's analysis of supply and demand in the market and the rates of return obtainable for investments with comparable risks should reveal that the development will make a profit.

Subtract development costs and entrepreneurial profit from the anticipated gross sales price. The remaining sum is the net sales proceeds, which represents what the indicated land value would be once the development is complete and all the developed sites are sold.

Select a discount rate that reflects the risks involved in the development project. This rate is applied to discount the net sales proceeds to present value over the anticipated development and selling period. If some of the finished units have to sell at a lower price than anticipated or do not sell at all, the risk of the development will be high and so will the discount rate.

The following example illustrates land valuation with subdivision development analysis.

Subdivision development example

A developer is planning to subdivide an eight-acre tract and develop 20 residential lots. The anticipated gross sales price of the finished lots is $500,000. The following development and absorption costs will be incurred.

Site development costs for grading, clearing, paving, and curbing; sewage and water lines; and design engineering	$150,000
Management and supervision	10,000
Contractor's overhead and profit[2]	50,000
Sales expenses	15,000
Carrying charges (e.g., taxes, insurance)	10,000
Entrepreneurial profit[3]	30,000
Total costs	$265,000

The net sales proceeds of the development may be estimated by deducting its total costs from the anticipated gross sales price of the finished lots ($500,000 − $265,000 = $235,000).[4] The development and selling period is projected to take three years. A discount rate of 10% is selected to reflect the risk incurred during this period. The average, annual net sales proceeds is $78,333 ($235,000/3). This sum is multiplied by the present value of $1 per period factor for three years at 10% to produce an indication of land value.

$$\$78,333 \times 2.4869 = \$194,806, \text{ or } \$194,800$$

Thus the developer can afford to pay $194,800 for the land.

---

2. Contractor's profit is a direct cost and should be distinguished from entrepreneurial profit.

3. Entrepeneurial profit may be estimated differently in different markets. Here it is approximately 7% of all direct costs, indirect costs, and land acquisition costs ($429,800 × 0.07).

4. In some cases it may be necessary to schedule costs and income over a number of years. For example, one-half of the costs might be phased in the first year with the sales beginning in the second year; the other half of the costs might be phased in the third year with sales continuing until all sites have been sold.

Applicability and limitations

Subdivision development analysis is complicated and can only be applied to tracts of land for which the highest and best use is subdivision development. The land value estimate in a typical appraisal need not be based on such detailed analysis. If the appraisal is being performed for a developer who is contemplating a land purchase and interested in the feasibility of subdivision development, the procedure is appropriate. The land value estimates produced with this procedure should always be checked against the prices of other similar parcels of raw land for which subdivision development is the highest and best use.

Ground Rent Capitalization

When the owner of a parcel of land charges ground rent for the right to occupy and use the land, the ground rent capitalization procedure can be used to arrive at the value of the lessor's interest in the land—i.e., the leased fee. Market-derived capitalization rates are used to convert ground rent into value. This procedure is useful when an analysis of comparable sales of leased land indicates a range of rents and capitalization rates. If the current rent corresponds to market rent, the indicated value will be equivalent to the market value of the fee simple interest in the land. If the ground rent paid under the terms of the existing contract does not correspond to market rent, the ground rent must then be adjusted for the difference in property rights to obtain an indication of the market value of the fee simple interest. An alternative method of ground rent capitalization involves discounting the anticipated cash flows (rental income) over the holding period and the reversion or lump-sum benefit received upon termination of the investment.

Applicability and limitations

Ground rent capitalization can be applied when ground rent is being charged for the use of land and the ground rent corresponds to the owner's leased fee interest in the land. This procedure is primarily used in states such as Hawaii, where much residential development is on leased land.[5] It is rarely applicable to residential properties, which are usually occupied by owner-occupants. To apply ground rent capitalization, an appraiser must derive a capitalization rate from the market which reflects the relationship between land sales and land rents. However, if sales are available to support such a derivation, the sales can often be used directly to value the land with sales comparison.

When ground rent is capitalized, differences in lease terms, escalation clauses, and option periods must also be ascertained

---

5. See the discussion of residences on leased land in Chapter 22 and the accompanying footnote.

and accounted for. When the current ground rent does not correspond to market rent, a property rights adjustment to the ground rent is needed to obtain a market value indication of the fee simple interest.

SUMMARY

Land or site valuation is a distinct phase of the valuation process. In appraisals performed to estimate the market value of improved residential property, a land value estimate is needed to complete the cost approach. This estimate can also be used to analyze comparability in the sales comparison approach. In many appraisal situations the land and improvement components of a property must be valued separately. Appraisals for income tax or insurance purposes, for example, may also call for a distinct land or site valuation.

Land refers to unimproved parcels, but a *site* is a parcel that has been improved so that it is ready to be used for a specific purpose. Site improvements *to* a site may also be distinguished from site improvements *on* a site. These terms must be used consistently throughout the valuation process.

The value of land is determined by its potential for a beneficial or profitable use. The market value of land is established by its highest and best use as though vacant. The present owner may or may not be using the site to its highest and best use. The existing improvements may contribute to or penalize the value of the land as though vacant.

A variety of techniques can be used to value land or sites. The most direct and most reliable procedure is the sales comparison approach. Sales of similar, unimproved parcels are analyzed, compared, and adjusted to derive an indication of value for the parcel being appraised. This procedure should be used whenever data on recent comparable sales are available to support the value indication.

To value land by allocation, sales of improved properties are analyzed to establish a typical ratio of land or site value to total value, which may then be applied to the property being appraised. Extraction also involves analysis of improved properties. With this technique, the contribution of the improvements is estimated and deducted from the total sale price of the property to arrive at the price of the land. This procedure is most reliable when the value contribution of the improvements is small and easily identified.

To apply the land residual technique, the highest and best use of the site is determined and the net operating income attributable to the land is capitalized with the land capitalization rate into an indication of land value. This procedure may be used when the highest and best use of the land is an income-producing use and data on building value, the stabilized net operating income to the property, and land and building capitalization rates can be derived from the market.

Subdivision development analysis is used when subdivision and development represent the highest and best use of an undeveloped parcel or tract of land. All development and sales costs as well as an entrepreneurial profit are deducted from the anticipated sales proceeds of the improved sites. The resulting sum is discounted to present value over the anticipated development and selling period to obtain an indication of the market value of the land.

When a parcel of land commands ground rent, its market rent can be capitalized into an indication of the value of the land. The ground rent capitalization procedure is useful when the ground rent of the subject is known and market rent and capitalization rates can be derived from comparable sales of leased land.

REVIEW QUESTIONS

1. Identify some appraisal situations in which a separate land or site value estimate is required.

2. Explain the distinction between a parcel of land and a site.

3. What six procedures can be used for land or site valuation?

4. Outline the basic steps in each land valuation procedure.

5. Discuss the specific applicability and limitations of each land valuation procedure.

6. Which procedure would an appraiser most likely use when

   a. market data are scarce, but the contributory value of the improvements is small and easy to identify?

   b. the land has an income-producing use, and data on market rent and capitalization rates are available?

   c. market data on comparable parcels of vacant land are readily available?

   d. the property has an income-producing use, and market data on building value, the stabilized net operating income to the property, and land and building capitalization rates are available?

   e. the highest and best use of the land is for subdivision and development?

   f. market data are scarce, but typical ratios of land value to property value can be derived for similar properties in comparable neighborhoods?

13 The Cost Approach

The cost approach is one of the three approaches commonly used to estimate property value. The approach is based on the reasoning that a purchaser will not normally pay more for a property than it would cost to purchase comparable land and have improvements of comparable utility constructed on that land without undue delay. To apply the cost approach an appraiser estimates the cost of reproducing or replacing the existing structure with a new building, deducts an appropriate amount for the loss in value caused by accrued depreciation in the existing structure, and then adds the depreciated value of the improvements to an estimate of the value of the land.

The cost approach is applied in five steps. An appraiser

1. Estimates the value of the site as though vacant and available for development to its highest and best use.
2. Estimates all reproduction or replacement costs required to construct the main improvement(s). This estimate includes direct costs, indirect costs, and an entrepreneurial profit, all estimated at current prices.
3. Estimates the amount of accrued depreciation due to physical deterioration, functional obsolescence, and external obsolescence and deducts this amount from the current reproduction or replacement cost of the improvements to obtain the depreciated cost of the improvements.
4. Estimates the current reproduction or replacement cost of any site improvements or accessory buildings and deducts accrued depreciation from these costs.
5. Adds the depreciated value of all improvements to the value of the site to obtain the value of the fee simple interest in the property.

RELATION TO APPRAISAL PRINCIPLES

The cost approach is based on appraisal principles and reflects the thinking of those buyers and sellers in the residential real estate market who relate value to cost. Market participants typically judge the value of an existing structure by considering the prices and rents of comparable, existing buildings. They may also consider the costs of creating a new building with similar physical and functional utility. Therefore, the principle of substitution, which holds that value is indicated by the prices of similar items, suggests that the appraiser should study the costs of new structures as well as the prices of existing structures. Buyers and sellers are most likely to consider building costs when a building is relatively new and offers maximum physical and functional utility. When structures are older or possess less-than-optimal utility, market participants adjust their opinions of value accordingly. Buyers and sellers may also give considerable weight to a value estimate based on cost when the property has unique features and there are few recent sales of similar property for comparison.

The cost of construction affects, and is affected by, the interplay of supply and demand in the marketplace. Even if the cost approach is not emphasized in an appraisal, the trend in construction costs has a significant influence on property value and should be identified. The value of existing properties may increase or decrease depending on the cost of creating competitive properties.

If total development costs rise faster than the prices of improved properties, the prospect of lower profits will reduce the incentive to develop new properties and the supply of new units may contract. The lack of development may push existing property prices upward. Similarly, if construction costs fall faster than the prices of improved properties, new properties will be developed and the prices of existing properties will fall. Changes in development costs may result from shifts in the prices of labor, materials, and land; financing charges; contractor profits; architects fees; and many other factors. Each of these costs is of concern to appraisers.

When improvements are new, their contribution to total property value tends to approximate the cost to construct them. Consequently, cost is frequently related to value when improvements are new. Developers who build overly expensive residences or are careless about costs may quickly suffer losses and be forced to abandon their projects. They leave room for other developers who more judiciously relate the costs of building improvements to the prices sustained by market demand. Often developers who find ways to lower their costs or build where property values are comparatively high are soon joined by a host of competitors. This competition further alters the relationship between costs and property values. The process may take time, but ultimately the market moves toward balance where the direct and indirect costs of a new building approximate the building's contribution to property value.

The cost approach is also based on the principle of balance and the concept of highest and best use. The principle of balance suggests that in a given location there is an optimal combination of the agents of production that creates the greatest value and utility for the property. The combination of land and improvements in the existing property must represent the optimal combination for that location. The optimal combination is the highest and best use of the site as though vacant, so a different use will result in a loss in value.

An existing structure and the site on which it is located may be out of balance in several ways. If a dwelling is an overimprovement, it may contribute value to the property, but not nearly as much value as a similar structure would have on a more appropriate site or a site in a different location. In effect, the building cannot realize its full potential to produce benefits or income on its present site. Conversely, a building that is an underimprovement or suffers depreciation will not contribute as much value as an improvement that represents the highest and best use of the site. In this situation, the full potential of the site is not being realized by the improvement that exists on it. The combination of the site and the improvement is less than optimal.

APPLICABILITY AND LIMITATIONS

Because cost and market value are often most closely related when properties are new, the cost approach is particularly useful in deriving market value indications for new or relatively new construction. The approach is especially persuasive when land value is well-supported and the improvements are new or suffer only minor accrued depreciation, and therefore represent a use that approximates the highest and best use of the land as though vacant.

The approach is widely used to estimate the market value of proposed construction, and properties that are not frequently exchanged in the market. Buyers of these properties often measure the price they will pay for an existing building by the cost to build a replacement minus accrued depreciation or by the cost to purchase an existing improvement and make any necessary modifications. Because comparable sales are not always available to analyze the market value of certain types of properties, current market indications of a building's depreciated cost or the cost to acquire and refurbish an existing building provide the best reflections of market thinking and thus of market value.

A number of factors limit the applicability of the cost approach. When improvements are older or do not represent the highest and best use of the land as though vacant, accrued depreciation is more difficult to estimate. Furthermore, collecting and updating data on construction costs is a time-consuming task; as an alternative an appraiser may rely on cost service manuals, but the data in these manuals do not always produce reliable results. When land sales are few, as in built-up urban areas, the land value estimate required in the cost approach may be difficult to support. Comparable properties may not provide sufficient relevant data or the data from comparables may be too diverse to suggest an appropriate estimate of entrepreneurial profit. Any one of these problems can seriously undermine the persuasiveness of the cost approach. It may be difficult to apply the cost approach to special-purpose residences because the unique features of these properties make it extremely difficult to estimate functional and external obsolescence.

Despite these limitations, the cost approach is an essential valuation tool. It is especially significant when a lack of market activity limits the reliability of the sales comparison approach. When sales data on comparable improved properties are available, the cost approach can be used to test the indication produced by sales comparison. The usefulness of the cost approach as a check on the value indication derived with the sales comparison approach is particularly important because these two approaches may be the only means available to value a single-family residence. The income capitalization approach is rarely applied to single-family residences.

Not only can the cost approach be used as an independent approach to market value, but information derived in the approach can also be applied in the other valuation approaches. For example, cost estimates can be used to support the size of the adjustments calculated in the sales comparison approach. If a feature of the subject property or a comparable property is deficient in comparison with market standards, the cost to cure the deficiency may serve as a basis for calculating the adjustment. Adjustments for special-purpose property features, which incur extensive obsolescence, and for any new accessory buildings or site improvements, which are standard in the market and often contribute value equal to their cost, may be estimated in this way. However, because cost does not necessarily equal value, sales comparison adjustments must be supported with direct market evidence.

Depreciation estimates are made in the cost approach by comparing the existing structure with a newly constructed, duplicate or replacement building. The subject property, as well as the comparables used in the sales comparison approach, generally suffers from various forms of depreciation, but the extent of physical deterioration and functional obsolescence varies among different properties. The adjustments made for property condition in the sales comparison approach should be related to depreciation estimates. To reconcile the value indications derived from the cost and sales comparison approaches, an appraiser often checks the depreciation estimates in the cost approach against the adjustments for property condition derived in the sales comparison approach.

The cost approach requires separate valuations of the land and the improvements, so it may be applied whenever land or the improvements must be valued separately. The segregation of land value from total property value is fundamental to certain methods of land valuation. These methods include the extraction, land residual, and subdivision development procedures. The cost approach may also be used in

- Appraisals performed to estimate insurable value, which usually call for an estimate of the replacement cost of the improvements alone
- Appraisals used as a basis for income tax calculations, which require estimates of building depreciation
- Appraisals used to calculate ad valorem property taxes, which require that property value be allocated to the land and the improvements.

Cost approach techniques can be especially useful when additions or renovations are being considered. The approach provides cost data that are essential to determine feasibility—i.e., whether the cost of the improvement can be recovered through an increase in the property's income stream or anticipated sale price. Cost approach data can help prevent the addition of overimprovements.

Finally, an estimate of probable building and development costs, which is one element of an appraisal based on the cost approach, is also an essential component of feasibility studies that test the assumptions on which investment land-use decisions are based. Financial feasibility is indicated when the market value of a property exceeds its total building and development costs and provides an allowance for entrepreneurial profit and risk.

STEPS IN THE COST APPROACH

Site Value

Usually the value of the site is estimated by sales comparison. Sales of comparable vacant parcels are analyzed and the sales prices are adjusted to reflect differences between the comparable properties and the subject. The results are reconciled into a land value indication. When sufficient data on recent comparable sales are unavailable, allocation, extraction, land residual, subdivision development, or ground rent capitalization procedures can be applied. These methods are described in detail in Chapter 12.

When a land value indication is derived in the cost approach, it is essential that the principle of consistent use be observed. This principle prohibits an appraiser from valuing land on the basis of one use and the improvements on the basis of another. In many residential valuations, the use of both the land and the improvements is obvious. Often the highest and best use of the land as though vacant is the same as the highest and best use of the property as improved. The existing improvements have utility, but suffer depreciation.

Problems can arise when the property being appraised is located in a transitional neighborhood, where it is more difficult to determine the highest and best use of a site. Appraisers must be careful not to base a land value estimate on properties that only appear similar to the subject property or properties that are similar only as improved. The comparable sites on which the value indication is based must have the same highest and best use as the subject property. A careful highest and best use analysis of the subject property and each comparable property is needed to make this determination.

Reproduction or Replacement Costs

Reproduction versus replacement

The terms *reproduction cost* and *replacement cost* are not synonymous. They reflect two different ways of looking at a new structure to be built in place of the existing improvements. Application of the two concepts may produce two different cost estimates. An appraiser must select one of these concepts and use it consistently throughout the cost approach. The use of reproduction or replacement cost also affects how accrued depreciation is estimated.

Reproduction cost is the estimated cost to construct at current prices an exact duplicate, or replica, of the building being appraised using the same materials, construction standards, design, layout, and quality of workmanship, and embodying all the deficiencies, superadequacies, and obsolescence of the subject building. To estimate the reproduction cost of a structure, an appraiser must ascertain the cost to construct a replica of the existing building using the same materials at their current prices. If the improvement contains superadequate features, the cost to reproduce these features is included in the reproduction cost estimate. An appraiser might estimate reproduction cost in valuing historic properties, houses that are more than 30 years old, and newly constructed improvements.

Replacement cost is the estimated cost to construct at current prices a building with utility equivalent to the building being appraised, using modern materials and current standards, design, and layout. To estimate replacement cost, an appraiser calculates the cost to construct an equally desirable, substitute improvement; this improvement will not necessarily be constructed with similar materials or to the same specifications. Because readily available materials would probably be substituted for the outdated or more costly materials used in the existing structure, the appraiser estimates the cost of construction with substitute materials. If the present structure contains a superadequacy such as high ceilings, the costs of producing this extra space in the existing building and all other costs resulting from the excessive ceiling height would be eliminated in the replacement cost estimate.

The use of replacement cost frequently results in a building cost estimate that is considerably lower than an estimate based on reproduction cost. However, fewer deductions are usually made for obsolescence when replacement cost is used. A replacement building has fewer items that are functionally obsolete than a reproduced building, so it suffers less depreciation.

Types of cost

Regardless of whether reproduction or replacement cost is used, three types of costs are involved in the creation of an improvement and each must be reflected in the cost estimate. The three types of cost are direct costs, indirect costs, and entrepreneurial profit.

Direct costs, or hard costs, are expenditures for the labor and materials used in the construction of the improvement(s). Included in this category are expenditures for

- Labor used to construct buildings
- Materials, products, and equipment
- Contractor's profit and overhead, including the cost of job supervision, workers' compensation, fire and liability insurance, and unemployment insurance

- Performance bonds
- Use of equipment
- Security
- Contractor's shack and temporary fencing
- Materials storage facilities
- Power-line installation and utility costs

An appraiser should be familiar with the types of labor and materials used in the subject property or an equivalent replacement property, and with current costs in local construction markets. Direct costs can vary considerably, depending on the quality of the labor and materials involved and on current conditions in the market—i.e., the supply of and demand for contractors' services. Even when the building specifications are the same, there may be a substantial difference between the bids submitted by different contractors. A contractor who is working at full capacity is often inclined to make a high bid, while one who is not so busy may submit a lower figure.

A building contractor's overhead and profit are treated as direct costs and usually included in the construction contract. These costs should not be confused with entrepreneurial profit, or the developer's profit, which is neither a direct nor an indirect cost. If the contractor is also the developer, both types of profit will probably be combined in the building contract; nevertheless, an appraiser must carefully distinguish between the two in cost calculations and in the appraisal report.

Indirect costs, or soft costs, are expenditures for items other than labor and materials such as administrative costs; professional fees; financing costs and interest paid on permanent and construction loans; taxes and insurance during construction; and marketing, sales, or leaseup costs incurred to achieve occupancy or a sale. Indirect, or soft, costs are usually calculated separately from direct costs. They include expenditures for

- Architectural and engineering fees for plans, plan checks, surveys to establish building lines and grades, and environmental and building permits
- Appraisal, consulting, engineering, accounting, and legal fees
- The cost of permanent financing as well as interest on construction loans, interest on land costs, and processing fees or service charges
- Builder's, or developer's, all-risk insurance and ad valorem taxes during construction
- Leaseup, marketing, and sales costs
- Administrative expenses of the developer
- Cost of title changes

Many indirect costs are calculated as a percentage of direct costs. The percentage is converted into a dollar amount and added to the direct costs of materials, labor, and contractor's overhead and profit. Some indirect costs such as professional fees are not related to the size and direct cost of the improvements. These costs are expressed as lump-sum figures and added to the direct costs.

Entrepreneurial profit is a market-derived figure that represents the amount an entrepreneur, who is actually the developer, expects to receive in addition to costs for providing coordination and expertise and assuming risk. Entrepreneurial profit is the difference between the total cost of development and market value. It may be considered a component of *coordination*, the fourth agent of production, which must be paid for along with expenditures for the other three agents of production—land, labor, and capital. Normally a development will not be undertaken without the expectation of a profit.

An appraiser estimates entrepreneurial profit by analyzing development activity in the local market. Entrepreneurial profit may be expressed as a percentage of direct costs, direct and indirect costs, direct and indirect costs plus land value, or the value of the completed project; an appraiser follows the practice of the local market. Entrepreneurial profit is always estimated at the rates prevailing in the market as of the date of the value estimate.

Because the amount of entrepreneurial profit varies considerably depending on economic conditions and the property type, a typical relationship between this cost and other costs may be difficult to establish. An appraiser may survey developers to establish the range of anticipated and actual profit in the market. Although it may be difficult to estimate precisely, entrepreneurial profit is an essential development cost and should, therefore, be recognized in the cost approach.

Methods of estimating cost

To estimate replacement or reproduction cost, an appraiser generally uses one of three methods—the comparative-unit method, the unit-in-place method, or the quantity survey method. To apply the *comparative-unit method*, an appraiser first derives an estimate of the cost per unit of area from the known costs of comparable new structures or from a recognized cost service. These unit costs are adjusted for the physical differences in the subject property and time, or cost-trend, changes and then applied to the dimensions of the subject.

In the *unit-in-place method*, costs for specific, individual construction components such as the cost per linear foot of brick wall or the cost per hour for masonry work are derived from market research or from cost service manuals. These unit-in-place costs are applied to the corresponding components of the subject property and are added together. If the unit-in-place method is applied using extremely detailed units, it approximates the quantity survey method.

The *quantity survey method* most closely simulates the procedure a contractor uses to develop a construction bid. The quantity and quality of all the materials used and all the labor required are estimated, and unit cost figures are applied to these estimates to arrive at a total cost estimate for materials and labor. All three cost-estimating methods are discussed more extensively in Chapter 14.

Accrued Depreciation

The accrued depreciation estimate is a critical element in the cost approach and one of the most difficult to develop. The procedures used to estimate accrued depreciation include sales comparison techniques, the economic age-life method, the modified economic age-life method, and the breakdown method. Chapter 15 covers accrued depreciation in great detail.

Accrued depreciation is the amount by which the replacement or reproduction cost of a new replica structure must be adjusted to reflect the value of the existing structure. There are three main types of accrued depreciation—physical deterioration, functional obsolescence, and external obsolescence. Existing, older structures usually suffer some *physical deterioration.* Normal wear and tear reduces the value of a building over time. Some forms of physical deterioration are economically feasible to cure, while others are *incurable* insofar as it would be impractical or uneconomic to correct them.

Many existing buildings suffer from design problems such as a poor floor plan, inadequate mechanical equipment, or excessively high ceilings. These forms of *functional obsolescence* can also reduce the value of a building. A replacement building may eliminate many forms of functional obsolescence, but it usually cannot eliminate them all. Some forms of functional obsolescence are curable, while others are incurable. Curable forms of functional obsolescence may include deficiencies requiring additions, substitution, or modernization. Deficiencies resulting from superadequacies in structural components or materials are rarely curable.

Finally, an existing structure may be located on land that is inappropriate to this type of development, in which case a further value penalty must be deducted for *external obsolescence.* External obsolescence generally results from conditions outside the property such as a change in land uses, proximity to incompatible land uses, mistaken forecasts of market demand, or a downswing in regional or national economic conditions. External obsolescence is always incurable on the part of the owner, landlord, or tenant.

All three types of accrued depreciation must be carefully estimated, added together, and deducted from the cost new of the improvements to arrive at the depreciated cost of the existing structure.

Site Improvements and Accessory Buildings

Once cost and depreciation figures for the main improvement are calculated, site improvements may be examined. The costs to replace or reproduce a garage, paving, landscaping, accessory buildings, fences and walls, patios, swimming pools, and other site improvements must be estimated along with the amount of depreciation observed in these items. If the land value estimate is based on raw land, an appraiser must also estimate expenses for clearing and grading the site, installing utilities, and preparing the site for development.

Final Value Indication

Normally the last step in the cost approach is accomplished by adding the depreciated costs of the improvements to the value of the land. The depreciated costs of all the structures on the property are combined to obtain the value contribution of the improvements. This sum is then added to the land value estimate to obtain a total property value indication by the cost approach.

This value indication will be the value of the fee simple interest in the subject property. If the property rights being valued represent a different ownership interest, the indicated fee simple value must be adjusted to reflect the interest being appraised.

SUMMARY

The cost approach is supported by many appraisal principles. The principle of substitution affirms that value is indicated by the prices of similar items—i.e., the building costs of new structures and the prices of existing structures. When improvements are new, their contribution to total property value tends to approximate the cost of their construction. Supply and demand in the market affect construction costs and the prices of existing properties. The principle of balance indicates that an optimal combination of the agents of production creates the greatest value and utility. The highest and best use of property identifies the optimal combination of land and improvements in a given location.

The cost approach is most applicable to new properties, properties that have little accrued depreciation, properties proposed for construction or renovation, and properties that are not frequently exchanged in the market. It has limited applicability to older improvements because accrued depreciation is difficult to estimate. The cost approach is inappropriate when land value cannot be supported. The approach is extremely useful in deriving adjustments in the sales comparison approach and can be applied in situations such as appraisals for insurance or tax purposes when separate valuations of land and improvements are required.

An appraiser begins the cost approach by estimating the value of the land as though vacant and available for development to its highest and best use. Next, the reproduction or replacement cost of the main improvements is estimated at current prices. Reproduction cost is the cost required to build an exact replica of the improvement; replacement cost is the expenditure necessary to build a structure with equivalent utility using modern materials and design. A reproduction or replacement cost estimate includes the direct costs of the labor and materials used in construction, indirect costs for items such as administrative, professional, financing, insurance, and marketing fees, and an entrepreneurial profit. This profit is a market-derived figure that represents the amount the entrepreneur, or developer, expects to receive for providing coordination and expertise and assuming investment risk.

All accrued depreciation incurred by the main improvements is then estimated and deducted from the cost new. Accrued depreciation may be broken down into physical deterioration, functional obsolescence, and external obsolescence. Both physical deterioration and functional obsolescence may be curable or incurable. External obsolescence is always incurable. The cost new of all site improvements is estimated and observed depreciation is deducted. Finally, the depreciated value of all the improvements is added to the value of the land to obtain the indicated value of the fee simple interest in the property by the cost approach.

REVIEW QUESTIONS

1. Discuss the applicability and limitations of the cost approach. When is the cost approach especially appropriate?

2. Explain the difference between reproduction cost and replacement cost. Why do cost estimates based on reproduction cost and replacement cost often differ?

3. Define *direct cost, indirect cost,* and *entrepreneurial profit.* Cite examples of direct and indirect costs and explain how entrepreneurial profit is estimated.

4. Describe the basic steps in the cost approach.

5. Identify the various types of accrued depreciation. To what aspect of the property does each type of depreciation apply?

14 Cost-Estimating Methods

Several methods may be used to estimate the costs of an existing or proposed building. The available techniques vary in their complexity, the time and effort required to apply them, and their relevance to the problem at hand. The comparative-unit method, the unit-in-place method, and the quantity survey method are described here.

COMPARATIVE UNIT

The comparative-unit method is the simplest cost-estimating technique and usually the easiest to apply. This is the technique used in most ordinary residential appraisals.

To apply the comparative-unit method, an appraiser estimates the replacement or reproduction cost of the subject building by comparing it with recently constructed, similar buildings for which cost data are available. Unit costs are derived from these buildings and applied to the building dimensions of the subject. Adjustments are made for physical differences and time, or cost-trend changes, if necessary. Indirect costs and entrepreneurial profit may be included in the unit costs or they may be computed separately. Variations exist, but the comparative-unit method typically is applied in seven steps. An appraiser

1. Finds and verifies several sales of recently constructed buildings that are similar to the subject building.

2. Subtracts land value from the sale price of each comparable to obtain the cost new of the improvements. Cost new includes all direct and indirect costs as well as entrepreneurial profit.

3. Adjusts the cost new of the improvements on the comparable properties to reflect how they differ from the subject. Adjustments are made for physical differences such as size, shape, finish, and equipment. In the cost approach, adjustments are based on the cost of the item; in the sales comparison approach, adjustments are based on the item's contributory value.

4. Divides the adjusted cost new of the improvement on each comparable property by the unit area to arrive at the cost per unit of area.

5. Studies the trend in costs between the time the comparable properties were constructed and the date of the appraisal. The unit costs of the comparables are then adjusted to reflect cost differences over time.

6. Relates unit costs to property size and interpolates to arrive at the appropriate cost new. Generally unit costs decline as property size increases.

7. Applies the adjusted unit cost of the comparables to measurements of the subject building to obtain the current reproduction or replacement cost of the main improvement.

The following example illustrates this cost-estimating method.

Comparative-Unit Example

The subject property is a two-story residence built three years ago. The quality of construction is average for similar, mass-produced homes in the area. The house has a concrete block foundation, attractive wood siding, asphalt shingle roofing, ½-in. drywall construction, and a good-to-average finish. It has three bedrooms, two-and-one-half baths, a full basement, and a roof dormer. The house does not have a fireplace. The mechanical equipment consists of combination forced-air heat and air-conditioning, a dishwasher, a garbage disposal, and a built-in microwave oven. The appraiser's measurements show that the structure contains 1,648 square feet of gross living area.

After inspecting comparable properties that were constructed and sold within the past three years, the appraiser decides to place the greatest emphasis on a single, similar property that has features typical of the subject neighborhood.[1] This comparable residence has 1,596 square feet of gross living area and was built and sold three years ago. It is located in the subject neighborhood and is similar to the subject, except that it has a foundation of poured concrete instead of concrete block and brick exterior walls instead of wood siding. This house does not have a roof dormer, but it does have a fireplace.

The sale price of the comparable, including entrepreneurial profit, was $116,000. By means of sales comparison, site value on the date of construction is estimated at $18,000. The appraiser calculates the cost of the comparable dwelling as follows:

Sale price	$116,000
Less site value	18,000
Equals cost of comparable	$98,000

This estimate is consistent with the costs listed in the construction contract and seems reasonable for the area.

Next, through discussions with local contractors and building suppliers, the appraiser derives adjustments for differences between the comparable and the subject. These adjustments are

---

1. This example is only an illustration. Data on the other comparables and the reconciliation of the varying cost estimates are not included.

applied to the cost of the comparable and the adjusted cost is converted into a comparative unit cost. Another adjustment is made to reflect changes in cost over the past three years. Finally, the adjusted unit prices are applied to the dimensions of the subject building. These calculations are shown below.

Cost of comparable structure three years ago	$98,000
Adjustments	
Brick siding	−6,800
Poured concrete foundation	−620
Fireplace	−3,600
Roof dormer	+1,200
Equals adjusted historical cost of comparable	$88,180
Divided by gross living area of comparable	1,596 sq. ft.
Equals adjusted historical unit cost	$55.25
Multiplied by time adjustment for cost-trend changes	119%
Equals adjusted current unit cost	$65.75
Times gross living area of subject (In this market, the difference in size was not significant enough to require a size adjustment)	1,648 sq. ft.
Equals estimate of current subject reproduction cost	$108,356

Using the comparative-unit method, the appraiser estimates the cost of the subject residence to be $108,400.

Sales comparison was used to derive a unit-cost figure in the example, but this figure can also be developed using data from a recognized cost service. Cost service manuals are discussed later in this chapter, but it should be noted that cost manuals usually do not include entrepreneurial profit. A unit cost calculated from cost service data must be adjusted for entrepreneurial profit; this unit cost can then be used to confirm the figures that the appraiser has developed in the local market.

Experienced appraisers recognize that the unit costs of structures typically decrease with size and increase with irregularity in shape. Larger buildings do not necessarily cost proportionately more than smaller ones. Doors and windows can make construction more expensive, but usually the number of doors and windows in any one residence is limited. Plumbing, heating units, and kitchen equipment represent major expenses, but the cost of these items is fairly stable. Equipment costs do not necessarily increase with the size of the building.[2]

Structures that are not designed in the conventional cube shape tend to have higher unit costs. Two buildings with the same area can have different unit costs if one is square and the other is rectangular or irregular in another way. A rectangular structure

---

2. Appraisers should note that the ratio of equipment costs to the cost of the basic building shell has been rising steadily over the years. Additional equipment tends to increase building costs and depreciate more rapidly than the rest of the structure.

is often more expensive to build because more linear feet of wall are needed to enclose it and it may have more windows and doors. Structures with many irregularities often incur higher costs for design, engineering, skilled labor, and additional building materials. Figure 14.1 shows how the shape of a structure can affect its costs.

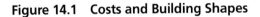

Figure 14.1   Costs and Building Shapes

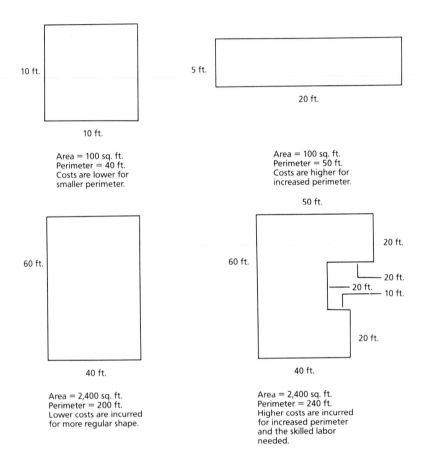

Applicability and Limitations

The apparent simplicity of the comparative-unit method can be misleading. To develop dependable unit-cost figures, an appraiser must carefully compare the subject building with similar or standard structures for which actual costs are known. Inaccuracies may result if the appraiser selects a unit cost that is not appropriate to the building being appraised. Correct application of the comparative-unit method can provide an appraiser with a reasonably accurate estimate of reproduction or replacement cost.

To apply the method correctly, an appraiser must assemble, analyze, and catalog data on actual building costs. Construction contracts for buildings similar to the subject are primary sources of cost data; discussions with local contractors can supplement this information. Many appraisers maintain comprehensive files on the current costs for completed structures. These costs may be classified according to types of residences. Appraisers should also follow cost trends in local and competitive markets so that they can adjust costs for market conditions and location if necessary. Unit costs can be derived from cost service manuals, but costs vary in different markets and a firsthand analysis of the market can often produce data that are more reliable.

UNIT IN PLACE

The unit-in-place, or segregated cost, method allows an appraiser to estimate costs in greater detail. The appraiser derives unit costs for individual structural components and applies them to the components found in the subject property. The unit-in-place method can be applied to all the improvements on the property or separately to the main improvements and any accessory improvements.

The unit-in-place method has six steps. An appraiser

1. Collects data on current direct costs for various building components. Data can be obtained from an analysis of recent construction contracts, surveys of builders and contractors, and recognized cost services. Then information on indirect costs and typical entrepreneurial profit are collected.

2. Measures the components of the subject building, studies plans, and determines the number of units of each component that were required to construct the building. Excavating costs are typically expressed in dollars per cubic yard. Foundation costs may be reported in dollars per linear foot of perimeter or per cubic yard of concrete. Floor construction costs are expressed in dollars per square foot. The basic unit for roofing, called a *square*, represents 100 square feet. Interior partitions may be reduced to dollars per linear foot. Costs for other items such as mechanical equipment are expressed in trade units such as cost per ton of air-conditioning or other selected units.

3. Applies the unit costs for each component to the units of the component found in the subject.

4. Estimates contractor's overhead and profit. If these items are already included in the unit costs, which is often the case, this step is omitted.

5. Estimates any indirect costs not included in the unit costs and adds them to the direct costs.

6. Estimates entrepreneurial profit and adds this amount to the direct costs and indirect costs to arrive at a cost new estimate.

Unit-in-Place Example

Table 14.1 shows unit-in-place costs for a $90,400, one-story ranch house.

Table 14.1 Unit-in-Place Costs

Component	Unit	Quantity	Unit Cost	Cost
General expense for engineering, plans, survey, site	sq. ft./GLA	1,442 sq. ft.	$1.38	$ 2,000*
Foundation	sq. ft./GLA	1,442 sq. ft.	2.22	3,200
Basement	sq. ft./GLA	1,442 sq. ft.	3.32	4,800
Floors	sq. ft./GLA	1,442 sq. ft.	3.60	5,200
Exterior walls & insulation, including windows & exterior doors	lin. ft./wall	1,450 lin. ft.	6.48	9,400
Roof	sq. ft./GLA	1,442 sq. ft.	4.16	6,000
Roof dormers	lin. ft. across face	None		
Interior walls, ceilings, doors, cabinets, trim & accessories	sq. ft./GLA	1,442 sq. ft.	6.52	9,400
Stairways	each	2 outside	400.	800
Attic finish	sq. ft. of fin. area	None		
Heating	sq. ft./GLA	1,442 sq. ft.	2.22	3,200
Cooling		None		
Electrical system	sq. ft./GLA	1,442 sq. ft.	2.78	4,000
Plumbing system	sq. ft./GLA	1,442 sq. ft.	5.54	8,000
Fireplaces & chimneys	each	1 chimney	1,600.	1,600
Built-in appliances	each	2	600.	1,200
Porches	sq. ft./porch	None		
Patios	sq. ft./patio	144 sq. ft.	2.78	400
Other doors & windows	each	22	36.36	800
Site improvements not included in land value	lump sum		1,200.	1,200
Garage	sq. ft./garage	460 sq. ft.	8.70	4,000
Indirect costs	sq. ft./GLA	1,442 sq. ft.	10.27	14,800
Total direct and indirect costs				80,000
Plus entrepreneurial profit @ 13%				10,400
Total reproduction cost				$90,400

*Figures are rounded

Applicability and Limitations

The unit-in-place method breaks down the cost of a building into the costs of its component parts. Such a cost estimate is useful for recording the quality of construction components and computing the cost of their reproduction or replacement. However, assembling the basic costs of the equipment, material, and labor used in the structure and combining these costs into a final cost estimate may require specialized knowledge. When fully developed, the unit-in-place method substitutes for a complete quantity survey and can provide an accurate estimate of reproduction or replacement cost with considerably less effort.

QUANTITY SURVEY

The quantity survey method, which is the most comprehensive method of estimating building costs, simulates how a contractor develops a bid. To complete a quantity survey, an appraiser must prepare a detailed inventory of all the materials and equipment needed to build a house. The cost of each item as of the date of the appraisal is estimated along with the number of labor hours needed to install each item at current rates. Finally, estimates of the contractor's overhead and profit, indirect costs, and the developer's profit are added to the cost of labor and materials.

The quantity survey method is similar to the unit-in-place method, but costs are identified in much greater detail. For example, the kitchen cabinets and plumbing in a structure might be broken down as follows in a quantity survey:

Item	Material			Labor			Total Cost
	Units	Price	Total	Hours	Rate	Total	
Cabinet work: base-finished w/formica top	16	$44	$704	14	$14.60	$204.40	$908.40
Plumbing: 60-gal. hot water heater	1	$590	$590	8	$31.50	$252.00	$842.00

Appraisers often summarize the details of a contractor's or cost estimator's cost breakdown in appraisal reports. The following example presents a building description that might appear in an appraisal report. This description is followed by a summary of a quantity survey that breaks down the costs of various building components. A complete quantity survey would contain more detailed information.

Quantity Survey Example

General Description

This is a one-family, one-story, ranch-style residence with seven rooms (living room, family room, dining room, kitchen, and three bedrooms), two full baths, and a full, unfinished basement. It has a two-car, attached garage but no porches. The gross living area is 1,442 square feet.

General Construction

The house has concrete footings and foundation walls. The exterior walls and roof covering are of cedar shingles. The wood, double-hung windows have combination aluminum storm windows and screens. The gutters and downspouts are aluminum and batt insulation is used. The structure has wood platform framing, plywood subfloors, and oak floors. The kitchen has vinyl flooring and the bathrooms have ceramic tile wainscot.

Mechanical Systems

Plumbing: Copper water pipes and cast-iron waste pipes connected to municipal services in street.
Electric, 60-gal. domestic hot water heater.
One double, stainless steel kitchen sink.
Each bathroom has a standard water closet, lavatory, and tub with a shower.
Laundry tub in basement and washer/dryer hook-up.
Heating: Oil-fired, hot water furnace; two circulators; base-board radiators.
Electrical: 100-ampere service; 16 circuits protected with circuit breakers; BX cable; adequate outlets and features.
Built-in appliances: Gas oven and range with hood and exhaust fan in kitchen.

General Quality

The house is of average quality throughout and meets FHA minimum standards.

Summary of Quantity Survey

Component	Cost
Survey and engineering	$ 400
Plans and plan checking	400
Site preparation	800
Excavation	400
Footings and foundation	3,200
Basement	4,800
Framing	6,000
Interior walls & ceilings	2,800
Exterior siding	2,400
Roof covering & flashing	4,000
Insulation	1,600
Fireplaces & chimneys (no fireplace)	1,600
Leaders & gutters	800
Exterior & interior stairs	800
Doors, windows & shutters	1,600
Storm windows, doors & screens	800
Main floor covering (carpeting)	2,400
Kitchen flooring	400
Bathroom and lavatory floors	400
Hardware	400
Water supply	800
Water disposal	800
Heating	3,200
Cooling (no central air-conditioning)	
Domestic hot water	800
Piping	3,200
Plumbing fixtures	2,400
Kitchen cabinets & counters	2,400
Built-in appliances	1,200
Shower doors	400
Bathroom accessories	400
Vanities, medicine cabinets & counters	400
Electric service	1,600
Electric wires & outlets	1,600
Lighting fixtures	800
Painting & decorating	3,200
Porches (none)	
Patios	400
Finish grading	400
Landscaping	800
Garages & carports	4,000
Clean up	400
Interest, taxes & insurance	800
Contractor's overhead & temporary facilities	3,200
Professional services, permits & licenses	800
Selling expenses & carrying costs	4,000
Contractor's profits	6,000
Direct & indirect costs	$80,000
Plus entrepreneurial profit (10%)	8,000
Total reproduction cost	$88,000

Applicability and Limitations

The quantity survey method is the most comprehensive and precise way to estimate building costs, but it is also the most costly and time-consuming. It provides more detail than is normally required in an appraisal. When a complete building cost breakdown is needed, the services of a trained cost estimator should be obtained.

COST SERVICE MANUALS

Data for estimating the current cost of improvements are published by cost-estimating services such as Marshall and Swift Publication Company; Boeckh Publications, a division of American

Appraisal Associates; and F. W. Dodge Corporation. Computer-assisted cost-estimating services can also provide useful data.

The cost manuals published by these services usually show direct unit costs, but an appraiser must conduct research to find which costs are most applicable to the appraisal problem. Depending on the source of the data, quoted construction costs may include other necessary expenses. Cost manuals almost always include indirect costs such as legal fees; escrow fees; interest on construction loans; financing fees; carrying charges; leasing, sales, and marketing costs; and property taxes. However, discounts or bonuses paid for financing may not be included.

Often the data furnished by national cost services do not include the costs associated with site improvements; these may include the costs of demolishing existing improvements, paving roads, installing storm drains, grading, and compacting soil as well as the fees and assessments for utility hookup. Estimates of entrepreneurial profit are rarely, if ever, provided by cost services. Appraisers estimate these costs separately and add them to the reproduction or replacement costs derived from published cost data.

Benchmark Buildings

The unit costs shown in cost-estimating manuals normally are given for a base, or benchmark, building of a certain size. Additions or deductions are made to these unit costs if the actual area or volume of the subject building differs from the area or volume of the benchmark building. If the subject is larger than the benchmark building, the unit costs will generally be lower. If the subject building is smaller, the unit costs will probably be higher.

Most buildings are somewhat dissimilar in size, design, and quality of construction, so the benchmark building used in the manual is rarely identical to the building being appraised. Variations in roof design, building shape, and types of mechanical equipment can substantially affect unit costs. Some published manuals indicate what adjustments should be made for such differences. Costs for materials and labor are different in different parts of the country; they often vary considerably from one construction market to another. Many cost manuals provide specific city multipliers so that benchmark building costs can be adjusted to reflect these variations. Ultimately, however, the best way for an appraiser to derive costs and cost adjustments is to research the local market.

Cost-Index Trending

Cost services often provide cost indexes, which can be used to translate a known historical cost into a current cost estimate. Cost-index trending is useful when the comparative-unit method is applied to buildings that were constructed several years prior to the appraisal. Base years and regional multipliers are identified in the manuals. Base year construction costs are based on an actual investigation of costs. Construction costs for subsequent years are calculated by multiplying these base year costs by a multiplier, or index. To estimate the current costs of a building constructed several years earlier, an appraiser divides the current cost index by the index as of the date of construction and applies this ratio to the known historical costs. The procedure can be expressed with the following formula:

$$\frac{\text{current cost index}}{\text{index as of construction date}} \times \text{historical cost} = \text{current cost}$$

Certain problems can arise when an appraiser uses cost-index trending to estimate current reproduction or replacement cost. The accuracy of the figures on which the indexes are based cannot always be ascertained, especially when the manual does not indicate which components are included—e.g., only direct costs and some indirect costs. Furthermore, historical costs may not be typical or normal for the time period and the construction methods applied in the base years may differ from those in use on the date of the appraisal. Appraisers who use cost-index trending should recognize that recent costs are more reliable than older costs adjusted with an index. Although cost-index trending may be used to confirm a cost estimate, it is not necessarily an accurate substitute for a firsthand analysis of cost trends.

BUILDING MEASUREMENT

To use a cost service or apply any cost-estimating method, the dimensions of the subject building must be measured. Building measurements are taken during the building inspection. There are many different ways to take measurements, but most appraisers follow the custom observed in their market area. When cost-service data are used, the appraiser should understand the measurement technique used by the service.

The total gross area of a building is measured from its outside dimensions. The building measurements are checked to make sure that the front equals the back, and the left side equals the right. The width is multiplied by the depth. The measurements of projections or cantilevers are added, and the area of insets or recesses are subtracted. The most common measurement applied to houses is *gross living area* (*GLA*), which is defined as the total area of finished, above-grade residential space. Unfinished basement areas and attics are not considered part of gross living area. *Gross building area* (*GBA*) is the sum of the areas of all floor levels, measured from the exterior of the walls. Superstructure floor area and the substructure basement are included in gross building area. In some locations dwellings are measured in terms of the area of ground floor coverage; in others *above-grade living area* (*AGLA*) is the area measured.

SUMMARY

Three methods can be used to estimate building costs. In the comparative-unit method, a dollar cost per unit of area is derived from the known costs of similar structures adjusted for physical differences such as size, shape, finish, and equipment and for time, or cost-trend, changes. The unit-in-place, or segregated cost, method establishes a total building cost by adding together the unit costs of various building components as installed. A complete unit-in-place estimate may be an adequate substitute for a comprehensive quantity survey. To apply the quantity survey method, an appraiser estimates the quantity and quality of all the materials and labor needed to construct the building and applies unit cost figures to arrive at a total cost estimate. This method recreates the procedure a contractor follows to develop a bid.

Cost manuals include direct and sometimes indirect costs, but rarely are the costs of site improvements and entrepreneurial profit considered. A benchmark building provides the base from which costs are estimated in these manuals. Adjustments are usually needed to apply these costs to the subject building. In cost-index trending, base years and multipliers are used to translate historical costs into current costs.

The building measurements taken should be appropriate in the local market. The most common measurement, gross living area (*GLA*), represents the total residential area excluding unfinished basement and attic areas. Gross building area (*GBA*) is the sum of the areas shown on the floor plans, measured from the exterior of the walls. Dwellings may also be measured in terms of ground floor coverage and above-grade living area (*AGLA*).

REVIEW QUESTIONS

1. Describe the three methods of estimating costs. Discuss the applicability and limitations of each.

2. What types of cost information do cost manuals provide? What data may not be included in cost manuals?

3. How can cost indexes be used to estimate the current costs of a building constructed several years ago?

4. Define the following area measurements: *gross living area, gross building area,* and *above-grade living area.*

15 Accrued Depreciation

In the cost approach a property value indication is derived by estimating the cost new of the improvements, which comprises direct costs, indirect costs, and entrepreneurial profit. Accrued depreciation is then subtracted from the cost new estimate, and land value is added to the depreciated cost estimate. Because existing improvements usually contribute less value than their reproduction or replacement cost, an appraiser must often make an adjustment to reflect the loss in value that the existing structure has incurred since its construction. This deduction represents the amount of *accrued depreciation* from which the improvements suffer.

Accrued depreciation is the difference between the reproduction or replacement cost of an improvement and its market value as of the date of the appraisal. Various factors may cause a building to lose value, or depreciate, over time. One common cause is *physical deterioration.* As a building ages, it is subject to wear and tear from regular use and the impact of the elements. Deterioration reduces the value of a building over its life as compared with the cost of a newly built replacement or reproduction. Careful maintenance may slow down this process, and neglect or improper maintenance may accelerate it.

A building may also suffer from *functional obsolescence* due to some flaw in the structure, material, or design that diminishes its function, utility, and value. As the term *obsolescence* suggests, this type of value loss is often caused by the obsolete features of older buildings, including buildings that are still in good repair. For example, older windows that do not provide sufficient insulation may cause functional obsolescence. Even a newly constructed building can have functional obsolescence due to a deficient feature such as a poor floor plan.

To test whether or not functional obsolescence is present, an appraiser decides whether the structure or its design conforms to current market standards. The quality of construction, materials, or design of a building may be inferior to current market standards for the neighborhood. In this case, any savings realized from the lower construction costs will probably result in a disproportionately greater loss in the price obtainable for the property.

If the structure and its design are superior to market standards, the additional utility provided may not justify the additional cost. In either case, functional obsolescence must be deducted from the cost new of the structure to reflect its diminished utility in comparison to market standards.

A building can also suffer from *external obsolescence,* an impairment of its utility or salability due to negative influences outside the property. A change in market conditions at the local or national level is a common cause of external obsolescence. Interest rates that are rising quickly, for example, may cause current construction costs to outpace building values. Similarly, overbuilding in certain markets may create a surplus of space and curb rents and values.

A loss in value also results when a neighborhood changes and an improvement that was formerly well-suited to its location is no longer appropriate. In this situation the site may or may not lose value; it may be more valuable as the site of a more intensive use. Although the existing improvements may be well-designed and well-maintained, if they are not what the market currently demands of that location they cannot contribute value commensurate with their cost.

External or economic changes can restore the appropriateness of the location for the existing improvements. Often, however, land value or entrepreneurial profit increases when such a change occurs, not the value contribution of the building. The contribution of a building to property value rarely rises above its cost. One exception to this general rule might be a residence of historical significance, which contributes more value than the cost of a new structure.

All three causes of accrued depreciation—physical deterioration, functional obsolescence, and external obsolescence—reduce the value of an existing structure in comparison with its reproduction or replacement cost new. An appraiser calculates the amount of accrued depreciation in a structure by applying one of four techniques: the sales comparison, economic age-life, modified economic age-life, and breakdown methods. Accrued depreciation is deducted from the reproduction or replacement cost new of the existing improvements to estimate their contribution to the total value of the property.

ACCRUED DEPRECIATION AND BOOK DEPRECIATION

The term *depreciation* is used in both accounting and appraisal, so it is important to distinguish between the two usages. *Book depreciation* is the amount of capital recapture written off an owner's books. This term is typically used in income tax calculations to identify the amount allowed for the retirement or replacement of an asset under the tax laws. Like accrued depreciation, book depreciation refers to a loss in value that accrues over time and applies only to improvements, never to land. Losses in book depreciation, however, are often measured against book value or original cost rather than current market value. Book depreciation amounts may be estimated to correspond to a depreciation schedule set by the Internal Revenue Service. Thus book depreciation is not market-derived, while accrued depreciation is. The estimate of accrued depreciation in an appraisal may help a client reach a conclusion about book depreciation, but the two concepts are distinct and should not be confused.

AGE AND LIFE OF RESIDENCES

The appraisal concept of accrued depreciation is closely related to economic life, physical life, remaining economic life, actual age, and effective age. Many techniques for estimating accrued depreciation make use of these terms.

Economic life is the period over which improvements to real estate contribute to property value. A building's economic life begins when it is built and ends when the building no longer contributes any value to the property above land value. This period is often shorter than the building's *physical life*, which is the total period the building lasts or is expected to last. If buildings are adequately maintained, they may remain on the land long after they cease to contribute economically to property value. More often, buildings are demolished shortly after the end of their economic lives and replaced with more suitable structures.

To estimate a building's economic life, an appraiser studies the typical economic life expectancy of structures similar to the subject in the market area. In other words, the quality of construction and functional utility of the existing residence are considered in the estimate of economic life. The existing condition of the subject property is reflected in estimates of remaining economic life and effective age.

Although the economic life expectancy of a structure is difficult to predict, it is shaped by a number of factors, including:

- Physical considerations—i.e., the rate at which the physical components of the residence wear out, given the quality of construction, the use of the property, maintenance standards, and the climate of the region.

- Functional considerations—i.e., the rate at which building technology, tastes in architecture, and family size and composition change. These factors can make a residence obsolete.

- External, economic considerations, especially long-term influences such as the stage in the neighborhood's life cycle.

Many of these considerations may become significant 20, 50, or even 100 years in the future, so they are obviously difficult to forecast with any accuracy. Nevertheless, market study and analysis of historical and geographical trends may provide important information.

Remaining economic life is the estimated period over which existing improvements continue to contribute to property value. This concept refers to the economic life that remains in the existing structure. It begins on the date of the appraisal or some other specified date and extends until the end of the building's economic life. A building's remaining economic life is always less than or equal to, never more than, its total economic life.

Actual age, which is sometimes called *historical age* or *chronological age*, is the number of years that have elapsed since building construction was completed. The prices of newly completed buildings are compared with the prices of similar, older structures to establish a correlation between actual age and the value of residences. (See Figure 15.1.)

Effective age is the age indicated by the condition and utility of the structure. Similar buildings do not necessarily depreciate at the same rate. The maintenance standards of owners or occupants can influence the pace of building deterioration. If a building is better maintained than others in the market area, its effective age will be less than its actual age. If a building is poorly maintained, its effective age may be greater. If a building has received typical maintenance, its effective age and actual age may be the same. Effective age is related to remaining economic life. The total economic life of similar structures, minus the effective age of the subject building, equals the remaining economic life of the subject.

METHODS OF ESTIMATING ACCRUED DEPRECIATION

Several methods may be used to estimate accrued depreciation. Each of these methods is acceptable so long as it reflects the manner in which informed, prudent buyers would react to the condition of the structure being appraised and the appraiser ap-

Figure 15.1   Hypothetical Correlation Between Actual Age and Property Value

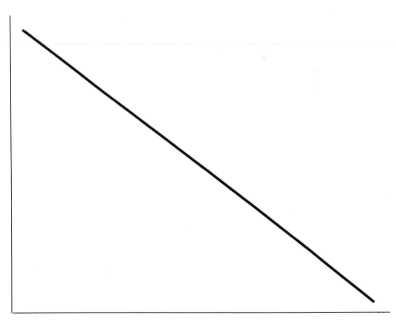

Current price of similar properties (less current land value)

Actual age

plies the method consistently, logically, and cautiously. The methods are summarized and demonstrated in the following sections. Their applicability and limitations are discussed in detail.

The four principal methods for estimating accrued depreciation are the sales comparison method, the economic age-life method, the modified economic age-life method, and the breakdown method. To apply the *sales comparison method,* an appraiser develops a depreciation estimate by studying sales of comparable properties that have depreciated to the same extent as the subject residence. Current land value is subtracted from the price of each comparable to obtain the depreciated value of the improvement. When this figure is subtracted from the reproduction or replacement cost of the comparable, the result is a lump-sum, dollar estimate of accrued depreciation. This dollar amount is converted into a percentage by dividing it by the reproduction or replacement cost. The percentage of lump-sum accrued depreciation is then annualized by dividing it by the actual age or, if there is a significant difference between the acutal age and effective age, by the effective age estimate. Once a range of annual percentages of accrued depreciation is established, the appraiser can apply an approximate rate to the cost of the subject improvement.

In the *economic age-life method,* an appraiser estimates the total economic life of the existing structure as well as its effective age based on an analysis of sales of similar structures. The ratio of effective age to total economic life is considered to represent the extent to which the building has depreciated. This ratio is directly applied to the replacement or reproduction cost of the structure to arrive at a lump-sum depreciation amount, which is then deducted from the cost figure.

The *modified economic age-life method* distinguishes between curable and incurable items of depreciation. An appraiser first estimates the cost to cure all curable items—i.e., items that can be repaired or replaced at a cost that is equal to or less than the amount of value that the item contributes to the total property. This amount is deducted from the replacement or reproduction cost of the structure to arrive at the depreciated replacement or reproduction cost. Then the appraiser estimates the effective age and total economic life of the structure assuming the curable items have been cured, and applies the ratio of effective age to total economic life to the depreciated replacement or reproduction cost. The sum for incurable depreciation is then deducted from the depreciated cost.

The *breakdown method* is a more detailed, expanded variation of the modified economic age-life method. Items of curable physical deterioration and incurable physical deterioration are estimated separately. Accrued depreciation for items of curable functional obsolescence, incurable functional obsolescence, and external obsolescence are also identified separately. The accrued depreciation for each category of depreciation is estimated by a specific method applicable to that form of depreciation. The sum of accrued depreciation for all items is then subtracted from the replacement or reproduction cost new of the structure.

Regardless of the method applied, the appraiser must ensure that the final estimate of accrued depreciation reflects the loss in value from all causes, and that no cause of depreciation has been considered more than once. For example, a residence should not be penalized for a superadequate component that should be removed and for the physical deterioration in that component. Double charges for depreciation may produce overly low value indications in the cost approach. Both the modified economic age-life and breakdown methods provide an estimate of the cost to cure curable items of depreciation, which should be recognized in the application of the other approaches. This estimate should be related to the adjustment for property condition in the sales comparison approach.

Reproduction and Replacement Cost Bases

An appraiser must estimate depreciation using the same basis from which costs were calculated—either reproduction or replacement cost. A reproduction is a virtual replica of the existing structure, employing the same design and similar building materials. A replacement is a structure of comparable utility constructed with the design and materials that are currently used in the building market. A reproduction may contain more items of functional obsolescence than a replacement structure does. These items might include high ceilings, an older floor plan, the lack of adequate electrical outlets and plumbing facilities, and the use of outdated, more expensive building materials and techniques. Obsolete items usually cost more in the current market and do not produce a proportionate increase in utility and value. An amount must be deducted from reproduction cost for these items of functional obsolescence.

The use of replacement cost usually eliminates the need to measure some, but not all, forms of functional obsolescence. Replacement structures usually cost less than reproductions because they are constructed with materials and techniques that are more readily available and less expensive in today's market. Thus a replacement cost figure is usually lower and may provide a better indication of the existing structure's contribution to value. A replacement structure typically does not suffer functional obsolescence resulting from superadequacies, but if functional problems are found in the existing structure, an additional amount must be deducted from the replacement cost. Estimating replacement cost generally simplifies the procedure for measuring accrued depreciation in superadequate construction components. Examples of functional obsolescence might include a structural defect in the existing residence such as an excessively thick foundation or a deficiency such as an inferior floor plan. Both would be corrected in a replacement building.

To avoid errors in measuring accrued depreciation, an appraiser must be consistent and clearly understand the purpose of this step in the cost approach. Accrued depreciation is estimated and deducted to adjust the cost to create a new reproduction or replacement improvement to reflect the value contribution of the existing improvement. Even a newly constructed improvement may not contribute as much value as it costs. Although it has no physical deterioration, a reproduction or replacement structure may suffer from external obsolescence and functional obsolescence. Any feature that creates a loss in value from the cost standard must be accounted for as an item of accrued depreciation.

Sales Comparison Method

If a large amount of sales data are available to support the appraiser's conclusion, sales comparison is often a reliable procedure for estimating accrued depreciation. There are seven steps in the sales comparison method. An appraiser

1. Finds and verifies at least two sales of similar improved properties that have approximately the same amount of accrued depreciation as the subject property.
2. Subtracts the land value from the sale price of each comparable property to obtain the depreciated cost of the improvements.
3. Estimates the cost new of the improvements on each comparable property.
4. Subtracts the depreciated cost of each improvement from the cost new of the improvement to obtain a lump-sum estimate of accrued depreciation in dollars.
5. Converts the dollar estimates of accrued depreciation into percentages by dividing each accrued depreciation estimate by the cost new.
6. Annualizes the percentages of lump-sum accrued depreciation by dividing each total percentage of accrued depreciation by the actual age estimate or, if there is a significant difference between the actual age and the effective age, by the effective age estimate.
7. Considers the range of annual percentage rates derived and applies an approximate accrued depreciation rate to the cost of the subject improvement.

The sales comparison method is demonstrated in the following example.

Sales comparison example

The subject property is a 12-year-old, frame structure with an effective age of 12 years. Typical neighborhood residences of equal quality normally have economic life expectancies of 55 years; this estimated economic life is supported throughout the area. The subject property contains 1,496 square feet of gross living area and is situated on a site that is valued at $26,000. The cost new of this residence is $43.85 per square foot of gross living area.

The appraiser has found three sales of neighborhood properties similar to the subject property. Property 1 was sold recently for $92,500. The appraiser estimates that the site is worth $22,000, and the reproduction cost new of the improvement is $96,750.

The property's actual age, which is 15 years, corresponds to its effective age.

Property 2 was sold recently for $98,500. The appraiser estimates that the site is worth $20,000, and the reproduction cost new of the improvement is $92,000. The property's actual age is 8 years, which is the same as its effective age.

Property 3 was sold recently for $113,500. The appraiser estimates the site is worth $25,000, and the reproduction cost new of the improvement is $138,750. The property's actual age, which is equal to its effective age, is 20 years.

To estimate the average annual rate of depreciation in the subject property, the appraiser compares the three sales.

	Property 1	Property 2	Property 3
Sale price	$92,500	$98,500	$113,500
Less site value	22,000	20,000	25,000
Depreciated cost of improvements	$70,500	$78,500	$ 88,500
Cost new	$96,750	$92,000	$138,750
Less depreciated cost of improvements	70,500	78,500	88,500
Lump-sum dollar depreciation	$26,250	$13,500	$ 50,250
Percentage depreciation (Lump-sum dollar depreciation divided by cost new)	27.13%	14.67%	36.22%
Average annual depreciation rate (Lump-sum percentage depreciation divided by effective age)	27.13/15 1.81%	14.67/8 1.83%	36.22/20 1.81%

With these figures the value of the subject property is estimated as follows:

Reproduction cost new	
1,496 sq. ft. @ $43.85	$65,600
Less depreciation	
10 years @ 1.8% × $65,600	11,808
Depreciated cost of improvements	$53,792
Plus site value	26,000
Total property value indication	$79,792, or $79,800

Applicability and limitations

When sales data are plentiful, sales comparison usually provides a reliable estimate of accrued depreciation. However, the properties compared must be very similar to the subject, and the amounts and types of depreciation from which they suffer must be fairly uniform. When the properties compared differ in design, quality or construction, it is difficult to ascertain whether differences in value are attributable to these differences or to a difference in accrued depreciation. The method is also difficult to apply when the type or extent of depreciation varies greatly among properties. If the sales analyzed were affected by special financing or unusual motivation, the problem is further complicated. The accuracy of the method depends heavily on the accuracy of the land value and cost-new estimates of the comparable properties.

If the sales are located in districts or neighborhoods that are not comparable, the method may not be appropriate. All types of depreciation are considered in a lump sum in the sales comparison method, and cannot be broken down into various types.

The sales comparison method has very stringent market data requirements. Methods that employ age-life estimates allow the appraiser to rely on data from buildings with considerably more or less depreciation than the subject. Thus a broader pattern of depreciation may be established, considering both the rate at which depreciation occurs in similar buildings and the period over which it occurs. Within this pattern the accrued depreciation in the subject property may then be found. The sales comparison method makes use of a static analysis rather than a patterned analysis, so it requires more comparable market data. Depreciation is forced into a straight line, which may not be the typical pattern for the market.

In spite of these limitations, sales comparison provides extremely reliable and convincing results and may be used to check the results obtained by applying other methods. Many appraisers use this method to measure accrued depreciation in single-family residences.

Economic Age-Life Method

The economic age-life method identifies the rate at which buildings similar to the subject depreciate and uses this rate along with the effective age of the subject to derive an estimate of accrued depreciation. Although it is not always as accurate as other techniques, the economic age-life method is the simplest way to estimate accrued depreciation. The method is applied in three steps. An appraiser

1. Conducts research to identify the total economic life of similar structures in the market area, and estimates the effective age of the subject building. (The effective age may be the same as the actual age if the building has received typical maintenance.)

2. Divides the effective age of the subject by the anticipated total economic life of similar structures. When this ratio is applied to the cost new of the subject, the result is a lump-sum estimate of accrued depreciation.

3. Subtracts the estimate of accrued depreciation from the cost new to arrive at the improvement's contribution to property value.

The example that follows illustrates the economic age-life method.

Economic age-life example

The subject property is located in a neighborhood that was developed during a land boom 20 years ago. Most of the properties nearby are similar to the subject in size and architectural style. These buildings appear to be maintained adequately and the appraiser estimates the typical economic life is 75 years. The subject has been especially well maintained, however, and the appraiser concludes that it has an effective age of only eight years. The replacement cost is estimated at $74,000 and land value is estimated at $12,900.

The appraiser estimates accrued depreciation with the following calculations:

$$\text{Depreciation ratio} = \frac{8 \text{ years (effective age)}}{75 \text{ years (total economic life)}}$$

$$= 0.107, \text{ or } 10.7\%$$

10.7% × $74,000 (replacement cost) = $7,918
Estimated accrued depreciation   = $7,900 (rounded)

Replacement cost	$74,000
Less accrued depreciation	7,900
Value contribution of the improvement	$66,100
Plus land value	12,900
Total property value indication	$79,000

Applicability and limitations

Although the economic age-life method is usually the simplest way to estimate accrued depreciation, it has certain limitations. First, because the percentage of depreciation is represented by the ratio of effective age to total economic life, this method assumes that every building depreciates on a straight-line basis over the course of its economic life. In other words, a residence that has twice the effective age is presumed to suffer from twice as much accrued depreciation. Thus the method is flawed because depreciation does not always occur on a straight-line basis. In some markets buildings tend to depreciate more rapidly as they approach the end of their economic lives. In other markets a different pattern may be observed. The straight-line pattern of depreciation is only an approximation, although it is usually a sufficiently accurate one.

Second, the economic age-life method does not divide accrued depreciation into subcategories such as curable or incurable physical deterioration, curable or incurable functional obsolescence, and external obsolescence. Like the sales comparison method, the age-life method does not distinguish these different kinds of value loss. Therefore, the method may not recognize differences in depreciation among residences as well as other methods which categorize different types of depreciation. In neighborhoods where residences suffer different types and amounts of accrued depreciation, the economic age-life method may be difficult to justify.

The economic age-life method does not recognize the difference between short-lived and long-lived items of physical deterioration. In other methods short-lived items are identified as those that are not expected to last for the remaining economic life of the rest of the structure. Examples of short-lived items include the roof cover and painting. Long-lived items are items such as structural components which will last at least as long as the remaining economic life of the structure. Because a single figure is used to reflect depreciation in the structure as a whole, varying amounts of depreciation in short-lived items are not directly reflected in the economic age-life ratio. For example, a building as a whole may be estimated to be 20% depreciated except for the roof which, unlike other roofs in the neighborhood, is estimated to be 90% depreciated. In this situation the breakdown method would allow an appraiser to make a more refined analysis.

Finally, the denominator in the economic age-life ratio—the total economic life of typical, similar structures—refers to a future period of time which may be difficult or impossible to measure. Any forecast of future events calls for judgment, so the estimates of effective age and economic life may be difficult to justify.

To minimize this problem, economic life estimates should be based on objective data as much as possible. Useful information can be obtained from historical studies of the actual lives of similar structures and by asking lenders, brokers, buyers, and sellers how much longer they anticipate neighborhood structures similar to the subject will be economically useful. Because depreciation is assumed to occur on a straight-line basis, a market-derived estimate of economic life can be obtained by identifying the annual rate of depreciation for similar structures and dividing this figure into 100%. The formula is

$$\text{Economic life} = \frac{100\%}{\text{annual \% depreciation}}$$

Market-derived information can help support the depreciation estimates used in the economic age-life method.

The economic age-life method can be used to derive depreciation estimates in a broad range of situations. This method is widely used in appraisals of single-family residences.

Modified Economic Age-Life Method

The modified economic age-life method provides greater accuracy by dividing accrued depreciation into curable and incurable components. A form of accrued depreciation is curable if, as of the date of the appraisal, the cost to cure the defect is equal to or less than the value that would be added by doing so. Otherwise, it is incurable. When an item is considered incurable it does not mean that the problem cannot physically be solved. It only means that it cannot be solved economically—i.e., the cure is simply not worth its cost.

The modified economic age-life method is applied in five steps. An appraiser

1. Estimates the cost to cure all items of curable depreciation.

2. Deducts the cost to cure these items from the cost new.

3. Estimates the effective age and remaining economic life of the structure *as cured*. Curing a major item can sometimes decrease the effective age of the building, prolong its remaining economic life, or both.

4. Applies the ratio between the adjusted effective age and the total economic life of the structure to the remainder of the cost new to obtain the amount of incurable depreciation found in the building.

5. Deducts the incurable depreciation from the remainder of the cost new.

The modified economic age-life method is demonstrated below.

Modified economic age-life example

A house with a current reproduction cost new of $100,000 had a total economic life expectancy of 60 years when it was built 18 years ago. The appraiser estimates that it now has an effective age of 15 years and a 45-year remaining economic life expectancy. Total curable physical deterioration and functional obsolescence in the structure amounts to $15,000. By curing these items, the effective age could be reduced to 5 years and the remaining economic life expectancy could be extended to 55 years.

To estimate lump-sum accrued depreciation using the modified economic age-life method, the appraiser performs these calculations.

Reproduction cost new		$100,000
Less physical and		
functional curable items		15,000
Depreciated reproduction cost		$ 85,000
Depreciated cost basis		
Total economic life	60 years	
Remaining economic life	55 years	
Effective age	5 years	
Ratio applied to cost		
less physical and functional		
curable items	5/60 = 8.33%	
Less incurable items $85,000 × 0.0833 =		$ 7,081
Total depreciated value of improvements		$ 77,919, or $77,900

Applicability and limitations

In the modified economic age-life method, curable items of depreciation are cured at the outset, before estimating the incurable depreciation. This is helpful for a number of reasons. Most importantly, this procedure closely approximates the reasoning of an informed buyer contemplating a purchase. A buyer frequently wants to know how much the residence will be worth after all problems that can be economically cured have been attended to. Most astute purchasers do not simply consider the property in its present, depreciated state; they are concerned with its potential after repairs have been made. The modified economic age-life method addresses these concerns, which are not considered in the simpler economic age-life method.

Furthermore, by curing the structure the appraiser brings it in line with existing market standards as far as possible. If the addition or repair of an item is so in demand that the market is prepared to award a value increase equal to or greater than its cost, the feature added or repaired usually conforms to neighborhood standards. For the appraiser, this procedure can enhance accuracy in three ways.

First, the amount of depreciation to be deducted for curable items can usually be established with some certainty. Typically it is simply the current cost to cure the defect. Once a defect is identified as curable, the amount to be deducted for it is known. Second, when curable items are cured the proportion of the estimate that depends on the judgmental economic age-life technique is smaller. The age-life ratio is applied only to items of incurable depreciation, so the potential for error is decreased. Third, when a building is cured of curable defects, incurable defects can usually be assessed more accurately. A partially cured building conforms more closely to market standards, so there may be more similar structures from which to derive an appropriate estimate of effective age and remaining economic life.

The modified economic age-life method, like the simpler unmodified method, does not divide incurable depreciation into physical, functional, and external subcategories or distinguish between short-lived and long-lived items. It assumes depreciation in incurable items occurs on a straight-line basis. Moreover, the estimates of effective age and remaining economic life still require judgment on the part of the appraiser. However, because these problems influence the incurable portion of the accrued depreciation estimate only, their effects are more limited.

Breakdown Method

The breakdown method is the most comprehensive and detailed way to measure accrued depreciation. Although this method is rarely used to estimate depreciation in single-family residences, the procedure should be understood because it provides the conceptual basis for the less-detailed methods described previously. Its techniques must be understood to determine the breakdown of accrued depreciation, which is necessary in most residential form reports. The five steps in the breakdown method are outlined below. An appraiser

1. Estimates curable physical deterioration, which is measured by the cost to cure.

2. Estimates all incurable physical deterioration, beginning with deteriorated short-lived items. The physical age-life method may be employed to measure the deterioration of short-lived items. The ratio of actual age to estimated total physical life is applied to the cost new of each short-lived item.

   Next the deterioration of long-lived items is estimated. The physical age-life method may be employed to measure the deterioration of long-lived items. The ratio of actual age to total physical life is applied to the cost new of all long-lived items.

   The estimates of curable and incurable physical deterioration in short-lived and long-lived items are added to arrive at the subtotal for physical deterioration.

3. Estimates all curable functional obsolescence in the form of

   a. curable deficiencies requiring additions, which are measured as the excess cost of the addition over the cost if the item were installed new at the time of construction;

b. curable deficiencies requiring substitution or modernization, which are measured as the cost of installing the modern fixture minus the physically depreciated value of the existing fixture or component; and

c. curable superadequacies, which are measured as the current cost of the item minus the physical deterioration already charged plus the cost to replace the superadequate item with a standard item.

Different estimates will result depending on whether replacement or reproduction cost is used.

4. Estimates all incurable functional obsolescence including

a. incurable deficiencies, which may be measured with paired data set analysis. If the property is income-producing, incurable functional deficiencies may also be measured by capitalizing the rent loss—i.e., multiplying the rent loss by the gross rent multiplier. The procedure is the same whether reproduction or replacement cost is used.

b. incurable superadequacies, which may be measured as the current cost of the superadequate item minus the current cost of the standard item minus the physical deterioration already charged. Because replacement cost does not include the cost of a superadequacy, this form of obsolescence usually applies only to reproduction cost estimates.

The estimates of curable and incurable functional obsolescence are added to arrive at the subtotal for functional obsolescence.

5. Estimates external obsolescence using paired data set analysis or, if the property is income-producing, income capitalization techniques. External obsolescence in income-producing property can be measured as the capitalized rent loss allocated between the improvement and the land. Only the proportion imputed to the improvement reflects the estimate of external obsolescence.

The subtotals for physical deterioration, functional obsolescence, and external obsolescence are added. The sum of all forms of accrued depreciation is then deducted from the reproduction or replacement cost.

In applying the breakdown method, some appraisers find it more appropriate to estimate all curable physical and functional items of accrued depreciation first, and then estimate all incurable physical, functional, and external items. Incurable items generally cannot be measured properly until all curable items have been measured. The steps outlined above and the discussion that follows reflect the traditional treatment of these items in appraisal reports, including the Uniform Residential Appraisal Report form.

Curable physical deterioration

The first step in the breakdown method is to estimate items of curable physical deterioration. Cosmetic repairs, touch-up painting, carpentry, plumbing, and electrical repairs fall into this category. REALTORS® have long recognized that most minor repairs add value that equals or exceeds their cost, so they encourage home owners to make these repairs before a house is offered for sale.

Items of curable physical deterioration are items in need of repair on the date of the appraisal. The amount of accrued depreciation to be deducted for these items is simply the cost to cure them. Often an appraisal client will request that these curable items be listed in the appraisal report along with an estimate of the cost to cure. In addition to items of curable physical deterioration, the appraiser may find evidence of damage. If severe enough, damage becomes curable physical deterioration and is treated accordingly. The measure of damage is the cost to cure. The significance of damage is that the life of the component that is damaged is not renewed or increased by the repair.

Cost-to-cure estimates should be based on actual contractors' bids or on the amounts indicated in contracts for similar work in recently completed properties. National cost services provide less reliable estimates of the cost of repair and maintenance work because the cost for such work usually depends on the specific problems found in the house.

Various types of accrued depreciation are calculated using the breakdown method in the examples that follow. The results of these calculations are summarized in a total estimate of accrued depreciation, which is the final example in the chapter.

Breakdown example: Curable physical deterioration

During a house inspection, an appraiser notes the need to repair the interior painting at a cost of $900 and the interior floor finish at a cost of $800. Curable physical deterioration is estimated as the total cost to cure these items.

Interior painting	$900
Plus interior floor finish	800
Total curable physical deterioration	$1,700

Incurable physical deterioration

Once curable physical deterioration has been deducted, the appraiser can estimate and deduct incurable physical deterioration. By distinguishing between curable and incurable items an appraiser can provide a more accurate estimate of depreciation which reflects the thinking of potential home buyers.

Items of incurable physical deterioration are divided into incurable short-lived and incurable long-lived items. The depreciation in long-lived items is often deducted in a lump sum. Depreciation in short-lived components is more variable and therefore must be estimated first. Short-lived building components typically include items such as the roof cover, gutters and downspouts, kitchen cabinets and counters, and exterior painting.

If direct market data are available, depreciation estimates for a component can be derived using sales comparison. If market data are not available, the physical age-life method can be used to estimate incurable short-lived physical deterioration.

In the physical age-life method, the typical physical life of a building component is estimated assuming a normal degree of maintenance. The actual age of the component is also established. The actual age divided by the physical life of the component is considered to represent the extent to which the component has physically deteriorated. This method assumes that physical deterioration occurs at a constant annual rate. The deterioration ratio derived is then applied to the cost of replacing each short-lived item as of the date of the appraisal.

Appraisers disagree about how to classify short-lived items that are only partially worn. Many believe that if there are still useful years left in an item, it cannot be economically repaired or replaced as of the date of the appraisal and must be classified as incurable. Others argue that partially worn short-lived items are curable, even if it is not economically practical to do so as of the date of the appraisal. They believe that market participants apply the term *incurable* only to defects that cause a permanent loss in building value. Both positions have merit and the classification does not matter so long as the appraiser estimates depreciation consistently and accounts for each item once and only once.

The incurable deterioration in short-lived items is calculated separately for each item, but deterioration in long-lived items is often based on a single estimate of the age and life of all items. Once again the physical age-life ratio can be used as the basis of the estimate. However, this ratio can only be applied after depreciation has been charged for curable and incurable physical deterioration in short-lived items.

Breakdown example: Incurable physical deterioration—short-lived items

An appraiser inspects a residence and notes that the exterior painting, which was done three years ago and generally lasts for seven years, would currently cost $7,000. The appraiser also estimates that the hot water heater, which is two years old and generally lasts for 12 years, would cost $600 to replace, including installation.

The incurable physical deterioration in these short-lived items is estimated as follows:

Item	Cost New	Actual Effective Age	Total Physical Life	Physical Age-Life Ratio	Incurable Physical Deterioration
Exterior painting	$7,000	3 yrs.	7 yrs.	3/7 (42.86%)	$3,000
Hot water heater	$600	2 yrs.	12 yrs.	2/12 (16.67%)	$ 100
Total physical deterioration in short-lived items					$3,100

Breakdown example: Incurable physical deterioration—long-lived items

An appraiser estimates the cost new of a residence to be $90,000. The cost to cure curable physical deterioration ($1,700) plus the cost to replace short-lived items of incurable physical deterioration ($7,600) equals $9,300. The actual age of the structure is 15 years and its total physical life expectancy is 75 years.

The incurable physical deterioration in the long-lived items is estimated with the following calculations:

Cost new	$90,000
Less total cost to cure curable physical items and to replace incurable physical short-lived items	9,300
Cost new of long-lived items	$80,700
Ratio of actual age to total physical life (15/75) =	× 0.20
Total incurable physical deterioration in long-lived items	$16,140

Curable functional obsolescence

Once the cost to cure all curable physical deterioration and the amount of incurable physical deterioration have been calculated, curable functional obsolescence can be estimated. Functional obsolescence may be evident in the original design of the residence or changes in market standards may have made some aspect of the structure, its design, or its component parts obsolete.

When functional obsolescence takes the form of a *deficiency requiring additions*, a component that is currently desired in the market such as an additional bath or powder room is not present in the existing structure. Expenditures for the addition would not be included in the reproduction or replacement cost. The deficiency might be curable, but an additional cost is required to bring the building up to market standards. Reproduction or replacement cost plus the cost of the addition is almost always greater than the cost of the building if it had conformed to market standards when it was constructed. Depreciation must be deducted for the extra expenditures the owner of the subject building must now incur. Curable functional obsolescence is measured as the difference between the cost of adding the component now, when the structure is complete, and the cost if the component had been included in the original structure.

Breakdown example: Curable functional obsolescence—deficiency requiring additions

The residence being appraised has no water closet on the first floor, which is standard in the market for this type of property. A water closet can be installed for $1,800, but it would have cost only $1,200 if it had been installed originally. The incurable functional obsolescence due to this deficiency is measured as the amount by which the cost of the addition exceeds the cost of the item installed new during construction.

Cost to install water closet in existing structure	$1,800
Less cost to install water closet during construction	1,200
Loss in value	$ 600

Another type of functional obsolescence that is sometimes curable is a *deficiency requiring substitution or modernization.* In this case, the component intended to satisfy market demand does exist and is represented in the reproduction or replacement cost, but it is inadequate or outmoded. Plumbing fixtures that need replacing, inadequate electrical service, and an insufficient hot water system are examples of deficiencies requiring substitution or modernization. The depreciation in such items is measured as the cost of the modern component plus installation minus the physically depreciated value of the existing component. To avoid charging for an item twice when curable functional obsolescence is deducted, the appraiser should make sure that no physical deterioration is charged for an item that is to be removed or replaced.

Breakdown example: Curable functional obsolescence— deficiency requiring substitution or modernization

A residence is being remodeled and outmoded plumbing fixtures are to be replaced with more modern ones. The current cost new of the old plumbing fixtures is $1,500, and the appraiser estimates that the existing fixtures are 90% depreciated. The current cost of installing modern fixtures is $2,500.

The curable functional obsolescence due to this type of depreciation is calculated as follows:

Cost of modern fixtures plus installation	$2,500
Less remaining value of existing fixtures (10% × $1,500)	150
Loss in value	$2,350

Superadequacies are structural components of a higher quality and cost than are required under current market standards. A superadequacy is a form of functional obsolescence that is rarely curable in single-family residences. There is usually nothing to be gained by diminishing the quality or capacity of the component— e.g., removing unnecessarily elaborate wainscotting—even though the item may contribute less value than its reproduction cost. Thus most superadequacies must be treated as items of incurable functional obsolescence in the breakdown method. However, if the superadequate component is not desired, the costs of removing it must be considered. For example, if a house has an unnecessary heating unit in the basement, it may pay to remove it and refinish the additional space. In this case, the curable depreciation to be deducted for the superadequacy would be the cost to remove the heating unit and refinish the space minus any physical deterioration already charged for the item.

Breakdown example: Curable functional obsolescence—superadequacy

The recreation room in a single-family residence is to be refurbished. A large, overhead lighting fixture will be replaced with track lighting. The cost new of the fixture is $250, the depreciation charged for physical deterioration of the item is $50, and the cost to remove the fixture and replace it with track lighting is $150.

To estimate the curable functional obsolescence caused by the superadequacy, the appraiser makes the following calculations:

Cost new of the overhead lighting fixture	$250
Less physical deterioration already charged	50
Plus cost to remove fixture and install track lighting	150
Total curable functional obsolescence	$350

Incurable functional obsolescence

There are two kinds of functional obsolescence that may be incurable in a residence. Any deficiency in the existing structure, such as a poor interior floor plan which cannot be economically cured, represents a form of functional obsolescence that must be deducted from the remainder of the reproduction or replacement cost. There are a number of ways to estimate the value loss due to such a deficiency. If the building generates a rental income, the appraiser may capitalize the income loss attributable to the deficiency. In this case, the income loss is multiplied by a gross rent multiplier to arrive at a lump-sum amount of depreciation. Alternatively, the appraiser can compare the prices of comparables that vary only in the presence or absence of the deficiency in question.

Breakdown example: Incurable functional obsolescence—deficiency

A large mansion was converted into a three-family residence several years ago. At the time of conversion, it could have been developed into a four-family dwelling, which represents the current highest and best use of the site. It is not economically feasible to make this change now. The appraiser estimates that the additional unit could have generated $200 per month in gross rental income. The current *GRM* is 48.

In this case, the appraiser estimates the incurable functional obsolescence due to this deficiency by capitalizing the rent loss.

$$\$200 \text{ per month} \times 48 = \$9,600.$$

A second form of incurable functional obsolescence is due to a superadequacy. The number of superadequacies found in a building tends to increase as the building ages. Building materials and techniques become outdated and owners often install superadequate features suited to their individual tastes. Superadequacies are treated differently depending on whether reproduction or replacement cost is used as the basis of the cost estimate.

If reproduction cost is used, the reproduced building, like the subject, will contain items that are superadequate by current market standards. The cost of the superadequate item minus the cost of an item considered adequate in the current market minus any physical deterioration already charged for the item equals the amount that must be deducted for the superadequacy. The appraiser should review the estimates of curable and incurable physical deterioration to see whether charges were included for superadequate items.

When the cost estimate is based on replacement cost, the replacement building usually will contain no superadequacies. The replacement building will have approximately the same utility as the existing building, but its cost reflects what the market is willing to pay for its utility without any excesses. No amount need be deducted for superadequacies because in a replacement building the cost of a component will not exceed its current utility and value.

Buildings that contain superadequacies may incur additional expenses for taxes, insurance, maintenance, and utilities. If these charges are not offset by a corresponding increase in value, they may represent a further value penalty which must be deducted from the reproduction or replacement cost estimate.

Breakdown example: Incurable functional obsolescence—superadequacy

A single-family residence in a very competitive market was equipped with a whirlpool bath in a misguided attempt to lure buyers. No other houses in the area have whirlpool baths. It currently costs $600 to install a regular bathtub and $900 to install a whirlpool. The whirlpool bath is physically 15% depreciated. The appraiser concludes that it is not economically feasible to replace the whirlpool bath and no additional ownership costs are associated with the superadequate item.

To estimate the incurable functional obsolescence due to this superadequacy, the appraiser makes the following calculations.

Cost of whirlpool tub	$900
Less cost of regular bathtub	600
Difference	$300
Less physical deterioration ($300 × 0.15)	45
Total incurable functional obsolescence	$255

External obsolescence

The last form of accrued depreciation to be deducted is external obsolescence. External obsolescence is a loss in value due to negative influences outside the property. It is usually incurable, but it is not always permanent. A home owner or landlord cannot cure an environmental problem such as a deteriorating neighborhood or an economic recession that creates a sluggish market.

External obsolescence results in a loss in the value contribution of the *improvement;* it does not lessen the value of the land. It may be caused by neighborhood decline, changes in market conditions, or the property's location near an airport, railroad, landfill, or commercial district. When market data are studied to estimate external obsolescence, it is important to isolate the effects of changes in land value from the effects of changes in the value of improvements. A building-to-property-value ratio may be used to allocate the value loss imputable to the building.

In appraisals of single-family residences, external obsolescence is usually estimated by sales comparison. Sales of properties that are subject to the negative external influence are compared with sales of properties that are not. Not only must the effects of land value differences be isolated, but the effects of differences in the physical deterioration and functional obsolescence of the comparable structures must also be studied. Many of the problems that limit the usefulness of the sales comparison method in estimating total depreciation create difficulties in this portion of the breakdown method as well.

Breakdown example: External obsolescence estimated with paired data set analysis

A single-family residence located on a noisy street is being appraised. The appraiser finds two very similar comparable properties that were recently sold; one is adjacent to the subject and the other is farther away from the noisy street. The adjacent property was sold for $89,000, while the other comparable was sold for $92,000. Using paired data set analysis, the appraiser estimates external obsolescence as follows:

$$\$92,000 - \$89,000 = \$3,000$$

When a property produces income, the rent loss caused by the external obsolescence can be capitalized into a loss in total property value. Then the amount of loss attributable to the improvement can be isolated from the loss attributable to the land. The procedure is applied in three steps. An appraiser

1. Compares the gross rents of similar properties that are subject to the same negative influence and others that are not. For purposes of this analysis, the properties are considered to be cured of all other problems.
2. Capitalizes the difference in rent—i.e., multiplies it by the gross rent multiplier—to obtain the value loss affecting the property as a whole.
3. Applies the building-to-property-value ratio typical of the area to the total loss in property value to isolate the value loss imputable to the improvement.

The building-to-property-value ratio is derived from a study of land values and property values in the area. When external influences are affecting property values and the neighborhood is in transition, the appraiser must make sure that the isolated land values reflect the highest and best use of the land for residential purposes, not for some other use. Land near a growing commercial district may remain stable or increase in value while residences situated on this land decrease in value.

Breakdown example: External obsolescence estimated by capitalization of rent loss

An income-producing residential property located on a noisy street is being appraised. The appraiser estimates a rent loss of $50 per month for the property due to the noise from the street. From a study of comparable properties, the appraiser derives a gross rent multiplier of 60 and a building-to-property-value ratio of 4:5. External obsolescence is calculated as follows:

Monthly rent loss	$50
GRM	× 60
Total loss in property value	$3,000
Building-to-property-value ratio	× 0.80
Total loss in improvement value	$2,400

After all items of physical deterioration, functional obsolescence, and external obsolescence have been estimated, a total estimate of accrued depreciation can be calculated. Although it is implausible that all the forms of depreciation described in the preceding examples would be present in one residential property, for purposes of illustration the estimates derived are combined in the following calculation of total accrued depreciation. (The estimate of the incurable functional obsolescence in the converted mansion and the estimate of external obsolescence derived through paired data set analysis are not included in the total estimate of accrued depreciation.)

Breakdown example: Total estimate of accrued depreciation

Physical deterioration		
Curable	$ 1,700	
Incurable, short-lived items	3,100	
Incurable, long-lived items	16,140	
Total		$20,940
Functional obsolescence		
Curable ($600 + $2,350 + $350)	$ 3,300	
Incurable ($255)	255	
Total		$3,555
External obsolescence		$2,400
Total accrued depreciation		$26,895

Total accrued depreciation is deducted from the cost new of the improvements to derive the depreciated value of the improvements. This value is added to land value to provide an indication of total property value by the cost approach.

Combined Methods

Different methods of estimating accrued depreciation can be combined to solve specific problems, or the results of one can be used to test the results of another. For example, if external obsolescence cannot be accurately determined through paired data set analysis or capitalization of an income loss, a lump-sum indication of total depreciation can be derived through sales comparison. Then an indication of depreciation from all causes other than external obsolescence can be derived with the breakdown method and this figure can be subtracted from the estimate of total depreciation to derive an estimate of external obsolescence. Sales comparison can also be used to derive or verify an estimate of the annual overall rate of depreciation, which is the basis of the economic life estimate (economic life = 100%/annual % rate of depreciation). The overall percentage of depreciation in each comparable is obtained by dividing its sale price minus the current land value of the comparable by its cost new. This overall percentage is divided by the actual age of the comparable or, if there is a significant difference between the actual age and the effective age, by the effective age, to estimate the annual percentage of depreciation.

SUMMARY

Accrued depreciation is the difference between the reproduction or replacement cost of an improvement and its market value as of the date of the appraisal. An improvement can suffer from three forms of accrued depreciation: physical deterioration caused by wear and tear as the building ages, functional obsolescence resulting from a structural or design flaw, and external obsolescence brought about by external factors such as changes in the neighborhood or economy. Accrued depreciation should not be confused with book depreciation, which is the amount of capital recapture written off an owner's books.

Many techniques for estimating accrued depreciation make use of the concepts of economic life, physical life, remaining economic life, actual age, and effective age. Economic life is the period over which improvements to real estate contribute to property value. The economic life of a building may be shorter than its physical life, which is the total period the building lasts or is expected to last. Remaining economic life is the estimated period over which existing improvements will continue to contribute to property value. Actual age, which is also called *historical* or *chronological age*, is the number of years that have elapsed since building construction was completed. Effective age is the age indicated by the condition and utility of the structure.

There are four methods for estimating accrued depreciation: the sales comparison, economic age-life, modified economic age-life, and breakdown methods. Either reproduction cost or replacement cost may serve as the basis for the cost new estimate, but the appraiser must consistently use one or the other. The principal difference between the two is that the use of replacement cost generally eliminates the need to measure certain forms of functional obsolescence.

To apply the sales comparison method, an appraiser first studies sales of comparable properties that have suffered the same amount of depreciation as the subject property. Current land value is subtracted from the sale price of each comparable to obtain the depreciated value of the improvement, which is subtracted from the cost new of that comparable. This lump-sum depreciation figure is then divided by the cost new, and the resulting percentage of depreciation is annualized by dividing it by the actual age or, if there is a significant difference between the actual age and the effective age, by the estimated effective age of the improvement. Once a range of annual percentage rates has been established, an approximate rate can be selected and applied to the subject. The sales comparison method can only be used to estimate accrued depreciation when data on extremely similar comparable properties are available.

In the economic age-life method, an appraiser estimates the total economic life and the effective age of the existing structure. The ratio of effective age to total economic life is then applied to the cost new of the improvement to obtain a lump-sum depreciation estimate, which is deducted from cost new. The economic age-life method assumes depreciation occurs on a straight-line basis. It does not divide depreciation into subcategories or distinguish between short-lived and long-lived building components. Estimates of total economic life require expert judgment.

In the modified economic age-life method, the appraiser estimates the cost to cure all curable items and deducts this amount from the cost new. Then the effective age and total economic life of the improvement are estimated and the ratio between the two is applied to the cost new to obtain the accrued depreciation estimate, which is deducted from the cost new. The advantage of this method is that the appraiser estimates curable items of depreciation separately, which enhances the accuracy of the estimate of incurable depreciation.

To apply the breakdown method, an appraiser analyzes all categories and subcategories of depreciation in detail. Separate estimates are made of curable and incurable physical deterioration in short-lived items and long-lived items; curable functional obsolescence due to a deficiency requiring addition, substitution, or modernization or a superadequacy; incurable functional obsolescence due to a deficiency or superadequacy; and external obsolescence, which is always incurable.

Specific procedures are applied to estimate each of these items. When the breakdown method is used, the appraiser must be very careful not to count any item of depreciation more than once.

The various methods for estimating accrued depreciation may be combined or used to test one another.

REVIEW QUESTIONS

1. Describe the characteristics of each of the following categories of accrued depreciation: physical deterioration, functional obsolescence, and external obsolescence.

2. Define the following terms: *economic life, remaining economic life, actual age,* and *effective age.* What ratio is used in the economic age-life and modified economic age-life methods?

3. Explain the difference between reproduction cost and replacement cost. How does the use of replacement cost affect a depreciation estimate?

4. How does an appraiser determine whether an item of physical depreciation or functional obsolescence is curable or incurable?

5. Describe the applicability and limitations of each of the following methods of estimating accrued depreciation: sales comparison, economic age-life, and modified economic age-life.

6. Discuss the procedures for estimating each of the following forms of accrued depreciation in the breakdown method:

   a. Curable physical deterioration
   b. Incurable physical deterioration in short-lived items
   c. Incurable physical deterioration in long-lived items
   d. Curable functional obsolescence—deficiency requiring addition
   e. Curable functional obsolescence—deficiency requiring substitution or modernization
   f. Curable functional obsolescence—superadequacy
   g. Incurable functional obsolescence—deficiency
   h. Incurable functional obsolescence—superadequacy
   i. External obsolescence

PART V

THE SALES COMPARISON APPROACH

16 The Sales Comparison Approach

The sales comparison approach is generally the most direct and reliable approach in many appraisal situations. Five basic steps are involved in the sales comparison approach. An appraiser

1. Finds recent sales, listings, and offers for properties that are comparable to the subject property.
2. Verifies that the data obtained are accurate.
3. Selects relevant units of comparison to analyze each sale.
4. Compares the subject property and the comparables using elements of comparison and adjusts the sales prices of the comparables to reflect how they differ from the subject.
5. Reconciles the various value indications derived into a single value indication or a range of values.

This chapter examines the strengths and limitations of the sales comparison approach, the importance of comparability, and the techniques employed to identify and select comparable properties. The elements of comparison used to isolate property differences are also discussed. Chapter 17 covers mortgages and financing adjustments and Chapter 18 focuses on how the sales comparison approach is applied and how the various value indications obtained in the approach are reconciled.

STRENGTHS OF THE APPROACH

The sales comparison approach is a powerful tool which appraisers apply in many situations with a variety of quantitative techniques. The approach derives its usefulness and analytic power from several factors. The sales comparison approach is a direct application of the principle of substitution. It is simple, makes use of observable market data, and has wide applicability.

The principle of substitution holds that when similar or commensurate objects or commodities are available for sale, the one with the lowest price will attract the greatest demand and the widest distribution. The price at which an item will most likely sell in a market is closely related to the prices at which similar items in the same market are selling. The sales comparison approach is firmly based on this principle. Properties similar to the subject are found and the sales prices of these properties are adjusted to account for differences between the comparables and the subject. These adjusted sales prices serve as the basis for a value estimate.

By applying the principle of substitution an appraiser simulates the comparisons which most informed buyers and sellers make to decide on a transaction price. The sales comparison approach is representative of the reasoning that shapes value in the market.

The sales comparison approach is generally easy to apply. A simple method based on reliable data and sound reasoning often results in extremely reliable conclusions. Furthermore, clients find the approach persuasive because the reasoning is easy to follow.

In the sales comparison approach, an appraiser focuses on the property characteristics that make a difference in the market. From the market an appraiser obtains quantifiable data which indicate the differences in price caused by differences in building features, site size, location, and other property characteristics. Adjustments for differences are based directly on the observed preferences of market participants. When objective market data are analyzed and presented in an appraisal report, they are often compelling.

The market data on which sales comparisons are based lend themselves to various types of quantitative analysis. Paired data set analysis, scatter diagrams, and other analytical tools can be used to isolate the effect of specific variables on market prices. Statistical sampling can be used in the selection of comparables. By selecting some comparables that may be slightly superior to the subject and others that may be slightly inferior, an appraiser can develop a good sense of the value range for the subject property. Tabulated or graphed historical data on sales of similar property can be used to recognize trends and discern changes in the market.

All three valuation approaches make use of sales comparison to some degree. The cost approach requires that land value be estimated separately, and this is often accomplished by analyzing the prices of comparable vacant land or land considered as though vacant. The cost of buildings and accrued depreciation may also be estimated by sales comparison. In the income capitalization approach, the rent that the subject property is likely to produce is estimated by analyzing the rents of comparable properties. Thus sales comparison techniques have broad application in the valuation process.

LIMITATIONS OF THE APPROACH

The sales comparison approach has some important limitations. A conclusion derived from comparable sales is only as reliable as the data which support it. If the only recent sales are of properties that differ substantially from the subject, the prices of these comparables will be subject to major adjustments and the reliability of the conclusion may be questionable. Properties with unique or special features often cannot be valued with sales comparison analysis. When the approach is applied in markets with few recent sales, the appraiser must proceed with extreme caution and pay careful attention to all factors that could affect current market conditions. The results of sales comparison reflect historical, rather than current, market conditions because market changes that have occurred since the sale dates of the comparables are not always readily discernible.

COMPARABLES AS COMPETITIVE PROPERTIES

For valuation purposes a property used as a comparable must be competitive with the subject property. Each potential comparable should be similar to the subject in important features and be located in the same market area. Properties that are markedly different from the subject property and similar properties that are far removed do not appeal to the same market population. The sales prices of such properties are of little use to the appraiser. The market forces that have shaped these prices may have little in common with the forces that shape the value of the subject.

What features must be similar for properties to be considered comparable? Individual features are important if the market population regards them as significant. Property characteristics established during the neighborhood analysis are used as a basis for the elements of comparison. An appraiser learns about the significance of property characteristics by observing variations and correlations in the sales prices of properties with different locations, sizes, designs, taxes, and other characteristics. Further insights can be gained by identifying the income levels, ages, and family sizes of prospective buyers. A careful highest and best use study can help identify which elements of comparison are important in the market.

There is also no set rule as to how far a property may be from the subject property and still remain competitive with it. The size of market areas can vary considerably depending on the size of the city, the distances that residents commute, the transportation available, and the property type. If there are many similar houses or neighborhoods which purchasers regard as more or less equal, the market area can be quite extensive. In other situations a market area may be quite small. It is best to select comparable properties from the immediate neighborhood of the subject. If sales data are not available, sales from the broader neighborhood may be acceptable. Sometimes appraisers need to search for sales in other competitive neighborhoods as well.

RESEARCH AND SELECTION OF COMPARABLE SALES

Researching and selecting comparable properties is accomplished in five steps. An appraiser

1. Researches and identifies potentially comparable properties.
2. Inspects the subject property, the neighborhood, and each potential comparable.
3. Analyzes the highest and best use of each potential comparable to test its comparability with the subject.

4. Verifies data and eliminates sales that are not arm's-length transactions if an accurate adjustment for atypical conditions of sale cannot be calculated.

5. Analyzes differences between the subject property and each potential comparable and selects true comparables for use in the sales comparison approach.

The process begins with the identification of potential comparables and concludes with the selection of the actual comparables to be used in the appraisal. Although the steps are not always followed in the order indicated, each task must be performed at some point in the valuation process. When the appraiser concludes that the differences between the subject property and a given comparable are not too great, the transaction may be used in sales comparison analysis.

Research and Identification of Comparables

Procedures for identifying comparables were discussed at length in Chapter 5. In brief, an appraiser first collects general information on the subject property which can be used to help identify comparables. Usually data on the property location, house type, size, number of stories, number of bedrooms and bathrooms, and site size are sufficient, but additional detail can be helpful. Next, the appraiser tries to generate a list of properties in the subject neighborhood and competitive neighborhoods that meet this general description. Information may be obtained from office files, multiple listing services, public records, news publications, title companies, and knowledgeable individuals such as appraisers, brokers, and bankers.

Figure 16.1 is a sample profile sheet from a multiple listing service. A completed sheet on a comparable property could provide an appraiser with a wealth of useful information.

An appraiser is primarily interested in comparable properties that have been sold recently. Contracts, offers, refusals, and listing prices of competitive properties may provide additional insights into the character of the local market.

How many comparables should be identified? An appraiser must have an adequate number of sales to establish a firm basis for the value conclusion. If the quality of the data collected is questionable, a larger pool of comparable properties should be considered. Increasing the number of comparables selected takes time and incurs expense, but a larger sample generally produces more reliable results.

The appraiser collects important data on each comparable transaction and records the legal, physical, and locational characteristics of the property as of the date of sale. The following items of information are generally needed:

Transactional characteristics
- Sale price
- Financing terms
- Date of sale

Figure 16.1   Sample Profile Sheet

MLS # (Assigned)

RES RESIDENTIAL
FREDERICKSBURG BOARD OF REALTORS
*Denotes Required Fields

*PROPERTY TYPE (✓ One)
- SD ☐ Single Family Detached
- TH ☐ Townhouse
- 1D ☐ Duplex (1 Unit)
- 2D ☐ Duplex (2 Units)
- AP ☐ Apts (3 or More)
- MO ☐ Mobile
- CN ☐ Condominium

*AREA (Major) (1-6)   Z

*SUBAREA (1-9) (See Map Book)   Y

(✓ One)
☐ For Sale
☐ For Rent Only
(If 'Rent', Form Must Be Submitted To Board For Entry)

*PRICE $

*LIST DATE (DD-MON-YY)

*EXP DATE (DD-MON-YY)

ZONING (See Reverse Side)   ***MAP COORD** (Page) (Grid)

ADDRESS #   *** STREET/STATE RT #** (Use Street Name Or VA State Rt. #. If None, Use Nearest VA Rt. #)   ***SUBDIVISION** (Do Not Abbreviate)

*LEGAL (Legal Description Lot-Block-Section Or Surveyor's Name)   ***TAX MAP**

*ROOMS (Finished — Do Not Include Baths or Utilities)

*BEDROOMS

BATHS
- ***FULL**   **PARTIAL**
- **DIM OF HOUSE**   X

*APPROX SQFT (Habitable Space) (Use Outside Dimensions Less Unfin Area)

(L = Lower, M = Main, U = Upper)

*LIVING ROOM   ***LR LVL**   X

DINING ROOM   **DR LVL**   X

*DIN TYPE (✓ Up To 2)
- C/B ☐ ESIK-Counter/Bar
- TS ☐ ESIK-Table Space
- KF ☐ Kit-Fam Rm-Dining Combo
- CK ☐ Country Kitchen
- BR ☐ Breakfast Room
- L/D ☐ LR-DR Combo
- SEP ☐ Separate

FAMILY ROOM/DEN   **FR LVL**   X

*KITCHEN   *** KIT LVL**   X

*MASTER BEDROOM   *** MBR LVL**   X

*2 BEDROOM   *** 2BR LVL**   X

3 BEDROOM   **3BR LVL**   X

OTHER ROOMS (✓ Up To 4)
- UL ☐ Unfinished Lower Level
- IL ☐ In-Law Suite
- REC ☐ Recreation Room
- SL ☐ Study/Library
- EF ☐ Entrance Foyer
- PN ☐ Pantry
- LR ☐ Laundry Room
- 1B ☐ 1st Flr Bedroom & Bath
- SP ☐ Screened Porch
- SUN ☐ Sun Room

* APPROX AGE (If New Constr Enter "0")

* DESIGN (✓ One)
- 1S ☐ 1 Story
- 1H ☐ 1½ Story
- 2S ☐ 2 Story
- SF ☐ Split Foyer
- BT ☐ Bi-Tri Level
- FM ☐ Farm House
- CN ☐ Contemporary
- OT ☐ Other (See Remarks)

NEW CONSTR (✓ One)
- TBB ☐ To Be Built
- FND ☐ Foundation
- URF ☐ Under Roof
- DRY ☐ Drywall
- COM ☐ Complete

* CONSTRUCTION (✓ Up To 2)
- BK ☐ All Brick
- PB ☐ Partial Brick
- FR ☐ Frame
- ST ☐ Stone
- AL ☐ Aluminum
- VY ☐ Vinyl
- RC ☐ Redwood/Cedar
- OT ☐ Other

* GARAGE (✓ Up To 3)
- N ☐ None
- 1C ☐ Carport-1 Car
- 2C ☐ Carport-2 or More
- 1G ☐ Garage-1 Car
- 2G ☐ Garage-2 or More
- DE ☐ Detached
- DU ☐ Drive Under

FOUNDATION (✓ Up To 3)
(Do Not Use For Bi-Tri Level or SF)
- SL ☐ Slab
- CS ☐ Crawl Space/Cellar
- PB ☐ Partial Basement
- FB ☐ Full Basement
- PF ☐ Partially Fin Basement
- FI ☐ Finished Basement
- OE ☐ Outside Entrance

* LOT SIZE SQFT (If Under 1 Acre Give SQFT-Enter "0" If 1 Acre Or More)

* ACRES (More Or Less) (Enter "0" If Less Than 1 Acre)

* HEAT/COOLING (✓ Up To 3)
- HP ☐ Heat Pump
- BB ☐ Baseboard
- FA ☐ Forced Air
- ST ☐ Steam/Hot Water
- FF ☐ Floor Furnace
- SH ☐ Space Heater
- CA ☐ Central Air
- WU ☐ Window Unit(s)
- OT ☐ Other
- N ☐ None

* FUEL (✓ Up To 3)
- GA ☐ Gas
- EL ☐ Electric
- OL ☐ Oil
- WD ☐ Wood
- SO ☐ Solar
- N ☐ None

* SEWER (Pub/Priv/Cen/Sep)

* WATER (Pub/Priv/Cen/Well)

FIREPLACE (#of/Loc/Type)

* FLOORING (✓ Up To 3)
- WW ☐ Wall-To-Wall Carpet
- HW ☐ Hardwood
- VY ☐ Vinyl
- TI ☐ Tile
- PQ ☐ Parquet
- PC ☐ Partial Carpet

* FRONTAGE (✓ Up To 4)
- ST ☐ State/City/U.S. Road
- PR ☐ Private Road
- RW ☐ R/W Easement
- WF ☐ Waterfront
- NV ☐ Navigable
- SC ☐ Stream/Creek/Pond
- WT ☐ Wooded/Treed

* POSSESSION

* SCHOOLS (ES/MS/HS)
(Use Codes On Reverse Side)

* FIRST TRUST (Balance Owed) $

* EXIST FINANCING (✓ Up To 3)
- CN ☐ Conventional
- VAR ☐ VA-Release
- VAS ☐ VA-Substitute
- FHA ☐ FHA
- GPM ☐ GPM
- VH ☐ VHDA
- FM ☐ FmHA
- WR ☐ Wrap/Land Contract
- FLB ☐ FLB
- PV ☐ Private
- 2/3 ☐ 2nd/3rd Trust(s)
- TAC ☐ TAC

* YRS REMAINING (On 1st Trust)

* PAYMENT $

* PMT INCLUDES (Circle What Is Included)
P I T I M N   (N=None)

* INTEREST RATE   %

* LENDER

* CASH TO ASSUME
(If Not Assumable, Enter List Price) $

* TAXES (Annual) $

HOME/CONDO FEE $

* PROPOSED FIN (✓ Up To 6)
(Owner Will Consider)
- CC ☐ Conventional/Cash
- ASM ☐ Assumption
- VA ☐ VA
- FHA ☐ FHA
- VH ☐ VHDA
- FM ☐ FmHA
- O1 ☐ Owner-1st Trust
- O2 ☐ Owner-2nd/3rd Trust
- WR ☐ Wrap/Land Contract
- RO ☐ Rent With Option
- LP ☐ Lease Purchase
- SMP ☐ Seller May Pay Some/ All Closing Costs

APPLIANCES (✓ Up To 7)
- RS ☐ Range/Stove
- MW ☐ Microwave
- RF ☐ Refrigerator
- DW ☐ Dishwasher
- DS ☐ Disposal
- WS ☐ Washer
- DY ☐ Dryer
- TC ☐ Trash Compactor
- CV ☐ Central Vacuum

EXTRAS (✓ Up To 6)
- CD ☐ Curtains/Drapes
- WB ☐ Wet Bar
- WA ☐ Walk-up Attic
- PS ☐ Pull Down Stairs
- CC ☐ Cathedral Ceiling
- SG ☐ Sliding Glass Doors
- FD ☐ French Doors
- PO ☐ Pool
- SW ☐ Storm/Insulated Windows
- SD ☐ Storm/Insulated Doors
- SS ☐ Security System
- AF ☐ Attic Fan
- TV ☐ TV Antenna
- FE ☐ Fireplace Equip.
- CA ☐ Cable Available
- PA ☐ Patio
- DK ☐ Deck
- FN ☐ Fence
- SB ☐ Storage Bldg
- BS ☐ Barn/Stable

*REMARKS (Begin Line 1 With Directions From Well-Known Landmark Or Major Road. On New Homes Include Type, Thickness & R Value of Insulation)

*OWNER   *** PH**

*LA   ***AP**   ***CM-SB**

*OFFICE ID   **SUPPLEMENT** (✓ One) 1 ☐ Yes   ☐ No

*PHOTO (✓ One)
- Y ☐ Take Photo
- P ☐ Submit Photo
- S ☐ Submit Sketch
- N ☐ No Photo
- U ☐ Under Construction

CODES (✓ Up To 3)
- O ☐ OLREA
- BA ☐ BA-Call Lister
- B ☐ B-Call Lister
- EA ☐ EA

Owner

Owner

Broker

*SHOW (✓ Up To 2)
- GO ☐ Lock Box-Go
- CF ☐ Lock Box-CF
- KO ☐ Key In Office
- AO ☐ Appt-With Owner
- AT ☐ Appt-With Tenant
- PT ☐ Pet-Call Lister/ Occupant
- CL ☐ Call Lister

Courtesy of Fredericksburg, Virginia, Board of Realtors®

- Names of parties (or others who can verify data)
- Motivations of parties
- Personalty included in sale

Legal, physical, and locational characteristics

- Legal description of the real estate
- Property rights conveyed
- Location and neighborhood
- Site size, shape, and location
- Assessments
- Public and private restrictions
- Building type and size
- Total number of rooms and number of bedrooms and bathrooms
- Age of building
- Physical condition
- Functional utility
- Size and type of garage
- Other pertinent property characteristics

Field Inspection

After the neighborhood and the subject property have been inspected, the appraiser can usually eliminate several potentially comparable properties from the list. Some of these properties may be located outside the boundaries of the subject neighborhood or competitive neighborhoods, which have now been more precisely identified. Other properties may no longer qualify as comparables because inspection of the subject has revealed that they are dissimilar.

Each remaining potential comparable must then be inspected. With the permission of the owners, properties may be inspected from the inside. Thorough analysis often requires that the interior of each comparable property used in sales comparison be inspected. However, many property owners are reluctant to allow strangers into their homes. In addition, a complete inspection of each comparable may be too time-consuming and costly. Information on construction features may be obtained from MLS data and tax assessment records and from building permits and blueprints kept on file at county and municipal offices. Photographs should be taken of each comparable for inclusion in the appraisal report.

Highest and Best Use Analysis

Each potential comparable should be analyzed to determine the highest and best use of the land as though vacant and the property as improved. When the sales comparison approach is used to value a residence, a detailed analysis of the highest and best use of comparables is often unnecessary. However, the appraiser's analysis must be sufficient to establish that the properties are indeed comparable. Highest and best use analysis is particularly important in transitional neighborhoods.

The appraiser must also consider the markets to which the potentially comparable properties appeal. Does the land considered as though vacant possess any special appeal to commercial users? Is the location of the improved site suitable for a nonresidential use? In some areas a residence located on a corner site or a busy street could potentially accommodate an office. If this property is a potential comparable and the subject property is located on an interior site or secondary street, the highest and best use of the improved subject and potential comparable may well differ. When the highest and best uses of the subject property and a potential comparable are dissimilar, the comparable must be eliminated from further consideration.

Verification of Data

Data on comparable sales transactions can be obtained by interviewing one of the parties to the transaction. However, appraisers must recognize that buyers and sellers are not disinterested parties. Any and all information provided by interested parties should be corroborated through other sources. Statements of fact can be verified by brokers, closing agencies, lending institutions, property managers, and lawyers involved in the sale. Owners and tenants of neighboring properties can sometimes provide important clues about the reasons for the sale. In verifying data, an appraiser must recognize that some sources of information may be more or less reliable and always ensure the confidentiality of the parties consulted.

The appraiser seeks answers to the following questions. What was the sale price and what were the terms of the financing? Were any concessions or incentives other than financing involved in the sale? Were items of personal property included? Exactly when was the closing price established? Are the parties to the transaction related? How old is the property? Sales used as comparables should be arm's-length transactions made in the open market by unrelated parties under no duress.

Analysis of Comparables: Elements of Comparison

Individual properties and the transactions in which they are exchanged may differ in many ways. From an appraiser's point of view, the important differences are those that affect the value of the property and the price obtained for it. These differences, which are called *elements of comparison,* include real property rights conveyed, financing terms, conditions of sale, market conditions (time), location, and physical characteristics. Other differences may be relevant in certain markets.

By studying transactions in the market area, an appraiser learns how much effect on value each different element of comparison produces. The comparables are analyzed in light of these differences and their sales prices are adjusted to reflect the value of the subject. When the differences are minor, adjusted sales prices of comparable properties provide a persuasive indication of value.

When differences are more substantial, greater adjustments are required and the results are less reliable.

Real property rights conveyed

At the outset an appraiser identifies the real property interest to be valued. For single-family residential properties, this is generally the fee simple estate. If the valuation assignment involves an unencumbered fee simple property, the appraiser should ascertain that the legal estate of each comparable is identical. Income-producing real estate may be subject to existing leases, which often limit the property's revenue-generating potential. In this case the real property interest being considered is the encumbered leased fee estate.

When an income-producing property is considered free and clear of all leases, its value is based on the market rent it can command. If the property is an encumbered leased fee, the appraiser must determine whether the contract rent is above, below, or equal to market rent. Then the difference between the contract rent and market rent may be used in estimating the property rights adjustment.

Financing terms

Financing terms can affect the price at which a property is sold. Sellers sometimes offer buyers a special inducement to purchase their property in the form of creative financing instruments. In contrast, appraisers sometimes find that above-market interest rates are paid to lower the purchase price. In these cases the final sale price reflects the value of both the financing inducement and the property, so the sale price of the comparable must be adjusted before it can be used as an indication of market value.

Financing plans can vary significantly. One common form of special financing is mortgage assumption, in which the buyer takes over the mortgage payments that the seller has been making to a lender. If these payments reflect an interest rate that is lower than current market rates, the buyer receives a substantial advantage. Other special financing terms include seller-paid points, FHA insurance, VA guarantees, wraparound mortgages, second mortgages, and buydown plans. These financing plans appear in the market when interest rates are high; they become less popular when rates fall. Sellers, lenders, and others use financing instruments to sustain demand for real estate at current price levels.

Various techniques can be used to measure how financing considerations affect price. Two such techniques are paired data set analysis and the calculation of cash equivalency with discounting procedures. Because of the importance of financing considerations, Chapter 17 is entirely devoted to this topic. Note that a financing adjustment is only required when the sale of a comparable was transacted with unusual financing terms.

Conditions of sale

Unusual conditions of sale can also cause a comparable property to sell at a price that does not reflect its value. The motivations of the buyer and the seller are important conditions of sale. For example, a buyer who owns an adjoining lot may be prepared to pay a price for the property that is higher than its market value. If a financial, business, or family relationship exists between the parties, the sale may not be an arm's-length transaction. One family member may sell property to another at a reduced price and an individual might pay a higher-than-market price to acquire a property built or owned by an ancestor.

If the buyer or seller in a transaction is subject to special pressure, duress, or undue stimulus that does not affect typical market participants, an atypical price may result. For example, the price paid for a property in a liquidation sale would probably not reflect its market value.

Market exposure is another important condition of sale. To qualify as an open-market transaction, the property should have received adequate exposure in the market. In many markets this means that a sign was posted in front of the house or an advertisement was placed in a local publication, and that the comparable property was exposed for sale for approximately the normal marketing time for similar properties. Bids and acceptable prices usually stabilize around market value in the normal marketing time. Some appraisal assignments may call for an indication of value based on a quick sale, a liquidation sale, or a transaction consummated within a specific number of days.

When a property sells much sooner than expected, the quick sale may suggest that the buyer was unusually motivated or that the seller was poorly informed. When a property is on the market for an unusually long time, it may be because the seller was holding out for a certain price or a certain buyer or because the property has problems that the market recognizes. Whatever the reason, the transaction is probably less reliable as a comparable sale and should be investigated further or eliminated from consideration.

No transaction is perfect. Appraisers must occasionally use sales data that do not precisely reflect open-market, arm's-length transactions. An appraiser should carefully judge each situation to determine how much the variance affects the price of the comparable. If the transaction is substantially different from the norm, the sales data should not be used regardless of how similar the subject and comparable may be in other ways. Only modest differences can be accounted for with an adjustment for conditions of sale.

Market conditions

Market conditions generally change over time. The date of the appraisal is a specific point in time, so sales transacted before this point must be examined and adjusted to reflect any changes that may have occurred in the interim. Otherwise the sales prices of the comparables will reflect the market conditions as of the date on which they were sold, not the current value of similar real estate. Changes in market conditions are usually measured as a percentage relative to previous price levels.

Market conditions can change for various reasons, but two of the most important considerations are inflation or deflation and changes in supply and demand.

Inflation and deflation generally can be observed throughout the regional economy. The rate of change in price levels is often easy to estimate. Tracking changes in supply and demand requires more research. Overbuilding is one common cause of an increase in supply; the unexpected departure of a major employer can cause demand to fall suddenly. Analyzing changes in supply and demand was discussed in Chapters 6 and 7.

The best indications of changes in market conditions are provided by the prices of properties that have been sold and resold several times. Because different types of properties are affected differently by changing market conditions, these properties should be similar to the subject property. If several property resales can be collected, they will provide an adequate data base.

The market conditions adjustment is sometimes referred to as a *time* adjustment. It should be emphasized, however, that it is not time which necessitates this adjustment, but shifts in the market. If market conditions have not changed although considerable time has elapsed, no adjustment is required.

Location

Adjustments for location are often difficult to make. The adjustment and the reasoning behind it should be carefully supported in the appraisal report. Generally, the largest adjustments for location are required when the comparable properties are not located in the subject neighborhood. Adjustments might also be required for properties in the same neighborhood that are subject to different influences. The character of the immediate neighborhood, traffic density, view, and siting are all significant factors in making location adjustments.

Every location has its advantages and disadvantages. The desirability of a location is judged in comparison with other alternatives. An appraiser investigates the effects of location by considering how the prices of physically similar properties in various locations differ.

Physical characteristics

A comparable may differ from the subject property in many physical characteristics, including building size, architectural style, functional utility, building materials, construction quality, age and condition of improvements, and site size. Overall attractiveness and special amenities can introduce other variables. Sometimes separate adjustments are required to reflect each major difference in physical characteristics.

Adjustments for the physical differences between the subject and improved properties usually cannot be made simply by adding or subtracting the difference in the cost of the varying components. Unless the subject and comparable improvements are both new, the cost of a component does not usually reflect its contribution to value accurately. The effect of a physical difference on value must be estimated through careful analysis of the market. To perform this analysis, an appraiser collects information on how variables such as age, size, and condition affect the prices of similar real estate in the local market.

Other characteristics

Other elements of comparison may also be relevant. In the appraisal of residential property, zoning, access, and view may be important. Income-producing characteristics such as tenant mix, the length of lease terms, lease conditions, and the management history of the property are significant in valuing income-producing property.

Market data grids

One important analytical tool used in the sales comparison approach is the market data grid. An appraiser may sketch a grid during the field inspection to record data quickly or fill in the spaces on a preprinted table. Market data grids can take many forms, but usually each comparable is identified in the top row of the grid. The sales prices of the comparables are entered in the next row and the gross living area and unit sale price of each comparable are shown in the following rows. The elements of comparison are listed on the left side of the grid.

The blank spaces across from each element of comparison are filled in with information which indicates the difference or similarity between the subject and each comparable property. The differences in value resulting from these variances are also noted once the amounts have been established by market analysis. Amounts of differences, or adjustments, may be expressed in dollars or percentages. Whenever adjustments are made, they should be applied in a particular sequence, which is discussed in Chapter 18. The market data grid shown in Figure 16.2 indicates dollar adjustments of value differences.

Market data grids are extremely useful in the analysis of comparables. They show at a glance which comparables are most similar to the subject and should therefore be accorded the most weight in reconciling the results. With a market data grid an appraiser can quickly locate pairs of comparables that are identical in all but one element of comparison. These paired data sets can be analyzed to pinpoint how much value the market ascribes to a particular property characteristic.

The total difference in value between the subject property and each comparable can also be calculated from the market data grid. The price of each comparable is adjusted for value differences ascribed to the elements of comparison. The resulting figures indicate a range of values for the subject property by the sales comparison approach.

Figure 16.2 Sales Comparison Analysis Section of the Uniform Residential Appraisal Report form

(Not Required by Freddie Mac and Fannie Mae)	Construction Warranty ☐ Yes ☐ No
Does property conform to applicable HUD/VA property standards? ☐ Yes ☐ No	Name of Warranty Program _____
If No, explain: _____	Warranty Coverage Expires _____

The undersigned has recited three recent sales of properties most similar and proximate to subject and has considered these in the market analysis. The description includes a dollar adjustment, reflecting market reaction to those items of significant variation between the subject and comparable properties. If a significant item in the comparable property is superior to, or more favorable than, the subject property, a minus (−) adjustment is made, thus reducing the indicated value of subject; if a significant item in the comparable is inferior to, or less favorable than, the subject property, a plus (+) adjustment is made, thus increasing the indicated value of the subject.

ITEM	SUBJECT	COMPARABLE NO. 1		COMPARABLE NO. 2		COMPARABLE NO. 3	
Address							
Proximity to Subject							
Sales Price	$		$		$		$
Price/Gross Liv. Area	$ ☑	$	☑	$	☑	$	☑
Data Source							
VALUE ADJUSTMENTS	DESCRIPTION	DESCRIPTION	+ (−) $ Adjustment	DESCRIPTION	+ (−) $ Adjustment	DESCRIPTION	+ (−) $ Adjustment
Sales or Financing Concessions							
Date of Sale/Time							
Location							
Site/View							
Design and Appeal							
Quality of Construction							
Age							
Condition							
Above Grade Room Count	Total ¦ Bdrms ¦ Baths	Total ¦ Bdrms ¦ Baths		Total ¦ Bdrms ¦ Baths		Total ¦ Bdrms ¦ Baths	
Gross Living Area	Sq. Ft.	Sq. Ft.		Sq. Ft.		Sq. Ft.	
Basement & Finished Rooms Below Grade							
Functional Utility							
Heating/Cooling							
Garage/Carport							
Porches, Patio, Pools, etc.							
Special Energy Efficient Items							
Fireplace(s)							
Other (e.g. kitchen equip., remodeling)							
Net Adj. (total)		☐ + ☐ −	$	☐ + ☐ −	$	☐ + ☐ −	$
Indicated Value of Subject			$		$		$

Comments on Sales Comparison: _____

INDICATED VALUE BY SALES COMPARISON APPROACH .... $ _____

(SALES COMPARISON ANALYSIS — vertical label)

SUMMARY

The sales comparison approach is a direct application of the principle of substitution. It is a simple method which relies on objective market data and can be used in a broad range of appraisal situations. The sales comparison approach cannot be applied when sales data are too limited to produce reliable conclusions and when the data available pertain to properties that are not comparable to the subject property.

To be comparable a property must be competitive with the subject property; similar in transactional, legal, and physical characteristics; and located in the same market area. The selection of comparables begins with research and identification of potentially comparable properties. The appraiser inspects the subject property, the neighborhood, and each of the potential comparables. To ensure comparability with the subject property, the highest and best use of each potentially comparable property is analyzed. The appraiser verifies the data collected. Finally the legal, transactional, physical, and locational differences between each potential comparable and the subject are analyzed to narrow down the list of potential comparables to include only truly comparable properties.

Elements of comparison are property characteristics that cause prices to vary. They include legal characteristics such as the property rights conveyed; transactional characteristics such as financing terms, conditions of sale (motivation), and market conditions (time); physical characteristics such as size and condition; and locational features such as the neighborhood and siting.

Most residential properties are held in fee simple, but income-producing property may represent an encumbered leased fee. In valuing leased property an appraiser must estimate the difference between contract and market rent and adjust the price of the comparable for the nonmarket, contract rent. Financing may be conventional or a creative instrument may affect the price of a comparable sale. The effect of unusual financing may be measured with paired data set analysis or cash equivalency calculations.

A conditions of sale adjustment may be needed if the parties to a transaction were subject to pressures uncharacteristic of those operating on typical market participants. Any comparable sales that are not arm's-length transactions may be eliminated if an accurate adjustment for atypical conditions of sale cannot be calculated. Analysis of market conditions identifies changes resulting from inflation or deflation and trends in supply and demand. The effects of market changes may be investigated by studying the prices of unchanged properties that have been resold several times.

An appraiser can isolate the effects of physical and locational characteristics by comparing the prices of properties that are similar except for a single physical or locational difference. Adjustments for zoning, access, and income-producing characteristics may be required in some appraisals.

A market data grid is a tabular representation of market data organized into useful, measurable units. A market data grid facilitates adjustments to the sales prices and unit prices of comparable properties using various elements of comparison.

REVIEW QUESTIONS

1. What criteria are applied to judge the comparability of a property? How does an appraiser narrow the list of potentially comparable properties and isolate properties that are truly comparable to the subject?

2. What are elements of comparison? Identify which elements of comparison pertain to the sales transaction and which pertain to the legal, physical, and locational features of the property.

3. What general rule do appraisers follow in deciding whether to adjust the sale price of a comparable or eliminate the property from consideration as a comparable?
4. How do existing leases affect the rent an income-producing property can generate?
5. Define *arm's-length transaction* and *creative financing.*
6. Explain what is meant by unusual conditions of sale and changes in market conditions.
7. How is a market data grid used in adjusting the prices of comparable properties?

17 Residential Financing and Cash Equivalency

Mortgage financing is especially important to residential appraisers, who are concerned with the topic for two reasons. First, appraisers observe market activity patterns to ascertain how changes in these patterns affect the availability of mortgage funds and the terms on which funds can be obtained. The market for residential property is strongly influenced by trends in mortgage financing and their effects on supply and demand. The types of financing plans currently available must be thoroughly researched and historical trends must be analyzed to make a reasonable forecast. Mortgage analysis is normally conducted as part of neighborhood and market analysis.

Second, appraisers must understand the different types of market and nonmarket financing plans available to apply the sales comparison approach. Whenever a comparable property is sold with nonmarket financing, the special financing may be considered an inducement to either the buyer or the seller. As an inducement, its value must be separated from the value of the property. Mortgage assumptions, seller financing at below-market rates, installment sales contracts, buydowns, and wraparound mortgages are all special financing arrangements. When a property that was sold with special financing is used as a comparable in a market valuation, the appraiser must calculate the value of the financing inducement and adjust the property's sale price accordingly. Financing inducements may also be tied to unusual conditions of sale—i.e., special motivations that encourage either the buyer or the seller to conclude the transaction. In these cases, adjustments must be made for the effects of both the financing and the conditions of sale.

This chapter focuses on the typical and atypical financing plans found in the market, sources of mortgage money, and factors that influence the mortgage market. Appraisals undertaken to estimate market value require a financing adjustment if special financing is involved. Thus the various techniques used to estimate adjustments for special financing are explained. These techniques include analysis of market-derived paired data sets, simple arithmetic for estimating the value of seller-paid points and considerations other than cash, and cash equivalency calculations that involve discounting. Before specific applications are demonstrated, however, the nature of residential mortgage financing must be examined.

FINANCING PLANS

Traditional Loans

Many kinds of financing are available to home buyers. The most common is the fully amortizing, fixed-rate, first mortgage loan. A fully amortizing loan is repaid with equal, periodic payments, usually on a monthly basis, which provide the lending institution with both a return on the investment in the form of interest, and a return of the investment through the recovery of principal over the term of the loan. Because the loan is fixed-rate, the interest rate does not vary over the life of the loan; it remains at the percentage that was agreed to initially. The mortgage payments are structured so that the first years' payments are mostly interest and the payments made in later years reduce the principal. This repayment schedule allows for level periodic payments and gradual equity buildup over the term of the loan. By the end of the term, the loan is fully amortized—i.e., the principal and the interest are entirely paid.

Variable-rate mortgages have become quite common in many parts of the country. A variable-rate mortgage has an interest rate that moves up or down according to a specified schedule or, more commonly, to follow the movements of a standard or index to which the interest rate is tied. Variable-rate mortgages protect the lender because their interest rates rise when interest rates in the general money market rise. In this situation the yield, or rate of return, from a fixed-rate mortgage investment may not be competitive with the yield from other real estate investments or securities.

Normally traditional mortgages cannot be obtained for the full purchase price of a property. Most institutional lenders are subject to state laws and federal regulations that prescribe maximum loan-to-value ratios between the amount of the mortgage loan and the value of the security pledged. Many lending institutions require a buyer to make a cash down payment of 10% to 20% of the sale price. Most loans are for a specified term, normally 25 to 35 years. If the mortgagor, or borrower, defaults on the loan, the mortgagee, or lender, can foreclose—i.e., take legal action to force a sale and recover all or part of the loan amount.

Mortgages are either conventional, guaranteed, or insured. The typical first mortgage is a conventional mortgage that is not guaranteed or insured by any institution. Nonconventional mortgages are guaranteed or insured by a governmental agency such as the Federal Housing Administration (FHA) or the Veterans Administration (VA) or by a private company. Since the 1930s the FHA has been insuring loans, principally but not solely to people with limited financial capacity. The VA, which is the largest source of guaranteed mortgages, provides a similar service to veterans. Both

FHA and VA mortgages tend to have lower interest rates than conventional loans, longer terms, and higher loan-to-value ratios. The U.S. Congress sets maximum interest rates for FHA and VA loans. In FHA and VA transactions, the points are usually paid by the seller.

Legal restrictions and requirements that apply to mortgages vary from state to state. These requirements provide home owners with protection and encouragement and also address the lender's risk. The interests of both parties must be balanced. This can be clearly seen in the foreclosure laws of various states. A state with foreclosure legislation that is extremely favorable to the borrower may attract few funds from outside the state. States that provide more protection for the lender by requiring short periods for foreclosure tend to attract more funds from around the country.

Other Types of Financing

In addition to a first mortgage, second or additional mortgages can be used to facilitate the purchase of a home. Such junior mortgages are subordinate to the rights of the first mortgagee, the primary lender. A junior mortgage is required when the buyer is unable to arrange for adequate financing on the basis of one mortgage. Because the first mortgagee has lien priority, a secondary lender can incur a substantial loss if the borrower defaults. To prevent the first lender from foreclosing, which would cut off or wipe out the junior position, the secondary lender is obliged to meet all first mortgage payments to keep that loan current. Interest rates on junior mortgages reflect this increased risk to the lender. They can, however, provide additional funds to the borrower and facilitate a purchase that might not be possible otherwise.

A mortgage is the traditional means of financing the purchase of a house, but in some states the same end is accomplished with different legal arrangements. In some western states, *deeds of trust* are used instead of mortgages. Money is borrowed in the same manner as it is with a mortgage loan, but a third party, the trustee, holds title to the property. When the borrower has met all his or her obligations, title is conveyed to the borrower.

Occasionally a buyer will purchase a residence with all cash, obtained from the sale of other property or from savings. A lump-sum cash payment often expedites a purchase and enhances the negotiating ability of the buyer.

A type of insured loan has been developed by private mortgage insurance companies that cover conventional mortgages. These companies insure the risk to lenders who advance 10% or 15% more than the amount traditionally loaned on a conventional mortgage. If an 80% loan-to-value mortgage is standard, a private mortgage company can provide insurance for an additional 10% or 15%, which increases the loan-to-value ratio to 90% or 95%.

Creative Financing

When interest rates are high, the monthly payments on typical loans can be higher than most consumers can afford to pay for housing. Faced with a shrinking market for their properties, sellers may entice buyers by adjusting prices. Sellers who are reluctant to lower their prices can sometimes appeal to buyers by offering alternative or creative financing. These plans may call for monthly payments that are lower than those required with typical financing. In some of these arrangements, the seller provides the financing rather than a lending institution; in others both the seller and a lending institution play a role.

Besides high interest rates, there are other reasons for using alternative financing arrangements such as mortgage assumptions and installment sale contracts. When mortgages do not prohibit assumptions or require lender approval, easier credit requirements may make creative financing attractive to buyers. Sellers who provide financing may have less stringent credit requirements than lending institutions. Furthermore, loan assumptions and sales contracts generally close faster and are less costly.

Several creative financing plans are described below.[1]

Mortgage assumption

In a mortgage assumption a buyer takes over the remaining payments on a loan originally made to the seller. Because this loan usually carries a rate of interest that is lower than current rates, the buyer may be willing to pay a higher price for the property to obtain the favorable financing terms. The interest rate, monthly payment, and maturity of the mortgage remain the same when the loan is assumed. Mortgages guaranteed by the VA may be taken over by a third party without the approval of the lender, but mortgages insured by the FHA are assumable only with lender approval.

Not all mortgages can be assumed. Some contain due-on-sale clauses stipulating that the outstanding loan balance will become due when the mortgaged property is sold or transferred.

Seller loan

A seller may be willing to finance all or part of the purchase price of a property at a below-market interest rate. If the seller finances the entire amount, the loan would usually represent a first mortgage, often in the form of a balloon mortgage. In a balloon mortgage the payments do not fully amortize the loan at maturity, so a lump-sum payment of the outstanding balance is required. More commonly, only a portion of the price is financed by the seller. In this case the loan represents a second mortgage which is subordinate to the first mortgage obtained from a financial institution. A buyer may be willing to pay a higher price for a property to obtain favorable, below-market financing terms from the seller.

Installment sale contract

Under an installment sale contract, a seller allows a buyer to purchase property by making periodic payments. The title does

---

1. See Halbert C. Smith and John B. Corgel, "Adjusting for Nonmarket Financing: A Quick and Easy Method," *The Appraisal Journal*, January 1984, and Bruce Foote, "A Glossary of Mortgage Terms and Financing Techniques," *The Appraisal Journal*, April 1984.

not pass from the seller to the buyer until the buyer has satisfied the contract by paying all or a specified portion of the purchase price. If the buyer defaults, he or she normally forfeits all payments made. Quite often the terms of a sale contract are different from those available for a first mortgage. An installment sale contract may have a shorter term, specify a balloon payment, or provide for a higher loan-to-value ratio. Interest rates may be higher or lower than those available through conventional means. If the terms are favorable, a buyer may be willing to pay a higher price for a property purchased in this manner.

Buydown plan

In a buydown plan, a home seller advances a lump-sum payment to the lender to reduce, or buy down, the interest payments of the borrower. The buydown period may range from one year to the entire term of the mortgage. Builders sometimes buy down interest rates on loans to increase sale activity in new subdivisions.

Wraparound mortgage

Wraparound mortgages can be used to preserve part of an existing, low-interest loan in periods of high interest rates. The buyer borrows the outstanding balance of the existing mortgage plus an additional amount from another lender. The existing mortgage is not paid off. Instead the borrower makes payments on the new mortgage, and the new lender assumes the debt service on the original loan. In a sense the new mortgage is wrapped around the existing loan. A wraparound mortgage is possible only if the existing mortgage on the property is assumable. The interest rate on a wraparound mortgage is a blend of the rate on the existing mortgage and the rate on the new money advanced. The purchase price of a property bought with a wraparound mortgage may be higher to reflect the favorable financing to the buyer.

The arrangements described above represent only the most common of the many creative financing instruments that came into existence in the early 1980s. Appraisers should be familiar with all creative financing plans and be aware of those that were typical of market practices at the time of sale and those that were not.

SOURCES OF MORTGAGE MONEY

Funds for financing the purchase of a single-family residence can come from either primary or secondary sources. Primary sources are institutions that assemble money deposited by savers and lend it directly to borrowers. Individuals who make mortgage loans are also included in this category. Institutions that are secondary financing sources do not raise money or make mortgage loans directly. These institutions facilitate financing opportunities by buying and selling existing mortgages, which increases the effectiveness of the lending market.

Savings and loan associations, banks, and mortgage companies provide funds to most residential buyers. Life insurance companies invest some money, but they tend to be interested in multi-family residences and other types of income-producing property.

Table 17.1 shows the percentage of mortgage funds loaned by various primary sources in 1985. The figures shown are based on HUD statistics.

Table 17.1 Distribution of Mortgage Funds

Loan Source	% of Loans
Savings & loan associations	50.0
Mortgage companies	27.0
Commercial banks	21.0
Federally supported agencies	1.0
Life insurance companies	0.5
Other	0.5
Total	100.%

Banks and savings and loan associations act as financial intermediaries. When other investments offer better interest rates, depositors withdraw their money and invest elsewhere. This is called *disintermediation,* and it affects the availability of mortgage funds. During the past ten years, disintermediation has reduced the funds available for home financing more than once. The operations of the secondary mortgage market can help offset these difficulties.

Secondary Mortgage Market

The development of the secondary mortgage market has greatly facilitated the financing of real estate over the past few decades. Formerly many lending institutions made home loans and held them until maturity. Now they can sell packages of mortgage loans in the secondary mortgage market and free additional funds for further home financing. Private investors and institutions purchase home mortgages as do governmental and quasi-governmental agencies. The Federal National Mortgage Association (Fannie Mae) is an independent government agency with lines of credit to the Federal Reserve System. The Federal Home Loan Mortgage Corporation (Freddie Mac) is a federal agency regulated by the VA and the FHA. The Government National Mortgage Association (Ginnie Mae) is a federally owned and financed corporation under the Department of Housing and Urban Development. Because governmental and monetary authorities believe that home buying and home building can improve a depressed economy, the secondary mortgage market is often used to stimulate housing activity.

Federal National Mortgage Association

Fannie Mae has a major influence on the secondary mortgage market. Its principal purpose is to purchase mortgages from the primary mortgage market, which increases the liquidity of primary lenders. Two important activities of the association are the over-the-counter program, in which Fannie Mae posts the prices it will pay for the immediate delivery of mortgages, and the free market system commitment auction, in which FHA, VA, and conventional mortgages are sold in separate, simultaneous auctions.

Federal Home Loan Mortgage Corporation

Freddie Mac was created in 1970 to increase the availability of mortgage funds and generate greater flexibility for mortgage investors. The Federal Home Loan Bank Board created and operates the organization, which is related to the system of federally chartered savings and loan associations. Freddie Mac helps expand and distribute capital for mortgage purposes by conducting both purchase and sales programs.

In its purchase programs, Freddie Mac buys single-family and condominium mortgages from approved financial institutions. This gives the institutions greater liquidity in times of credit stringency so they can continue making mortgage funds available for housing. While Fannie Mae programs include insured and guaranteed mortgages, most Freddie Mac activity is in the conventional mortgage field. In its sales programs, Freddie Mac sells its mortgage inventories, thus acquiring funds from organizations that have excess capital. These funds are used to purchase mortgages from organizations with shortages. Because Freddie Mac operations are conducted nationally, they help make mortgage capital available in all regions of the country.

Government National Mortgage Association

Ginnie Mae is a third major influence on the secondary mortgage market. Its operations also make mortgage capital available to housing markets. Fannie Mae is an independent agency, but Ginnie Mae is a government organization that gets financial support from the U.S. Department of the Treasury. Ginnie Mae has special assistance programs which facilitate mortgage loans that could not be handled without its support. The organization also manages and liquidates certain mortgages acquired by the government, but its most important role in the secondary mortgage market is in the Mortgage Backed Security Program.

Ginnie Mae is authorized to guarantee the timely payment of principal and interest on long-term securities that are backed by pools of insured or guaranteed mortgages. The most popular security is called a *pass-through certificate* because it is based on mortgage payments that are passed on to the holder of the security. In the Mortgage Backed Security Program, mortgage originators pool loans in groups of $1 million or more, issue covering securities, and obtain a Ginnie Mae guarantee. Through this program, investors who do not have the capacity to make mortgages can still be involved in home finance markets. Ginnie Mae securities make excellent investments, so these securities are traded extensively.

The recent development of Collateralized Mortgage Obligations (CMOs) as a major investment banking activity is due in part to Ginnie Mae guarantee arrangements. These investment instruments are attractive because the debt is usually secured by Ginnie Mae certificates covering pools of residential mortgages. Due to Ginnie Mae's participation, these bonds receive a AAA rating, the highest-quality risk rating. Ginnie Mae guarantees also allow these bonds to be sold at low interest rates. As CMOs have proliferated, some have been secured using Fannie Mae, Freddie Mac, and even conventional institutional mortgages as collateral. The CMO vehicle has provided great liquidity for the mortgage industry and has helped monetize the mortgage element in real estate investment.

Private sector transactions

Although most secondary mortgage market activity is generated by Fannie Mae, Freddie Mac, and Ginnie Mae, many private sector transactions also take place. Banks and insurance companies that make mortgages often sell loan portfolios, or participations, to private or institutional investors. Real Estate Investment Trusts (REITs) also purchase mortgages from institutions, which gives the sellers the liquidity needed to continue their lending programs.

The development and growth of private mortgage insurance programs has facilitated private activity in the secondary mortgage market. In the residential field, private programs have been successful in insuring mortgage loan increments that exceed legal ratios. This has encouraged private secondary mortgage market operations, which could not occur without insurance.

INFLUENCES ON THE MORTGAGE MARKET

The availability of mortgage financing is influenced by many organizations and by developments at various levels. The decisions of the Federal Reserve are of great importance because they affect the amount of credit available throughout the nation. The activities of the Treasury Department, which reflect the economic policy of the federal government, also influence mortgage rates. Competition in international financial markets and fluctuations in the business cycle can also have pronounced effects. These forces combine to create the economic climate within which the secondary mortgage market operates. In turn the secondary mortgage market influences the availability of funds in the primary mortgage market.

Primary lenders are subject to other constraints in addition to those imposed by secondary mortgage market conditions. To measure the risk associated with a mortgage loan, primary lenders must also consider the economic health of the region, the community, and the neighborhood as well as the location of the specific property, the property type, and the income level and credit rating of the potential buyers. Lenders adjust the terms of financing by raising interest rates, charging points, or using other devices to reflect the risks they associate with the loan.

Mortgage loan underwriters frequently call on appraisers for the unbiased value estimates they need to assess loan risk. The underwriter analyzes the property based on the appraisal and judges the property's acceptability as security for the loan being sought.[2] Neighborhood analysis is critical to the underwriter's

---

2. "An Underwriter's Guide to Single Family Appraisals," Fannie Mae, Southwestern Regional Office. Revised July 1986.

determinations. Properties in neighborhoods characterized by instability or declining values usually are not eligible for maximum financing.

The Federal Reserve System

The policies of the Federal Reserve System have the most significant influence on the terms and availability of mortgage financing. Through its actions, the Federal Reserve regulates the supply of credit available throughout the national economy. To a limited extent, the Federal Reserve can even influence the timing and severity of the major economic shifts which create business and real estate cycles.

The Federal Reserve System is composed of 12 regional banks, which serve the 12 Federal Reserve regional districts, and numerous member banks, which include all nationally chartered commercial banks and many state-chartered banks. The Federal Reserve can act independently to further national economic goals. "The function of the Federal Reserve System is to foster a flow of credit and money that will facilitate orderly economic growth, a stable dollar, and long-run balance in our international payments. Its original purposes, as expressed by the founders, were to give the country a lasting currency, to provide facilities for discounting commercial paper, and to improve the supervision of banking." As the economy changed, broader objectives were outlined, namely "to help counteract inflationary and deflationary movements, and to share in creating conditions favorable to a high level of employment, a stable dollar, growth of the country, and a rising level of consumption."[3]

Credit regulation devices

The Federal Reserve uses three devices to regulate the supply of money and credit: the reserve requirement, the federal discount rate, and the Federal Open Market Committee (FOMC). The *reserve requirement* establishes the amount of deposit liabilities that member banks must keep in reserve accounts. These funds cannot be made available for business loans. The Federal Reserve can expand or contract the supply of available credit by changing its reserve requirement, which alters the amount of money banks can lend.

The *federal discount rate* is the rate of interest at which member banks can borrow funds from the Federal Reserve. This borrowing privilege gives member banks an important advantage over other banks in times of great demand. The Federal Reserve can encourage or discourage borrowing by raising or lowering the interest rate charged. When borrowing is discouraged by the Federal Reserve, banks have fewer funds available for loan programs.

The third credit regulation device, the *Federal Open Market Committee* (FOMC), is the most potent of the Federal Reserve's

---

3. The Federal Reserve Board, *The Federal Reserve System: Purposes and Functions,* Washington, D.C., 1985.

tools and the most commonly used. To increase the supply of credit, the FOMC writes Federal Reserve checks and buys U.S. government securities from securities dealers who deposit the checks with their banks. This increases balances in the reserve accounts of these banks and permits them to make more loans. To restrict credit, the FOMC sells securities to dealers who pay with their checks, which reduces their banks' reserve account balances. Thus business loans and economic growth are discouraged.

U.S. Department of the Treasury

The U.S. Department of the Treasury implements the fiscal policies of the United States government and exerts a substantial influence on credit and mortgage markets. The treasury helps manage the government's finances by raising funds and paying bills. To raise funds, the treasury prints currency, collects taxes, and borrows money. Bills are paid when Congress appropriates funds for various national projects. The treasury department does not have a day-to-day regulative influence on money markets like the Federal Reserve, but it does have a sizable impact. When the government borrows heavily to meet its deficit payments, less money is usually available to the private sector. When the government prints money to meet its obligations, it weakens the buying power of the dollar and contributes to inflation.

Impact on Real Estate Activities

Restricted credit can have a severe impact on activities that require borrowed funds, including property purchases and home construction. When the Federal Reserve pursues a tight monetary policy and interest rates rise, the market for real estate can go into a steep decline. In 1981 and 1982 the prime rate, which is the interest rate that banks charge their best customers, rose to 21½%. Mortgage loans are usually about two percentage points higher than the prime. Consequently, during these years very few home loans were made. Mortgage funds were scarce because lenders were reluctant to lend for long terms without knowing how high money costs might run. As a result, variable-rate mortgages were introduced and for a time they dominated the market. Rollover mortgages, periodic adjustable-rate mortgages, and other renewable mortgages were common. Still many buyers kept away from the market entirely due to high rates and unfamiliar financing arrangements.

To bring people back into the real estate market, many sellers offered nonmarket financing terms geared to the buyers' ability to pay. Builders arranged to buy down institutional mortgage charges by making initial lump-sum payments for buyers to sell off existing housing stock and increase the pace of development.

The experience of the market in the early 1980s demonstrates how sensitive the mortgage market is to conditions in the money market. In 1984 and 1985, a less restrictive climate returned to the money market; the Federal Reserve relaxed its credit policy, interest rates fell, and more funds were available. The mortgage market was quick to respond. Variable-rate mortgages became less popular and long-term, fixed-rate, fully amortizing first mortgages once again became the dominant form of financing for most single-family residences. These changes have improved the volume and velocity of real estate market activity.

Loan Risk and Points

Institutions and individuals who lend money analyze the risks associated with a residential loan in the same way they would consider any other investment. The security of real estate provides an added incentive for many institutions and individuals to make mortgage loans. Real estate is typically considered excellent collateral because it is fixed in location and likely to remain useful for a long period. Its utility and therefore its value are protected by a wide range of public services and governmental organizations. However, certain risks are involved in making mortgage loans. Delinquencies and foreclosures can be costly and, at some point, the loan may be greater than the price the real estate would bring in a forced sale. These risks could result in loss to the financial institution.

To analyze the relationship between financing and real estate values, an appraiser must consider the mortgage lending system and the specific risks involved. The interest rate is quoted for a mortgage loan represents the cost of the money. This annual rate of return reflects the risks of the specific investment given the property type, the neighborhood and region where the property is located, and the credit rating of the borrower. The rates for residential real estate mortgages, however, also depend on the cost of money in money markets. Home buyers must compete with other groups for funds. When the supply of money available in money markets is substantially reduced, the housing market is one of the first areas to suffer.

To compete in the market, lenders often find it necessary to charge points or use a discount rate. For example, a lender making a $10,000 loan at the going rate of 9% may feel that conditions in financial markets warrant some adjustment of the loan. The lender may ask the borrower to pay points for the right to borrow the money. One point equals 1% of the loan amount. If four points are required on a $10,000 loan, the buyer would pay $400. Alternatively, the lender might adjust the loan by applying a discount rate. If the loan is discounted at 3%, the amount of money actually advanced at the time of closing is 3% less than the original $10,000. Thus the borrower pays 9% interest on $10,000 even though only $9,700 was loaned. The discount increases the yield to the lender; it can compensate for higher risk or make the mortgage yield meet the yields obtainable on other investments.

CASH EQUIVALENCY

Whenever a property sells with atypical financing, the financing plan may have influenced the sale price. Most creative financing plans are inducements offered by the seller which allow the buyer to make periodic payments that are lower than those required with market financing. If comparables with unusual financing are to be used in sales comparison, the value of the financing incentive must be distinguished from the value of the real property. The price of the comparable must be adjusted to reflect the amount of cash the seller would have received if no special financing agreement had been made.

Nonmarket financing plans can be translated into terms that represent the cash paid to the seller as of the date of the sale. This is called rendering the terms *cash equivalent.*[4] Cash equivalency is estimated in several ways. The effect of special financing can be measured by analyzing market-derived paired data sets or the amount can be calculated with simple arithmetic or discounting techniques.

Comparison of Sales Transactions

Adjustments for estimating cash equivalency derived by comparing recent sales transactions are generally the most reliable. These adjustments can be obtained from paired data set analysis. To apply this technique an appraiser finds several pairs of comparable sales that are essentially similar in all characteristics except the form of financing used. The effect of financing is indicated by the difference between the prices of the paired sales. Similarly, if a newspaper advertisement quotes a sale price for a new home and indicates that the developer is offering a $5,000 or 5% discount for an all-cash purchase, the appraiser has a solid basis for estimating the effect of the financing arrangement on the price of the house.

Deriving cash equivalency directly from sales transaction data may be problematic because sales with financing terms that require adjustment are, by definition, atypical for the market. Therefore, it is unlikely that an appraiser will find sufficient comparables to conduct a reliable paired data set analysis. One or two sets of matched data may not be an adequate sample. However, even a limited sample can be useful if the reasonableness of the adjustment derived from paired data set analysis is tested against the results of other cash equivalency techniques.

In purchases transacted with atypical financing, one of the parties involved often has a special motivation to complete the sale. When paired data set analysis is used to derive an adjustment, the price difference between comparables usually reflects both a financing inducement and a special motivation. Consequently, financing and conditions of sale may be combined into a single adjustment. Comparable sales that do not reflect arm's-length transactions should only be used with extreme caution.

Adjusting for Seller-Paid Points

An adjustment for seller-paid points is one cash equivalency adjustment that is relatively easy to calculate. The points are applied to the mortgage amount, and the result is deducted from the

---

4. See the Appraisal Institute's Guide Note 2, "Cash Equivalency in Value Estimates."

total price. For example, consider a comparable property that was sold for $130,000. The buyer made a $30,000 cash down payment, and financed the balance of the sale price with a $100,000 FHA-insured mortgage. The seller paid the lender three points, which is 3% of the *mortgage amount* of $100,000, or $3,000. The cash equivalent price of the comparable is therefore $127,000 ($100,000−$3,000 + $30,000). This cash equivalent price is then used as the basis for further sales comparison adjustments.

Some clients may not require that seller-paid points be converted into cash-equivalent terms. However, to satisfy the cash-equivalent assumptions in the definition of market value, an appraiser must calculate the adjustment. Although adjustments for points are easy to calculate, the VA and FHA handle points differently. Appraisers who work for these agencies must use procedures that are consistent with agency regulations.

Adjusting for Considerations Other Than Cash

In a property sale, the seller and buyer may agree on a price that includes items of real or personal property. To determine the cash equivalency of the sale price in this situation, the appraiser focuses on the cash amount that the seller received for the items traded.

For example, an appraiser is analyzing a complicated sale in which the seller reportedly sold the property for $86,000. The sale was financed with a 10% cash down payment and the buyer assumed the existing mortgage balance of $50,000 at current market rates. The seller also received a trade property from the buyer. The seller believed that this property was worth $15,000, but was only able to sell it for $10,000. The seller also received a new car with a sticker price of $7,500. The seller sold the car for $9,400.

To estimate the cash equivalent value of the sale, the appraiser totals the following figures:

Cash down payment	$ 8,600
Mortgage balance	50,000
Trade property	10,000
Car	9,400
Cash equivalent sale price	$78,000

Some might argue that the cash equivalent sale price should reflect what the seller thought he or she was getting at the time of the sale. This is incorrect, however, because financing adjustments must reflect the value that is ultimately determined in the market.

Discounting Cash Flows

Many techniques for deriving cash equivalency adjustments involve discounting cash flows. Lenders and investors commonly discount cash flows to estimate what a future stream of payments is worth at present. They use discounting procedures and financial function tables to make these calculations. Appraisers can apply the same principles to convert future payments into the present value of any financing plan when the pattern of the anticipated payments is known. Such cash-equivalent adjustments should only be used with extreme caution; they should always be checked against more reliable adjustments derived directly from sales data.

A stream of income expected in the future is not currently worth the sum of all the anticipated payments to be received. Normally, money that is invested today is expected to earn interest and produce more money in the future. This is why a future income stream must be *discounted*. A *discount factor* is applied to the income stream to obtain its present value.

Several terms used in cash equivalency analysis are defined below.

Present value (PV) is the value of a future payment or series of future payments discounted to the current date or to time period zero. The present value of a series of payments depends on the size of the payments, the schedule of the payments, and the interest rate that applies to each portion of the schedule. When these variables are known, present value can be estimated using an appropriate financial function table, a financial function calculator, or a computer program.

Present value of $1 ($1/S^n$) is a compound interest factor that indicates how much $1 due in the future is worth today. A future payment is multiplied by this factor to obtain its present value. When the payment amount and the interest rate are known, the present value factor can be found with an appropriate financial function table, a financial function calculator, or a computer program.

Present value of $1 per period ($a_n$) is a compound interest factor that indicates how much $1 paid periodically is worth today. An amount payable periodically is multiplied by this factor to obtain its present value. When the payment amount and the interest rate are known, the present value factor can be found with a financial function table, a financial function calculator, or a computer program.

Mortgage constant (R_M) is a rate that reflects the relationship between debt service and the principal of the mortgage loan. It is used to convert debt service into mortgage loan value. The monthly or annual mortgage constant equals the monthly or annual debt service payment divided by the mortgage loan value. If either the debt service payment or the mortgage loan principal is known as well as the interest rate and the term, R_M can be obtained with a direct-reduction loan factor table, a financial function calculator, or a computer.

Procedures for estimating the present value of a financing instrument vary, depending on what information is known about the financing plan and how future repayment is scheduled. When a mortgage at a below-market rate is assumed or the seller makes a mortgage loan at a below-market rate, the cash flow for the entire stated term of the mortgage can be discounted in three steps.

1. Determine the monthly payment. When the mortgage amount, the contract interest rate, and the term are known, the monthly mortgage constant can be obtained from the appropriate table and the monthly payment can be calculated.

2. Determine the present value of the monthly payments over the stated term at the market interest rate by applying a present value of $1 per period factor. The result is the market value of the mortgage.

3. Add the down payment to the market value of the mortgage. This sum is the cash equivalent sale price.

The procedure is illustrated in the following example.

Example

A comparable single-family residence was sold for $110,000 with a down payment of $25,000 and an $85,000 mortgage from the seller for a 20-year term. The seller charged 10% interest when market rates were 13%. The cash equivalent sale price can be calculated as follows.

Monthly payment on $85,000 for 20 years @ 10%
$85,000 × 0.00965 (direct-reduction loan factor) = $820.25

Present value of $820.25 for 20 years @ market rate of 13%
(monthly conversion frequency) = $820.25 × 85.3551
(*PV* of $1 per period) = $70,012.52

Cash equivalent value of mortgage (rounded)	$70,000
Plus down payment	$25,000
Sale price adjusted for financing	$95,000

A slightly more complicated calculation can be used to estimate the cash equivalency of mortgage assumptions and seller loans. Many mortgage loans are not held for the entire mortgage term, but are repaid early. A more elaborate calculation is used to reflect this fact. Present value is determined separately for two distinct phases of the loan repayment schedule: the period during which scheduled payments are being made and the point at which the balance is repaid in a lump sum. The following five-step procedure is recommended.

1. Determine the monthly payment.

2. Research the average mortgage life of loans for the type of property in question. The *average mortgage life* is the length of time a typical home owner holds the mortgage before paying off the remainder in a lump sum. Repayment normally takes place when the property is resold. Information on average mortgage life can be obtained from local lenders.

3. Estimate the present value of the portion of the mortgage that will be repaid over the average mortgage life. A present value of $1 per period factor is applied to the monthly payment at the market interest rate for the average mortgage life.

4. Estimate the present value of the balance to be repaid at the end of the average mortgage life. This is done in two steps. First, the amount of the balance is calculated. The present value of the monthly payment for the remaining period is computed at the *contract* interest rate by applying a present value of $1 per period factor. Then this future lump sum is discounted by applying the present value of $1 factor for the number of years until the sum will be repaid—i.e., for the average life of the mortgage. The result is the present value of the balance payment.

5. Add together the present value of the mortgage to be repaid during the average life, the present value of the balance payment, and the down payment amount. The resulting sum is the cash equivalent sale price of the comparable.

This procedure is demonstrated below using the data presented in the previous example.

Example

Monthly payment: $820.25

Average mortgage life for similar property (from lenders): 7 years

Present value of $820.25 per month for 7 years at market rate of 13% (monthly conversion frequency)

$820.25 × 54.9693 ($PV$ of $1 per period) = $45,090 (rounded)

Present value of future mortgage balance

Number of years remaining: 20 − 7 = 13
PV of $820.25 per month @ 10% contract rate for 13 years (monthly conversion frequency)

$820.25 × 75.6712 ($PV$ of $1 per period) = $62,070 (rounded)

Future balance payment converted to present value
PV of one factor for 7 years @ 13% market rate (monthly conversion frequency)

$62,070 × 0.4045 ($PV$ of $1) = $25,110 (rounded)

$45,090 ($PV$ of mortgage paid in 7 years) + $25,110 ($PV$ of balance) = $70,200 (cash equivalent value of total mortgage)

Plus down payment   + $25,000

Adjusted sale price of comparable $95,200

This second procedure requires more calculations, but it more accurately reflects the accounting method used by lending institutions.

Financing plans that involve balloon payments may be adjusted using a similar technique. A *balloon mortgage* is not fully amortized at maturity; a lump-sum, or balloon, payment of the outstanding balance is required. The cash equivalency calculation demonstrated above is used, but the average mortgage life is replaced with the length of period preceding the balloon payment and the balance of the mortgage is replaced with the known balloon payment.

Limitations of discounting procedures

Discounting procedures for estimating cash equivalency can provide mathematical solutions to a wide range of financing problems. However, appraisers should only use these calculations when they are confident that they reflect market behavior accurately. Calculated adjustments are often somewhat larger than market-derived adjustments. Adjustments derived by comparing recent sales transactions are more reliable than adjustments based on discounting procedures alone.

SUMMARY

Financing is important in appraising residential real estate because the availability of money influences the supply of and demand for residential housing and special financing plans affect property sales prices. Conventional fixed-rate, fully amortizing first mortgage loans are repaid with equal, periodic payments, which provide the lending institution with both a return on the investment, in the form of interest, and a return of investment, through recovery of principal over the term of the loan. A variable-rate mortgage has an interest rate that may move up or down following a specified schedule or the movements of a standard or index. Most traditional mortgages conform to established loan-to-value ratios and are not insured or guaranteed. Nonconventional mortgages are insured or guaranteed and may be offered by a governmental agency such as the FHA or VA or by a private insuring company. These mortgages tend to have lower interest rates and higher loan-to-value ratios.

Other types of financing include second or additional mortgages which are subordinate to the rights of the primary lender. Such junior mortgages, which are obtained to acquire additional funds, usually have higher interest rates to reflect the greater risks to the lender. The high interest rates of the early 1980s necessitated the development of a profusion of creative financing arrangements. These nonmarket mortgage instruments include mortgage assumptions, seller loans, installment sale contracts, buydown plans, and wraparound mortgages.

Financing for residential properties may be obtained from primary or secondary sources. Primary sources are institutions that assemble money from savers and lend it directly to borrowers. Savings and loans associations, banks, and mortgage companies are the primary sources used by most residential buyers. The secondary mortgage market includes governmental and quasi-governmental agencies as well as private investors and institutions such as banks, insurance companies, and real estate investment trusts. By purchasing packages of mortgage loans, these secondary sources increase the liquidity of the primary sources of residential financing.

The Federal National Mortgage Association (Fannie Mae) is an independent government agency that conducts two important activities: an over-the-counter program and a free market system commitment auction. The Federal Home Loan Mortgage Corporation (Freddie Mac), a federal agency regulated by the Veterans Administration and the Federal Housing Administration, purchases and sells mortgage packages. The Government National Mortgage Association (Ginnie Mae), a federally owned and financed corporation under the Department of Housing and Urban Development, provides housing assistance by sponsoring mortgage loans that require special support. Collateralized Mortgage Obligations (CMOs) have developed to take advantage of Ginnie Mae guarantee arrangements.

The mortgage market is affected by the policies of the Federal Reserve System and the activities of the U.S. Treasury Department. The Federal Reserve has three devices to regulate credit: the reserve requirement that member banks must maintain; the federal discount rate at which member banks borrow funds from the Federal Reserve; and the Federal Open Market Committee, which buys and sells U.S. government securities to increase or restrict credit. The treasury prints currency, collects taxes, and borrows money to meet budget deficits. Competition in international financial markets and fluctuations in business cycles also influence the mortgage market.

The mortgage market is very sensitive to conditions in the money markets. Risk analysis for real estate is very much like risk analysis for other investments. The annual interest rate on a mortgage represents the cost of using the money; this rate must remain competitive with the rate of return on other investments of similar risk. If a lender believes the current interest rate is not competitive, the lender may charge the borrower points or discount the loan.

The cash equivalency of a special financing plan may be calculated with paired data set analysis. Simple arithmetic calculations can be applied to estimate cash equivalency in sales involving seller-paid points and considerations other than cash. Discounting procedures are sometimes used to find the cash equivalent value of mortgage assumptions, seller loans, and balloon mortgages.

Paired data set analysis is extremely reliable, but appraisers often have difficulty finding a sufficient number of comparables. To adjust a sale price for seller-paid points, the dollar equivalent of the points is deducted from the mortgage amount. In estimating the cash equivalency of considerations other than cash, only the actual prices that can be obtained for trade items should be considered, not the amounts that the seller may have attributed to the items.

Discounting is used to calculate the present value of a future payment or income stream by applying financial function factors— i.e., PV of $1 and PV of $1 per period—to the payment or income stream at the stated interest rate for the specified term. When the mortgage principal, the interest rate, and the term of the loan are known, the monthly mortgage payment can be calculated using the mortgage constant (R_M) found in the direct-reduction loan factor table. The calculation of cash equivalency with discounting procedures is a valid mathematical technique, but it should only be applied when the appraiser is confident that the calculations accurately reflect market behavior.

REVIEW QUESTIONS

1. Describe the characteristics of a conventional mortgage, a variable-rate mortgage, an unconventional mortgage, and a second or junior mortgage.

2. Explain the profusion of creative financing plans. Define these terms: *mortgage assumption, seller loan, investment sales contract, buydown plans,* and *wraparound mortgage.*

3. Describe the difference between primary and secondary sources of mortgage financing. How are the two sources related? Which agencies and institutions constitute the secondary mortgage market.

4. What three devices does the Federal Reserve System use to regulate the supply of credit? How does the U.S. Treasury Department influence the availability and the cost of credit? What other factors influence the supply of credit available for mortgage financing?

5. Why do lenders charge points and discount mortgage loans?

6. What techniques can be used to estimate an adjustment for nonmarket financing? How would an appraiser adjust a sale price for seller-paid points or considerations other than cash? What technique might be applied to estimate an adjustment for mortgage assumptions, seller loans, and balloon mortgages?

7. Define the following terms: *discounting, present value, financial functions of a dollar* (PV of $1 and PV of $1 per period), and mortgage constant (R_M). How is a lump sum payment projected into the future such as a mortgage balance or balloon payment discounted? How is an income stream of monthly mortgage payments discounted? How is the monthly mortgage payment calculated when the mortgage loan principal, contract interest rate, and term are known?

18 Application of the Sales Comparison Approach

After all potentially comparable properties have been identified and inspected and the transaction data have been verified, the appraiser selects the comparables that will actually be used in the appraisal. Comparable properties are often quite similar to the subject property, but they can never be exactly identical to it. Therefore, the prices of the comparables must be adjusted to reflect their differences from the subject.

The appraiser first identifies the effect on value produced by each difference. This is accomplished through analysis of market data. Paired data set analysis may facilitate this task. Next the appraiser applies dollar or percentage adjustments to the price of each comparable. Adjustments are usually made in a particular sequence. As the sequence of adjustments proceeds, the price of each comparable is reshaped until it ultimately approximates a current, open-market sale price and corresponds to the value of the subject property. The adjusted prices of the comparables are reconciled to provide an indication of the value of the subject property by the sales comparison approach.

PURPOSE OF ADJUSTMENT

A sales comparison adjustment is made to account for a specific difference between the subject property and a comparable property. As the comparable is made more like the subject, its price is brought closer to the subject's unknown value. If the comparable is *superior* to the subject, a *downward* adjustment must be applied to the price of the comparable; if the comparable is *inferior* to the subject, the price of the comparable must be adjusted *upward* to reflect the difference. Because only the price of the comparable is known, only it can be adjusted. The unknown value of the subject is suggested by the price of the comparable once it has been adjusted for all differences from the subject.

UNITS OF COMPARISON

Units of comparison are the components into which a property may be divided for purposes of comparison. When units of comparison are used to organize the data, the comparison of the subject and comparable properties is facilitated. Because only like units can be compared, each sale price is stated in the same units of comparison. All units must be appropriate to the appraisal problem. When unit prices related to size are used, adjustments for differences in size may be unnecessary. Single-family residential properties are usually compared on the basis of gross living area or above-grade living area. Apartment properties are often analyzed on the basis of price per apartment and price per room. Price per square foot of gross building area or leasable building area may also be used.

Many properties can be analyzed with several different units of comparison, so an appraiser should apply all appropriate units of comparison, compare the results of each application, and examine the reasons behind any wide variation. This procedure will help the appraiser determine which unit or units are the most appropriate and reliable. The units of comparison selected can have a significant bearing on the reconciliation of value indications in the sales comparison approach.

Adjustments can be made either to the total sale price of the comparable property or to a unit price such as price per square foot of gross living area. Income multipliers are units of comparison that are not adjusted in sales comparison analysis, but an appraiser should consider why these units vary among the comparable sale properties. Income multipliers are applied in the income capitalization approach to value, but it is quite appropriate to extract them from comparable properties in sales comparison analysis.

Units of comparison can help an appraiser decide whether a potentially comparable property is in fact comparable to the subject property. For example, if an appraiser finds that one potentially comparable parcel of land was sold for $15 per square foot while most other parcels similar to the subject are selling for about $8 per square foot, the discrepancy would suggest that there is something unique about the more expensive parcel. It may have a different highest and best use. In any case, the reasons for the discrepancy should be investigated and, if the potential comparable is not truly comparable, it must be eliminated from further consideration. In this example, the unit of comparison applied was price per square foot of land. Because several units of comparison may be applicable in a given appraisal situation, all relevant units should be applied to each potential comparable to reveal any significant discrepancies.

SCATTER DIAGRAMS

A scatter diagram is an analytical instrument that can be used to help organize data and set up a market data grid. Scatter diagrams used in sales comparison typically have a unit of comparison as one coordinate axis and the unit price as the other axis. The coordinates of each comparable are plotted on the graph. Table 18.1 lists the gross living areas, sales prices, and price per gross living area of nine comparable properties. These data are then portrayed on the scatter diagram in Figure 18.1.

Table 18.1 Tabular Representation of Data

	Sale A	Sale B	Sale C	Sale D	Sale E	Sale F	Sale G	Sale H	Sale I
Price	$84,000	$72,000	$96,000	$92,000	$89,000	$83,000	$79,000	$81,000	$85,000
Gross living area in sq. ft.	2,150	1,800	2,700	2,500	2,400	2,100	1,900	2,060	2,300
Price/ gross living area	$39	$40	$35.60	$36.80	$37.10	$39.50	$41.60	$39.30	$37

Figures are rounded

Figure 18.1 Scatter Diagram

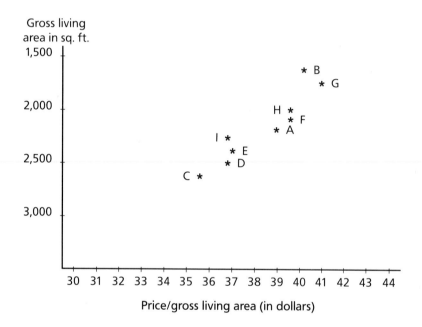

An appraiser could analyze this scatter diagram to derive an estimate of the unit price of the subject property. A line or curve that corresponds to the central tendency of the scatter pattern is plotted. Then the position of the subject property along this line or curve is located by drawing a perpendicular line from the gross living area of the subject on the vertical axis of the graph to the point where it intersects the curve. A perpendicular line drawn from this point to the horizontal axis will indicate the unit price of the subject property.

The sales properties' comparability with the subject is also depicted in the diagram. This analytical tool allows an appraiser to distinguish readily between closely comparable properties and those that are less comparable. However, the points in a scatter diagram do not always fall into a roughly linear pattern. When no line approximating a central tendency is suggested by the graph, the scatter diagram technique is unreliable.

DOLLAR AND PERCENTAGE ADJUSTMENTS

Adjustments may be applied to the prices of comparables in two ways. The dollar amount of the difference can be calculated and added to or subtracted from the total price or unit price of the comparable. Adjustments derived from paired data set analysis are often entered on a market data grid as dollar adjustments. Alternatively, the relationship between the subject and a comparable property can be expressed in terms of a percentage of value. When percentage adjustments are employed, the price of the comparable is adjusted to reflect a percentage of increase or decrease in value.

The adjustments required for certain elements of comparison are frequently derived in percentages. Sales data may indicate that market conditions have resulted in a 5% increase in overall prices during the past year, or that prices for a particular category of property have recently increased 0.5% per month. Similarly, an appraiser may analyze market data and conclude that properties in one location command prices that are approximately 10% higher than similar properties in another location. Adjustments for market conditions and location are often derived in percentages. These percentages can be converted into dollar amounts that are added to or subtracted from the price of the comparable, or they can be applied directly to the total price or unit price of the comparable.

In making adjustments appraisers should keep in mind that the sale price of a comparable property is known while the value of the subject property is unknown. An appraiser considers whether the subject property is superior, equal, or inferior to the comparable property. If the subject is superior, a positive adjustment is made to the comparable sale price. If the subject and the comparable are equal, no adjustment is needed. If the subject is inferior, a negative adjustment is made to the comparable sale price.

Whether they are expressed in dollars or percentages, all adjustments are based on the sale price of the comparable property.

SEQUENCE OF ADJUSTMENTS

Once adjustments are derived they must be applied to the price of the comparable. In applying both percentage and dollar adjustments, the sequence of the adjustments is important. Percentage adjustments are not transitive—i.e. their order is not interchangeable. Consequently, whenever percentage adjustments are added to or subtracted from an intermediate price in the adjustment process, a particular sequence should be followed.[1] It is recommended that appraisers adhere to the sequence in applying dollar adjustments as well.

---

1. This sequence was first presented by Halbert C. Smith in *Real Estate Appraisal* (Columbus, Ohio: Grid, Inc., 1976).

The sequence of adjustments is:

1. Property rights conveyed
2. Financing (cash equivalency)
3. Conditions of sale (motivation)
4. Market conditions (time)

After applying these four adjustments, additional adjustments may be made for

5. Location
6. Physical characteristics
7. Other characteristics—e.g., zoning, access, view, income-producing characteristics

The sequence of adjustments is illustrated in Table 18.2.

MARKET DATA GRID

Data on the subject property and comparable properties may be organized and analyzed on a market data grid. Each important difference between the subject and the comparable properties that can affect value is considered an element of comparison. Each element is assigned a row on the grid and the total prices or unit prices of the comparables are adjusted to reflect the value of these differences.

Market data grids can be extremely useful. They identify which comparables have the fewest differences from the subject and should be accorded the most weight in reconciliation. They can reveal pairs of comparables that are identical in all but one characteristic; by analyzing these pairs an appraiser can estimate the difference in value attributable to the dissimilar feature. Market data grids also facilitate the totaling of adjustments to calculate the value differences between the subject property and each comparable.

Table 18.2 is a sample market data grid that reflects typical elements of comparison and the proper sequence of adjustments. The sample grid has a separate line for each element of comparison. When the subject and a comparable are similar in regard to a given element of comparison, no adjustment is required for that element. This grid includes separate lines for comparison and adjustment to ensure that adjustments are made in a consistent manner. In this market data grid, adjustments are applied on a gross dollar basis.

ANALYSIS OF COMPARABLE SALES

Sales of comparable properties are analyzed so an appraiser can make a judgment about how property differences affect price. Any recent sale of the subject property would also be analyzed to see whether it falls within the range reflected by the comparable sales. Several methods can be used to study market data, including paired data set analysis and units of comparison.

Table 18.2 Market Data Grid
Adjustments Applied on a Gross Dollar Basis

Element	Subject	Sale 1	Sale 2	Sale 3	Sale 4	Sale 5
Sale price	?	$67,000	$66,500	$71,000	$61,000	$71,500
Real property rights conveyed						
Comparison	Fee simple	Same	Same	Same	Same	Same
Adjustment		0	0	0	0	0
Financing Comparison	Conv.	Seller Superior	Conv. Similar	Seller Superior	Seller Superior	Conv. Similar
Adjustment		−3,500	0	−3,500	−3,500	0
Conditions of sale						
Comparison	Arm's-length	Same	Same	Same	Same	Same
Adjustment		0	0	0	0	0
Adjusted*		$63,500	$66,500	$67,500	$57,500	$71,500
Date of sale	Current	One year ago Inferior	Current Similar	Current Similar	One year ago Inferior	Current Similar
Comparison Adjustment		+5,000	0	0	+5,000	0
Adjusted**		$68,500	$66,500	$67,500	$62,500	$71,500
Location Comparison	Average	Good Superior	Average Similar	Average Similar	Average Similar	Average Similar
Adjustment		−6,000	0	0	0	0
Garage Comparison	2-car	1-car Inferior	2-car Similar	1-car Inferior	1-car Inferior	2-car Similar
Adjustment		+4,000	0	+4,000	+4,000	0
Pool Comparison	No	No Similar	No Similar	Yes Superior	No Similar	Yes Superior
Adjustment		0	0	−5,000	0	−5,000
Adjustment***		−2,000	0	−1,000	+4,000	−5,000
Final adjusted sale price		$66,500	$66,500	$66,500	$66,500	$66,500
For reconciliation purposes:						
Total adjustment****		$18,500	0	$12,500	$12,500	$5,000
Total adjustment as percentage of sale price		27.61%	0.00%	17.60%	20.49%	6.99%

*Sale price adjusted for financing

**Sale price further adjusted for market conditions

***Difference between positive and negative adjustments made for location, garage, and the absence or presence of a pool

****Total positive and negative adjustments applied to each comparable

Paired Data Set Analysis

Through paired data set analysis, an appraiser can derive the amount of value attributable to a difference in an element of comparison directly from the market data. When two comparable sales are identical or very similar in all but one characteristic, the appraiser may be able to conclude that the difference in this single characteristic accounts for the difference in their prices.

For example, assume that a property is sold twice within a short period of time and no changes have occurred in the property or the neighborhood during this period. An adjustment for market conditions may be derived from the prices of the two transactions. Similarly, if two very similar properties located in different neighborhoods are sold within a limited period, an adjustment for location can be calculated from their sales prices. After adjustments are made for market conditions and location, it may be possible to isolate the effects of other variables on price. In practice, several matched pairs should be isolated from the sales of comparable or similar properties so that the appraiser's conclusion will be based on an adequate sample. Listings and offers to buy can also be used for this analysis, but they provide less reliable results.

Usually the number of available comparables is limited and an appraiser will rarely find pairs that directly indicate the effect of each element of comparison. Many pairs of comparables on the market data grid differ from one another in more than one element, so it can be difficult to isolate the effects of each individual variation. Often a more complicated procedure must be applied to obtain the necessary information. To apply this procedure the appraiser makes a series of repeated paired data identifications and adjustments directly on the market data grid. Each step in this procedure is demonstrated in the following example.

Step 1

On a market data grid, the appraiser notes the significant differences between each comparable property and the subject property in the appropriate spaces. If a comparable is identical to the subject in a given respect, "same" is indicated on the grid.

Table 18.3

	Subject	Sale 1	Sale 2	Sale 3	Sale 4	Sale 5	Sale 6
Price	?	$105,000	$101,000	$96,000	$109,800	$103,000	$103,800
Element*							
View	Yes	No	Yes (same)	No	Yes (same)	No	Yes (same)
Access	Poor	Poor (same)	Poor (same)	Poor (same)	Good	Poor (same)	Good
Site shape	Irreg.	Reg.	Reg.	Irreg. (same)	Irreg. (same)	Reg.	Irreg. (same)
Cond. of improv.	Good	Good (same)	Poor	Poor	Good (same)	Good (same)	Poor
Garage	1-car	2-car	1-car (same)	1-car (same)	2-car	1-car (same)	2-car

*Throughout this example it will be assumed that the sales prices of the comparables have already been adjusted for property rights, financing, market conditions, conditions of sale, and location.

Step 2

Find a pair of comparables that differ from one another only in one respect. In this case, Sales 4 and 6 can be paired because they differ only in the condition of the improvements.

Table 18.4

	Subject	Sale 1	Sale 2	Sale 3	**Sale 4**	Sale 5	**Sale 6**
Price	?	$105,000	$101,000	$96,000	**$109,800**	$103,000	**$103,800**
Element							
View	Yes	No	Yes (same)	No	**Yes (same)**	No	**Yes (same)**
Access	Poor	Poor (same)	Poor (same)	Poor (same)	**Good**	Poor (same)	**Good**
Site shape	Irreg.	Reg.	Reg.	Irreg. (same)	**Irreg. (same)**	Reg.	**Irreg. (same)**
Cond. of improv.	Good	Good (same)	Poor	Poor	**Good (same)**	Good (same)	**Poor**
Garage	1-car	2-car	1-car (same)	1-car (same)	**2-car**	1-car (same)	**2-car**

Appraising Residential Properties

Step 3

Using paired data analysis, determine whether the presence of the feature in question is an advantage or a disadvantage, and how much value the market ascribes to it.

Next, the direction of the adjustment must be determined. If the comparable is inferior to the subject, an upward adjustment is called for. If the comparable is superior to the subject, a downward adjustment is needed. If the comparable is equal to the subject in this respect, no adjustment is made. The goal of the analysis is to find what the price of the comparable would be if the comparable were more like the subject.

An adjustment amount is entered on the grid *only* when the comparable differs from the subject. In this example, the good condition of the improvements in Sale 4 is an advantage valued at $6,000.

Table 18.5

	Subject	Sale 1	Sale 2	Sale 3	Sale 4	Sale 5	Sale 6
Price	?	$105,000	$101,000	$96,000	$109,800	$103,000	$103,800
Element							
View	Yes	No	Yes (same)	No	Yes (same)	No	Yes (same)
Access	Poor	Poor (same)	Poor (same)	Poor (same)	Good	Poor (same)	Good
Site shape	Irreg.	Reg.	Reg.	Irreg. (same)	Irreg. (same)	Reg.	Irreg. (same)
Cond. of improv.	Good	Good (same)	Poor +$6,000	Poor +$6,000	Good (same)	Good (same)	Poor +$6,000
Garage	1-car	2-car	1-car (same)	1-car (same)	2-car	1-car (same)	2-car

Step 4

Adjust the price of each comparable that differs from the subject by the amount indicated. After all necessary adjustments are made, the impact of a single difference will have been identified in the market data grid. Once one variable has been eliminated, other pairs of comparables that are identical in all but one characteristic can be identified by repeating Steps 2, 3, and 4.

Table 18.6

	Subject	Sale 1	Sale 2	Sale 3	Sale 4	Sale 5	Sale 6
Price	?	$105,000	$101,000 + $6,000	$ 96,000 + $6,000	$109,800	$103,000	$103,800 + $6,000
Adjusted			$107,000	$102,000			$109,800
Element							
View	Yes	No	Yes (same)	No	Yes (same)	No	Yes (same)
Access	Poor	Poor (same)	Poor (same)	Poor (same)	Good	Poor (same)	Good
Site shape	Irreg.	Reg.	Reg.	Irreg. (same)	Irreg. (same)	Reg.	Irreg. (same)
Garage	1-car	2-car	1-car (same)	1-car (same)	2-car	1-car (same)	2-car

Step 5

Repeat Steps 2, 3, and 4 until the values of all elements of comparison have been found. The adjusted figures are the prices the comparable properties would have sold for if they resembled the subject property more closely. These figures provide the basis for a value indication of the subject property using paired data set analysis.

Table 18.7

	Subject	Sale 1	Sale 2	Sale 3	Sale 4	Sale 5	Sale 6
Price	?	$105,000	$101,000	$ 96,000	$109,800	$103,000	$103,800
Cond. of improv.			+ $6,000	+ $6,000			+ $6,000
Adjusted			$107,000	$102,000			$109,800
Site shape		− $1,000	− $1,000			− $1,000	
Adjusted		$104,000	$106,000			$102,000	
Garage		− $2,000			− $2,000		− $2,000
Adjusted		$102,000			$107,800		$107,800
View		+ $4,000		+ $4,000		+ $4,000	
Adjusted		$106,000		$106,000		$106,000	
Access					− $1,800		− $1,800
Adjusted					$106,000		$106,000
Comp. prices after adjustment		$106,000	$106,000	$106,000	$106,000	$106,000	$106,000

In this example the adjusted prices of the comparables are identical. The adjusted prices will not coincide when two sets of paired data yield different adjustments for the same element of comparison, or when other techniques are applied to produce different adjustments. In practice the adjusted prices of comparable properties are almost never identical.

Limitations of Paired Data Set Analyses

This brief discussion of paired data set analysis may seem to suggest that identifying the effects of property differences from market data is a straightforward procedure which can produce accurate, complete mathematical results in all appraisals. However, such an impression would be misleading. Appraisal is an art in which appraisers apply their judgment to the analysis and interpretation of data. Paired data set analysis is a tool that an appraiser can apply to market data in some circumstances. When used in conjunction with other tools, this type of analysis supports and guides the appraiser's judgment, but it does not take its place.

Perfect sets of comparables that vary in a single identifiable respect are rarely found. Because properties that are sufficiently similar to the subject are usually limited in number, the decision to apply paired data set analysis in a given situation is a matter of judgment. Often the sampling size may not be large enough to provide a solid statistical foundation for the appraiser's conclusions.

Nevertheless, paired data procedures are important valuation tools which appraisers should use whenever possible. Identifying matched pairs and isolating the effects of variables is a practical methodology for studying market data, even if a comprehensive paired data set analysis cannot be performed.

When only a narrow sample of market data is available, which would not lend itself to statistical analysis, paired data set analysis can be used to test the results of other analytical procedures. To complete an appraisal, the appraiser should use any and all analytical tools that are pertinent to the assignment and amenable to the available data.

Units of Comparison

Units of comparison can also be used to identify the effects of variations in property characteristics. Units of comparison play various roles in different parts of the valuation process, but they are especially significant in the analysis of comparables. They can be applied to derive adjustments.

Although properties can be divided into many different component parts, only a few units of comparison are commonly used in residential valuations. One property is generally compared with another in terms of the total property price, the price per square foot of gross living area, the price per room, or the price per living unit. The ratio between the sale price and the gross rental income of a property is called a *gross rent multiplier* (*GRM*). This is an important unit of comparison in the income capitalization approach. Parcels of land may be compared in terms of total price, price per acre, price per lot, price per square foot, or price per front foot.

With units of comparison an appraiser can make adjustments for size differences between the subject and comparable properties. After adjustments are made for financing, conditions of sale, market conditions, and location, an appraiser may need to isolate the amount of value difference attributable to size. The appraiser can use a scatter diagram, plotting the square footage of gross living area on one axis and price per square foot on the other. The results may then be reconciled to derive the amount of the size adjustment.

The adjustment may be applied on a unit sale price basis as the market data grid in Table 18.8 illustrates. Units of comparison may also facilitate paired data set analysis. They can help isolate the effects of differences and resolve problems. Units of comparison are applied to paired data set analysis in four steps.

1. Select a relevant unit of comparison such as price per square foot of gross living area.

2. Divide the sale price of each comparable by the number of units in that comparable. If, for example, the price of the comparable is $64,000 and its gross living area is 1,600 square feet, the calculation would be

$$\$64{,}000/1{,}600 \text{ sq. ft.} = \$40 \text{ per sq. ft.}$$

The derivation of a unit price helps reveal relationships and facilitates analysis of paired data sets and scatter diagrams.

3. Analyze paired data sets making adjustments to the unit sale price of the comparable rather than the total sale price.

4. After all adjustments have been made, multiply the adjusted unit sale price of each comparable by the number of units of comparison in the subject to obtain a value indication for the subject property.

Table 18.8 Market Data Grid
Adjustments Applied on a Unit Sale Price Basis

Element	Subject	Sale 1	Sale 2	Sale 3	Sale 4	Sale 5	Sale 6
Sale price	?	$49,500	$56,550	$49,600	$56,000	$51,200	$60,000
Gross living area in sq. ft.	1,425	1,650	1,450	1,550	1,600	1,600	1,500
Unit sale price	?	$30	$39	$32	$35	$32	$40
Real property rights conveyed Comparison	Fee simple	Same	Same	Same	Same	Same	Same
Adjustment		0	0	0	0	0	0
Financing Comparison	Conv.	Conv. Similar	Special Superior	Conv. Similar	Conv. Similar	Conv. Similar	Conv. Similar
Adjustment		0	−2	0	0	0	0
Conditions of sale Comparison	Arm's-length	Same	Same	Same	Same	Same	Same
Adjustment		0	0	0	0	0	0
Adjusted*		$30	$37	$32	$35	$32	$40
Date of sale Comparison	Current	Current Similar	6 mos. Inferior	Current Similar	Current Similar	6 mos. Inferior	Current Similar
Adjustment		0	+3	0	0	+3	0
Adjusted**		$30	$40	$32	$35	$35	$40
Location Comparison	Average	Fair Inferior	Average Similar	Fair Inferior	Fair Inferior	Average Similar	Average Similar
Adjustment		+5	0	+5	+5	0	0
Garage Comparison	2-car	1-car Inferior	2-car Similar	2-car Similar	2-car Similar	1-car Inferior	2-car Similar
Adjustment		+2	0	0	0	+2	0
Quality of construction Comparison	Average	Fair Inferior	Average Similar	Fair Inferior	Average Similar	Fair Inferior	Average Similar
Adjustment		+3	0	+3	0	+3	0
Adjustment***		+10	+0	+8	+5	+5	0
Adjusted unit sale price		$30	$40	$32	$35	$35	$40
Final adjusted unit price		$40	$40	$40	$40	$40	$40
For reconciliation purposes:							
Total adjustment****		$10	$ 5	$ 8	$ 5	$ 8	0
Total adjustment as percentage of sale price		33.33%	12.82%	25.00%	14.29%	25.00%	0.00%

*Unit sale price adjusted for financing
**Unit sale price further adjusted for market conditions
***Total adjustments for location, garage size, and quality of construction
****Total positive and negative adjustments applied to each comparable

OTHER ADJUSTMENT TECHNIQUES

There are several other adjustment techniques that can be applied in the sales comparison approach. Cost and depreciated cost data can be used in making adjustments, especially data on the costs of upgrading existing homes and installing additional amenities in new houses. Interviews with contractors, construction experts, buyers, sellers, and brokers can provide an appraiser with this information. Regression analysis can be used to isolate and test the significance of specific value determinants. The difference in rent attributable to a difference between otherwise similar income-producing properties can also be capitalized to derive an indication of the difference in their values.

RECONCILIATION

The final step in the sales comparison approach is the reconciliation of data. In this phase of the valuation process the appraiser reviews the quality of the data and analyzes the appropriateness of the methodology applied. How reliable were the sources that supplied data on each comparable sale? Did the field inspection corroborate the factual data obtained from secondary sources? Was all information from the parties to the sale verified? To begin the process of reconciliation, an appraiser asks, "What could possibly be wrong with the data I have collected?"

After the legal, transactional, physical, and locational data on each comparable sale have been reviewed, the appraiser analyzes the data sources and the procedures used to derive adjustments. What sales information was used? Was the sample large enough? If listings and offers were used as well as sales, how reliable are these data? How similar to the subject are the properties used in the data base? How old are the data and do they conform to current market patterns? If they do not, why not?

The analytical procedures used to derive adjustments are also investigated. Was paired data set analysis used? If so, how well-matched were the paired sales? Were scatter diagrams drawn? Which of the procedures applied is most reliable given the constraints of the data? All relevant analytical procedures should be applied to the data so the results of each analysis can be tested against the results of others. If these results vary widely, the appraiser should find out why; if the results are similar, they must be reconciled. The greatest weight is given to the most reliable procedure.

Each adjustment must be fully understood before it is applied. Often appraisers erroneously reward or penalize a comparable twice for the same difference. Certain differences between properties may represent mixed blessings. For example, a property may suffer from special tax assessments but benefit from the additional services that these taxes support. It is inconsistent to penalize a property for an obvious disadvantage without considering a compensating advantage, which may be less obvious.

Once all the prices of the comparables have been adjusted, a range of prices is indicated for the value of the subject property.

These different prices must be reconciled. Greater reliance is generally placed on comparables that were sold most recently and those that are most similar to the subject property. Comparables that require few adjustments are also highly reliable. Near the bottom of the market data grid there is a line labeled "For reconciliation purposes." Here the appraiser indicates the total adjustment to the sale price of each comparable and the total adjustment as a percentage of the price. This figure can help the appraiser assess each sale's comparability and aid in reconciliation.

Because the market is not perfect, many appraisers arrive at a range of values for the subject property in the reconciliation phase of the sales comparison approach. Often a single value estimate can be obtained only after all three approaches are completed. An appraisal is more credible if the indications of value derived in the other approaches fall into the range suggested by the sales comparison approach.

SAMPLE APPLICATION

The following appraisal problem illustrates paired data set analysis and the correct sequence of adjustments in the sales comparison approach. The problem solution is presented as it might appear in an appraisal report.

The house being appraised is a 1,200-sq.-ft., frame, ranch-style structure with a finished basement. It is situated on a 10,000-sq.-ft. lot and has six rooms, three bedrooms, one and one-half baths, and no garage. It is in average condition and is located in the same neighborhood as the comparable properties described below.

Comparable A is a 1,200-sq.-ft., frame ranch house situated on a 10,000-sq.-ft. lot with an unfinished basement and an attached, two-car garage. It has six rooms, three bedrooms, and one and one-half baths. It was sold three weeks before the date of the appraisal for $67,000. Through a seller-paid buydown arrangement, the buyer obtained a below-market interest rate, which resulted in a price that was $5,000 higher than it would have been otherwise.

Comparable B is a 1,450-sq.-ft., frame ranch house situated on a 12,000-sq.-ft. lot with an unfinished basement and an attached, two-car garage. It has seven rooms, three bedrooms, and one and one-half baths. It was sold one month before the date of the appraisal for $75,000. Again, a below-market interest rate resulted in a price that was $5,000 higher than it would have been otherwise.

Comparable C is a 1,200-sq.-ft., frame ranch house situated on a 10,000-sq.-ft. lot with an unfinished basement and an attached, two-car garage. It has six rooms, three bedrooms, and one and one-half baths. It was sold one year before the date of the appraisal for $56,500 with market financing.

Comparable D is a 1,450-sq.-ft., frame ranch house situated on a 12,000-sq.-ft. lot with a finished basement and an attached, two-car garage. It has seven rooms, three bedrooms, and one and one-half baths. It was sold one year before the date of the appraisal for $70,000 with market financing.

Comparable E is a 1,200-sq.-ft., frame ranch house situated on a 10,000-sq.-ft. lot with an unfinished basement and no garage. It has six rooms—three bedrooms, and one and one-half baths. It was sold one year before the date of the appraisal for $53,200 with market financing.

A market data grid for comparative analysis is shown in Table 18.9. The comparable properties differ from the subject property in terms of financing, date of sale, size—i.e., livable area and number of rooms—and the presence or absence of a garage and a finished basement. To derive adjustments for these elements of comparison, paired data analysis is used.

Comparables A and C differ only in their financing terms and dates of sale. The financing adjustment is given as $5,000. After this adjustment is applied, the market conditions (date of sale) adjustment can be made using the sale price of Comparable C and the adjusted sale price of Comparable A. The adjustment for market conditions is calculated as:

$$(\$62,000 - \$56,500)/\$56,500 = 0.097345$$

This 9.7% adjustment can be rounded to 10%.

The difference in size between Comparables A and B can be attributed to the additional room in Comparable B. The size adjustment is made after both prices are adjusted $5,000 downward for financing terms.[2] The adjustment for size is calculated as:

$$\$70,000 - \$62,000 = \$8,000$$

A comparison of Comparables C and E indicates that the adjustment for the lack of a garage in Comparable E can be calculated as:

$$\$62,150 - \$58,520 = \$3,630, \text{ or } \$3,600$$

An adjustment for the finished basement in Comparable D is calculated by comparing Comparables B and D after Comparable D is adjusted $7,000 upward for market conditions and Comparable B is adjusted $5,000 downward for financing:

$$\$77,000 - \$70,000 = \$7,000$$

All these adjustments are made directly from the market data. The financing adjustment specified is based on the actual dollar amount needed to recapture the seller's buydown payment to the lender. In this sample application none of the comparables is given greater weight because no sale is considered a better indicator than the others. No comparable is exactly like the subject and all of the comparables required at least two adjustments. The range of adjusted sales prices is very narrow, so the value indication can be rounded to the nearest $100. The market value of the subject property is estimated to be between $65,400 and $65,550.

---

2. The adjustment in this example is derived from an analysis of one paired data set. Several comparables, however, may vary in size. After all other adjustments have been made, the comparable sales prices may be reduced to unit prices, which are then analyzed and adjusted.

Table 18.9 Market Data Grid
Single-Family Residence Appraisal

	Subject	Comparables A	B	C	D	E
Sale price	—	$67,000	$75,000	$56,500	$70,000	$53,200
Real property rights conveyed	Fee simple	Same	Same	Same	Same	Same
Adjusted price	—	$67,000	$75,000	$56,500	$70,000	$53,200
Financing terms	—	Nonmarket	Nonmarket	Market	Market	Market
Adjustment for financing	—	−$5,000	−$5,000	0	0	0
Conditions of sale	—	Arm's-length	Same	Same	Same	Same
Adjustment for conditions of sale	—	0	0	0	0	0
Adjusted price	—	$62,000	$70,000	$56,500	$70,000	$53,200
Date of sale	—	3 weeks ago	1 month ago	1 year ago	1 year ago	1 year ago
Adjustment for date of sale	—	0	0	+10% ($5,650)	+10% ($7,000)	+10% ($5,320)
Adjusted price	—	$62,000	$70,000	$62,150	$77,000	$58,520
Location	—	Similar	Similar	Similar	Similar	Similar
Adjustment for location	—	0	0	0	0	0
Size in sq. ft.	1,200	1,200	1,450	1,200	1,450	1,200
Adjustment for size	—	0	−$8,000	0	−$8,000	0
Garage	None	2-car	2-car	2-car	2-car	None
Adjustment for garage	—	−$3,600	−$3,600	−$3,600	−$3,600	0
Finished basement	Yes	No	No	No	Yes	No
Adjustment for basement	—	+$7,000	+$7,000	+$7,000	0	+$7,000
Adjusted price	—	$65,400	$65,400	$65,550	$65,400	$65,520

SUMMARY

The purpose of the adjustment procedure is to bring the known price of each comparable property as close as possible to the unknown value of the subject property. Adjustments can be applied as dollar amounts or as percentages of the comparable sales prices. Using units of comparison, the sales prices of the comparables may be converted into unit prices such as price per square foot. Adjustments are then applied to the unit sale price of each comparable.

Units of comparison and scatter diagrams can help an appraiser organize data and decide whether or not a potentially comparable property is in fact comparable. If the subject is superior to the comparable property, a positive adjustment is applied to the price of the comparable; if the subject is inferior to the comparable, a negative adjustment is applied to the price of the comparable.

When percentage and dollar adjustments are applied to the sales prices of comparables, a particular sequence must be followed. The sequence of adjustments is: 1) property rights conveyed, 2) financing, 3) conditions of sale, and 4) market conditions. After these four adjustments are made, further adjustments can be made for location, physical characteristics, and other characteristics.

The use of market data grids helps ensure that adjustments are made in a consistent manner.

Various analytical procedures facilitate the study of comparable data. Paired data set analysis can be applied when two comparable properties are identical or very similar in all but one characteristic. The difference in their sales prices is attributed to the dissimilar characteristic. Paired data set analysis can also be applied to several comparables. Adjustments are made for specific differences between individual paired sales and these adjustments are applied to other comparables that require adjustment; in this way adjustments for property characteristics are successively resolved. The use of paired data set analysis is limited because perfect sets of comparables that differ in only one respect are rarely found.

Unit prices may be adjusted in market data grids with paired data set analysis. The application of units of comparison provides a different set of figures to compare, and facilitates paired data set analysis. Other adjustment techniques make use of cost and depreciated cost data, especially data on the costs of upgrading existing housing and outfitting new residences with additional amenities. Interviews with contractors, construction experts, buyers, sellers, and brokers can provide useful information. Regression analysis can be used to isolate differences and test the significance of special value determinants.

The final step in the sales comparison approach is reconciliation of the data. An appraiser reviews the reliability, type, and scope of the data and evaluates the analytical procedures used. The value penalty or reward attributed to a specific characteristic should not be considered more than once; the relative advantages and disadvantages of property features with mixed benefits must be weighed. In reconciliation the greatest reliance is placed on comparables which have been sold most recently, are most similar to the subject, and are subject to the fewest price adjustments.

REVIEW QUESTIONS

1. What is meant by a dollar adjustment, a percentage adjustment, and a unit price adjustment?

2. Explain how the sale price of a comparable property is adjusted.

3. What is the sequence of adjustments and when must it be applied?

4. Discuss how paired data set analysis and units of comparison assist an appraiser in estimating the size of an adjustment.

5. What specific limitations apply to paired data set analysis?

6. Discuss other adjustment techniques that an appraiser may use.

7. What is involved in the reconciliation of data? What principles does an appraiser follow in weighing the value indications of comparable properties?

P A R T   V I

THE INCOME CAPITALIZATION APPROACH

19 The Income Capitalization Approach (Gross Rent Multipliers)

The income capitalization approach is one of the three traditional approaches to value. In the valuation of residential property, however, it is only applicable to properties for which an active rental market exists. To apply the approach, an appraiser estimates the gross monthly income a property is expected to generate and capitalizes this income into a value indication using a gross rent multiplier.

The income capitalization approach is based on the assumption that the value of a rental property is directly related to its ability to produce income. The approach reflects the appraisal concept of anticipation, which affirms that value is created by the expectation of benefits to be derived in the future. *Capitalization* is the process of converting income into value. In one common capitalization procedure, a multiplier is applied to the anticipated income of a property to derive an indication of its value.

Different property types are valued with different income capitalization methods. The method and procedure selected should closely correspond to the market's perception of the relationship between income and value for the property being appraised. Only income capitalization with a gross rent multiplier (*GRM*) is discussed here. This is usually the most appropriate procedure for valuing single-family residences. A similar procedure can be applied to two- to four-unit buildings. Generally the rental income of these properties is analyzed by applying additional units of comparison such as monthly rent per square foot of gross living area, per room, and per unit.[1] Appraisals of larger income-producing residential properties usually call for capitalization techniques and procedures which are beyond the scope of this text.

---

1. A refinement of this simple capitalization procedure is applied to two- to four-unit buildings. This procedure employs an *effective gross rent multiplier*, which is the ratio between the value or sale price of a property and its *effective gross rent*—i.e., gross monthly rental income minus vacancy and collection loss.

OUTLINE OF THE APPROACH

Income capitalization with a *GRM* is applied in three steps. To obtain a value indication for the subject property, an appraiser

1. Derives a *GRM* from market data. To do this, the appraiser finds recent sales of similar properties that were rented at the time of sale, divides the sale price of each property by its monthly rental income, and reconciles the results.

2. Estimates the monthly market rent the subject property should command. This estimate is based on the actual rents of competitive properties that are adjusted for the advantageous or disadvantageous features of the subject.

3. Multiplies the estimated monthly market rent for the subject by the estimated *GRM* to obtain a value indication for the subject property.

APPLICABILITY AND LIMITATIONS

The income capitalization approach is only applicable to properties for which reliable sales and rental data exist. Residential properties that can produce income but are more typically used for owner occupancy may be valued with this approach if data are available. Assume, for example, that due to unfavorable economic conditions home purchases have declined. As a result, 20 units have to be rented in a 200-site residential subdivision intended for owner-occupants. Some of these rental units are eventually sold to owners or investors. In this case, meaningful comparative data can be derived for application of the income capitalization approach.

An active rental market for the subject property must exist to ensure a sufficient quantity of sales and rental data. The quality of the data is also important. The properties from which the gross rent multiplier is derived should be competitive with the subject property and similar to it in terms of market appeal, size, occupancy levels, lease characteristics, and expense ratios. The estimated market rent for the subject property should also be based on data from properties that are sufficiently comparable.

The applicability of the income capitalization approach may be limited by legal and economic restrictions on property use. If, for example, the owner-occupant of a property is considering converting it to a rental use, zoning regulations must be investigated to determine the legal permissibility of the contemplated use. Assuming the use is permitted, the costs and benefits of conversion must also be weighed.

The prevalence of rent control programs in some metropolitan areas affects the reliability of market rent data and the *GRM*s derived. Rent control makes future rental income less certain, but most rent control ordinances allow for some growth in rents and increased operating expenses can often be passed on to tenants. If rents are prevented from increasing in line with operating expenses, property owners may try to further reduce operating expenses or to divest themselves of the property through sale or condominium conversion. Therefore, rent controls can represent a value penalty. To determine the impact of rent control on property values in a given area, an appraiser might compare income-producing properties subject to rent control with similar properties that are not.[2]

DERIVATION OF A *GRM* FROM MARKET DATA

The first step in the income capitalization approach is the derivation of a *GRM* from market data. An appraiser begins by gathering recent sales of properties that are competitive with the subject and similar to it in terms of lease, expense, and income characteristics. The price of each property is divided by the monthly rent from all units in the property as of the date of sale. The resulting *GRM* indications are then reconciled into a single figure. Differences in the properties are usually reflected in their rents, so *GRM*s are never adjusted. The derivation of a *GRM* is illustrated in the following example.

Example

After gathering sales of similar properties and verifying their prices and rents, the appraiser arranges the market data in the following table.

Comparable Sale	Verified Sale Price	Verified Monthly Rent	Indicated Gross Rent Multiplier (*GRM*)
1	$199,500	$1,865	107
2	290,000	2,636	110
3	206,000	1,900	108
4	212,500	1,900	112
5	214,750	1,925	112
6	270,000	2,432	111
7	160,000	1,467	109
8	265,000	2,410	110
9	222,500	2,025	110
10	224,500	2,025	111
11	220,000	2,000	110

The appraiser selects a gross rent multiplier of 110 because this is the multiplier derived from the properties that are most similar to the subject in terms of location, size, property features, and expense characteristics.

A *GRM* reflects a typical ratio between the value or sale price of a property and its *gross rent,* which is the gross monthly rental income at the time of sale before expenses or vacancy and collection losses are deducted. When this ratio is applied to the subject property's market rent it will provide a reliable value indication if the properties from which it was derived are truly comparable. The division of utility expenses between tenants and the landlord must be similar. The properties analyzed must also be competitive with the subject, and have similar expense-to-income ratios and lease terms.

---

2. Harold A. Davidson, "The Impact of Rent Control on Apartment Investment," *The Appraisal Journal,* October 1978, and Robert J. Strachota and Howard E. Shenehon, "Market Rent vs. Replacement Rent: Is Rent Control the Solution?" *The Appraisal Journal,* January 1983.

The rental properties from which the *GRM* is derived need not be identical to the subject, but they should be competitive with it. They should be located in the same neighborhood as the subject property or a similar neighborhood and appeal to tenants of approximately the same income levels and household sizes. Four-bedroom houses are usually not in direct competition with two-bedroom houses. Sales should be fairly recent, especially if the market appears to be changing. In some areas a *GRM* derived from data that are more than six months old may prove unreliable; in others, a *GRM* derived from two-year-old data may still be valid.

At this point in the income capitalization approach, the appraiser is concerned with the relationship between property value and rent. Thus a competitive property that has a slightly higher rent than the subject because of its larger size or additional amenities can still be used to derive a *GRM* provided the competitive property has a correspondingly higher value. The ratio between property value and income usually changes more slowly than either value or income. The comparability of market data becomes even more critical in the second step of the income capitalization approach when the appraiser analyzes the current rents of the most comparable properties to estimate the rent that the subject property can command.

Expense Characteristics

The ratio between the operating expenses that the landlord incurs and the rent the building can command must be similar for the subject and all comparable properties used in the analysis. Houses that appear similar to tenants may have different expense-to-income ratios; from a landlord's point of view these properties will be regarded quite differently. It may be less profitable to own and operate one building than to own and operate another. A building that requires extraordinary maintenance or has higher taxes without higher rental income is obviously worth less. When such variations are found in the market data, the reliability of the *GRM* is diminished.

The typical operating expenses of residential properties can be divided into two categories:

1. Fixed expenses such as taxes and insurance charges which must be paid regardless of the level of occupancy.

2. Variable expenses that vary with the level of occupancy. These include charges for electricity and other utilities paid by the landlord; routine cleaning, repair, and maintenance; interior and exterior painting; and garbage removal, pest control, and other items.

An appraiser studies fixed and variable expenses by analyzing operating statements for the subject property and similar properties or by reviewing published statistics. This investigation is part of the rent survey and data collection effort.

Lease Provisions

The lease provisions of the comparable properties should be similar to those of the subject property. Because leases specify the obligations of the landlord and the tenant, differences in leases can influence the expenses the landlord must pay or the rent the property can attract. Thus unusual lease provisions may distort the relationship between income and value in a property. A lease that is especially favorable to the tenant, for example, may attract a higher-than-normal rent, although the value of the property is not proportionately higher.

The important lease provisions listed below often vary in residential properties.

- Lease period
- Amount of security deposit. Some landlords may not require a security deposit; others may insist on one-half the monthly rent, a full month's rent, or more.
- Division of expenses between tenant and landlord
- Penalty for breaking lease
- Penalty for late payment of rent
- Restrictions on tenant activities
- Conditions that constitute violation of the lease by the tenant
- Provisions for termination of the lease by the tenant or landlord
- Landlord's maintenance obligations
- Landlord's landscaping obligations
- Furniture included in the lease agreement
- Options to renew the lease
- Conditions under which the tenant may sublet

Reconciling *GRMs*

After the market data are assembled and several indicated *GRMs* are derived, the appraiser reconciles the results and selects a *GRM* that is appropriate for the subject property. The greatest emphasis is placed on *GRMs* derived from properties that are most comparable to the subject. Rent and property value generally move in tandem so *GRM* ratios should remain fairly stable. The indicated *GRMs* are not adjusted because property differences are already reflected in the *GRMs*. By adjusting *GRMs* an appraiser would consider these differences twice. Adjustments are only made in the second step of the income capitalization approach when the market rent of the subject property is estimated.

MONTHLY MARKET RENT ESTIMATE

To derive a value indication, the *GRM* is multiplied by the subject property's market rent. Appraisers must distinguish between market rent and contract rent. *Market rent* is the rental income a property would most probably command in the open market as of the date of the appraisal. *Contract rent* is the actual rent specified in a lease or received on a month-to-month basis. The subject's market rent is the rent that would be received under the terms of the lease that would most probably be applied to the subject property as of the date of the appraisal.

The rent that the subject property currently generates may differ from market rent for a number of reasons. At the time of the lease agreement, the landlord or tenant may have been poorly informed or acting under duress. Market conditions may have changed since the lease was signed or for some reason the lease terms may be unusually favorable to the tenant or the landlord. Contract rent is often lower than market rent if the parties are related or if the tenant has agreed to work for the landlord in exchange for lower monthly payments. To maintain full occupancy, the landlord may keep rent slightly below market value.

An appraiser estimates the market rent the subject property should command by studying the rents of the most comparable rental properties and adjusting these rents for differences in lease terms and provisions.[3] The appraiser also examines the rent the subject is currently generating, studies the existing lease, and asks the tenant and the landlord whether they believe the lease terms and rent are fair. This investigation is supported by the appraiser's analysis of the rents of competitive rental properties in the subject neighborhood.

When differences among properties influence the amount of income that the properties can generate, adjustments must be made. The size of these adjustments can be derived with paired data set analysis or other techniques. Data are arranged on a market data grid, differences for properties that vary in only one feature are isolated, and adjustments are made. The example that follows illustrates this process. The market data grid that accompanies the example is presented for purposes of illustration; all the adjustments shown will not be required in every application. Percentage adjustments for differences are provided.

Rental income for single-family residences is typically stated as a dollar amount per month or as the monthly rent per square foot of gross living area. For two- to four-unit apartment properties, rental income is typically broken down into monthly rent per square foot of gross living area or monthly rent per unit. Monthly rent per square foot of gross living area is used in the example, so a separate adjustment for differences in size is not needed. Note that the lot sizes of the comparable properties also vary slightly. No adjustment is made for lot size because the difference is negligible.

Example

In analyzing the market for a subject property, an appraiser finds a number of closely comparable rental properties. However, these properties vary in terms of size, leasing dates, lease provisions (payment of utilities), expense ratios, location, construction qual-

---

3. The data used to estimate the market rent the subject should command may come from the same comparable properties used for the derivation of the *GRM* or from different comparable properties.

ity, room count, and lot size. The rent data are displayed below and adjusted in the market data grid that follows.

	Subject	Rental 1	Rental 2	Rental 3	Rental 4
Monthly rent	?	$915	$1,100	$950	$1,100
Gross living area in sq. ft.	1,450	1,450	1,475	1,500	1,475
Date of lease	–	6 mos.	Current	Current	Current
Lease provisions Payment of utilities	Tenant	Tenant	Owner	Tenant	Owner
Expense ratio*	–	35%	30%	30%	30%
Location	–	Inferior	Similar	Superior	Similar
Construction	–	Similar	Similar	Similar	Superior
Room count	6	6	7	6	6
Basement	Finished	Finished	Finished	Finished	Finished
Garage	2-car	2-car	2-car	2-car	2-car
Lot size in sq. ft.	9,450	9,450	9,475	9,450	9,475

*Expense ratios are derived by dividing total operating expenses by rental income.

Table 19.1   Market Data Grid for Market Rent Analysis

	Subject	Rental 1	Rental 2	Rental 3	Rental 4
Element					
Monthly rent	?	$915	$1,100	$950	$1,100
Gross living area in sq. ft.	1,450	1,450	1,475	1,500	1,475
Rent per sq. ft. of gross living area	–	$0.63	$0.75	$0.63	$0.75
Market conditions and lease provisions					
Date of lease Comparison Adjustment (5%)	–	6 mos. −0.03	Current	Current	Current
Lease provisions: Payment of utilities Comparison Adjustment ($0.75−$0.63=$0.12)	Tenant	Tenant	Owner −0.12	Tenant	Owner −0.12
Operating expenses					
Expense ratio Comparison Adjustment (5%)	–	35% −0.03	30%	30%	30%
Characteristics influencing income					
Location Comparison Adjustment (5%)	–	Inferior +0.03	Similar	Superior −0.03	Similar
Construction Comparison Adjustment (5%)	–	Similar	Similar	Similar	Superior −0.03
Room count Comparison Adjustment (5%)	6	6	7 −0.03	6	6
Adjustment*		−0.03	−0.15	−0.03	−0.15
Adjusted rent/sq. ft. of gross living area		$0.60	$0.60	$0.60	$0.60

*Difference between all positive and negative adjustments applied to each comparable or total adjustments if only negative or positive adjustments have been applied to the comparable.

The indicated market rent of the subject is $0.60 per square foot of gross living area.

Elements of Comparison

In estimating the monthly market rent the subject should command, adjustments are made to actual rents of comparable properties for transactional variations, chiefly market conditions and lease conditions; characteristics that influence the amount of income the property can generate such as location, size, quality, condition, and amenities; and variations in operating expenses.

Market conditions and lease conditions

Changing market conditions can alter property income over time. When this is the case, the rental data of the comparable properties must be adjusted to reflect changes in market conditions. A percentage adjustment for market conditions is derived by analyzing the trend in rentals of income-producing property over several years. If all the rent data are current, a separate adjustment for market conditions is not needed unless market conditions have changed appreciably.

At times a market conditions adjustment may be needed when the data are only a few months old. If the rent data analyzed reflect a seasonal peak or trough, the estimate of rent derived from these data may be distorted. Many markets experience seasonal fluctuations in supply and demand which may affect property rents, particularly in areas where most leases turn over once a year. An appraiser should adjust comparable rents for these seasonal fluctuations in estimating the typical monthly rental for the subject property over the course of an entire year.

Rents can only be truly comparable if lease conditions are similar. An adjustment must be made for any significant lease difference that affects the rent a property can command or the obligations and expenses of the landlord. Adjustments for lease conditions are common when a property owner pays for utilities and when off-street parking is provided as part of the lease agreement. Downward adjustments are made for lease terms that are more favorable to the tenant than those contemplated for the subject property; upward adjustments are made for leases that are favorable to the owner. An appraiser would also consider the effect of a long-term lease at below-market levels.

A landlord's reputation for honoring lease terms and performing maintenance and repairs punctually may also influence the actual rent of a property. If the appraiser finds that a comparable property is generating a lower rent because the landlord has an unusually poor maintenance record, an upward adjustment of the comparable rent may be justified.

The amount of rent charged is an important provision of the lease. An overly high rent can discourage prospective tenants and reduce the property's occupancy rate.

Property characteristics that influence income

Many features influence the rent a property is able to command. Location is a primary consideration. Tenants usually prefer a secure, central location with a pleasant view, adequate light, and available parking. Access to public transportation, proximity to places of entertainment and schools, and good linkages with workplaces and commercial centers are advantages in most rental markets.

Size is another important factor. Size needs vary with typical household sizes, the income of tenants, and the sizes of competitive properties in the area. Adjustments for size differences are based on an analysis of the trend in rents per square foot of gross living area in the market region.

The quality and condition of the rental property and the amenities it provides have a substantial impact on its rent. Residences with sunny, eat-in kitchens and an extra half-bathroom are popular in many areas. Compact designs are usually preferred over linear layouts and high ceilings, large windows, and cross ventilation are advantageous in hot climates. Closet space is generally more critical in rental properties than owner-occupied dwellings because tenants usually have less room in which to store their possessions.

Private access to units in a rental property is desirable, particularly if the owner lives on the first floor. Building entrances should be secure; intercoms and buzzers are standard in some locations. Built-in appliances such as microwave ovens and dishwashers and any furniture included in the lease can influence the rent. Fireplaces, fine woodwork, clean carpeting, freshly painted or papered walls, soundproofing, adequate climate control, well-placed light fixtures and electrical outlets, sufficient hot water, and good water pressure are all appreciated by tenants. The value of personalty included under the lease terms should also be identified and its effect on income should be measured.

Operating expenses

Adjustments for variations in leases and the characteristics that influence the income a property can generate must be made before the market rent of the subject property can be estimated. Some further adjustment may be necessary if the subject property has an expense-to-income ratio that is especially high or low. Variations in this ratio can affect the value of properties even when the income they produce remains constant. Because the *GRM* is never adjusted in the income capitalization approach, an adjustment for the subject's atypical expense ratio is made in deriving the estimated market rent of the subject property.

DATA COLLECTION AND RENT SURVEY

An appraiser may have difficulty compiling all the rental data needed to complete the first two steps of the income capitalization approach. Experienced appraisers collect relevant information continuously and keep it on file for use in specific appraisal assignments. Newspaper advertisements are a good source of data for analyzing trends in rents. Asking rents and actual rents do not vary as much as asking prices and sales prices for similar property. Interviews with landlords, tenants, real estate brokers, property managers, and neighbors can also provide useful information. In addition to rents and sales, data on typical expenses for a variety of residential properties should be collected. The appraiser can file these data chronologically and by property type for future use.

In performing an appraisal the appraiser may collect required market data by conducting a *rent survey.* The focus of a rent survey is the subject property. The appraiser notes the size and characteristics of the subject property and interviews the tenant or tenants that currently occupy the property. The appraiser asks about the rent being paid, anticipated rent increases or decreases, the benefits and drawbacks of the property, whether the rent and lease provisions are fair, and whether the tenant plans to leave when the lease expires. The actual rent and lease provisions may not be supported in the current market, but these data provide a good starting point for the appraiser's investigation.

The appraiser then investigates the properties from which the *GRM* and comparable rents are to be derived. A separate form can be completed for each rental property to help organize the data and ensure that the appraiser has collected all the necessary information. The location of the property, the names of the tenant and the landlord, and a brief rental history can be recorded on the form along with the property size, condition, special features, and other pertinent data.

Neighbors and tenants frequently supply valuable information on the desirability of the property in question. Rental data should always be verified if possible by interviewing both the tenant and the landlord. The appraiser is interested in the amount of rent that is actually being paid, not in the landlord's wishful thinking.

Data are collected for each rental property separately and additional information is often needed. A brief sales history of the property and a schedule of expenses can be useful. Sometimes expenses are detailed in a published operating statement compiled by the property owner for tax purposes. Accounting methods vary, so figures obtained from operating statements should be examined critically.

APPLICATION OF *GRM* TO MONTHLY MARKET RENT

To arrive at the market value of a residence using the income capitalization approach, the monthly market rent of the residence is estimated and then multiplied by the *GRM* selected. If, for example, a *GRM* of 140 is selected based on market analysis and the monthly market rent of the subject property is estimated to be $1,200, the property's market value would be estimated as follows:

Estimated monthly market rent of property being appraised	$1,200
Times gross rent multiplier	× 140
Indicated market value	$168,000

In some situations it may be necessary to calculate market rent on an annual basis. Assume the property in question rents for $1,300 per month during the 9-month school year and $900 per month during the remaining three months. The annual property rent is $14,400 (9 × $1,300 + 3 × $900) and the average monthly rent is \$14,400/12, or \$1,200. When this rent is multiplied by the *GRM* of 140, the indicated value of the property is calculated.

$$\$1,200 \times 140 = \$168,000$$

SUMMARY

The income capitalization approach is applicable to properties for which an active rental market exists. To value an income-producing, single-family residential property, an appraiser estimates the rental income the property is expected to generate and converts this income into an indication of value by applying a gross rent multiplier. The procedure has three steps: 1) derivation of a *GRM*, which is the ratio between the sales prices of comparable properties and their gross monthly rental income; 2) estimation of the monthly market rent the subject property should command; and 3) multiplication of the subject property's market rent by the *GRM*.

Gross rent multipliers can be used when reliable sales and rental data are available. If a property cannot be used for an income-producing use due to legal or economic restrictions or because sufficient, appropriate data are not available, the income capitalization approach is inapplicable.

The comparable properties that provide data for deriving a *GRM* must be similar to and competitive with the subject in terms of lease provisions, expenses, and income characteristics. The reliability of the *GRM* depends on the comparability of the properties from which it is derived. Comparable properties should be located in the same neighborhood or similar neighborhoods and appeal to households of similar sizes and income levels. The ratios of operating expenses to income must be similar for the comparable properties and the subject. The expenses incurred by residential properties can be divided into fixed expenses and variable expenses. The lease provisions applicable to the comparable properties should be similar to those of the subject property because differences can affect the expenses that the landlord must pay or the rent the property can generate.

In the reconciliation of *GRM*s, the greatest emphasis is placed on multipliers derived from properties that are most comparable to the subject. No adjustments are made to *GRM*s because differences between the comparable properties are already reflected in their *GRM*s.

The market rent of the subject property is the rental income the property would most probably command in the open market as of the date of the appraisal. Contract rent, which is the actual rent specified in the lease, may differ from market rent. One of the parties to the lease may have been under duress or market conditions may have changed since the lease was signed. Special circumstances can influence lease provisions, which in turn affect property income.

The actual rent of a comparable property can be adjusted to reflect the market rent the subject is capable of generating. Adjustments may be made for market conditions and lease provisions; for characteristics that influence the income a property can generate such as location, size, quality, condition, and amenities; and for differences in operating expense ratios. To estimate the market rent of property, appraisers keep files of data on rental trends and typical operating expenses. Rent surveys are conducted to determine current rents, anticipated rent changes, lease provisions, and the benefits and drawbacks associated with specific rental properties.

REVIEW QUESTIONS

1. What is a gross rent multiplier (*GRM*)? How are *GRM*s derived?

2. When is the income capitalization approach applicable to the valuation of residential properties? What factors limit its usefulness?

3. Explain why expense-to-income ratios and lease provisions are examined in analyzing the comparability of properties.

4. How are *GRM*s reconciled? Why are *GRM*s never adjusted?

5. Discuss the distinction between contract rent and market rent. Why does the actual rent of a property sometimes differ from the market rent it is capable of generating?

6. What three categories of adjustments are made to bring the actual rent of a property in line with its market rent?

7. How does an appraiser analyze the monthly rent of a single-family residence? How is the rent of a two- to four-unit building analyzed?

8. What kinds of data are gathered in a rent survey?

PART VII

CONCLUDING THE APPRAISAL

20 Final Reconciliation

The final reconciliation of value estimates is the last analytical step in the valuation process. Typically an appraiser applies different valuation approaches and obtains a number of different estimates. Sometimes different results may be obtained from a single approach; in the sales comparison approach, for example, the adjusted sales prices of comparable properties can be considered value estimates. Some appraisers choose to reconcile these variations only after the data associated with the other valuation approaches have been considered. In any case, all remaining differences in the value estimates derived must be reconciled at this stage in the valuation process.

Final reconciliation begins with a review of the entire appraisal. The purpose and use of the appraisal, the methods of data collection, and the analytical tools employed are reexamined in reconciliation. Each step of the valuation process is tested for logic, consistency, and appropriateness. Mathematical errors are corrected and gaps in the data are filled in with further research. If data are inadequate or additional data are not available, the effect of the incomplete data on the valuation conclusion is explained.

The results produced by each of the approaches to value are weighed. The greatest emphasis is placed on the approach or approaches that are most applicable to the problem and make use of the most reliable, accurate, and representative data. Finally, a single value indication or a range of value is selected. The figures are rounded to reflect the appraiser's confidence in their accuracy, and the value conclusion is presented to the client with the reasoning and documentation in the appraisal report.

In final reconciliation the different value estimates are *not* averaged. No mechanical formula can be used to select one indication over the others. An appraisal depends on the application of appraisal judgment and experience. The appraiser's judgment, experience, and sound application of appraisal techniques are all critical in final reconciliation.

REVIEW

To provide a basis for final reconciliation, an appraiser reviews the entire valuation process. The nature of this review and the need for it depends on the complexity of the assignment and the appraiser's confidence in the data and the analytical techniques applied. Even experienced appraisers review their valuations before submitting the conclusions to their clients to reduce the chances of error.

To perform a comprehensive review, the appraiser proceeds methodically through each step of the valuation process. Typically an appraiser considers whether 1) the appraisal is logical and the conclusion is appropriate to the purpose and use of the appraisal; 2) the data are accurate, adequate, and properly analyzed; 3) the data have been used in a consistent manner within each approach and are correlated from one approach to another; and 4) the calculations are correct.

Logical Answer to the Client's Question

An appraisal is designed to provide an answer to a client's specific question, which the client will use to make some decision concerning the real estate in question. The appraiser must make sure that the solution provided is appropriate and presented in a way that is meaningful and useful to the client.

Thus, the first question to ask is Do the approaches and methods applied lead to meaningful conclusions that relate to the purpose and use of the appraisal? In most residential appraisals the purpose of the valuation will be to estimate market value, and the use of the appraisal will be to serve as a basis for a mortgage loan decision or a relocation purchase offer. The definition of value employed should be reviewed along with the assumptions and limiting conditions applicable to the appraisal to ensure that the value estimate derived satisfies all of the client's requirements as well as those of the appraisal profession.

If a valuation is to be used in court, the value definition should be closely scrutinized. The definition used in a particular jurisdiction may contain subtleties that merit special attention. The value conclusion must be consistent with the property interests being appraised. The court may seek specific evidence regarding the amount a seller could obtain for a property in the open market or the amount a buyer would be willing to pay in the same market. A value indication reflecting the current highest and best use of the property may be sought, rather than one that considers other uses for which the property might be legally, physically, and economically suited. Various legal considerations may affect the character of the assignment and the appraiser's conclusions.

Accuracy and Adequacy of Data and Analysis

The data an appraiser collects must be accurate. They must support the conclusions drawn and provide a convincing representation of market patterns. Accuracy is enhanced if the appraiser is knowledgeable about the sources of the data and their relative reliability. At times certain information cannot be taken too seriously. For example, market projections issued by local chambers of commerce can sometimes be inaccurate. Nevertheless, this type of information should be considered because it may supply important leads and suspect information can be checked against data from independent sources. As a general rule, firsthand research is more persuasive than outdated, generalized information obtained from reference manuals.

Critical details pertaining to the subject and comparable properties and aspects of transactions that may have influenced sales prices must always be verified personally. The appraiser should interview one of the parties to the transaction, preferably the buyer or the seller; attorneys, real estate agents, brokers, and lenders can also be contacted. Often documented evidence that is verified by one of these individuals is the most reliable and compelling form of data for appraisal purposes.

Appraisers should avoid using suspicious or questionable data. A property sale between related parties may not qualify as an arm's-length transaction, and, therefore, the property should not be used as a comparable. The comparable sales selected must be truly representative of the market.

Using a reliable data source may not be enough. The appraiser must also be satisfied that the data accurately represent the thinking and behavior of market participants. To ensure that the data are representative, an appraiser attempts to locate and study a broad sample of comparable properties located in the neighborhood delineated for the subject property. A large base of general market data can also provide support for the valuation conclusion, even if these data are not derived from perfectly comparable properties. General information on market trends can be almost as revealing as specific sales of very similar properties. Therefore, it is very important that appraisers maintain good records on all kinds of real estate transactions.

To review the data collection effort, the appraiser first reexamines the purpose of the appraisal, the property interests being valued, and the assumptions and limiting conditions. Given these parameters, was the data collection effort complete? Were city and regional data collected to provide a background for neighborhood analysis? If these data were collected, how reliable and current are they? Do market trends in real estate values support the adjustments for market conditions applied to the comparable properties?

Next, the appraiser scrutinizes the neighborhood analysis. How were the neighborhood boundaries drawn? In light of what the appraiser has learned from his or her field inspection, should these boundaries be redrawn? If so, does this change affect the selection or reliability of the data used? The comparables selected should all be located within the boundaries of the subject neighborhood or in similar, competitive neighborhoods.

By the reconciliation stage of the valuation, the appraiser has a broader picture of the market and can better judge whether the comparables are truly comparable. Do they provide the best indications of the value of the subject property in the market area? If they do not, what other evidence would be more persuasive? Would it be worthwhile to replace a comparable or include additional comparables? Have all available data on the subject property been used? If the subject property has been sold recently, has all information about the transaction been considered? How confident is the appraiser of the reasonableness of the adjustments made for property differences?

The observations made during the field inspection are also examined. Does this information correspond to published information about the subject and comparable properties? Are the sketches and maps used accurate and up-to-date? Any changes in property boundaries, additions to the improvements since their original construction, and subsequent encroachments or easements should be carefully noted. Such changes can alter the appraiser's conclusion of market value.

The accuracy and reliability of transactional data should be ascertained. What sources were contacted for this information? How were the data verified—by the buyer, the seller, an attorney, or a lender? Is the information complete? Are sales prices, sales concessions, and special financing arrangements specified? Are any items of personal property included in the transactions listed? How were adjustments for special financing derived—through paired data set analysis, cash equivalency calculations, or some other method? Were the methods appropriate?

Finally, cost and income and expense data are reviewed. If a cost service was used, is the appraiser satisfied with the reliability of the cost estimates? Should these costs be confirmed by local contractors? Were costs for all the components of the subject property taken into account? Was a reasonable amount added for entrepreneurial profit? How reliable is the appraiser's estimate of land value? Are the estimates of various types of accrued depreciation well supported?

Consistency

An appraiser checks the consistency of the data and reasoning applied in each valuation approach and the correlation between the approaches. Although the valuation approaches reflect different appraisal strategies, the data considered in the different approaches should be consistent. For example, the depreciation estimate calculated in the cost approach should usually correlate with the total adjustments made for the quality, age, and condition of the improvements in the sales comparison approach.

To ensure consistency, the same highest and best use conclusion must be used throughout the appraisal. In the cost approach the appraiser values the land or site as though vacant and the property as though improved on the basis of the same use. The appraiser must also ascertain that the site improvements included in the land or site value estimate have not been cited again in the estimate of the depreciated value of the improvements.

In reconciliation an appraiser checks to see that no item has been mistakenly counted twice in any portion of the appraisal. In the sales comparison approach, for example, adjustments should not be made twice for the same difference under two separate headings. Sometimes an adjustment for an age difference is partially duplicated in an adjustment for physical condition. If these adjustments reflect the same difference, only one should be used.

In the cost approach an appraiser could mistakenly penalize a property twice by considering the same item of accrued depreciation under two separate categories. If, for example, the functional obsolescence of a kitchen appliance is measured in terms of the cost to remove and replace it, additional depreciation cannot be charged for the deteriorated physical condition of the same appliance.

Review of Calculations

All mathematical calculations should be checked, preferably by someone other than the person who originally made them. Errors in arithmetic can lead to erroneous value indications and undermine the credibility of the entire appraisal. It is easy for a person to overlook his or her own errors, so an independent check of numerical calculations is an important part of the appraiser's review.

RECONCILIATION CRITERIA

After the appraisal has been reviewed and the appropriateness of the value estimates derived in the various approaches has been determined, differences in the value estimates must be reconciled. There is no simple arithmetical or statistical procedure for reconciling value estimates. Rather, an appraiser reaches a final value indication or range of indications by assessing his or her confidence in each preliminary estimate. The degree of confidence associated with a given estimate usually depends on the appropriateness of the valuation approach to the problem at hand and the quality and quantity of the data used.

Appropriateness

The criterion of appropriateness helps an appraiser decide how much weight to accord the value estimate derived from a particular approach. The appropriateness of a given approach is usually related to the type of property being appraised and the viability of the market. Market value reflects how the market perceives value, so the approach that most closely mirrors market perceptions usually yields the most credible results.

In most residential appraisals the sales comparison approach is accorded the greatest weight. Sales comparison reflects the thinking of most buyers and sellers who study and compare the prices of similar property to find a reasonable price at which to buy or sell. However, this approach may not be applicable in areas where sales are few or when the property being appraised has unique features.

In these situations, market participants may base their value decisions on cost factors. The cost approach is more appropriate than the sales comparison approach when the highest and best use of the property is to demolish the existing structure and build a new improvement on the land. Cost analyses might also be important if typical purchasers interested in the property would plan on making substantial repairs or renovations.

In valuing older properties with a great deal of incurable depreciation, the cost approach tends to be less appropriate. Market participants, like real estate appraisers, have difficulty deciding how much accrued depreciation the property has incurred.

When an active rental market exists and potential purchasers are interested in the property's ability to generate an income, income capitalization may be the most reliable approach. The income capitalization approach is applicable when sufficient rental and sales data exist; if such data for residential properties are unavailable, the income capitalization approach is not appropriate.

Quality of Data

The specific items of data used in an appraisal may have different degrees of accuracy. Therefore, an appraiser should consider the relative quality of the data used in each approach to weigh the reliability of the estimates derived. For example, are the cost data and accrued depreciation estimates used in the cost approach as accurate as the adjustments made in the sales comparison approach or the market rent data and gross rent multipliers used in the income capitalization approach? An appraiser may have more confidence in the accuracy of the data used in one approach than those used in another.

There are several ways to measure the quality of the data used in the sales comparison approach. If the adjustments made to the comparable prices are too large or too numerous, the margin of error is broad and accuracy is diminished. The need for many adjustments suggests that the comparable properties are not truly comparable.

To judge the quality of the data, an appraiser may look at the number of adjustments made to each comparable. As the number of adjustments increases, the reliability of the value indication derived from that comparable decreases.

Another important measure is the size of the net adjustments as a percentage of the comparable's unadjusted sale price. The net adjustments to a comparable are calculated by adding the dollar amounts of all positive adjustments and deducting the sum of all negative adjustments. One problem with this test is that the appraiser cannot assume that positive and negative adjustments canel each other out. With this test a comparable with a net adjustment similar to those of other comparables may seem reasonable when actually either the positive or the negative side has been incorrectly weighted. For this reason appraisers also consider *gross adjustments*.

The gross adjustment to a comparable is the sum of the amounts of all the adjustments made to the comparable's sale price, regardless of whether these adjustments are positive or negative. This sum is expressed as a percentage of the unadjusted sale price.

At times, however, the gross size of dollar adjustments may not be a good indicator of the quality of the comparable data, particularly if few adjustments are needed. A single large adjustment may be more accurate and defensible than many smaller adjustments. For example, an appraiser may find abundant market evidence in a community to indicate the value added by a swimming pool, a garage, or an extra bedroom. An adjustment for the presence or absence of such a large item in a comparable might result in a gross adjustment that is larger than the gross adjustments made to the other comparables. However, greater accuracy may be attributed to this adjustment because the market evidence of its contribution to value is more reliable.

The tests described above are applied to check the reliability of each comparable sale as a basis for deriving a value indication for the subject property. These tests may also be used to reconcile different value estimates in the sales comparison approach and to determine the relative applicability of the approach.

The overall persuasiveness of the sales comparison approach is often enhanced by using a large number of comparable sales, but using a certain number of sales cannot guarantee a reasonable conclusion. The number of sales examined depends on the reliability of the sales and the client's requirements. Some clients insist on a minimum number of sales. The appropriateness of the valuation approach applied and the quality of the data employed determine the relevance of the value estimate derived from a given approach or comparable sale. In addition to quality, however, the quantity of evidence provided must be considered.

Quantity of Data

Although the data used in a given approach meet the criteria of appropriateness and quality, they may still be insufficient. When few reliable, recent sales are available but cost and depreciation data are abundant, increased emphasis may be given to the cost approach. Similarly, abundant data on one comparable may increase the appraiser's confidence in the value indication derived from this sale.

Of course, an appraiser must not be persuaded by the quantity of data alone. The data considered must be both relevant and accurate. When these data are interpreted by an experienced appraiser in a manner consistent with the purpose of the appraisal, a reliable value estimate will result. Sound appraisal conclusions rest on the application of reasoning and judgment to market data, not merely on the manipulation of data.

FINAL VALUE INDICATION

After the various value estimates are weighed, the appraiser must reconcile them. The final value indication may be expressed as a *point estimate*, as a *range* of value, or as a value within a designated range.

A point estimate is the traditional way of expressing a valuation conclusion. The estimate of the subject property's value is stated as a single dollar amount—e.g., $92,000, $187,000, or $365,000. A point estimate that reflects the appraiser's best opinion as to the approximate value of a property is required in many types of appraisals. Point estimates are requested for real estate tax purposes, just compensation estimates, and certain property transfer decisions; they are also used to calculate federal income tax depreciation deductions and to determine lease terms based on value. Clients may expect a point estimate even when they have not specifically requested one because this type of estimate has been customary in the past.

One problem associated with point estimates is that the presentation of a single figure may suggest greater precision than is warranted. Properly understood, a point estimate implies a range of value in which the property value most probably lies. The opinion on which a value indication is based is impartial, well-reasoned, and the very best a professional appraiser can provide in view of the evidence gathered and analyzed. Nevertheless, a point estimate is an opinion of the most likely dollar value of the interest being appraised subject to certain qualifying conditions. This opinion may, in fact, be too high or too low.

Occasionally an appraiser may have reason to avoid offering a "best" opinion and specify a range of value between two dollar figures. By reporting a range, the appraiser is indicating that the actual value is probably no lower than the low end of the range and no higher than the high end.

Stating a range of value can present serious problems, however. A wide range is of no use to a client, but a narrow range can be incorrectly interpreted as a guarantee that the price will fall between the extreme values. A client who is provided with a value range is likely to hold fast to whichever extreme suits his or her purposes.

Rounding

It is customary to round appraisal conclusions to reflect the lack of precision associated with them. Rounding may be based upon rules of significant digits, but often a value conclusion is simply rounded to two or three digits.

Rounding also reflects how prices are expressed in the market. If market study reveals a pattern in pricing, the appraiser should round accordingly.

SUMMARY

Final reconciliation of value estimates begins with a review of the entire appraisal. There is no prescribed formula for selecting the final indication; rather, the appraiser applies reasoning, judgment, and experience in this process. The logic, consistency, and appropriateness of each step of the valuation are reexamined. Errors are corrected and insufficient data are supplemented. The greatest emphasis is placed on the approach or approaches that are most applicable to the problem and employ the most accurate and representative data. The final value conclusion is presented to the client with all supporting reasoning and documentation in the appraisal report.

In reviewing the appraisal, the appraiser considers whether 1) the appraisal is logical and results in a conclusion that is appropriate to the purpose and use of the appraisal; 2) the data are accurate, adequate, and properly analyzed; 3) the data have been used in a consistent manner; and 4) the calculations are correct.

The appraiser must ascertain that the methods employed lead to a meaningful conclusion that relates to the purpose and use of the appraisal. Data on general market trends, neighborhood conditions, and specific comparables are verified; data obtained from primary sources, the physical inspection, and published records are cross-checked. Sales comparison data and adjustments are reviewed for consistency with cost data, depreciation estimates, and land value indications. The appraiser makes sure that the same highest and best use conclusion is used to value the land and the improved property and that no adjustment or item of depreciation has been counted more than once. Numerical calculations are also checked.

Once the review is completed and the appropriateness of the value estimates derived in the various approaches is determined, the appraiser must reconcile the differing indications. Three criteria are used to weigh the reliability of the preliminary value indications: the appropriateness of the approach to the specific problem, the quality of the data collected, and the quantity of the data analyzed.

The sales comparison approach generally reflects the thinking of market participants; it is appropriate when sales data are abundant and the property is fairly typical for its market. If data are insufficient or the property is unique, greater reliance may be placed on the cost approach to value. When a residence produces an income and sufficient rental and sales data are available, use of the income capitalization approach is appropriate.

The appraiser considers the quality of the data used in each approach—e.g., adjustments in the sales comparison approach, cost data and estimates of accrued depreciation in the cost approach, market rent data and gross income multipliers in the income capitalization approach. Appraisers examine the number and size of adjustments to check the reliability of sales data and the probability of error. The appraiser may choose to expand the number of comparables analyzed if the results are inconclusive. The quantity of data employed also is considered in deciding which approach or comparable provides the most reliable indication of value.

The final value indication may be expressed as a point estimate, a range of value, or a value within a designated range. A point estimate is a single dollar amount that reflects the impartial, expert, and reasoned opinion of the appraiser. An appraiser may choose to provide a range of value, but difficulties may arise if the range is too broad to be useful or too narrow and restrictive. Value estimates may be rounded to significant digits or simply carried out to two or three places.

REVIEW QUESTIONS

1. Which specific aspects of the appraisal does an appraiser consider in the review process?

2. How do the valuation methods applied in an appraisal problem lead to a meaningful conclusion that relates to the purpose and use of the appraisal?

3. What four criteria does an appraiser use to weigh the preliminary value estimates?

4. How does an appraiser check the reliability and probability of error in the adjustments made in the sales comparison approach?

5. Identify three ways in which an appraiser may express a final value indication.

21 The Appraisal Report

An appraisal report leads its reader from the definition of the appraisal problem through the appraiser's reasoning and relevant descriptive data to a specific value conclusion. The appraiser must present all facts, analysis, and conclusions clearly and succinctly. The length, type, and content of appraisal reports are dictated by the client, regulatory requirements, the courts, the type of property being appraised, and the nature of the valuation problem.

Every appraisal report is prepared to answer a particular question and provide information needed by a client. Some common appraisal questions are: What is the market value of the property? What is the highest and best use of the land as though vacant and the property as improved? What is the value of the part taken in condemnation? What is the damage or benefit to the remainder of the property as a result of the taking?

INSTITUTE STANDARDS FOR WRITTEN REPORTS

Each analysis, opinion, or conclusion that results from an appraisal must be communicated in a manner that is meaningful to the client and will not be misleading to concerned parties or the public. To ensure the quality of appraisal reports, professional appraisal organizations have set minimum standards for the factual content, descriptive material, and statements of work and purpose included in all types of appraisal reports. To comply with the requirements set by the American Institute of Real Estate Appraisers, an appraiser should

- Identify and describe the real estate being appraised
- Specify the real property interest(s) being appraised by analyzing the ownership, financial, and legal interests in the property
- Define the opinion that is the purpose of the appraisal and describe the use of the appraisal
- Specify the date of valuation and the date when the report was completed
- Determine the highest and best use of the real estate being appraised, when this is necessary and appropriate

- Describe the appraisal procedures used
- Provide supporting data and the reasoning behind the analyses, opinions, and conclusions in the report
- Explain all assumptions and limiting conditions that affect the analyses, opinions, and conclusions set forth in the report and disclose any extraordinary assumptions and limiting conditions in the relevant sections of the report
- Identify related personal property that is included in the appraisal opinion
- Discuss the history of the property, including recent sales transactions and current listings, offers, leases, and contracts
- Discuss the effect of leases and existing or assumed financing upon value[1]

Written appraisal reports prepared by members or candidates of the Appraisal Institute must contain a certification that includes the following items:

- A statement that, to the best of the appraiser's knowledge and belief, the facts in the report are true and correct and all assumptions and limiting conditions that affect the appraiser's analyses, opinions, and conclusions are set forth in the report
- A statement disclaiming or acknowledging any personal interest in the subject property
- A statement disavowing or disclosing any personal bias on the part of the appraiser with respect to the parties involved
- A statement that the appraiser's compensation is or is not contingent on any action or event resulting from the analyses, opinions, or conclusions in, or the use of, the report
- A statement that the analyses, opinions, and conclusions in the report have been developed in conformity with the requirements of the Code of Professional Ethics and the Standards of Professional Practice
- A statement that the use of the report is subject to the requirements of the Appraisal Institute regarding review by its duly authorized representatives
- A statement that the appraiser is or is not currently certified under the Appraisal Institute's voluntary continuing education program (Not required for candidates)
- A statement confirming that a personal inspection of the subject property was or was not made and identifying the individual(s) who carried out the inspection
- An acknowledgment of any significant professional assistance that the appraiser received in conducting the appraisal

---

1. See the Uniform Standards of Professional Appraisal Practice and Supplemental Standards for greater detail and the specific requirements that apply to appraisal reports signed by Appraisal Institute members and candidates.

TYPES OF REPORTS

An appraisal report may be oral or written. Written reports include letter, form, and narrative reports. Usually a report is presented in the manner requested by the client. Sometimes, however, a client asks for the appraiser's opinion without detailed documentation. In this case, the appraiser must perform the analysis required for a complete appraisal and keep all the material, data, and working papers used to prepare the report in permanent file. Although the appraiser may never need to provide written substantiation for the opinion rendered in abbreviated form, he or she may be asked to explain or defend the opinion at a later time.

Oral Reports

An appraiser may make an oral report if the circumstances or the needs of the client do not permit or warrant a written report. Expert testimony whether presented in deposition or in court is considered an oral report. Most oral reports are not made under oath; they are communicated to the client in person or by telephone.

Each oral report should include a property identification and the facts, assumptions, conditions, and reasoning on which the value conclusion is based. Before communicating an oral report, the appraiser should file all notes and data relating to the assignment and prepare a complete memorandum of the appraisal analysis, conclusion, and opinion.

Letter Reports

At times, by prior agreement with the client, an appraiser submits the results of an appraisal in a letter report. A letter report must comply with all reporting and certification requirements. Although much data and reasoning are omitted from a letter report, certain items must be included if the report is to be meaningful. A letter report must

- Adequately identify the property and the property rights being appraised
- State the purpose of the appraisal
- Describe the analysis or analyses performed
- Set forth the date of valuation, the date of the report, and all limiting conditions
- Include a certification statement[2]

Some of the minimum reporting requirements may be avoided, provided the appraiser meets the precise departure provision requirements of the Uniform Standards and complies with Ethical Rule 1-1. As in the case of an oral report, the appraiser must keep all notes and data on file along with a complete summary of the analysis, conclusions, and opinion. In addition the client should be informed that many regulatory agencies and other users of appraisal reports do not accept letter or short narrative reports.

---

2. Members and candidates of the Appraisal Institute must include a certification that complies with the Uniform Standards of Appraisal Practice.

Narrative Reports

A narrative appraisal report gives an appraiser the opportunity to support and explain his or her opinions and conclusions and convince the reader of the soundness of the final value indication. This type of report answers the client's questions in writing and substantiates these answers with facts, reasoning, and conclusions. To be most useful to the client, a narrative appraisal report must present adequate, pertinent supporting data and logical analysis that lead to the appraiser's conclusions.

A narrative report summarizes all the facts and appraisal methods and techniques that have been applied in the valuation process to arrive at the value estimate or another conclusion. The report demonstrates the appraiser's ability to interpret relevant data, select appropriate valuation methods and techniques, and ultimately estimate a specifically defined value.

In an appraisal report, descriptive material should be separated from analysis and interpretation. Typically factual and descriptive data are presented in the early sections of the report so that subsequent sections on data analysis and interpretation can refer to these facts and discuss how they influence the final value estimate. Unnecessary repetition is undesirable, but the presentation of data may depend on the nature and length of the report. Narrative reports are organized to follow the steps in the valuation process.

The appraiser may not be present when the report is reviewed or examined, so the report is the appraiser's representative. A good narrative report will give the client a favorable impression of the appraiser's professional competence.

Format

A narrative appraisal report should be designed for maximum communication with the reader, who may be the client or the client's representative. Because readers may scan rather than study a narrative report, the report should be organized to highlight the property description, the essential analysis of the problem, and the value conclusion.

In addition to thorough research, logical organization, and sound reasoning, a well-prepared report should reflect good composition, a fluid writing style, and clear expression. Technical jargon and slang should be avoided. To communicate with the reader most effectively, the content of the report should be set forth as succinctly as possible.

Outline

Narrative appraisal reports vary in content and organization, but they all contain certain elements. Generally a narrative report follows the order of the valuation process.

Most narrative reports have three major parts: an introduction, factual descriptions, and an analysis of data and the opinions of the appraiser. These parts may be further divided with subheadings or presented in a continuous narrative. In either case, the major divisions of the report should be identified with headings and separated from one another. Many reports also have a fourth section, an addenda, which contains supplemental information and illustrative material that would interrupt the narrative. The organization of individual narrative reports may vary, but the following outline can be used as a general guide.

Part I—Introduction
    Title page
    Letter of transmittal
    Table of contents
    Photograph (optional)
    Summary of important facts and conclusions
    Purpose and use of the appraisal
    Date of value estimate
    Property rights appraised
    Definition of value and property rights

Part II—Factual Descriptions
    Identification of the property
    History, including sales history
    Regional and city data
    Neighborhood data
    Zoning
    Tax and assessment data
    Site description
    Improvement description

Part III—Analysis of Data and Opinions of the Appraiser
    Highest and best use analysis
    Site value estimate
    The cost approach
        Estimate of current reproduction or replacement cost
        Estimate of accrued depreciation
        Summary of conclusions
    The sales comparison approach
        General content and depth of the market research
        Choice of the most indicative comparable sales
        Description of each selected comparable sale
        Analysis of major value-influencing characteristics of the comparable properties
        Market-oriented adjustments for differences between the comparables and the subject
    The income capitalization approach
        Estimate of market rent for subject
        Estimate of *GRM* for subject
    Reconciliation and final value estimate
    Certification of value
    Assumptions and limiting conditions
    Qualifications of the appraiser

Addenda
    Additional photographs of the subject property
    Photographs of street views in the immediate area
    Maps of secondary importance

City and regional statistical data

Supplemental material that may help the reader visualize the
property or understand the appraisal

The arrangement of items in this outline is flexible and can be
modified to fit nearly all appraisal assignments on any type of real
property. In practice, an appraiser would adapt this outline to
meet the particular requirements of the assignment and to suit
his or her personal preference. Appraisals of certain types of
property may require special treatment.[3]

Form Reports

In many appraisal situations, form reports meet the needs of
financial institutions, insurance companies, and government agencies. In the secondary mortgage market created by government
agencies and private organizations, form reports are required for
the purchase and sale of most existing mortgages on residential
properties. Because these clients review many appraisals, using a
standard report form is more efficient and convenient. When a
form is used, those responsible for reviewing the appraisal know
exactly where to find each category or item of data in the report.
By completing the form, an appraiser ensures that no item required by the reviewer has been overlooked. The Appraisal Institute's Guide Note 3 applies to the use of form reports for residential
property. Each form report must comply with all reporting and
certification requirements.

The method of valuation employed in an appraisal is determined by the nature of the specific appraisal problem. If a report
form seems too rigid and does not provide for the inclusion of all
the data that the appraiser believes to be pertinent, the relevant
information and the appraiser's comments should be added as a
supplement.

An appraiser should make sure that the completed report is
consistent in its description of the property and provides all the
data indicated by the categories listed. If the appraiser's determination of the highest and best use of the property does not conform to the use for which the form is appropriate, the form cannot
be used. All data must be presented in a clear and comprehensi-
ble manner and all form reports should include a proper certification and statement of limiting conditions.

A form appraisal report is unacceptable if the appraiser fails to
1) consider the purpose of the report, the value definition, and
the assumptions and conditions inherent in the report; 2) question the client about any underwriting criteria that might conflict with proper appraisal practice and explain how such criteria
affect the value estimate, given the value definition on the form;
3) conduct an appropriate review before signing the report as a
review appraiser; and 4) consider and discuss any prior sales,

---

3. For a comprehensive guide to writing a narrative report, see William C. Himstreet,
   The Narrative Report in the Communicating the Appraisal series, published by the
   American Institute of Real Estate Appraisers, Chicago, 1988.

offers, or listings of the property within one year of the date of the appraisal.[4]

The most widely used form report for residential appraisals is the *Uniform Residential Appraisal Report* (URAR) form, which is required by HUD/FHA, the VA, the Farmers Home Administration (FMHA), Fannie Mae, and Freddie Mac. Other forms used by government agencies include the *Individual Condominium or PUD Unit Appraisal Report* and the *Small Residential Income Property Appraisal Report.* The *Employee Relocation Council* (ERC) *Residential Appraisal Report* form was developed for use by members of the ERC, which is an independent organization that assists in the transfer of corporate employees. The URAR form is reproduced in Figure 21.1; the other forms can be found in Appendix B.

Uniform Residential Appraisal Report (URAR)

The Uniform Residential Appraisal Report (FHLMC Form 70/ FNMA Form 1004) was adopted in 1987 and is used by all major real estate-oriented government agencies. The form has two parts: a property description and analysis section and a valuation section. On the first part of the form, an appraiser fills in the following information:

- *Subject* (property address, legal description, owner/occupant, sale price and date, seller-paid loan charges or concessions, real estate taxes, and property rights appraised)
- *Neighborhood* (location—urban/suburban/rural, degree of development, growth rate, trend in property values, demand and supply balance, marketing time, neighborhood analysis, present land use, likelihood of change in use, predominant type of occupancy, and price and age range of single-family housing)
- *Site* (dimensions, area, zoning classification, zoning compliance, highest and best use, utilities, site improvements, and physical characteristics)
- *Improvements* (general description, exterior description, foundation, basement, and insulation)
- *Room list*
- *Interior* (surfaces, heating, kitchen equipment, attic, and improvement analysis)
- *Car storage facility*

Space is provided at the bottom of the first page for comments on any additional features of the subject property, accrued depreciation, and general market conditions and financing in the subject area.

The valuation section of the URAR includes entries for the following items:

- *Cost approach* (building sketch; estimates of the reproduction cost of the main improvement and accessory buildings, accrued depreciation, and site value; and construction warranty)

---

4. The Appraisal Institute's Guide Note 3, "The Use of Form Appraisal Reports for Residential Property."

Figure 21.1 The Uniform Residential Appraisal Report Form

Property Description & Analysis **UNIFORM RESIDENTIAL APPRAISAL REPORT** File No. _____

SUBJECT

Property Address	Census Tract _____
City _____ County _____ State _____	Zip Code _____
Legal Description	
Owner/Occupant	Map Reference _____
Sale Price $ _____ Date of Sale _____	PROPERTY RIGHTS APPRAISED
Loan charges/concessions to be paid by seller $ _____	☐ Fee Simple
R.E. Taxes $ _____ Tax Year _____ HOA $/Mo. _____	☐ Leasehold
Lender/Client	☐ Condominium (HUD/VA)
	☐ De Minimis PUD

LENDER DISCRETIONARY USE

Sale Price	$ _____
Date	
Mortgage Amount	$ _____
Mortgage Type	
Discount Points and Other Concessions	
Paid by Seller	$ _____
Source	

NEIGHBORHOOD

LOCATION	☐ Urban	☐ Suburban	☐ Rural
BUILT UP	☐ Over 75%	☐ 25-75%	☐ Under 25%
GROWTH RATE	☐ Rapid	☐ Stable	☐ Slow
PROPERTY VALUES	☐ Increasing	☐ Stable	☐ Declining
DEMAND/SUPPLY	☐ Shortage	☐ In Balance	☐ Over Supply
MARKETING TIME	☐ Under 3 Mos.	☐ 3-6 Mos.	☐ Over 6 Mos.

PRESENT LAND USE %	LAND USE CHANGE	PREDOMINANT OCCUPANCY	SINGLE FAMILY HOUSING
Single Family ____	Not Likely ☐	Owner ☐	PRICE $ (000) — AGE (yrs)
2-4 Family ____	Likely ☐	Tenant ☐	Low
Multi-family ____	In process ☐	Vacant (0-5%) ☐	High
Commercial ____	To: ____	Vacant (over 5%) ☐	Predominant
Industrial ____			—
Vacant ____			

NEIGHBORHOOD ANALYSIS	Good	Avg.	Fair	Poor
Employment Stability	☐	☐	☐	☐
Convenience to Employment	☐	☐	☐	☐
Convenience to Shopping	☐	☐	☐	☐
Convenience to Schools	☐	☐	☐	☐
Adequacy of Public Transportation	☐	☐	☐	☐
Recreation Facilities	☐	☐	☐	☐
Adequacy of Utilities	☐	☐	☐	☐
Property Compatibility	☐	☐	☐	☐
Protection from Detrimental Cond.	☐	☐	☐	☐
Police & Fire Protection	☐	☐	☐	☐
General Appearance of Properties	☐	☐	☐	☐
Appeal to Market	☐	☐	☐	☐

Note: Race or the racial composition of the neighborhood are not considered reliable appraisal factors.

COMMENTS: _____

SITE

Dimensions _____	Topography _____
Site Area _____ Corner Lot ☐	Size _____
Zoning Classification _____ Zoning Compliance _____	Shape _____
HIGHEST & BEST USE: Present Use _____ Other Use _____	Drainage _____

UTILITIES	Public	Other	SITE IMPROVEMENTS	Type	Public	Private		
Electricity	☐		Street		☐	☐	View	_____
Gas	☐		Curb/Gutter		☐	☐	Landscaping	_____
Water	☐		Sidewalk		☐	☐	Driveway	_____
Sanitary Sewer	☐		Street Lights		☐	☐	Apparent Easements	_____
Storm Sewer	☐		Alley		☐	☐	FEMA Flood Hazard Yes* ___ No ___

FEMA* Map/Zone _____

COMMENTS (Apparent adverse easements, encroachments, special assessments, slide areas, etc.): _____

IMPROVEMENTS

GENERAL DESCRIPTION	EXTERIOR DESCRIPTION	FOUNDATION	BASEMENT	INSULATION
Units ____	Foundation ____	Slab ____	Area Sq. Ft. ____	Roof ☐
Stories ____	Exterior Walls ____	Crawl Space ____	% Finished ____	Ceiling ☐
Type (Det./Att.) ____	Roof Surface ____	Basement ____	Ceiling ____	Walls ☐
Design (Style) ____	Gutters & Dwnspts. ____	Sump Pump ____	Walls ____	Floor ☐
Existing ____	Window Type ____	Dampness ____	Floor ____	None ☐
Proposed ____	Storm Sash ____	Settlement ____	Outside Entry ____	Adequacy ____
Under Construction ____	Screens ____	Infestation ____		Energy Efficient Items:
Age (Yrs.) ____	Manufactured House ____			
Effective Age (Yrs.) ____				

ROOM LIST

ROOMS	Foyer	Living	Dining	Kitchen	Den	Family Rm.	Rec. Rm.	Bedrooms	# Baths	Laundry	Other	Area Sq. Ft.
Basement												
Level 1												
Level 2												

Finished area **above** grade contains: _____ Rooms; _____ Bedroom(s); _____ Bath(s); _____ Square Feet of Gross Living Area

INTERIOR

SURFACES	Materials/Condition	HEATING		KITCHEN EQUIP.		ATTIC	
Floors	____	Type	____	Refrigerator	☐	None	☐
Walls	____	Fuel	____	Range/Oven	☐	Stairs	☐
Trim/Finish	____	Condition	____	Disposal	☐	Drop Stair	☐
Bath Floor	____	Adequacy	____	Dishwasher	☐	Scuttle	☐
Bath Wainscot	____	COOLING		Fan/Hood	☐	Floor	☐
Doors	____	Central	____	Compactor	☐	Heated	☐
		Other	____	Washer/Dryer	☐	Finished	☐
		Condition	____	Microwave	☐		
Fireplace(s) # ____		Adequacy	____	Intercom	☐		

IMPROVEMENT ANALYSIS	Good	Avg.	Fair	Poor
Quality of Construction	☐	☐	☐	☐
Condition of Improvements	☐	☐	☐	☐
Room Sizes/Layout	☐	☐	☐	☐
Closets and Storage	☐	☐	☐	☐
Energy Efficiency	☐	☐	☐	☐
Plumbing-Adequacy & Condition	☐	☐	☐	☐
Electrical-Adequacy & Condition	☐	☐	☐	☐
Kitchen Cabinets-Adequacy & Cond.	☐	☐	☐	☐
Compatibility to Neighborhood	☐	☐	☐	☐
Appeal & Marketability	☐	☐	☐	☐
Estimated Remaining Economic Life				____ Yrs.
Estimated Remaining Physical Life				____ Yrs.

AUTOS

CAR STORAGE					
No. Cars	Garage ____	☐ Attached	☐ Adequate	House Entry ☐	
Condition	Carport ____	☐ Detached	☐ Inadequate	Outside Entry ☐	
	None ____	☐ Built-In	☐ Electric Door	Basement Entry ☐	

Additional features: _____

COMMENTS

Depreciation (Physical, functional and external inadequacies, repairs needed, modernization, etc.): _____

General market conditions and prevalence and impact in subject/market area regarding loan discounts, interest buydowns and concessions: _____

Valuation Section   **UNIFORM RESIDENTIAL APPRAISAL REPORT**   File No. _____

Purpose of Appraisal is to estimate Market Value as defined in the Certification & Statement of Limiting Conditions.

COST APPROACH

BUILDING SKETCH (SHOW GROSS LIVING AREA ABOVE GRADE)
If for Freddie Mac or Fannie Mae, show only square foot calculations and cost approach comments in this space.

ESTIMATED REPRODUCTION COST - NEW - OF IMPROVEMENTS:

Dwelling _____ Sq. Ft. @ $ _____ = $ _____
_____ Sq. Ft. @ $ _____ = _____
Extras _____ = _____
_____ = _____
Special Energy Efficient Items _____ = _____
Porches, Patios, etc. _____ = _____
Garage/Carport _____ Sq. Ft. @ $ _____ = _____
Total Estimated Cost New .... = $ _____

     Physical | Functional | External
Less
Depreciation _____ = $ _____
Depreciated Value of Improvements .... = $ _____
Site Imp. "as is" (driveway, landscaping, etc.) = $ _____
ESTIMATED SITE VALUE .... = $ _____
(If leasehold, show only leasehold value.)
INDICATED VALUE BY COST APPROACH .... = $ _____

(Not Required by Freddie Mac and Fannie Mae)
Does property conform to applicable HUD/VA property standards? ☐ Yes ☐ No
If No. explain:

Construction Warranty ☐ Yes ☐ No
Name of Warranty Program _____
Warranty Coverage Expires _____

The undersigned has recited three recent sales of properties most similar and proximate to subject and has considered these in the market analysis. The description includes a dollar adjustment, reflecting market reaction to those items of significant variation between the subject and comparable properties. If a significant item in the comparable property is superior to, or more favorable than, the subject property, a minus (−) adjustment is made, thus reducing the indicated value of subject; if a significant item in the comparable is inferior to, or less favorable than, the subject property, a plus (+) adjustment is made, thus increasing the indicated value of the subject.

SALES COMPARISON ANALYSIS

ITEM	SUBJECT	COMPARABLE NO. 1		COMPARABLE NO. 2		COMPARABLE NO. 3	
Address							
Proximity to Subject							
Sales Price	$		$		$		$
Price/Gross Liv. Area	$	$		$		$	
Data Source							
VALUE ADJUSTMENTS	DESCRIPTION	DESCRIPTION	+ (−) $ Adjustment	DESCRIPTION	+ (−) $ Adjustment	DESCRIPTION	+ (−) $ Adjustment
Sales or Financing Concessions							
Date of Sale/Time							
Location							
Site/View							
Design and Appeal							
Quality of Construction							
Age							
Condition							
Above Grade Room Count	Total / Bdrms / Baths	Total / Bdrms / Baths		Total / Bdrms / Baths		Total / Bdrms / Baths	
Gross Living Area	Sq. Ft.	Sq. Ft.		Sq. Ft.		Sq. Ft.	
Basement & Finished Rooms Below Grade							
Functional Utility							
Heating/Cooling							
Garage/Carport							
Porches, Patio, Pools, etc.							
Special Energy Efficient Items							
Fireplace(s)							
Other (e.g. kitchen equip., remodeling)							
Net Adj. (total)		☐ + ☐ − $		☐ + ☐ − $		☐ + ☐ − $	
Indicated Value of Subject			$		$		$

Comments on Sales Comparison: _____

INDICATED VALUE BY SALES COMPARISON APPROACH .... $ _____
INDICATED VALUE BY INCOME APPROACH (If Applicable) Estimated Market Rent $ _____ /Mo. x Gross Rent Multiplier _____ = $ _____

This appraisal is made ☐ "as is" ☐ subject to the repairs, alterations, inspections or conditions listed below ☐ completion per plans and specifications.
Comments and Conditions of Appraisal: _____

RECONCILIATION

Final Reconciliation: _____

This appraisal is based upon the above requirements, the certification, contingent and limiting conditions, and Market Value definition that are stated in
☐ FmHA, HUD &/or VA instructions.
☐ Freddie Mac Form 439 (Rev. 7/86)/Fannie Mae Form 1004B (Rev. 7/86) filed with client _____ 19 ____ ☐ attached.
I (WE) ESTIMATE THE MARKET VALUE, AS DEFINED, OF THE SUBJECT PROPERTY AS OF _____ 19 ____ **to be $** _____

I (WE) certify: that to the best of my (our) knowledge and belief the facts and data used herein are true and correct; that I (we) personally inspected the subject property, both inside and out, and have made an exterior inspection of all comparable sales cited in this report; and that I (we) have no undisclosed interest, present or prospective therein.

Appraiser(s) SIGNATURE _____   Review Appraiser SIGNATURE _____ ☐ Did ☐ Did Not
     NAME _____   (if applicable) NAME _____   Inspect Property

Freddie Mac Form 70   10/86   Fannie Mae Form 1004   10/86

- *Sales comparison approach* (market data grid for transactional, locational, physical, and other adjustments)
- *Value indication from the income approach*
- *Conditions* of the valuation (as is or subject to repairs or completion according to plans)
- *Conditions* of the appraisal (itemized cost of necessary repairs)
- *Final reconciliation*
- *Certification signature*

To complete the URAR form, the appraiser provides the appropriate information for each entry. If a line or section is not applicable to the appraisal, *not applicable* (N/A) or a similar term should be indicated in the appropriate space. The appraiser should make sure that the entries in the property description and analysis section are consistent with the data entered in the valuation section. Space is provided for comments so any considerations not specifically addressed on the form can be covered.

A certification and statement of limiting conditions (FHLMC Form 439/FNMA Form 1004B) must be attached to all URAR form reports unless the appraiser has placed the attachment on file with the client. This document provides the definition of market value used in the analysis, the certification of the professional ethics employed in performing the appraisal assignment, and the applicable contingent and limiting conditions. An appraiser might want to list additional conditions because the form may not cover all the specific points required.

Other useful attachments to the form might include photographs of the front and one side of the subject property, the rear of the property and the other side, and a street scene as viewed from the property; a floor plan sketch; a legal description; and a location map. The type and number of attachments are determined by the requirements of the appraisal assignment. A properly executed, well-documented report includes all necessary supplementary attachments.[5]

Individual Condominium or PUD Unit Appraisal Report

The Individual Condominium or PUD Unit Appraisal Report (FHLMC Form 465/FNMA Form 1073), which is shown in Appendix B, is a two-page form with entries for the following items:

- Names of the mortgagor, lender, and occupant; legal description of the unit; property rights appraised; and transactional and tax data
- Neighborhood land use, occupancy, and rating
- Site dimensions, zoning, utilities, and offsite improvements
- Project improvements, type, and rating
- Description and rating of the condo or PUD unit
- Budget analysis for the unit

---

5. For detailed instructions on filling out the URAR form, see Arlen C. Mills, *The Uniform Residential Appraisal Report* in the Communicating the Appraisal series, published by the American Institute of Real Estate Appraisers, Chicago, 1988.

- Cost approach value indication
- Market data analysis
- Market data and income approach value indications
- Final reconciliation
- Certification signature

Freddie Mac requires that an appraiser complete Addendum A for project analysis. Part I of this addendum must be completed if fewer than 70% of the individual units in the project have been sold. Part II must be completed if the project is in the process of conversion or has been converted within the past two years. Freddie Mac also requires that Addendum B/FNMA Form 1073A be completed by the seller/servicer or an agent for the owners association or property management. This form calls for a detailed analysis of the income and expenses—i.e., operating budget—for the entire project.

Small Residential Income Property Appraisal Report

The Small Residential Income Property Appraisal Report (FHLMC Form 72/FNMA Form 1025), which is included in Appendix B, is a two-page form that contains the following entries:

- Names of the mortgagor, lender, and occupant; legal description of the property; property rights appraised; and transactional and tax data
- Neighborhood land use, occupancy, and rating
- Site dimensions, zoning, utilities, and offsite improvements
- Description and analysis of the improvements
- Cost approach value indication
- Rental data on comparable properties
- Schedule of actual and forecast rents for subject property
- Analysis of market data for deriving gross rent multipliers and reconciliation of *GRM*s
- Market data approach value indication
- Analysis of actual and forecast expenses
- Certification signature

Employee Relocation Council Residential Appraisal Report

The Employee Relocation Council Residential Appraisal Report form shown in Appendix B is published by the ERC, a nonprofit membership organization founded in 1964. Its members include corporations, relocation service companies, brokers, and appraisers involved in the transfer of corporate employees. The ERC is concerned with providing relocation assistance to transferred employees who are selling their existing homes and acquiring new ones.

The first page of the form provides definitions relating to relocation appraisals—the purpose and definition of a relocation appraisal and the market data approach to value. This material is followed by general and procedural guidelines for appraisers. A grid for a building sketch is included on the second page.

On the third page information on the description and analysis of the property is recorded. The information to be provided includes

- Address and legal description of the subject property and the property rights appraised
- Neighborhood land use and occupancy
- Site dimensions, zoning, and utilities
- Description of the improvements and basement
- Room list
- Description of the interior finish and equipment
- Property rating

The valuation section on the fourth page of the form contains a market data grid, a supplementary section for reconciling value-related differences between the subject property and individual comparables, and a line for recording the indicated value of the subject by the market data approach.

Information on competing listings and value-related differences between these properties and the subject is filled in on the top of page five. The entries on the bottom of this page and the top of page six are concerned with the subject property.

- Special features
- Condition
- Acreage, taxes, and fees
- Personal property included
- Special financing
- Information on the current list price and length of market exposure

The next section of the form addresses current market conditions, including the availability of financing, the present supply and demand situation, and future economic trends. Additional comments may be listed in the space that follows. The final entry on the form is the certification signature.

A Condominium Addendum may be attached to the ERC Residential Appraisal Report when supplemental information on the condominium unit and complex, its management, financing, and marketability is required by the client.

Special Pointers for Completing Form Reports

All form reports have entries for a highest and best use conclusion. The response most often recorded is "present use"; if "other use" is indicated, the appraiser must explain the reasoning that supports this use conclusion.

The Appraisal Institute's Guide Note 3 states that highest and best use appears as a box to be checked on most forms because the form itself is a statement of highest and best use. Therefore, it is inappropriate to use a single-family residential form or another type of form report if the appraiser has concluded that the highest and best use of the property being appraised is different from the property type specified on the form.

When improvements are rated, the terms *good, average, fair,* and *poor* may be used to indicate how the subject property compares to market standards. Average is not a negative rating, but ratings of fair and poor should be documented and explained. The ratings of improvements should be consistent with quality and condition statements that appear elsewhere in the appraisal report.

The type and number of attachments to a form report are determined by the client's requirements and the scope and character of the appraisal assignment. An appraiser should consider adding attachments if the form does not provide sufficient coverage of a relevant subject. Standard addenda are attached to the Individual Condominium or PUD Unit Appraisal Report form. To provide a valid valuation analysis, a form report must be properly documented and supported with all necessary attachments.

SUMMARY

An appraisal report should lead the reader from the definition of the appraisal problem through the reasoning and analysis of relevant data to a specific conclusion. An appraisal should be communicated in a meaningful and straightforward manner. The American Institute of Real Estate Appraisers has specific requirements for the content of appraisal reports and for the appraiser's certification of value. Appraisal Institute members and candidates should consult the applicable Uniform Standards and Supplemental Standards rules for these requirements.

Appraisal reports may be communicated orally or in writing. Written reports may be letter, narrative, or form reports. Regardless of how the report is conveyed, all data and notes that pertain to the assignment and a summary of the appraiser's analysis and conclusions should be kept in a permanent file.

An oral report must include a property description and all the facts, assumptions, conditions, and reasoning on which the conclusion is based. Expert testimony is considered an oral report, as are other presentations made in person or by telephone. A letter report identifies the property and the property rights appraised, states the purpose of the appraisal, describes the analysis performed, cites the date of valuation and the date of the report, sets forth all limiting conditions, and includes the required certification.

In a narrative report an appraiser provides a written explanation of the pertinent data analyzed and the methods employed to estimate a specifically defined value. Appraisers should keep factual and descriptive data separate from analysis and interpretation and not include repetitive or unnecessary material in their reports. Narrative reports follow the steps in the valuation process and often have three major parts: an introduction, factual descriptions, and an analysis of data and opinions of the appraiser. Addenda may be attached to include supplemental information and illustrative material.

Form reports are often used by financial institutions, insurance companies, and government agencies. They provide a standard, comprehensive format for recording data and may be supplemented with attachments.

To prepare an acceptable form report an appraiser must 1) consider the purpose of the report, the value definition, and the assumptions and limiting conditions inherent in the report; 2) question the client about any underwriting criteria that might conflict with proper appraisal practice; 3) conduct an appropriate review before signing the report as a review appraiser; and 4) consider any prior sales, offers, or listings of the property within one year of the date of the appraisal.

The Uniform Residential Appraisal Report (URAR) form was adopted in 1987 and is used by all major real estate-oriented government agencies. Other form reports include the Individual Condominium or PUD Unit Appraisal Report, the Small Residential Income Property Appraisal Report, and the Employee Relocation Council (ERC) Residential Appraisal Report.

REVIEW QUESTIONS

1. Discuss the Appraisal Institute's requirements for appraisal reports. What specific statements are required in the certifications used by Appraisal Institute members and candidates?

2. Describe the contents of oral, letter, narrative, and form reports.

3. What four things must an appraiser do to ensure that a form report is acceptable?

4. Identify situations in which the Uniform Residential Appraisal Report (URAR) form would be used. Describe the general organization of the URAR form.

5. What attachments can be submitted to supplement a form report? What specific attachment is required for all URAR form reports?

PART VIII

SPECIAL PROBLEMS

22 Special Problems in Residential Appraisal

The special characteristics of certain categories of single-family residences set them apart from more typical houses. These residences often present problems for appraisers. The ownership of condominiums and cooperatives, for example, includes interests in both privately held and commonly held areas. Timeshare properties and residences on leased land represent limited ownership interests. Resort and vacation homes, housing for the elderly, and farm and ranch houses are examples of special-purpose residences. In planned unit developments (PUDs), owners of privately held, single-family residences or townhouses have access to commonly held amenities. These PUDs exist because special zoning is enacted to facilitate the creation of neighborhoods. Other residences with special characteristics include mobile homes, modular and prefabricated houses, mansions, historic houses, log cabins, solar homes, and experimental houses.

CONDOMINIUMS

Condominium ownership is a form of fee ownership of separate units or portions of multiunit buildings that provides for formal filing and recording of a divided interest in real property. A condominium owner holds title to an individual unit in a multiunit property and has an undivided interest in common areas of the property. The owner of a condominium is the sole proprietor of the three-dimensional space within the outer walls, roof or ceiling, and floors of the individual unit. He or she can lease, sell, mortgage, or refinance this unit separately from the other units in the property. In addition, the owner, together with the owners of the other units, has an undivided interest in common areas such as the site on which the building stands, the public portions of the building—e.g., entryways, corridors, elevators—the building foundation, the outer walls, the parking areas, and all driveways and recreational facilities.

The condominium deed must contain an exact horizontal and vertical description of the location of the condominium unit. The boundaries of the common areas and the individual units are shown on the plot plan, or plat, and the architectual plans, which must be publicly recorded in many states.

Condominium owners usually form an association to manage the real estate in accordance with adopted bylaws. A typical condominium or home owners association is governed by a board of directors elected by the individual owners. It operates under a set of bylaws which is recorded in the master deed and complies with state laws concerning condominiums. Usually a majority of the owners must vote to change the bylaws and all of the owners must agree to change the master deed. Management and maintenance expenses are generally divided on a pro rata basis and levied as a monthly, quarterly, or annual fee.

Condominiums can be new units or existing units that have been converted to condominium ownership. They may be units in high rises, townhouses, small groups of party-wall units, or free-standing units.

Appraisal Techniques

Individual condominium units are typically appraised using the sales comparison approach. A value indication derived from sales comparison may be supported by application of the income capitalization approach if rental data on units comparable to the subject unit are available. Resales of similar units in the same or similar condominium projects make the best comparables. Because it is difficult to make accurate adjustments for differences in common charges, recreational facilities, size, and design, comparables must be selected from very similar complexes. The form of condominium ownership—i.e., fee simple or leasehold—is especially important in comparing properties. Adjustments for market conditions are also difficult to make because the market for condominiums is very volatile. Although the price of new, similar units should be considered, the resale prices of condominium units in some projects are substantially lower than the prices of comparable new units.

Many lenders require an analysis of the entire project when the value of an individual unit is estimated. An appraiser should examine the common charges and the expected rate of increase in these charges carefully because similar units in different projects may be subject to dissimilar charges.

COOPERATIVES

Cooperative ownership is a form of ownership in which each owner of stock in a cooperative apartment building or housing corporation pays a proportionate share of operating expenses and debt service on the underlying mortgage, which is paid by the corporation. A co-op is created when a stock corporation is organized to issue an authorized number of shares of stock at a specified par value. The corporation takes title to an apartment building and prices the various units. The price per unit determines the number of shares that a tenant, who is a shareholder in the cooperative apartment corporation, must purchase to acquire a *proprietary lease*. Under the lease the tenant-shareholder must pay a monthly maintenance fee, which may be adjusted later by the corporation's board of directors. The fee covers the costs of management, operations, and the maintenance of public areas. Shareholders use their shares in the corporation to vote on the election of directors, which gives them some control over property conditions.

Appraisal Techniques

The most persuasive indication of the value of a cooperative apartment is obtained by analyzing the sale of ownership shares to comparable units in the same building or similar buildings. However, there may be some confusion about what constitutes the sale price of a cooperative apartment. For example, a share entitling an owner to exclusive occupancy of a three-bedroom apartment may be offered for $30,000. This price appears to be very low, but this amount is not the total price. If the entire building is subject to a $600,000 mortgage and the shareholder's portion of this mortgage is $60,000, the real price of the unit is approximately $90,000. Therefore, in addition to normal operating expenses, the owner will have to make payments on a $60,000 share of the mortgage debt.

When sales of comparable units in the same cooperative corporation are available for analysis, no adjustment is needed to reflect the mortgage. However, the price of similar units in different cooperative corporations may differ because the two corporations may have dissimilar mortgage obligations.

Some cooperative corporations allow individual units to be rented to tenants, while others restrict the use of cooperative units to actual shareholders. If rentals are permitted in a given building, the appraiser can establish a correlation between rent and value and apply the income capitalization approach.

TIMESHARE PROPERTIES

Timesharing is the sale of limited ownership interests in residential property: single units, apartments or hotel rooms. The timeshare purchaser receives a deed that conveys title to the unit for a specific part of the year. Timesharing generally applies to resort and vacation housing. Under this arrangement, one property is purchased by several owners, each of whom has the right to use the property for a predetermined period of time. For example, 10 timeshare owners may buy a house at a ski resort. The owners share the cost of the property equally, and each has the right to use the property for two weeks during the ski season and three weeks at another time.

Appraisal Techniques

To value a timeshare an appraiser first identifies the rights to be valued. These rights pertain to both the ownership and the use of the property. The ownership of the shared property may be fee simple, tenancy in common, joint tenancy, condominium, cooperative, limited partnership, or a real estate investment trust. The part of the property that is allocated for use by the shareholder must also be established. The personal property included is an important consideration because many timeshare properties are sold furnished and equipped with appliances and utensils.

Resales of the timeshare property being appraised or similar properties may provide reliable value indications. Resales are better evidence because new sales may be motivated by the developer's aggressive promotional campaign. If some of the units are rented during part of the year, the income capitalization approach may be applicable. Market research can help the appraiser establish the relationship between the rent a timeshare unit can command and its resale value.[1] If new timeshare units are being sold in the area and vacant land is available for construction of additional units, the cost approach may also be applied.

RESIDENCES ON LEASED LAND

In states such as Hawaii, residences have long been built on leased land.[2] Leases may be for as long as 99 years or for 50 years or less. To protect the mortgage, some leases provide that the interest of the fee owner is subordinate to the interest of the mortgagee or lender. However, most leases give the mortgagee the right to take over the land rent payments if the mortgagor defaults. Usually the mortgagee also has the right to find a new mortgagor to continue the lease payments. When the lease expires, the improvements become the property of the landowner, who may extend the lease after modifying it to reflect current market conditions.

Appraisal Techniques

To value a residence on leased land an appraiser uses the same techniques applied to residences subject to other forms of ownership. The value of the leasehold interest may be estimated by capitalizing the ground rent. An adjustment is usually required to reflect differences between the ground rents and lease terms of the subject property and the comparable properties. Depending on the appraisal problem, it may be necessary to estimate the value of both the leased fee interest and the leasehold interest.[3]

RESORT AND RECREATION HOMES

There are several million resort and recreation homes in this country; most of these second homes are occupied by their owners on a seasonal basis. Some second homes are mansions in resort areas for the wealthy, but the majority are modest homes located near a body of water or other recreational area. Many developers are very active in the second home market, subdividing

1. Weekly rental rates for similar timeshare units are compared with the rent of the subject unit and adjusted for the location, recreational amenities, and construction quality of the overall property and for the size, layout, and furnishings of the rental unit. See Kathleen Conroy, *Valuing the Timeshare Property* (Chicago: American Institute of Real Estate Appraisers, 1981), p. 35.

2. To reduce the social and economic evils of concentrated land ownership, the Hawaii legislature adopted the Land Reform Act of 1967. In a 1983 decision, the Court of Appeals for the Ninth Circuit held the reform act unconstitutional. This ruling was reversed the following year when the Supreme Court upheld that the state of Hawaii had indeed met the public use requirement in exercising its power of eminent domain. See Jerome G. Rose, "From the Courts: Supreme Court Upholds Redistribution of Ownership of Hawaii Land," *Real Estate Law Journal*, Winter 1985, pp. 263-269.

3. Edith J. Friedman, ed., *Encyclopedia of Real Estate Appraising* (Englewood Cliffs, N.J.: Prentice-Hall, Inc., 1978), pp. 291-295.

Figure 22.1   Special Types of Residential Properties

Condominium

Resort/Recreation Home

Elderly Housing

Planned Unit Development

Mobile Home

Solar Home

Experimental Home

large tracts of land and building extensively. Although there was some discussion about prohibiting the deduction of mortgage interest and real estate taxes on second homes for income tax purposes, the Tax Reform Act of 1986 did not eliminate these deductions.

Appraisal Techniques

The second home market tends to be volatile. Resales are a persuasive indication of the value of these residences; initial sales, which are often the result of developer promotions, tend to be less reliable. When data on rents for seasonal residences are available, the income capitalization approach is applicable. When land is available for development and new homes are still being built, the cost approach may also be used.

HOUSING FOR THE ELDERLY

Housing for the elderly encompasses a variety of options, ranging from single-family residences and senior apartments to adult congregate living facilities (ACLF) and continuing-care retirement centers (CCRC). The elderly market may be divided into two age groups: 50 to 65 and 65 and over.[4] The first segment is composed of preretirement or empty-nester individuals who range in age from 50 to 64. Many are still employed, but find that their changing lifestyles warrant a different type of housing. They tend to prefer scaled-down single-family homes and townhouses in affluent neighborhoods or condominiums and cooperative apartments that require little maintenance.

The second segment of the elderly housing market consists of seniors over 65. This group can be broken down into three subgroups: those 65 to 74 years of age who are enjoying their leisure time and may live in retirement communities, those 75 to 84 years of age who require some care but wish to preserve their independence and privacy, and those age 85 and over who are frail or disabled. Congregate housing facilities for the elderly are generally designed with special equipment and have safety features such as fire-resistant construction. These features add to their cost. Elderly housing units generally have less square footage than conventional housing. Functional adequacy also dictates that facilities for the dependent elderly have special characteristics. Individual units may not have kitchens if residents take their meals in central dining areas. Similarly, rooms may be arranged for convenient access to facilities and public areas.

Appraisal Techniques

Many neighborhoods for the elderly are restricted to individuals who are at least 50 or 55 years of age. Age restrictions in senior citizen developments have been upheld by the courts. Because these restrictions affect the value of properties, comparable sales and rentals must be located in the same community or similar communities. Some facilities designated as elderly housing receive

---

4. Arthur E. Gimmy and Michael G. Boehm, *Elderly Housing: A Guide to Appraisal, Market Analysis, Development and Financing* (Chicago: American Institute of Real Estate Appraisers, 1988), pp. 24-31.

government subsidies to finance the costs of development or help residents pay their rent. Appraising these units may be difficult because the appraiser may need to search a wide geographic area for comparables. If a project has special construction and design features, locating comparables becomes even more problematic.

FARM AND RANCH HOUSES

The appraisal of rural property requires special skills and experience. In many ways, however, appraising a farm or ranch house is similar to appraising other single-family residences.

Appraisal Techniques

Two approaches are employed to value rural houses and acreage. If most of the property's value is in the land, the value of the residential improvement may be estimated with the cost approach. If most of the property's value is in the improvement, the sales comparison approach may be used. As an example, consider a property that consists of 50 acres valued at approximately $10,000 per acre improved with a 1,200-sq.-ft., six-room, one-story, ranch-style house valued at $30,000 based on its depreciated cost. To derive a total property value indication, the appraiser should investigate comparable land sales to establish the land value estimate and then add the $30,000 depreciated cost of the improvement.[5]

For contrast, consider an eight-room, two-story farmhouse valued at approximately $80,000 located on two acres of land. To value this property an appraiser would examine comparable sales of similar farmhouses and make adjustments for differences in the acreage on which these houses are situated. An accurate analysis of highest and best use is critical. Excess land that could be separated from the property may have its own highest and best use and should be valued separately based on this use.

In the appraisal of a small farm, it may be possible to extract the value of the house and homesite—i.e., the one or two acres that include the well, septic system, and site improvements—from the total property value. The appraiser then compares these property components with similar houses and homesites on other farms to derive an indication of their value. (The extraction procedure is discussed in detail in Chapter 12.)

PLANNED UNIT DEVELOPMENTS (PUDs)

A *planned unit development* (PUD) is a type of land development in which buildings are clustered or set on lots that are smaller than usual. Large, open, park-like areas are included in the development. Residential PUDs exist because special zoning allows groups of housing units, often townhouses, to be built on lots

---

5. If the property being appraised was also improved with farm buildings, the relationship between these buildings and the agricultural enterprise would have to be considered. The appraiser would need to understand the management and operation of the farm to analyze the role and suitability of the various improvements. Cost comparisons based on local standards could be used to estimate the value contribution of farm buildings. *The Appraisal of Rural Property* (Chicago: American Institute of Real Estate Appraisers, 1983), pp. 101-102.

smaller than those normally required for residential construction. In exchange for the right to build on smaller lots, the developer agrees to set aside some vacant land to be used by the community or a home owners association. In PUDs streets, landscaping, and public facilities can be designed with greater flexibility than is possible in conventional neighborhoods.

The individual single-family residences in a PUD are owned in fee simple or as condominiums with joint ownership of open areas; in some areas local law requires that open areas be deeded to the city. Driveways, parking areas, and recreational facilities may also be jointly owned by the residents. An undivided interest in these common areas runs with the title to each property. Consequently, these areas must be inspected as part of the site when individual properties are appraised.

A *de minimis PUD* is a special category of PUD. Before construction of such a project begins, the developer must submit the project plans to Fannie Mae for approval. Early application facilitates the loan processing. Three criteria are used to determine whether a project qualifies as a de minimis PUD. The project plan must specify that the owner of each unit will 1) possess fee simple title to the lot for the unit delineated in the subdivision plans; 2) maintain both the interior and exterior of the unit under the terms set forth in the conditions, covenants, and restrictions (CC&Rs) of the project; and 3) base the purchase decision on the dwelling unit, not the special rights to use project amenities, depending on the extent of these amenities.

Appraisal Techniques

The problems encountered and the methods applied in appraising PUD residences are similar to those associated with the appraisal of condominiums and fee simple properties.

MOBILE HOMES

A mobile home, or house trailer, is a complete, livable dwelling unit that is equipped with wheels so it can be towed from place to place with a truck or automobile. Mobile homes make up almost 10% of all existing single-family residences in the United States. The most popular size for a mobile home is 12 or 14 feet wide by 60 feet long; larger units are 24 feet wide and 47 feet long or 28 feet wide and 60 feet long. Smaller units are manufactured, but these are rarely occupied year round. When mobile homes are not on the road, they can be settled on pads or foundations in *mobile home parks*, or trailer parks, which have permanent parking facilities for mobile homes. Mobile home parks offer a range of recreational amenities and many are situated near shopping centers and public transportation.

Mobile homes offer substantial living space at a typical cost of $40,000 to $60,000, which is less than the cost of comparable conventional housing. A mobile home park can also be a community of rental units. Typical park residents include senior citizens, young couples, students, and military personnel.

Appraisal Techniques

Mobile homes may be valued by applying the sales comparison, cost, and income capitalization approaches. Like models must be compared because the quality of construction varies widely among different models and manufacturers. Valuation books are available for mobile homes. These books are similar to the books used by car and truck dealers to determine the value of used vehicles. The books contain data collected from mobile home dealers all over the country; the figures shown are derived by averaging sales in many areas. These data are useful, but they cannot substitute for the data obtained in a complete appraisal.

Most mobile homes that are sold in place are not moved, so their value is affected by their environment. Like a house, a mobile home can either benefit from its location or incur external obsolescence. An appraisal based solely on data published in a valuation book would not reflect the influence of external factors.

MODULAR AND PREFABRICATED HOUSES

Modular and prefabricated houses are partially constructed in a factory and transported to a site for installation and assembly. When set up on a site, a small modular home may resemble a mobile home. A typical home measures 12 feet by 60 feet and is joined together in the middle. Larger modular houses may consist of several segments, which are shipped by rail or truck and assembled on the site. Prefabricated houses, often called *prefabs*, are factory-built shells that are assembled on site.

Modular houses and prefabs represent a small, but growing, part of the housing market. Companies that manufacture modular and prefabricated housing make use of efficient assembly line and mass production methods to create affordable housing. On-site assembly of these factory-produced houses generally takes only a few days, which reduces costs for builders and home buyers. Lot owners can see complete model houses and be assured that they will get a house very similar to the model. Buyers of conventional new houses must often base their purchase decisions on architectural plans and specifications, which they may find confusing.

Appraisal Techniques

Traditional appraisal techniques and procedures can be applied to prefabricated and modular houses. There is generally little difference in value between these houses and conventionally built houses of similar size, design, and quality. The short construction period and reduced cost of modular housing may benefit the original owner, but these benefits do not affect the properties' resale value.

MANSIONS

Mansions are large, imposing residences for wealthy individuals who can sustain high maintenance costs and enjoy gracious living. Mansions usually have extra rooms for recreation, entertaining, and accommodating guests and servants. Most mansions are designed to reflect the individual tastes of their owners and some may have historical value.

Appraisal Techniques

Mansions can present unique valuation problems because they are few in number and are sold infrequently. The amenities these houses afford, their size, and their sales histories vary. If the highest and best use of a mansion is to remain as a single-family residence, the sales comparison approach will produce the most reliable value indication. To find comparable property sales, an appraiser will probably have to investigate sales in neighboring or competitive communities. The adjustment for location is extremely important, but it may be difficult to determine.

The highest and best use of a mansion may be other than a single-family residential use. Many mansions are suitable for conversion into multifamily units or for institutional use. The sites may include excess land that could be developed separately. In these situations the appraiser may need to conduct further investigation and analysis.

HISTORIC HOUSES

Until the middle of the twentieth century, most historic houses were structures associated with well-known figures and events of great national significance. Since the 1960s and 1970s, however, the preservation movement has become increasingly focused on architecturally significant buildings and historic neighborhoods. In the late 1970s historic district zoning and federal tax incentives for rehabilitation emerged along with adaptive uses through which old railroad stations, factories, and churches were converted into shopping malls, apartments, and offices. The preservation movement has also proven that restoring neighborhoods has a stabilizing effect on communities.[6]

Houses designated as historic landmarks are protected by special national, state, or local legislation, which is often concerned primarily with the exterior of the structures. Because the significance of many buildings in registered districts lies mainly in their location and contribution to the appearance of the street, private easements and restrictions may affect only the building facade.[7] Historic designation may enhance the value of property, but some owners feel that restrictions limit their ownership rights.

Special tax legislation may benefit property owners who grant historic easements that control interior and exterior renovations. The National Trust for Historic Preservation, state preservation organizations, and state or local governments are qualified to accept such easements. Property owners can deduct the value of these historic easements as gifts on their income tax returns. Some communities also reduce property taxes in exchange for easements.

---

6. Judith Reynolds, *Historic Properties: Preservation and the Valuation Process* (Chicago: American Institute of Real Estate Appraisers, 1982), pp. 2-3, 49-50; Virginia O. Benson and Richard Klein, "The Impact of Historic Districting on Property Values," *The Appraisal Journal*, April 1988, pp. 223-232.

7. For a more detailed discussion of preservation easements, which may be called *historic, open space, scenic, conservation,* or *facade easements*, see Chapter 9 of Reynolds' *Historic Properties*.

Because of the complexity of appraising historic properties, appraisers should consult current literature published by the National Trust for Historic Preservation.

Appraisal Techniques

Appraising a historic house can be a difficult task. Application of the sales comparison approach may be more complex because market data are usually scarce. Often a very wide area must be searched to find comparable historic properties. The applicability of the cost approach is weakened because it is impossible to put a price on the building's historical significance or to duplicate the conditions under which the building was constructed. The income capitalization approach is often inapplicable because there is rarely a discernible relationship between the rental value of a historic house and its value.

Despite its complexity, the sales comparison approach may be the only suitable method available to the appraiser. To apply the approach an appraiser must consider the historic importance of each comparable property. Does the event, figure, or architectural style associated with the comparable make that property as significant as the subject? The location of the comparable is especially important.

Consider, for example, two fairly similar historic houses that an appraiser is using as comparables. One is located in a neighborhood that is part of a redevelopment program. Residents have formed a neighborhood association, renovated their properties, rebuilt the sidewalks and streets, and imposed controls to maintain the exterior appearances of the buildings. The other house is located in a neighborhood that has reached the end of its economic life cycle. Several nearby houses have been gutted by fire and left unrepaired. Many of the structures need exterior painting and carpentry. Buildings in the area are tenant-occupied and many are up for sale. In this case, the first comparable would most likely have a far higher value than the second. Although they appear similar, the properties are not really comparable.

Estimating the value of a historic easement also requires a search for relatively scarce market data. Ideally an appraiser will be able to find information on the value of properties before and after historic easements were granted or data on properties that were sold and then resold after an easement was granted. An appraiser could also apply paired data set analysis to the sales of similar properties that do and do not carry historic easements.

In valuing historic properties appraisers should keep in mind that tax incentives may actually create value in addition to the value attributable to the real estate. Many older properties are acquired and renovated by developers who then pass the tax benefits through to the purchasers of the renovated structure.

LOG CABINS AND OTHER HISTORIC REPRODUCTIONS

The popularity of historic houses has generated interest in historic reproductions. Owners of reproductions wish to enjoy the amenities of a historic style without having to endure the inconveniences of living in an older home. Modern plumbing and heating systems are installed in reproduction houses. Log cabins and colonial, mission, and Victorian style houses have become popular in different parts of the country.

Appraisal Techniques

The sales comparison approach provides the best indication of the value of a reproduction house. An appraiser should find and analyze market evidence to estimate the amenity value created by the property's reproduced style as well as any value penalty attributable to the property's lack of conformity to other properties in the neighborhood.

SOLAR AND UNDERGROUND HOUSES

Solar heat is an alternative to heating systems that depend on fossil fuels. Because solar houses are built with special materials and designed for a particular orientation on their lots, they usually are more expensive to build. However, owners anticipate that long-term energy savings will offset the additional cost. Solar houses are still in the experimental stage, but their popularity is increasing.

Houses built underground benefit from the fact that temperatures below grade are moderate year round. Because the heating and cooling equipment in these houses operates with less power, energy costs are significantly reduced. Earth-covered dwellings of poured concrete and concrete block are usually located on grade and bermed—i.e., set into a site that is partly or completely excavated.

Appraisal Techniques

Application of the sales comparison approach is difficult because solar houses are scarce. Paired data set analysis may be used if developers have built solar and nonsolar homes together. Solar houses are experimental, so part or all of the excess costs involved in their construction may add to the property's value. Some buyers will pay a premium for a solar home because they believe that the status associated with living in solar housing increases its value. On the other hand, the market may impose a value penalty on a solar home for its nonconformity. In some areas a solar home may represent an overimprovement. In each case the appraiser must carefully determine whether the value to be estimated is the actual market value or the use value to a specific owner.

In the United States, most underground housing is found in the Central Plains states where storm protection and reduced energy costs are important concerns. The sales comparison approach is generally applied to value these properties.

EXPERIMENTAL HOUSES

Experimental houses are often built of unconventional materials such as plastic, fiberglass, and foams. These homes may be the work of nationally known architects and may incorporate unusual design features.

Appraisal Techniques

The sales comparison approach is the best method for appraising experimental houses. Location is important, of course, and the status and amenity value associated with living in an experimental house may add to the property's value. However, the property's lack of conformity with neighborhood structures may affect market value adversely. As in the appraisal of solar houses, the appraiser should determine whether the value being sought is market value or use value to a specific owner.

SUMMARY

Certain categories of residences present appraisers with particular problems.

Condominiums are held in fee simple but their ownership includes both a divided interest in an individual unit and an undivided interest in common building areas. To apply the sales comparison approach to the valuation of condominiums, an appraiser must study similar units in complexes that are truly comparable in terms of common charges, recreational facilities, unit size, and design. The sales prices of new units and the resale prices of similar units may vary substantially.

Cooperative apartments are owned by tenant proprietors or stockholders who pay a proportionate share of operating expenses and the debt service on the underlying mortgage, which is held by the corporation. Sales of ownership shares provide the most persuasive evidence of the value of cooperative apartments. The actual price of a cooperative is determined by two factors: the ownership share that entitles the stockholder to occupy an apartment and the owner's portion of the mortgage payment for the entire building. If rental data are available, the income capitalization approach is applicable to the appraisal of these properties.

Timeshares are limited ownership interests. A timeshare purchaser receives a deed that conveys title to a residential apartment or hotel room for a specified portion of the year. Resales of a timeshare property are better indicators of value than new sales because new sales usually result from developer promotions. If rental data are available, the income capitalization approach can be applied.

Residences are built on leased land in some states. Safeguards are written into the leases on these properties to protect the interests of the mortgagee, or lender. When the sales comparison approach is applied to the appraisal of residences on leased land, an adjustment may be required to reflect any differences between the land rents for the subject property and the comparable properties.

Resort and recreation houses are usually second homes occupied by their owners on a seasonal basis. Resales of these properties are generally more persuasive value indicators than initial sales, which may be motivated by developer promotions. If data on seasonal rentals exist, the income capitalization approach may produce a reliable value indication.

Housing for the elderly includes the scaled-down houses and apartments of individuals 50 to 64 years in age and a variety of options for people 65 and older. Retirement communities are attractive to older men and women who wish to enjoy their leisure; congregate and lifecare facilities may be more appropriate for those in their 70s and 80s who are no longer able to care for themselves. Appraisers valuing elderly housing should consider neighborhood age restrictions, the availability of government support, and any special size, design, and construction materials that may affect the value of such housing.

If most of a rural property's value is in the land, the value of ranch and farm houses is generally estimated using the cost approach. If most of the property's value is in the residential improvements, the sales comparison approach may be more appropriate.

A planned unit development (PUD) is a development project in which buildings are clustered or set on lots that are smaller than usual. These properties exist because special zoning is passed to create neighborhoods. The individual units in a PUD are owned in fee simple or as condominiums; open areas, parking, and recreational facilities are held in joint ownership. To qualify as a de minimis PUD the individual units in the project must be owned in fee simple and meet certain maintenance requirements. Moreover, owners must be motivated to purchase a dwelling unit rather than the rights to project amenties.

Mobile homes or house trailers are movable dwelling units that are usually settled in mobile home parks or trailer parks. All three approaches can be used to value mobile homes, but data from valuation books should be used with caution.

Modular and prefabricated houses are constructed in a factory and assembled on site. Modular units and prefabs cost less to build, but there is little difference between the values of these homes and similar conventional houses.

Mansions are few in number and are sold relatively infrequently. A highest and best use analysis is critical to determine whether the single-family use should continue or the property should be converted to multifamily or institutional use.

In the 1960s and 1970s historic houses and districts became the focus of preservationists who sought to save architecturally significant buildings and adapt them to economic uses, thereby stabilizing neighborhoods and communities. Special legislation and private easements are used to ensure that the exterior appearance of historic structures is maintained. Special income tax consideration for easements and lower property taxes provide incentives for preservation. Appraising a historic house can be a difficult task. When the sales comparison approach is applicable, a location adjustment may be especially important. Log cabins and other historic reproductions have increased in popularity. Market evidence is needed to estimate any special amenity value attributable to the historic style of these structures.

A solar or experimental house may give special status to its owners and therefore have amenity value. However, some markets may ascribe a value penalty to these nonconforming properties. In either case, an appraiser should determine whether the value to be estimated is the actual market value of the property or the use value to a specific owner.

REVIEW QUESTIONS

1. What procedures are followed in the appraisal of condominiums and cooperatives?
2. Why do resales provide better indications of the value of timeshare properties and resort and vacation houses?
3. Identify the segments into which the market for elderly housing can be divided.
4. What is a planned unit development (PUD)? What distinguishes a de minimis PUD?
5. Describe the advantages of modular and prefabricated houses to developers and buyers.
6. Why is highest and best use analysis so important in the appraisal of mansions?
7. What special difficulties does an appraiser encounter in the valuation of a historic property?
8. In valuing solar and experimental houses, why must the appraiser determine whether the value to be estimated is market value or use value?

Appendix A
Professional Practice

The body of knowledge that comprises the discipline of appraisal is the foundation of professional practice. In solving most appraisal problems, however, the final conclusions depend to a great extent on the ability, judgment, and integrity of individual appraisers. To form a sound conclusion, relevant data must be available and the appraiser must be committed to finding and analyzing the data; a valid analysis also depends on the skillful application of appraisal techniques. Because appraisal is an inexact science, appraisers must reach their conclusions in an impartial, objective manner, without bias or any desire to accommodate their own interests or the interests of their clients. Professional appraisers have the requisite knowledge and the ability to apply it capably and objectively.

A profession is distinguished from a trade or service industry by a combination of the following factors:

1. High standards of competence in a specialized field

2. A distinct body of knowledge that is continually augmented by the contributions of members and can be imparted to future generations

3. A code of ethics or standards of practice and members who are willing to be regulated by peer review

These criteria guided the individuals who founded the American Institute of Real Estate Appraisers in 1932. At that time the United States was in a period of unparalleled economic chaos and a sound basis was needed to establish the value and utility of real estate. The Appraisal Institute was formed for three purposes.

1. To establish criteria for selecting and recognizing individuals with real estate valuation skills who were committed to competent and ethical practice

2. To develop a system of education to train new appraisers and sharpen the skills of practicing appraisers

3. To formulate a code of professional ethics and standards of professional conduct to guide real estate appraisers and serve as a model for other practitioners

The first act of the new organization was to publish a code of ethics and standards of professional practice to protect the public and its members. Through the years these guidelines were refined and in 1984 the Code of Professional Ethics and the Standards of Professional Practice were separated into two discrete documents. The heart of these documents is contained in the six canons of the Code of Professional Ethics and the Standards of Professional Practice, which have been incorporated into the Uniform Standards of Professional Appraisal Practice.

Canon 1

A Member or Candidate of the Appraisal Institute must refrain from conduct that is detrimental to the Appraisal Institute, the real estate appraisal profession, and the public.

Canon 2

A Member or Candidate must assist the Appraisal Institute in carrying out its responsibilities to the users of appraisal services and the public.

Canon 3

In the performance of an appraisal assignment, each analysis and opinion of a Member or Candidate must be developed and communicated without bias and without the accommodation of the Member's or Candidate's personal interests.

Canon 4

A Member or Candidate must not violate the confidential nature of the appraiser-client relationship.

Canon 5

In promoting an appraisal practice and soliciting appraisal assignments, a Member or Candidate must use care to avoid advertising or solicitation that is misleading or otherwise contrary to the public interest.

Canon 6

A Member or Candidate must comply with the requirements of the Standards of Professional Practice.

Effective January 1, 1989, the Uniform Standards of Professional Appraisal Practice and Supplemental Standards 1 and 2 apply to all members and candidates of the Appraisal Institute. Additional explanatory comments and guide notes have been designed to help appraisers understand the standards and illustrate their application to specific appraisal problems.

Standard 1

In developing a real estate appraisal, an appraiser must be aware of, understand, and correctly employ those recognized methods and techniques that are necessary to produce a credible appraisal.

Standard 2

In reporting the results of a real estate appraisal, an appraiser must communicate each analysis, opinion, and conclusion in a manner that is not misleading.

Standard 3

In reviewing an appraisal and reporting the results of that review, an appraiser must form an opinion as to the adequacy and appropriateness of the report being reviewed and must clearly disclose the nature of the review process undertaken.

Standard 4

In developing a real estate analysis, an analyst must be aware of, understand, and correctly employ those recognized methods and techniques that are necessary to produce a credible analysis.

Standard 5

In reporting the results of a real estate analysis, an analyst must communicate each analysis, opinion, and conclusion in a manner that is not misleading.

Standard 6

In developing and reporting a mass appraisal for ad valorem tax purposes, an appraiser must be aware of, understand, and correctly employ those recognized methods and techniques that are necessary to produce and communicate credible appraisals within the context of the property tax laws.

Standard 7

In developing a personal property appraisal, an appraiser must be aware of, understand, and correctly employ those recognized methods and techniques that are necessary to produce a credible appraisal.

Standard 8

In reporting the results of a personal property appraisal, an appraiser must communicate each analysis, opinion, and conclusion in a manner that is not misleading.

Standard 9

In developing a business appraisal, an appraiser must be aware of, understand, and correctly employ those recognized methods and techniques that are necessary to produce a credible appraisal.

Standard 10

In reporting the results of a business appraisal, an appraiser must communicate each analysis, opinion, and conclusion in a manner that is not misleading.

Standards 7 through 10 will not be enforced by the Appraisal Institute.

Two supplemental standards follow. These standards apply only to members and candidates of the American Institute of Real Estate Appraisers.

Supplemental Standard 1

The Uniform Standards of Professional Appraisal Practice shall apply to all activities of a Member or Candidate involving an analysis, opinion or conclusion relating to the nature, quality, value or utility of specified interests in, or aspects of, identified real estate.

Supplemental Standard 2

The form of certification used by a Member or Candidate in a written report that contains an analysis, opinion or conclusion relating to the nature, quality, value or utility of specified interests in, or aspects of, identified real estate must include a statement indicating compliance with the Code of Professional Ethics and Standards of Professional Practice and a statement advising the client and third parties of the Appraisal Institute's right to review the report. The form of certification used by a Member in a written report that contains an analysis, opinion or conclusion relating to the nature, quality, value or utility of specified interests in, or aspects of, identified real estate must include a statement indicating the current status of the Member under the Appraisal Institute's continuing education program.

Appendix B
Appraisal Report Forms

In addition to the Uniform Residential Appraisal Report (URAR) form, which appears in Chapter 21, government agencies and lending institutions use three other forms:

- Individual Condominium or PUD Unit Appraisal Report
- Small Residential Income Property Appraisal Report
- Employee Relocation Council (ERC) Residential Appraisal Report (Only two of the six pages are shown)

These forms are provided in this appendix.

☐☐☐

To be completed by Lender

Borrower_____ Census Tract _____ Map Reference _____

Unit No. _____ Address _____ Project Name/Phase No. _____

City_____ County _____ State _____ Zip Code _____

Actual Real Estate Taxes $ _____ (yr.) Sales Price $ _____ Property Rights Appraised ☐ Fee ☐ Leasehold

Loan Charges to be Paid by Seller $ _____ Other Sales Concessions _____

Lender/Client _____ Lender's Address _____

Occupant _____ Appraiser_____ Instructions to Appraiser _____

☐ FNMA 1073A required   ☐ FHLMC 465 Addendum A required   ☐ FHLMC 465 Addendum B required

NEIGHBORHOOD

				NEIGHBORHOOD RATING	Good	Avg	Fair	Poor
Location	☐ Urban	☐ Suburban	☐ Rural	Adequacy of Shopping	☐	☐	☐	☐
Built up	☐ Over 75%	☐ 25% to 75%	☐ Under 25%	Employment Opportunities	☐	☐	☐	☐
Growth Rate ☐ Fully Developed	☐ Rapid	☐ Steady	☐ Slow	Recreational Facilities	☐	☐	☐	☐
Property Values	☐ Increasing	☐ Stable	☐ Declining	Adequacy of Utilities	☐	☐	☐	☐
Demand/Supply	☐ Shortage	☐ In Balance	☐ Oversupply	Property Compatibility	☐	☐	☐	☐
Marketing Time	☐ Under 3 Mos.	☐ 4-6 Mos.	☐ Over 6 Mos.	Protection from Detrimental Conditions	☐	☐	☐	☐

Present Land Use_____ % 1 Family____ % 2-4 Family____ % Apts____ % Condo

_____ % Commercial _____ % Industrial _____ % Vacant

Change in Present Land Use ☐ Not Likely ☐ Likely* ☐ Taking Place*

*From _____ Tp _____

				Good	Avg	Fair	Poor
Police and Fire Protection				☐	☐	☐	☐
General Appearance of Properties				☐	☐	☐	☐
Appeal to Market				☐	☐	☐	☐

Predominant Occupancy ☐ Owner ☐ Tenant _____ % Vacant

Condominium: Price Range $ _____ to $_____ Predominant $_____

Age _____ yrs. to _____ yrs. Predominant _____ yrs.

Single Family: Price Range $ _____ to $_____ Predominant $_____

Age _____ yrs. to _____ yrs. Predominant _____ yrs.

	Distance	Access or Convenience			
Public Transportation		☐	☐	☐	☐
Employment Centers		☐	☐	☐	☐
Neighborhood Shopping		☐	☐	☐	☐
Grammar Schools		☐	☐	☐	☐
Freeway Access		☐	☐	☐	☐

Describe potential for additional Condo/PUD units in nearby area _____

NOTE: FHLMC/FNMA do not consider race or the racial composition of the neighborhood to be reliable appraisal factors.

Describe those factors, favorable or unfavorable, affecting marketability (e.g. public parks, schools, noise, view, mkt. area, population size and financial ability).

SITE

Lot Dimensions (if PUD) _____ = _____ Sq. Ft. ☐ Corner Lot Project Density When Completed as Planned _____ Units/Acre

Zoning Classification _____ Present improvements ☐ do ☐ do not conform to zoning regulations

Highest and best use: ☐ Present use ☐ Other (specify) _____

	Public	Other (Describe)	OFF-SITE IMPROVEMENTS		Project Ingress/Egress (adequacy) _____
Elec.	☐		Street Access: ☐ Public ☐ Private		Topo _____
Gas	☐		Surface		Size/Shape _____
Water	☐		Maintenance: ☐ Public ☐ Private		View Amenity _____
San. Sewer	☐		☐ Storm Sewer ☐ Curb/Gutter		Drainage/Flood Conditions _____
	☐ Underground Elec. & Tel.		☐ Sidewalk ☐ Street Lights		Is the property located in a HUD Identified Special Flood Hazard Area? ☐ No ☐ Yes

Comments (including any easements, encroachments or other adverse conditions) _____

PROJECT IMPROVEMENTS

☐ Existing   Approx. Year Built 19 _____ Original Use _____

☐ Condo ☐ PUD   ☐ Converted (19 _____)

TYPE	☐ Proposed	☐ Under Construction
PROJECT	☐ Elevator	☐ Walk-up No. of Stories _____
	☐ Row or Town House	☐ Other (specify) _____
	☐ Primary Residence	☐ Second Home or Recreational

If Completed: No. Phases _____ No. Units _____ No. Sold _____

If Incomplete: Planned No. Phases _____ No. Units _____ No. Sold _____

Units in Subject Phase: Total _____ Completed _____ Sold _____ Rented _____

Approx. No. Units for Sale: Subject Project _____ Subject Phase _____

PROJECT RATING	Good	Avg.	Fair	Poor
Location	☐	☐	☐	☐
General Appearance	☐	☐	☐	☐
Amenities and Recreational Facilities	☐	☐	☐	☐
Density (units per acre)	☐	☐	☐	☐
Unit Mix	☐	☐	☐	☐
Quality of Constr. (mat'l & finish)	☐	☐	☐	☐
Condition of Exterior	☐	☐	☐	☐
Condition of Interior	☐	☐	☐	☐
Appeal to Market	☐	☐	☐	☐

Exterior Wall _____ Roof Covering _____ Security Features _____

Elevator: No. _____ Adequacy & Condition _____ Soundproofing: Vertical _____ Horizontal _____

Parking: Total No. Spaces _____ Ratio_____ Spaces/Unit _____ Type _____ No. Spaces of Guest Parking _____

Describe common elements or recreational facilities _____

Are any common elements, rec. facilities or parking leased to Owners Assoc.? _____ If yes, attach addendum describing rental, terms and options.

SUBJECT UNIT

☐ Existing ☐ Proposed ☐ Under Constr.   Floor No. _____ Unit Livable Area _____ ☐ Basement _____ % Finished _____

Parking for Unit: No. _____ Type _____ ☐ Assigned ☐ Owned Convenience to Unit _____

Room List	Foyer	Liv	Din	Kit	Bdrm	Bath	Fam	Rec	Lndry	Other
Basement										
1st Level										
2nd Level										

UNIT RATING	Good	Avg.	Fair	Poor
Condition of Improvement	☐	☐	☐	☐
Room Sizes and Layout	☐	☐	☐	☐
Adequacy of Closets and Storage	☐	☐	☐	☐
Kit. Equip., Cabinets & Workspace	☐	☐	☐	☐

Floors:	☐ Hardwood	☐ Carpet over _____	☐
Int. Walls:	☐ Drywall	☐ Plaster	
Trim/Finish:	☐ Good	☐ Average	☐ Fair ☐ Poor
Bath Floor:	☐ Ceramic	☐ Wainscot	☐ Ceramic
Windows (type):		☐ Storm Sash ☐ Screens ☐ Combo	
Kitchen Equip:	☐ Refrig.	☐ Range/Oven ☐ Fan/Hood ☐ Washer ☐ Dryer	
	☐ Intercom ☐ Disposal	☐ Dishwasher ☐ Microwave ☐ Compacter	

	Good	Avg	Fair	Poor
Plumbing—Adequacy and Condition	☐	☐	☐	☐
Electrical—Adequacy and Condition	☐	☐	☐	☐
Adequacy of Soundproofing	☐	☐	☐	☐
Adequacy of Insulation	☐	☐	☐	☐
Location within Project or View	☐	☐	☐	☐
Overall Livability	☐	☐	☐	☐
Appeal and Marketability	☐	☐	☐	☐

HEAT: Type _____ Fuel _____ Cond _____

AIR COND: ☐ Central ☐ Other _____ ☐ Adequate ☐ Inadequate

Est. Effective Age _____ to _____ yrs.

Est. Remaining Economic Life _____ to _____ yrs.

☐ Earth Sheltered Housing Design ☐ Solar Design/Landscape ☐ Solar Space Heat/Air Cond. ☐ Solar Hot Water

☐ Flue Damper ☐ Elec./Mech. Gas Furn. Ignition ☐ Auto Setback Thermostat ☐ Dble./Triple Glazed Windows ☐ Caulk/Weatherstrip

INSULATION (state R-Factor if known) _____ ☐ Walls _____ ☐ Ceiling _____ ☐ Floor _____ ☐ Water Heater

If rehab proposed, do plans and specs provide for adequate energy conservation? _____ If no, attach description of modification needed.

ENERGY EFFICIENCY APPEARS: ☐ High ☐ Adequate ☐ Low   Energy Audit ☐ Yes (attach, if available) ☐ No

COMMENTS (special features, functional or physical inadequacies, modernization or repairs needed, etc.) _____

MARKET DATA ANALYSIS

The appraiser, whenever possible, should analyze two comparable sales from within the subject project. However, when appraising a unit in a new or newly converted project, at least two comparables should be selected from outside the subject project. In the following analysis, the comparable should always be adjusted to the subject unit and not vice versa. If a significant feature of the comparable is superior to the subject unit, a minus (—) adjustment should be made to the comparable; if such a feature of the comparable is inferior to the subject, a plus (+) adjustment should be made to the comparable.

LIST ONLY THOSE ITEMS THAT REQUIRE ADJUSTMENT

ITEM	Subject Property	COMPARABLE NO. 1	COMPARABLE NO. 2	COMPARABLE NO. 3
Address-Unit No: Project Name				
Proximity to Subj.				
Sales Price	$	$	$	$
Price/Living Area	$	$	$	$
Data Source				
Date of Sale and Time Adjustment	DESCRIPTION	DESCRIPTION / +(—)$ Adjustment	DESCRIPTION / +(—)$ Adjustment	DESCRIPTION / +(—)$ Adjustment
Location				
Site/View				
Design and Appeal				
Quality of Constr.				
Age				
Condition				
Living Area, Room Count & Total Gross Living Area	Total / B-rms / Baths / Sq. Ft.	Total / B-rms / Baths / Sq. Ft.	Total / B-rms / Baths / Sq. Ft.	Total / B-rms / Baths / Sq. Ft.
Basement & Bsmt. Finished Rooms				
Functional Utility				
Air Conditioning				
Storage				
Parking Facilities				
Common Elements and Recreation Facilities				
Mo. Assessment				
Leasehold/Fee				
Special Energy Efficient Items				
Other (e.g. fireplaces, kitchen equip., remodeling)				
Sales or Financing Concessions				
Net Adj. (total)		☐ Plus ☐ Minus $	☐ Plus ☐ Minus $	☐ Plus ☐ Minus $
Indicated value of Subject		$	$	$

Comments on Market Data Analysis _____

INDICATED VALUE BY MARKET DATA APPROACH _____ $ _____

INDICATED VALUE BY INCOME APPROACH (If applicable) Economic Market Rent $ _____ /Mo. x Gross Rent Multiplier _____ = $ _____

This appraisal is made ☐ "as is" ☐ subject to repairs, alterations, or conditions listed below ☐ subject to completion per plans and specifications.

Comments and Conditions of Appraisal: _____

Final Reconciliation: _____

Construction Warranty ☐ Yes ☐ No Name of Warranty Program _____ Warranty Coverage Expires _____

This appraisal is based upon the above requirements, the certification, contingent and limiting conditions, and Market Value definition that are stated in

☐ FHLMC Form 439 (Rev. 7/86)/FNMA Form 1004B (Rev. 7/86) filed with client _____ 19____ ☐ attached.

I ESTIMATE THE MARKET VALUE, AS DEFINED, OF SUBJECT PROPERTY AS OF _____ 19____ to be $_____

Appraiser(s) _____ Review Appraisal (if applicable) _____

Date Report Signed _____ 19____ ☐ Did ☐ Did Not Physically Inspect Property

APPRAISAL REPORT - SMALL RESIDENTIAL INCOME PROPERTY

File No.

To be completed by Lender

Borrower	Census Tract — Map Reference
Property Address	
City	County — State — Zip Code
Legal Description	
Sale Price $ — Date of Sale — Loan Term — yrs. — Property Rights Appraised: ☐ Fee ☐ Leasehold ☐ Other
Actual Real Estate Taxes $ — (yr) Loan charges to be paid by seller $ — Other sales concessions
Lender/Client — Address
Occupant — Appraiser — Instructions to Appraiser

NEIGHBORHOOD

Location .... ☐ Urban ☐ Suburban .... ☐ Rural
Built-up .... ☐ Over 75% ☐ 25% to 75% .... ☐ Under 25%
Present land use .... ___ % Condominiums ___ % 1-Family ___ % 2-4 Family
___ % Apartments ___ % Commercial ___ % Vacant ___ %
Change in present land use ☐ Not likely ☐ Likely (*) ☐ Taking Place (*)
(*) From ___ To ___
Property values .... ☐ Increasing ☐ Stable ☐ Declining
Housing demand/supply ☐ In balance ☐ Shortage ☐ Oversupply
Predominant occupancy ☐ Owner ☐ Tenant ___ % Vacant
Single Family: Price range ___ to $ ___ Predominant $ ___
Age ___ yrs. to ___ yrs. Predominant ___ yrs.
Typical multifamily bldg. Type ___ No. Stories ___ No. Units ___
Age ___ yrs. Condition ___
Typical rents $ ___ to $ ___ ☐ Increasing ☐ Stable ☐ Declining
Est. neighborhood apt. vacancy ___ % ☐ Decreasing ☐ Stable ☐ Increasing
Rent controls ☐ No ☐ Yes ☐ Not likely ☐ Likely

OVERALL RATING	Good	Avg	Fair	Poor
Adequacy of Shopping				
Adequacy of Utilities				
Employment Opportunities				
Police and Fire Protection				
Recreational Facilities				
Property Compatibility				
Protection from Detrimental Conditions				
General Appearance of Properties				
Appeal to Market				

	Distance	Access or Convenience
Public Transportation		
Employment Centers		
Shopping Facilities		
Grammar Schools		
Freeway Access		

Note: FHLMC/FNMA do not consider race or the racial composition of the neighborhood to be reliable appraisal factors.

Describe those factors, favorable or unfavorable, affecting marketability (incl. mkt. area population size & financial ability).

SITE

Dimensions ___ = ___ Sq. Ft. or Acres ☐ Corner Lot
Zoning classification ___ Present improvements ☐ do ☐ do not conform to zoning regulations
Highest and best use: ☐ Present use ☐ Other (specify)

	Public	Other (Describe)	OFF-SITE IMPROVEMENTS		Topo
Elec.	☐		Street Access: ☐ Public ☐ Private		Size
Gas	☐		Surface		Shape
Water	☐		Maintenance ☐ Public ☐ Private		View
San. Sewer	☐		☐ Storm Sewer ☐ Curb/Gutter		Drainage
		☐ Underground Elec. & Tel	☐ Sidewalk ☐ Street Lights		Is the property located in a HUD Identified Special Flood Hazard Area? ☐ No ☐ Yes

Comments (favorable or unfavorable conditions including any apparent adverse easements or encroachments)

DESCRIPTION OF IMPROVEMENTS

☐ Existing ☐ Proposed ☐ Under Construction Type: ☐ Elevator ☐ Walk-up ☐ Det. ☐ Semi-Det. ☐ Row No. Stories ___
No. Bldgs. ___ No. Units ___ No. Rooms ___ No. Baths ___ Parking Spaces: No. ___ Type ___
Basic Structural System ___ Exterior Walls ___ Roof Covering ___
Foundation Walls ___ Basement ___ % Finished ___ % Describe use ___
Interior Walls ___ Floors ___ Bath Floor and Walls ___
Insulation ___ Adequacy ___ Adequacy of Soundproofing ___
Heating: ☐ Central ☐ Individual Type ___ Fuel ___ Adequacy & Condition ___
Air Conditioning: ☐ Central ☐ Individual Fuel ___ Make ___ Adequacy & Condition ___
Kitchen Cabinets, Drawers and Counter space ☐ Adequate ☐ Inadequate
Total No. Appliances: ___ Range/Oven ___ Fan/Hood ___ Dishwasher ___
___ Disposal ___ Refrigerator ___ Washer ___ Dryer ___ Compactor ___
Water Heater(s) (make, capacity, fuel) ___
Plumbing Fixtures (make) ___
Electrical Service (amps per unit) ___
Security Features ___
Special Features (including energy efficient items) ___

OVERALL PROPERTY RATING	Good	Avg	Fair	Poor
Quality of construction (materials and finish)				
Condition of improvements				
Room sizes and layout				
Closets and storage				
Plumbing--adequacy and condition				
Electrical--adequacy and condition				
Kitchen equipment--adequacy and condition				
Amenities and parking facilities				
Overall livability				
Appeal to market				

Age: Actual ___ yrs., Effective ___ yrs. to ___ yrs. Est. Remaining Economic Life ___ yrs. to ___ yrs. Explain if less than Loan Term
COMMENTS: (Including functional or physical inadequacies, repairs needed, modernization, etc.)

COST APPROACH

ESTIMATED REPRODUCTION COST NEW

___ x ___ = ___	sq. ft. x ___	(Stories) = ___	sq. ft. x ___	$ ___	$ ___
___ x ___ = ___	sq. ft. x ___	(Stories) = ___	sq. ft. x ___	$ ___	___
___ x ___ = ___	sq. ft. x ___	(Stories) = ___	sq. ft. x ___	$ ___	___

OTHER IMPROVEMENTS (Including special energy efficient items) ___

SITE IMPROVEMENTS ___

TOTAL ESTIMATED COST NEW OF IMPROVEMENTS .... $ ___

LESS DEPRECIATION: Physical $ ___ Functional $ ___ Economic $ ___ (___)
DEPRECIATED VALUE OF IMPROVEMENTS .... $ ___
ADD-ESTIMATED LAND VALUE (If leasehold, show only leasehold value — attach calculations) .... $ ___
INDICATED VALUE BY THE COST APPROACH ☐ FEE SIMPLE ☐ LEASEHOLD .... $ ___

FHLMC Form 72 7/79
2-12 Units

ATTACH LAYOUT SKETCHES SHOWING UNIT ENTRIES, LOCATION MAP AND
DESCRIPTIVE PHOTOGRAPHS OF SUBJECT PROPERTY AND STREET SCENE

FNMA Form 1025 7/79
2-4 Units

FHLMC Form 72 7/79
2-12 Units

COMPARABLE RENTAL DATA

ITEM	COMPARABLE No. 1	COMPARABLE No. 2	COMPARABLE No. 3
Address			
Proximity to subject			
Rent survey date			
Description of property and conditions	No. Units ___ No. Vac ___ Yr. Blt.: 19 ___	No. Units ___ No. Vac ___ Yr. Blt.: 19 ___	No. Units ___ No. Vac ___ Yr. Blt.: 19 ___

Individual unit breakdown

Rm. Count / Tot BR b	Size / Sq. Ft.	Monthly Rent $ / □ / Rm	Rm. Count / Tot BR b	Size / Sq. Ft.	Monthly Rent $ / □ / Rm	Rm. Count / Tot BR b	Size / Sq. Ft.	Monthly Rent $ / □ / Rm

Utilities, furniture and amenities incl. in rent

Compare comps to subj.

RENT SCHEDULE

Utilities included in actual rents: □ Water □ Gas □ Heat □ Electric □ Air Conditioning □ _____
Utilities included in forecasted rents: □ Water □ Gas □ Heat □ Electric □ Air Conditioning □ _____

No. of Units	Individual Unit Rm Count — Tot.	BR	b	Total Rooms	Sq. Ft. Area Per Unit	No. Units Vacant	ACTUAL RENTS — Per Unit Unfurnished	Furnished	Total Rents	FORECASTED RENTS — Per Unit Unfurnished	Furnished	Per Sq. Ft. or Room	Total Rents
							$	$	$	$	$	$	$
TOTAL									$				$

Other Monthly Income (Itemize) _____ $ _____

Vacancy: Actual last yr. ____ % Prev. yr. ____ % Forecasted: ____ % $ _____ Total Gross Monthly Forecasted Rent $ _____

Discuss rental concessions, forecasted rents: _____

MARKET DATA ANALYSIS

ITEM	SUBJECT	COMPARABLE No. 1	COMPARABLE No. 2	COMPARABLE No. 3
Address				
Proximity to subject				
Price	$ □ Unf. □ F.	$ □ Unf. □ F.	$ □ Unf. □ F.	$ □ Unf. □ F.
Date of sale				
	Yr. Blt.: 19 ___ No. Vac ___	Yr. Blt.: 19 ___ No. Vac ___	Yr. Blt.: 19 ___ No. Vac ___	Yr. Blt.: 19 ___ No. Vac ___

Individual unit breakdown	No. of Units	Individual Unit Room Count — Tot.	BR	b	No. of Units	Tot.	BR	b	No. of Units	Tot	BR	b	No. of Units	Tot.	BR	b

Compare to subject including condition, terms of sale/financing

Gross Bldg. Area (GBA)	sq. ft.	sq. ft.	sq. ft.	sq. ft.
Gross Monthly Rent	$	$	$	$
Gross Mo. Rent Mult. (1)				
Price Per Unit	$	$	$	$
Price Per Room	$	$	$	$
Price Per S.F. GRA	$ /sq. ft. GBA	$ /sq. ft. GBA	$ /sq. ft. GBA	$ /sq. ft. GBA

(1) Sale Price ÷ Gross Monthly Rent   Value indication for Subject _____

Val. Per Unit $ ____ X ____ Units = $ ____ ; Val. Per S.F. G.B.A. $ ____ X ____ S.F. Bldg. Area = $ ____
Val. Per Rm. $ ____ X ____ Rms = $ ____ ; G.R.M. ____ X ____ Total Monthly Rent = $ ____

Reconciliation: _____

INDICATED VALUE BY MARKET DATA APPROACH .... $ _____

EXPENSE ANALYSIS

ANNUAL EXPENSE SUMMARY - (If for FNMA - Lender must prepare operating data on sep. form for appraiser to review, comment on & attach to appraisal)

		ACTUAL	FORECAST	CALCULATIONS OR COMMENTS
1. Utilities: □ Heat $ ____ □ Electric $ ____				
□ Gas $ ____ □ Water & Sewer $ ____	Total:	$	$	
2. Real Estate Taxes $ ____ 3. Insurance $ ____	Total:			
4. Management $ ____ Salaries $ ____	Total:			
5. Maint. & Decor. $ ____ Repairs $ ____ Reserves $ ____	Total:			
6. Other ____	Total:			
TOTAL EXPENSES & REPLACEMENT RESERVES		$	$	

This appraisal is made □ "as is" □ subject to the repairs, alterations, or conditions listed below □ completion per plans and specifications.

Comments, Conditions and Final Reconciliation: _____

This appraisal is based upon the above requirements, the certification, contingent and limiting conditions, and Market Value definition that are stated in

□ FHLMC Form 439 (Rev. 10/78)/FNMA Form 1004B (Rev. 10/78) filed with client _____ 19 ___ □ attached

I ESTIMATE THE MARKET VALUE, AS DEFINED, OF SUBJECT PROPERTY AS OF _____ 19 ___ to be $ ____

Appraiser(s) _____   Review Appraiser (If applicable) _____

□ Did   □ Did Not Physically Inspect Property

FHLMC Form 72 7/79
2-12 Units

Forms and Worms Incorporated, 315 Whitney Ave., New Haven, CT 06511   BF   FNMA Form 1025 7/79
2-4 Units

EMPLOYEE RELOCATION COUNCIL
RESIDENTIAL APPRAISAL REPORT

SUBJECT INFORMATION

Homeowner

Property Address

City _____ County _____ State _____ Zip Code

Legal Description

Property Rights Appraised | Fee | Leasehold | DeMinimis PUD

Client _____ Address

Occupant _____ Appraiser

NEIGHBORHOOD

						Good	Avg.	Fair	Poor
Location	☐ Urban	☐ Suburban	☐ Rural						
Built Up	☐ Over 75%	☐ 25% to 75%	☐ Under 25%	Employment Stability		☐	☐	☐	☐
Growth Rate ☐ Fully Dev.	☐ Rapid	☐ Steady	☐ Slow	Convenience to Employment		☐	☐	☐	☐
Property Values	☐ Increasing	☐ Stable	☐ Declining	Convenience to Shopping		☐	☐	☐	☐
Demand/Supply	☐ Shortage	☐ In Balance	☐ Over Supply	Convenience to Schools		☐	☐	☐	☐
Marketing Time	☐ Under 4 Mos.	☐ 4-6 Mos.	☐ Over 6 Mos.	Adequacy of Public Transportation		☐	☐	☐	☐

Present Land Use ___ % 1 Family ___ % 2-4 Family ___ % Apts. ___ % Condo ___ % Commercial — Recreational Facilities ☐☐☐☐
___ % Industrial ___ % Vacant ___ % — Adequacy of Utilities ☐☐☐☐

Change in Present Land Use ☐ Not Likely ☐ Likely (*) ☐ Taking Place (*) — Property Compatibility ☐☐☐☐

(*) From _____ To _____ — Protection from Detrimental Conditions ☐☐☐☐

Predominant Occupancy ☐ Owner ☐ Tenant ___ % Vacant — Police and Fire Protection ☐☐☐☐

Single Family Price Range $ _____ to $ _____ Predominant Value $ _____ — General Appearance of Properties ☐☐☐☐

Single Family Age _____ Yrs. to _____ Yrs. Predominant Age _____ Yrs. — Appeal to Market ☐☐☐☐

Comments including those factors, favorable or unfavorable, affecting marketability (e.g. public parks, schools, view, noise)_____

SITE

Dimensions _____ = _____ Sq. Ft. or Acres ☐ Corner Lot

Zoning Classification _____ Present Improvements ☐ do ☐ do not conform to zoning regulations

Highest and Best Use ☐ Present Use ☐ Other (specify)_____

	Public	Other (Describe)	OFF SITE IMPROVEMENTS			Topo _____
Elec.	☐	_____	Street Access: ☐ Public ☐ Private			Size _____
Gas	☐	_____	Surface _____			Shape _____
Water	☐	_____	Maintenance: ☐ Public ☐ Private			View _____
San. Sewer	☐	_____	☐ Storm Sewer ☐ Curb/Gutter			Drainage _____

☐ Undergrnd. Elect. & Tel. ☐ Sidewalk ☐ Street Lights — Is the property located in a HUD Identified Special Flood Hazard Area? ☐ No ☐ Yes

Comments (favorable or unfavorable including any apparent adverse easements, encroachments or other adverse conditions) _____

IMPROVEMENTS

☐ Existing ☐ Under Constr. VALID PERMIT? No. Units ___ Type (det., duplex, semi/det., etc.) _____ Design (rambler, split level, etc.) _____ Exterior Walls _____

Yrs. Actual _____ Effective _____ to _____ No. Stories _____

Roof Material _____ Gutters and Downspouts ☐ NONE Window (Type): _____ Insulation ☐ None ☐ Floor

☐ Storm Sash ☐ Screens ☐ Combination — ☐ Ceiling ☐ Roof ☐ Wall

☐ Manufactured Housing — **BSMT.** ☐ % Basement ☐ Floor Drain Finished Ceiling _____

Foundation Walls _____ ☐ Outside Entrance ☐ Sump Pump Finished Walls _____

☐ Concrete Floor ___ % Finished Finished Floor _____

☐ Slab on Grade ☐ Crawl Space Evidence of: ☐ Dampness ☐ Termites ☐ Settlement

Refer comments on improvements and property condition to page 5 in the Supplement under "PROPERTY CONDITION."

ROOM LIST

Room List	Foyer	Living	Dining	Kitchen	Den	Family Rm.	Rec. Room	Bedrooms	No. Baths	Laundry	Other
Basement											
1st Level											
2nd Level											

Finished area above grade contains a total of _____ rooms _____ bedrooms _____ baths. *Gross Living Area _____ Sq. Ft. Bsmt. Area _____ Sq. Ft.

INTERIOR FINISH AND EQUIPMENT

Kitchen Equip.: ☐ Refrigerator ☐ Range/Oven ☐ Disposal ☐ Dishwasher ☐ Fan/Hood ☐ Compact. ☐ Washer ☐ Dryer

HEAT: Type _____ Fuel _____ Cond. _____ AIR COND.: ☐ Central ☐ Other _____ ☐ Adequate ☐ Inadequate

							Good	Avg.	Fair	Poor
Floors	☐ Hardwood	☐ Carpet Over _____			**PROPERTY RATING**	Quality of Construction (Materials and Finish)	☐	☐	☐	☐
Walls	☐ Drywall	☐ Plaster				Condition of Improvements	☐	☐	☐	☐
Trim/Finish	☐ Good	☐ Average ☐ Fair	☐ Poor			Room sizes and layout	☐	☐	☐	☐
Bath Floor	☐ Ceramic	_____				Closets and Storage	☐	☐	☐	☐
Bath Wainscot	☐ Ceramic	_____				Insulation - adequacy	☐	☐	☐	☐

Energy related (including energy efficient items) _____ — Plumbing - adequacy and condition ☐☐☐☐
— Electrical - adequacy and condition ☐☐☐☐

ATTIC: ☐ Yes ☐ No ☐ Stairway ☐ Drop-Stair ☐ Scuttle ☐ Floord. — Compatibility to Neighborhood ☐☐☐☐
☐ Heated — Overall Livability ☐☐☐☐

Finished (Describe)_____

CAR STORAGE ☐ Garage ☐ Blt. In ☐ Attached ☐ Detach ☐ Car Port — Appeal and Marketability ☐☐☐☐

No. Cars _____ ☐ Adequate ☐ Inadequate Condition _____

Describe specialty items (e.g. FIREPLACES, PATIOS, POOL, FENCES, etc.) and detail your comments of functional or physical inadequacies, repairs needed, modernization, etc. on page 5 of the Supplement under "SPECIAL FEATURES" and/or "PROPERTY CONDITION."

*See definition on page 4 and reflect same in the "Gross Living Area" section of the "MARKET DATA ANALYSIS."

VALUATION SECTION

IMPORTANT

*GROSS LIVING AREA (square footage) is defined as the calculation of the total living area, which is a measurement taken around the outside of the house and includes finished and habitable above-grade living area only. Finished (and unfinished) basement areas are calculated and shown separately (in both the Room List and Market Data Analysis sections of the appraisal report) but are not included in the total gross living area.

The appraiser has recited three recent sales of properties most similar and proximate to subject and has considered these in the market analysis. The description includes a dollar adjustment, reflecting market reaction to those items of significant variation between the subject and comparable properties. If a significant item in the comparable property is superior to, or more favorable than, the subject property, a minus (-) adjustment is made, thus reducing the indicated value of subject; if a significant item in the comparable is inferior to, or less favorable than, the subject property, a plus (+) adjustment is made, thus increasing the indicated value of the subject.

MARKET DATA ANALYSIS

ITEM	Subject Property	COMPARABLE NO. 1	+ (-) $ Adjustment	COMPARABLE NO. 2	+ (-) $ Adjustment	COMPARABLE NO. 3	+ (-) $ Adjustment
Address							
Proximity to Subj.							
Sales Price		$		$		$	
Closing Date							
Data Source							
Market/Time Adjustments	DESCRIPTION	DESCRIPTION		DESCRIPTION		DESCRIPTION	
Location							
Site/View							
Design and Appeal							
Quality of Const.							
Age							
Condition							
Living Area Room Count and Total	Total / B-rms. / Baths	Total / B-rms. / Baths		Total / B-rms. / Baths		Total / B-rms. / Baths	
*Gross Living Area	Sq. Ft.	Sq. Ft.		Sq. Ft.		Sq. Ft.	
Basement & Bsmt.							
Finished Rooms							
Functional Utility							
Air Conditioning							
Garage/Car Port							
Porches, Patio, Pools, etc.							
Energy Related Items (e.g. solar, heat pumps, etc.)							
Special Features (e.g. fireplaces, kit. equipment, remodeling, etc.)							
Other							
Sales or Financing Concessions							
Net Adj. (Total)		Plus Minus $		Plus Minus $		Plus Minus $	
Indicated Value of Subject		$		$		$	

Describe "other" for Subject: _____

SUPPLEMENT TO MARKET DATA ANALYSIS

The Market Data Analysis for each comparable sale should include adjustments as appropriate for market condition and **days-on-market** under the heading "Market/Time Adjustment." "Sales or Financing Concessions" should include adjustments for terms of sale
Reconcile each of the value-related differences between the subject property and the individual comparables, including but not limited to *financing, terms, condition, location, appeal, deferred maintenance, utility, style, view, days-on-market, and other amenities.*

Comparable Sale #1 _____

_____

_____

_____

Comparable Sale #2 _____

_____

_____

_____

Comparable Sale #3 _____

_____

_____

_____

Comments on Market Data and Final Reconciliation: _____

_____

_____

_____

INDICATED VALUE BY MARKET DATA APPROACH . . . . $ _____

The above indicated value by the market data approach is also to appear on page 6.

Construction Warranty ☐ Yes ☐ No   Name of Warranty Program _____ Warranty Coverage Expires _____

If yes, is it transferable? ☐ Yes ☐ No

TO ORDER: BLAKEWOOD BUSINESS FORMS 1 (800) 443-1004
© Copyright 1986, Employee Relocation Council

ERC-2 Rev. 4-86

Appendix C
Anatomy of a House

Professional appraisers must know residential construction details and local building codes. The following pages contain descriptive data on the construction components of a sample residence as well as floor plans and diagrams of the building's dimensions.

ANATOMY OF A HOUSE©

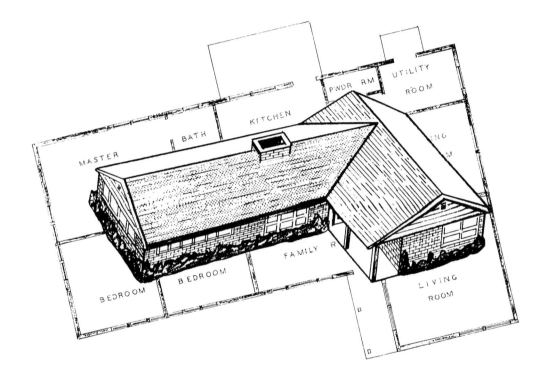

Copyright 1988 by Joseph H. Polley. Reprinted with permission.

Residential construction details vary greatly in different sections of the country. In Louisiana, basements are not built because of a high water table. In Florida, it is unnecessary to build a deep foundation wall since there is no long period of freezing weather. In the midwest, wide overhangs are used to get added protection from the hot sun.

Building codes often are different in adjoining municipalities within the same county. Therefore, what might be considered good construction in one area, could be below acceptable standards just five miles away.

The following is offered to show construction details generally accepted as quality workmanship in southeastern Pennsylvania. It must be pointed out, however, that certain differences may exist when compared to a local building code. Obviously, the local building code takes precedence.

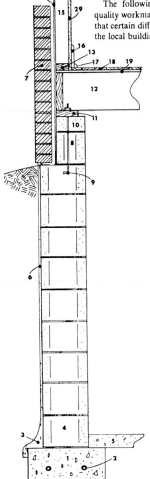

Foundation

1. *Concrete Footing*—Usually 8″ high and 4″ wider (on each side) than the foundation wall.
2. *Reinforcing rods*—⅜″ or ½″ in diameter and used to strengthen the concrete footing, especially where the soil is porous or not firm.
3. *Cement Cove*—Part of the cement parging on the exterior of the basement wall.
4. *Foundation Wall*—Good construction requires 12″ concrete block—sometimes 10″ poured concrete is used. In small basements, 8″ block is used to reduce cost. Cinder block should not be used below grade because it will deteriorate in certain soils.
5. *Concrete Basement Floor*—Usually 3″ thick. Sometimes a plastic vapor barrier is installed under the slab.
6. *Cement Parging and Waterproofing*—Applied to the exterior to keep the basement dry.
7. *Brick Veneer*—Standard size brick, used on the exterior to give the effect of a masonry dwelling. Often, only part of the front wall is done this way.

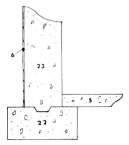

Poured Concrete Foundation

Section of Basement Wall
With Brick Veneer   Scale: ¾″ = 1′

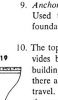

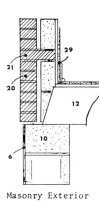

Frame Wall

Masonry Exterior

8. When brick veneer is used, the tenth course of basement block is an 8″ block to allow the 4″ brick to bear on the outer edge of the 12″ block.

9. *Anchor Bolt*—½″ in diameter—16″ or 18″ long—Used to secure frame construction to masonry foundation.

10. The top course of block is a solid block which provides better bearing for the frame section of the building and also acts as a termite repellent since there are no openings through which termites could travel. Note the grading is held at least 12″ below the nearest frame member.

11. *Sill Plate*—A 2 × 6 or a 2 × 8 which is the first wood member installed in a building.

12. *Floor Joists*—Depending on the span, 2 × 8, 2 × 10, or larger joists are used to support the floor load. Variances in type of lumber, grade of lumber, and size all have a bearing on the maximum permissible span.

13. *Sole Plate*—The bottom member of frame wall section 2 × 4 in a bearing wall and 2 × 3 in a non-bearing wall. Bearing walls support joists and rafters.

14. *Wall Sheathing*—Usually asphalt impregnated celotex or gypsum. Sometimes ⅜″ sheathing plywood or 1 × 8 sheathing boards are used.

15. *Wall Stud*—2 × 4 in bearing walls and 2 × 3 in non-bearing walls. They are placed directly over floor joists for strength and are spaced 16″ on centers since most building materials come in four-foot increments.

16. *Baseboard*—Usually 1 × 4 white pine trim lumber.

17. *Quarter Round*—Usually ¾ × ¾ —used to finish joint of baseboard and flooring. It is not installed when wall to wall carpeting is used.

18. *Finish Flooring*—$\frac{5}{16}$″ strip hardwood, top-nailed. $\frac{25}{32}$″ tongue and groove hardwood in better floors and nails are concealed.

19. *Sub-Flooring*—Usually ½″ sheathing plywood. Better floors use 1 × 5 tongue and groove sub-floors for extra strength and rigidity.

20. A masonry exterior wall above the basement level is about 9″ thick. It consists of 4″ face brick, a 1″

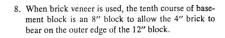
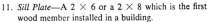
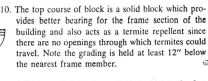
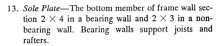
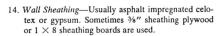
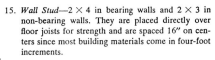

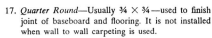
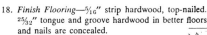
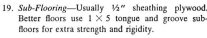

Center Beam and
Bearing Partition Above

First Floor Section With Brick Veneer Below Window and Frame Construction Above.

air space, and a 4″ back-up cinder block. Wood stripping is nailed to the blockwood on the inside so that lath can be installed.

21. Every seventh course of brick is installed so as to bond the brickwork and blockwork together. Sometimes corrugated metal strips called wall ties are used in the mortar instead of bonding with brick.

22. Poured concrete foundations are usually 4″ wider (on each side) than the foundation wall. Note the keyway built into the footing so that the wall will lock into the footing.

23. A poured concrete foundation is usually 10″ wide in residential construction. Plywood forms are erected to joist level. The forms are removed after the concrete has hardened and used again on another job.

24. Wood siding as applied over sheathing on frame exterior walls. Asbestos and aluminum siding are installed the same way.

Center Wall

25. The concrete footing under a lolly column is usually 24″ × 24″ × 10″ high. The extra size is used to disburse the weight over a greater area and to prevent settling of the column.

26. A lolly column is a steel post, usually 4″ in diameter and filled with concrete. It supports the steel center beam above it. Flanges are used as end caps to distribute the load.

27. Steel center beams vary in size according to the weight above. Typically, this beam is an 8″ wide flange weighing 17 lbs. per linear foot of length.

28. A rowlock of brick, laid on edge beneath window sills.

29. *Drywall* or *Plaster*—Drywall is usually ½″ on walls and ⅜″ on ceilings. Plaster is ⅜″ rocklath plus two coats of wet plaster or a total thickness of ¾″. Good plaster wall is three coats and ⅞″ thick.

First Floor Wall

30. *Double Top Plate*—Two 2 × 4 members used to tie framing together at the ceiling line of all frame construction.

31. *Window Header*—Double 2 × 6 over standard window rough opening to support load above windows. Wide windows require heavier headers.

32. White pine trim lumber around window on the inside.

33. Lower sash of double hung window.

34. *Stool*—Part of window assembly.

35. *Apron*—Part of window assembly.

36. *Rough Header*—Part of opening prepared to receive window assembly.

37. Short stud called cripple stud.

38. Wood drip cap which sheds rain water.

39. *Wood Casing*—Part of exterior window frame.

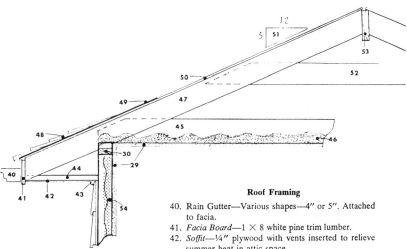

Roof Framing

40. Rain Gutter—Various shapes—4″ or 5″. Attached to facia.
41. *Facia Board*—1 × 8 white pine trim lumber.
42. *Soffit*—¼″ plywood with vents inserted to relieve summer heat in attic space.
43. *Quarter Round*—Used to seal joint between shingles and soffit.
44. *Outlooker*—2 × 3 or 2 × 2 on 16″ centers to support soffit.
45. *Ceiling Joist*—2 × 6 or heavier. Size depends on attic floor load above it.
46. *Insulation*—Loose spun glass or batts of glass wool.
47. *Roof Rafter*—2 × 6 on 16″ centers placed over studs which are directly over joists for maximum support.
48. *Roof Shingles*—Wood, asbestos, or asphalt. Usually asphalt weighing 235# per square (10′ × 10′ or 100 sf).
49. *Felt Paper*—15# roofing paper.
50. *Roof Sheathing*—½″ sheathing plywood or 1 × 8 roofing boards.
51. Diagram which indicates pitch of roof. This roof rises 5″ for every 12″ of run (horizontal).
52. *Collar Beam*—2 × 8 used on alternate roof rafters to strengthen roof framing in order to support snow loads.
53. *Ridge Rafter.*—2 × 8 center beam—ties roof rafters together.
54. *Sidewall Insulation*—Usually 2″ batts.

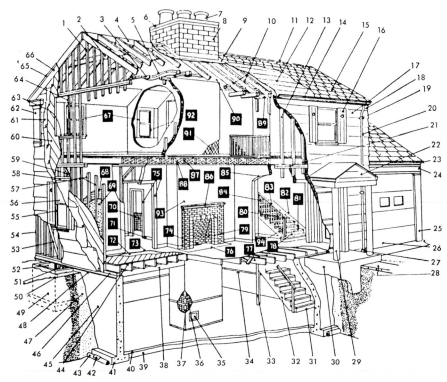

1. Gable stud	33. Girder post	65. Cornice moulding
2. Collar beam	*34. Chair rail	66. Frieze board
3. Ceiling joist	35. Cleanout door	67. Window casing
4. Ridge board	36. Furring strips	68. Lath
5. Insulation	37. Corner stud	69. Insulation
6. Chimney cap	38. Girder	70. Wainscoting
7. Chimney pots	39. Gravel fill	71. Baseboard
8. Chimney	40. Concrete floor	72. Building paper
9. Chimney flashing	41. Foundation footing	73. Finish floor
10. Rafters	42. Paper strip	74. Ash dump
11. Ridge	43. Drain tile	75. Door trim
12. Roof boards	*44. Diagonal subfloor	76. Fireplace hearth
13. Stud	45. Foundation wall	77. Floor joists
14. Eave gutter	46. Sill	78. Stair riser
15. Roofing	47. Backfill	79. Fire brick
16. Blind or shutter	48. Termite shield	80. Newel cap
17. Bevel siding	49. Areaway wall	81. Stair tread
18. Downspout gooseneck	50. Grade line	82. Finish stringer
19. Downspout strap	51. Basement sash	83. Stair rail
20. Downspout leader	52. Areaway	84. Balusters
21. Double plate	53. Corner brace	85. Plaster arch
22. Entrance canopy	54. Corner stud	86. Mantel
23. Garage cornice	55. Window frame	87. Floor joists
24. Frieze	56. Window light	88. Bridging
25. Door jamb	57. Wall studs	89. Lookout
26. Garage door	58. Header	90. Attic space
27. Downspout shoe	59. Window cripple	91. Metal lath
28. Sidewalk	*60. Wall sheathing	92. Window sash
29. Entrance post	61. Building paper	93. Chimney breast
30. Entrance platform	62. Pilaster	94. Newel
31. Stair riser	63. Rough header	
32. Stair stringer	64. Window stud	

*These items are found only in older homes.

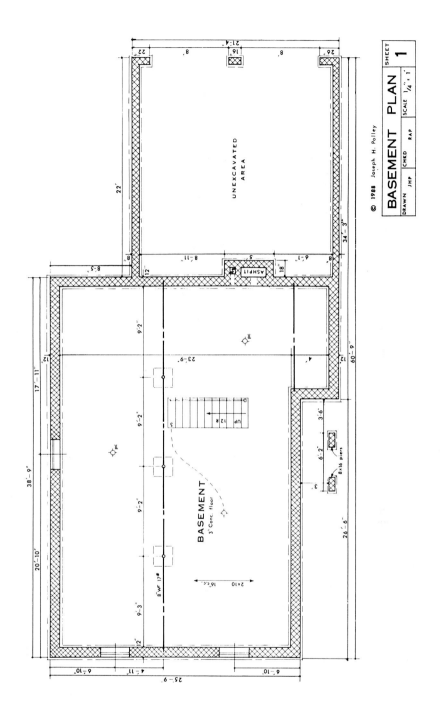

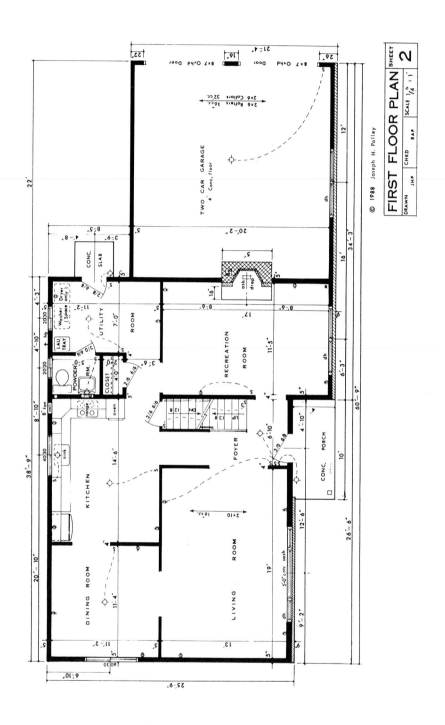

FIRST FLOOR PLAN
SHEET 2
SCALE ¼" = 1'

DRAWN	CHKD
JHP	RAP

© 1988 Joseph H. Polley

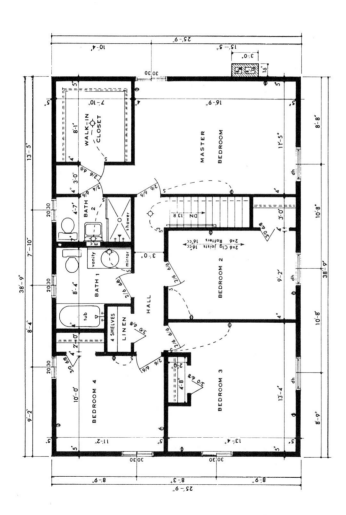

© 1988 Joseph H. Polley

2ND FLOOR PLAN	SHEET 3	
	CHKD	SCALE ¼"=1'
DRAWN JHP	RAP	

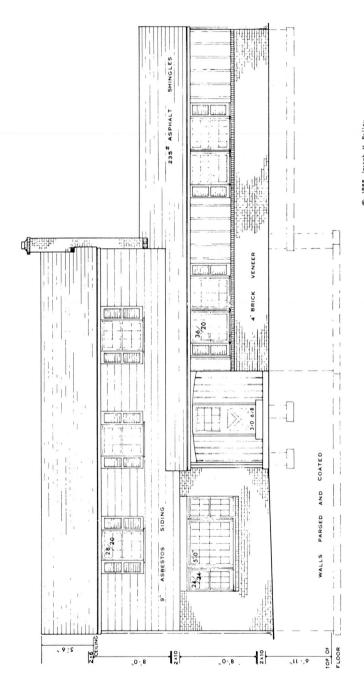

FRONT ELEVATION

SHEET 4

SCALE 1/4" = 1'

DRAWN RAP CHKD JHP JHP

© 1988 Joseph H. Polley

235# ASPHALT SHINGLES

4" BRICK VENEER

9" ASBESTOS SIDING

WALLS PARGED AND COATED

36/20

28/20

24/24

5'-0"

3'-0 6'-8

5'-6"
CEILING
2x6

8'-0"

2x10

8'-0"

2x10

6'-11"

TOP OF
FLOOR

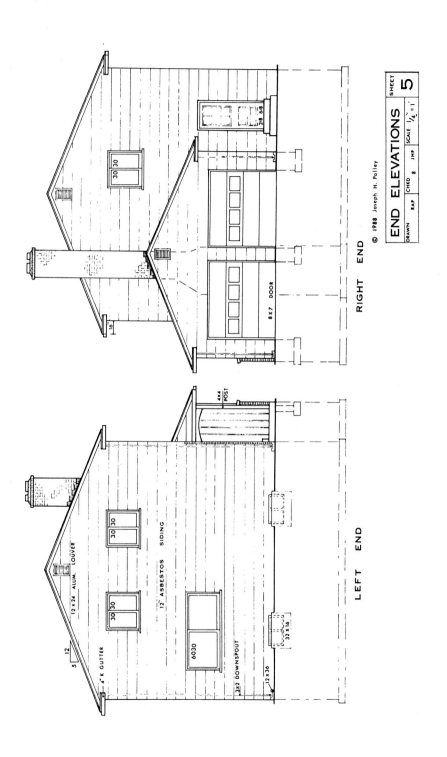

© 1988 Joseph H. Polley

END ELEVATIONS		SHEET 5
DRAWN RAP	CHKD JHP	SCALE ¼" = 1'

RIGHT END

LEFT END

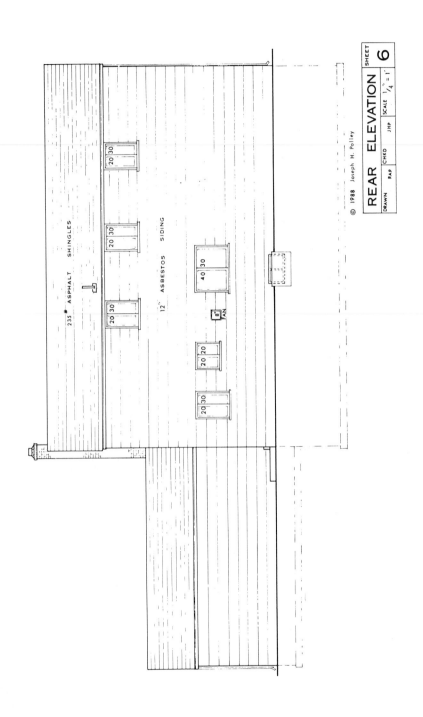

REAR ELEVATION

SHEET 6

DRAWN RAP CHKD JHP SCALE $\frac{1}{4}'' = 1'$

© 1988 Joseph H. Polley

Bibliography

BOOKS AND EDUCATIONAL MATERIALS

American Institute of Real Estate Appraisers. *The Appraisal of Real Estate.* 9th ed. Chicago, 1988.

_____. *The Appraisal of Rural Property.* Chicago, 1983.

_____. Basic Valuation Procedures course handbook. Chicago, 1987.

_____. *The Dictionary of Real Estate Appraisal.* 2nd ed. Chicago, publication forthcoming.

_____. Residential Valuation course handbook. Chicago, 1987.

Betts, Richard M., and Silas J. Ely. *Basic Real Estate Appraisal.* New York: John Wiley & Sons, 1982.

Bloom, George F., and Henry S. Harrison. *Appraising the Single Family Residence.* Chicago: American Institute of Real Estate Appraisers, 1980.

Boyce, Byrl N., and William N. Kinnard, Jr. *Appraising Real Property.* Lexington, Mass.: D.C. Heath and Company, 1986.

Conroy, Kathleen. *Valuing the Timeshare Property.* Chicago: American Institute of Real Estate Appraisers, 1981.

Dombal, Robert W. *Residential Condominiums: A Guide to Analysis and Appraisal.* Chicago: American Institute of Real Estate Appraisers, 1976.

Friedman, Edith J., ed. *Encyclopedia of Real Estate Appraising.* Englewood Cliffs, N.J.: Prentice-Hall, Inc., 1978.

Gimmy, Arthur E., and Michael G. Boehm. *Elderly Housing: A Guide to Appraisal, Market Analysis, Development and Financing.* Chicago: American Institute of Real Estate Appraisers, 1988.

Harrison, Frank E. Evaluating Residential Construction seminar. Chicago: American Institute of Real Estate Appraisers, 1984.

Harrison, Henry S. *Houses — The Illustrated Guide to Construction, Design, and Systems.* Rev. ed. Chicago: REALTORS® National Marketing Institute, 1976.

Himstreet, William C. *The Narrative Report* in the Communicating the Appraisal series. Chicago: American Institute of Real Estate Appraisers, 1988.

Hines, Mary Alice. *Real Estate Appraisal.* New York: Macmillan Publishing Co., Inc., 1981.

Jackson, Kenneth T. *Crabgrass Frontier: The Suburbanization of the United States.* New York: Oxford University Press, 1985.

Jacobs, Jane. *The Death and Life of Great American Cities.* New York: Random House, 1961.

Kostof, Spiro. *America by Design.* New York: Oxford University Press, 1987.

Kratovil, Robert, and Raymond J. Werner. *Real Estate Law.* 8th ed. Englewood Cliffs, N.J.: Prentice-Hall, Inc., 1983.

Miller, George H., and Kenneth W. Gilbeau. *Residential Real Estate Appraisal, An Introduction to Real Estate Appraising.* Englewood Cliffs, N.J.: Prentice-Hall, Inc., 1980.

Mills, Arlen C. *The Uniform Residential Appraisal Report* in the Communicating the Appraisal series. Chicago: American Institute of Real Estate Appraisers, 1988.

Reynolds, Judith. *Historic Properties: Preservation and the Valuation Process.* Chicago: American Institute of Real Estate Appraisers, 1982.

Shenkel, William M. *Modern Real Estate Appraisal.* New York: McGraw-Hill, 1978.

Stern, Robert. *Pride of Place: Building the American Dream.* Boston, Mass.: Houghton Mifflin, 1986.

BUILDING COST MANUALS

Boeckh Building Valuation Manual. Milwaukee: American Appraisal Co., 3 vols.
Vol. 1—*Residential and Agricultural;* Vol. 2—*Commercial;* Vol. 3—*Industrial and Institutional.* Includes wide variety of building models. Built up from unit-in-place costs converted to cost per square foot of floor or ground area. *Boeckh Building Cost Modifier* is published bimonthly for updating with current modifiers.

Building Construction Cost Data. Duxbury, Mass.: Robert Snow Means Co., annual.
Lists average unit prices on many building construction items for use in engineering estimates. Components arranged according to uniform system adopted by the American Institute of Architects, Associated General Contractors, and Construction Specifications Institute.

Dodge Building Cost Calculator & Valuation Guide. New York: McGraw-Hill Information Systems Co.
(looseleaf service, quarterly supplements).
Lists building costs for common types and sizes of buildings. Local cost modifiers and historical local cost index tables included. Formerly *Dow Building Cost Calculator.*

Marshall Valuation Service. Los Angeles: Marshall and Swift
Publication Co.
(looseleaf service, monthly supplements).
Cost data for determining replacement costs of buildings and
other improvements in the United States and Canada.
Includes current cost multipliers and local modifiers.

Residential Cost Handbook. Los Angeles: Marshall and Swift
Publication Co.
(looseleaf service, quarterly supplements).
Presents square-foot method and segregated-cost method.
Local modifiers and cost-trend modifiers included.

PERIODICALS

American Right of Way Proceedings. American Right of Way
Association, Los Angeles.
Annual. Papers presented at national seminars.

Appraisal Institute Magazine. Appraisal Institute of Canada,
Winnipeg, Manitoba.
Quarterly. General and technical articles on appraisal and
expropriation in Canada. Includes information on institute
programs, news, etc.

The Appraisal Journal. American Institute of Real Estate
Appraisers, Chicago.
Quarterly. Oldest periodical in the appraisal field. Includes
technical articles on all phases of real property appraisal and
regular feature on legal decisions. Bibliographies for
1932-1969, 1970-1980, and 1981-1987 available.

The Appraiser. American Institute of Real Estate Appraisers,
Chicago.
Monthly. News bulletin covering current events and trends in
appraisal practice.

Buildings. Stamats Communications, Inc., Cedar Rapids, Iowa.
Monthly. Journal of building construction and management.

Editor and Publisher Market Guide. Editor and Publisher,
New York.
Annual. Standardized market data for more than 1,500 areas
in the United States and Canada, including population estimates
for trading areas. List of principal industries, transportation,
climate, chain store outlets, etc.

Journal of the American Real Estate and Urban Economics Association.
Bloomington, Ind.
Quarterly. Focuses on research and scholarly studies of
current and emerging real estate issues.

*Journal of the American Society of Farm Managers and Rural
Appraisers.* Denver.
Semiannual. Includes appraisal articles.

Journal of Property Management. Institute of Real Estate Management, Chicago.
Bimonthly. Covers a broad range of property investment and
management issues.

Just Compensation. Sherman Oaks, Calif.
Monthly. Reports on condemnation cases.

Land Economics. University of Wisconsin, Madison.
Quarterly. Devoted to the study of economics and social institutes. Includes reports on university research and trends in land utilization. Frequently publishes articles on developments in other countries.

Property Tax Journal. International Association of Assessing Officers, Chicago.
Quarterly. Includes articles on property taxation and assessment administration.

The Quarterly Byte. American Institute of Real Estate Appraisers, Chicago.
Quarterly. Addresses use of computers in appraising.

The Real Estate Appraiser and Analyst. Society of Real Estate Appraisers, Chicago.
Quarterly. Technical articles, society news, and regular feature on legal cases. Consolidated bibliographies for 1935-1960 and 1961-1970 available. Previously published as *The Review, The Residential Appraiser,* and *The Real Estate Appraiser.*

Real Estate Issues. American Society of Real Estate Counselors, Chicago.
Semiannual.

Real Estate Law Journal. Warren, Gorham and Lamont, Inc., Boston.
Quarterly. Publishes articles on legal issues and reviews current litigation of concern to real estate professionals.

Right of Way. American Right of Way Association, Los Angeles.
Bimonthly. Publishes articles on all phases of right-of-way activity—e.g., condemnation, negotiation, pipelines, electric power transmission lines, highways. Includes association news.

Survey of Buying Power. Sales Management, New York.
Annual. Includes population totals and characteristics and income and consumption data presented in national, regional, metropolitan area, county, and city categories. Separate section for Canadian information. Population estimates between decennial censuses.

Survey of Current Business. U.S. Bureau of Economic Analysis, U.S. Department of Commerce, Washington, D.C.
Monthly. Includes statistical and price data. Biennial supplement, *Business Statistics.*

Valuation. American Society of Appraisers, Washington, D.C.
Three issues per year. Articles on real property valuation and the appraisal of personal and intangible property. Includes society news. Previously published as *Technical Valuation.*

Index

Appraiser(s)
education of, 9
employment as a, 10-11
experience of, 9-10
licensing and certification, 8
need for objectivity, 6
role of, 3-4
professional practice requirements, 405-408
skills and characteristics of, 8-10
Appropriateness, criterion of, in final reconciliation of value, 367-368
Appurtenant easements, 16
Architectural compatibility, 150-151
Architectural style(s), 149-159
Class, Type, Style (CTS) System, 149-150
common, 153
definition of, 149
and housing types, 154-159
trends in, 151-154
Area, formulas for calculating, 132-133
Asbestos, effect of, on value of income-producing property, 188-189
Asbestos-containing materials (ACMs), 120, 188
Asbestos Hazard Emergency Response Act (AHERA), 189
Asphalt shingles, 186
Assessed value, 24, 78
relation of, to market value, 78-79
Assessment ratio, 79
Assumption of mortgage, 302, 314

Balance, principle of, 53-54
and cost approach, 249
Balconies, 204
Balloon framing, 178
Balloon mortgage, 314, 326
Balloon payment, 315
Baseboards, 192
Baselines, 72
Basements, 176
entrance to, 160
Bathrooms, 168
Bay windows, 204
Beams, 180
Bedrooms, 167-168
Benchmark buildings, 267
Bi-level house, 158
Block clubs, 110
Blueprints, 145
Boeckh Publications, 266
Book depreciation, 271-272
Breakdown method
of estimating accrued depreciation, 274-275, 282-283
curable functional obsolescence, 286-288
curable physical deterioration, 284
external obsolescence, 289-291
incurable functional obsolescence, 288-289
incurable physical deterioration, 284-286
Breezeways, 204
Building codes, 145
and highest and best use, 216
and neighborhood stability, 113-114
as public limitation on property rights, 76
Building construction analysis, 172-173
attachments, 203-204
equipment and mechanical systems, 195
air-conditioning system, 202
electrical system, 203
heating system fuels, 201-202

heating systems, 197-201
hot water system, 197
miscellaneous systems and equipment, 203
plumbing system, 195-197
ventilation system, 202
exterior
substructure, 173-177
superstructure, 177-190
interior
interior covering and trim, 191-194
protection against decay and insect damage, 194-195
Building description, 144-170
architectural compatibility, 150-151
architectural styles, 149-159
background data and building inspection tools, 145
building size, 148-149
describing and rating, 145-146
house zones, 160-162
photographs in appraisal report, 149
purposes of, 144
rooms in residential properties, 162-169
site improvements, 147-148
steps in, 147-149
Building line, width at the, 130
Building size, 148-149
Built-up roof, 186
Bungalow, 153
Business cycles, and real estate, 90-92
Buydown plan, 302, 315

Cabinets, 194
California ranch architectural style, 153
Cape Ann house, 180
Cape Cod architectural style, 153, 154
Capital, 51, 89
Capitalization, 349
Capitalization of rent loss, to estimate external obsolescence, 290-291
to estimate incurable functional obsolescence, 288
Cash equivalency, 321-326
adjusting for considerations other than cash, 323
adjusting for seller-paid points, 322-323
comparison of sales transactions, 322
and determining effect of financing considerations on price, 302
discounting cash flows, 323-326
Ceilings, 180
Celotex™, 183
Center wall, 420
Central business district (CBD), 93-94
Chimneys, 186-187
Chronological age of building, 273
Circulation areas, 160
Circulator, 198
Clean Air Act, 188-189
Climate, 138
Closing, 71
Coal, 201
Collateralized Mortgage Obligations (CMOs), 317-318
Column footings, 174
Commercial district, definition of, 100
Communities. See also Districts, Neighborhoods
development of contemporary, 94-96
shape of, 93-96
Community associations, 110
Comparability, concept of, 63
Comparable properties. See also Sales comparison approach
collection of descriptive data on, 80-81

data sources for, 66-70
data verification, 80
identifying, 65-70
subject property and, 80-81
Comparable sales analysis, 334
paired data set analysis, 335-339
reconciliation of indications in, 341-342
units of comparison, 339-340
Comparative-unit method of estimating cost, 255, 259-260
applicability and limitations of, 262-263
example of, 260-262
Competition, 43
Concrete slabs, 191
Condition of improvement, 146
Conditions of sale, analysis of, in sales comparison, 305
Condominium deed, 389
Condominiums, 389-390
appraisal of, 390
appraisal report for, 379, 382-383, 410-411
conversion of rental properties to, 95
Conformity, concept of, 54-55
Consistency, as factor in final reconciliation of value, 366-367
Consistent use, 56
and highest and best use, 214-215
Constructive notice, 69
Consumer Product Safety Commission, banning of urea-formaldehyde foam insulation by, 189
Contemporary architectural style, 153
Contraction in the business cycle, 91
Contractor's profit, 244
Contract rent, 354
Contribution, concept of, 52
Convectors, 200-201
Cooperatives, 390-391
appraisal techniques, 391
conversion of rental properties to, 95
Coordination, 51, 89
Corner lots, 136
Cornices, 186
Corridor kitchen, 166
Cost approach, 34-35, 248-292
accessory buildings in, 256
accrued depreciation in, 256
applicability and limitations, 250-252
depreciation estimates, 251
final value indication, 248
identifying comparable for, 65
and principle of substitution, 44
relation to appraisal principles, 248-250
site improvements in, 256
steps in
methods of estimating cost, 255
reproduction versus replacement cost, 252-253
site value, 252
types of cost, 253-255
use of sales comparison in, 298
Cost-estimating methods, 255, 259
building measurement, 268
comparative unit, 255, 259-260
applications and limitations of, 262-263
example of, 260-262
cost service manuals, 266-267
benchmark buildings, 267
cost-index trending, 267-268
quantity survey, 255, 264-265
applicability and limitations, 266
survey, 265
unit in place, 255, 263
applicability and limitations, 264

example of, 263-264
Cost-index trending, 267-268
Cost-push inflation, 90-91
Cost service manuals, 266-267
benchmark buildings, 267
cost-index trending, 267-268
Cost to cure, 205
Council of Governments (COG), 116
Crawl space, 176
Creative financing, 313-315
Credit regulation devices, 319-320
Crime, in the neighborhood, 110
Crime watch groups, 110
Cul-de-sac lots, 136
Curability, of depreciation, 256
Curable functional obsolescence, in breakdown method, 286-288
Curable physical deterioration, in breakdown method, 284

Damage, 284
Data
collection of, 31-33, 64-65
quality of, in final reconciliation of value, 368-369
verification of, in sales comparison, 301
Data analysis, accuracy and adequacy in, 364-366
Data needs, 31-33
Data sources, on property rights, 77
Decay, protection of wood against, 194-195
Decks, 204
Decline, in neighborhood life cycle, 103
Decreasing returns, concept of, 52-53
Deed restrictions, 77
and neighborhood stability, 114
Deeds of trust, 313
Deficiency requiring additions, 286
and curable functional obsolescence, 286-287
Deficiency requiring substitution or modernization, and curable functional obsolescence, 287
Demand-pull inflation, 91
Depreciation
accrued. See Accrued depreciation
book, 271-272
Depreciation estimates, in the cost approach, 251
Desire, 41
Dining areas, 167
Direct costs, in cost approach, 253-254
Direct-reduction loan factor table, 324
Discount factor, 324
Discounting cash flows, 323-326
Disintermediation, 316
Disposable income, 86
District(s). See also Communities, definition of, 99-100
Dodge, F. W., Corporation, 267
Dollar adjustments, in sales comparison approach, 333
Doors, 192, 193
exterior, 184
interior, 192, 193
Dormers, 204
Downdraft, 194
Downspouts, 186
Drain systems, 184, 186
Drain tile, 174
Driveways, as site improvements, 142
Dutch Colonial house, 153, 180

in sales comparison approach, 300
sewage disposal, 140
size and shape of lot, 130-131
soil conditions, 134-135
street improvements, 137
tools for, 128-129
transportation, 135
utilities, 139
view, 138
water, 140
Final reconciliation, 363-371
  accuracy and adequacy of data analysis, 364-366
    consistency, 366-367
    review of calculations, 367
  criteria for, 367-369
  final value indication, 369-370
  quality of data, 368-369
  quantity of data, 369
  reconciliation criteria, 367-369
    appropriateness, 367-368
  review, 363-364
  rounding, 370
Financial feasibility
  and highest and best use
    of property as improved, 219-220
    of site as vacant, 218-219
Financing plans, 312-318
  assumption of mortgage, 314
  buydown plan, 315
  creative financing, 313-315
  installment sale contract, 314-315
  mortgage money sources, 315-318
    Federal Home Loan Mortgage Corporation, 317
    Federal National Mortgage Association, 316
    Government National Mortgage Association, 317-318
    private sector transactions, 318
    secondary mortgage market, 316-318
  and neighborhood analysis, 111
  seller loan, 314
  traditional loans, 312-313
  wraparound mortgage, 315
Financing terms, analysis of, in sales comparison
  approach, 302
Finish grading, 177
Fireplaces, 194
Fire protection, and neighborhood stability, 114
Fixed-rate, first mortgage loan, 312
Fixture, 13-14
Flag lot, 136
Flashing, 183, 186
Flood hazards, 138
Flooding, 176
Floor construction, 179-180
Floor covering, 191
Floor plans, 149, 160-162
Flue, 187
Footings, 174, 177
Form reports, 37, 378-385
  Employee Relocation Council Residential Appraisal
    Report, 379, 383-384, 411-415
  Individual Condominium or PUD Unit Appraisal Report,
    379, 382-383, 410-411
  Small Residential Income Property Appraisal Report,
    379, 383, 412-413
  special pointers for completing, 384-385
  Uniform Residential Appraisal Report (URAR),
    107, 379-382, 409
Foundation walls, 174-177
Framing, 177-180, 182

Freddie Mac, *See* Federal Home Loan
  Mortgage Corporation
French Provincial architectural style, 153
Front footage, 130
Fuel oil, 201
Functional obsolescence, 270
  in breakdown method, 282
  in cost approach, 256
  curable, 286-288
  incurable, 288-289
  and use of replacement cost, 275
Functional utility, 146

Galley kitchen, 166
Garages, 204
Garbage collection, 140
Garrison Colonial architectural style, 153
Gentrification, 95, 104
Geodesic domes, 159
Georgian architectural style, 153
Governmental forces, impact of, on value, 48, 112-116
Government National Mortgage Association (GNMA),
  87, 317-318
Government survey system, 72, 74
Grading, 177
GRM. See Gross rent multiplier (*GRM*)
Gross adjustments, 368
Gross building area (*GBA*), 268
Gross living area (*GLA*), 148, 268
Gross rent, 352
Gross rent multiplier (*GRM*), 339, 349. *See also* Income
  capitalization approach
  application of, to monthly market rent, 358
  derivation of a, from market data, 351-354
  reconciling, 353-354
Ground rent, 231
Ground rent capitalization, 233
  as land valuation technique, 245
    applicability and limitations, 245-246
Growth, in neighborhood life cycle, 101-105
Guest entrance, 160
Gutters, 186

Hard costs, in cost approach, 253-254
Hardwood floors, 191
Hazardous wastes
  definition of, 119
  presence of, and neighborhood value, 119-120
Hazards, in field inspection, 137-138
Heat pumps, 200
Highest and best use, 5, 33, 55, 105, 211, 249
  anticipated zoning changes, 114
  availability of utilities, 139
  for comparable sales, 234
  and concept of consistent use, 214-215
  definition of, 211-214
  and excess land, 217, 223
  on form reports, 384
  influence of taxation on, 78
  interim uses, 220-221
  financial feasibility, 219-220
  legally nonconforming use, 221-222
  multiple uses, 222-223
  of property as improved, 55, 213-214, 216
    financial feasibility, 219-220
    legal permissibility, 216
    maximum productivity, 220

Purchasing power, 86-88
  in real estate market, 45

Quadrangles, 73
Quality and condition survey, 146
Quantity survey method for estimating accrued
    depreciation, 255, 264-265
  applicability and limitations, 266
  example of, 265
Quarter sections, 73
Queen Anne architectural style, 153

Radon gas, 120, 138, 222
Raised ranch house, 158
Ranch houses, 395
  appraisal of, 395
Range lines, 72-73
Rate of return, 312, 321
Real estate
  and business cycles, 90-92
  creation and productivity of, 50-51
  definition of, 13
  identification of, 27-28
  legal descriptions of, 70-76
    lot and block system, 74-76
    metes and bounds system, 71-72
    rectangular or government survey system, 72-74
Real estate economics, 40-57
  changes in local and regional markets, 50
  characteristics of real estate markets, 45-49
  creation and productivity of real estate, 50-51
  forces in the local residential market, 49-50
  forces that influence value, 47-49
  general economic theory, 40-45
Real estate investment trusts (REITs), 87, 318
Real estate markets, characteristics of, 45-49
Real estate taxes
  and assessed value, 78-79
  and neighborhood value, 113
  and property rights, 78-80
  and special assessments, 79, 113
Real estate values, affect of seasonal cycles on, 90
Real property, 14-17
Real property rights conveyed, analysis of, in sales
  comparison, 302
Reconciliation, 341-342
  final See Final reconciliation
Reconciliation criteria, in final reconciliation of
  value, 367-369
Recreational areas, as site improvements, 142
Recreation homes, 392, 394
  appraisal of, 394
Recreation room, 169
Rectangular survey system, 72
Reflective insulation, 189
Remaining economic life, 272
Rental properties, conversion of, to condominiums and
  cooperatives, 95
Rent controls, 350-351
Rent levels, and neighborhood analysis, 111
Rent survey, 357
Replacement cost
  basis of, 275-276
  in cost approach, 252-253
Reproduction cost
  basis of, 275-276
  in cost approach, 252-253

Residence(s). See also House(s), Improvement(s)
  age and life of, and accrued depreciation, 272-273
  on leased land, 392
    appraisal techniques, 392
  overall condition of, 204
    items requiring immediate repair, 205
    long-lived items, 206-207
    short-lived items, 205-206
  operating expenses of, 352-353
Residential appraisals. See Appraisals
Residential appraiser. See Appraiser
Residents, economic profile of, and neighborhood
  analysis, 111
Resort homes, 392,394
  appraisal of, 394
Revitalization, in neighborhood life cycle, 104-105
Right-of-way, 16, 18, 77
  and site analysis, 129-130
Riparian rights, 78
Rolled roofing, 186
Rollover mortgages, 320
Roof attachments, 204
Roof covering, 184, 186
Roof framing, 421
Roofs, types of, 180
Rough grading, 177
Rounding, of value conclusions, 370
Rural estates, 100

Sales comparison approach, 35, 297-307, 330-345
  analysis of comparables, 301-302
    conditions of sale, 305
    financing terms, 302
    location, 306
    market conditions, 305-306
    market data grids, 307
    physical characteristics, 306-307
    real property rights conveyed, 302
  comparable sales analysis, 334
    paired data set analysis, 335-339
    reconciliation, 341-342
    units of comparison, 339-340
  comparables as competitive properties, 299
  dollar and percentage adjustments, 333
  for estimating accrued depreciation, 274, 276
    applicability and limitations of, 277-278
    example of, 276-277
  field inspection, 300
  highest and best use analysis, 300-301
  identifying comparables for, 65
  for land valuation, 233-238
    adjusting sales price to reflect differences, 235-236
    analyzing data for comparability, 234-235
    applicability and limitations, 238
    collecting data, 234
    example of, 236-237
    reconciling results, 236
  limitations of, 298-299
  market data grid, 334
  and principle of substitution, 44
  purpose of adjustment, 330
  research and identification of comparables, 300
  research and selection of comparable sales, 299-300
  sample application, 342-344
  scatter diagrams, 331-332
  sequence of adjustments, 333-334
  strengths of, 297-298
  units of comparison, 330-331

Tax(es), 17, *See also* Real estate taxes
Tax assessors, 6
Tax burden, 78
Tax rate, 78, 79
Tax records, 69-70
Tax Reform Act (1986), 394
Tax rolls, 78
Tax status, and property rights, 78-80
Terrazzo flooring, 191
Test borings, 174
Three-story houses, 159
Time adjustment, 306
Timeshare properties, 391
    appraisal techniques, 391-392
Title insurance companies, 69
Title reports, 69
    property rights in, 78
Topography and climatic conditions, and neighborhood
    value, 118
Township, 73
Township lines, 72-73
Toxic Substances Control Act, 189
Transfer records, 69
Transfer tax stamp, 80
Transportation systems and linkages, and neighborhood
    value, 117
Treasury, U.S. Department of, 320
Trend, definition of, 89
Trough, in the business cycle, 91-92
Trusses, 180, 182
Tudor architectural style, 153
Two-and-one-half-story houses, 159
Two-story house, 158

Underground houses, 400
    appraisal techniques, 400
Uniform Residential Appraisal Report (URAR), 107,
    379-382, 409
Uniform Standards of Professional Appraisal Practice,
    8, 22-23, 62, 64, 65, 76, 406-408
Unit costs, 259
U.S. Housing Authority, 94
Unit-in-place method of estimating cost, 255, 263
    example of, 263-264
    applicability and limitations of, 264
Units of comparison, in sales comparison, 339-340
Urea-formaldehyde foam insulation (UFFI), 189
Use value, 23-24
Utilities
    adequacy and quality of, and neighborhood value, 119
    onsite and offsite, 139
Utility, 41

Vacancy rates, 88-89
    and neighborhood value, 112
Vacant land, and neighborhood analysis, 111-112
Valuation process, 27-38. *See also* Appraisal(s)
    cost approach, 34-35
    date of value estimate, 29
    definition of value, 29-30
    description of scope of appraisal, 30
    highest and best use analysis, 33
    identification of property rights to be valued, 28-29
    identification of real estate, 27-28
    income capitalization approach, 35-36
    limiting conditions and assumptions, 30
    preliminary analysis, data selection, and collection, 30-33

reconciliation of value estimates and final value, 36-37
report of defined value, 37
sales comparison approach, 35
site value estimate, 34
use of appraisal, 29
Value
    concept of, 19-20
    definition of, 4, 29-30
    final reconciliation of. *See* Final reconciliation
    influences effecting subject property, 100-101
    report of defined, 37
Value estimate
    date of, 29
    reconciliation of, and final value, 36-37
Variable-rate mortgages, 312, 320
Ventilation, 190, 202
Vents, 186-187
Veterans Administration (VA), 87, 312
    guaranteed loan, 94, 302, 312-313
        assumption of, 314
    use of Uniform Residential Appraisal Report form by, 379
Victorian architectural style, 138
Voluntary associations, 110

Wainscoting, 192
Walks, as site improvements, 142
Wall attachments, 204
Wall footing, 174
Walls, 191-192
    center, 420
    exterior, 183
    as site improvements, 142
Wall siding, 183
Warm air heating systems, 197
Water, 140
Waterfront improvements, as site improvements, 142
Western row houses, 153
Width of lot, average, 130
Windows, 184, 185
Window wells, 204
Working-service zone, 160
Work schedule, 31
Work triangle, 163
Wraparound mortgages, 302, 315

Yield, 312, 321

Zone heating control, 200
Zoning, 103, 145
    as criterion in selection and analysis of comparables, 235
Zoning ordinance(s), 76-77, 94
    changes in, 77
    and highest and best use, 216, 222-223
    and neighborhood stability, 113-114
    and nonconforming use, 76
    as public limitation on property rights, 76